THE WELSH LANGUAGE

**studies in its syntax
and semantics**

The Schools Council project in WELSH AS A FIRST LANGUAGE AT THE SECONDARY STAGE was set up in 1969 and continued 1975. It was based at the University College of North Wales, Bangor, under the direction of Dr T. Emrys Parry, and covered the 11-16 age range. The research phase was directed by Alan R. Thomas, with Morris Jones as research officer.

Classroom materials in Welsh have been developed by the project, and are distributed by the Welsh Books Council, Aberystwyth. They consist of two series of source materials on a variety of themes, one for pupils aged 11-14/15 and another for those aged 14/15-17.

SCHOOLS COUNCIL PROJECT IN WELSH AS A
FIRST LANGUAGE AT THE SECONDARY STAGE

THE WELSH LANGUAGE

studies in its syntax and semantics

MORRIS JONES
ALAN R. THOMAS

UNIVERSITY OF WALES PRESS
FOR THE SCHOOLS COUNCIL

First published 1977

ISBN 0 7083 0671 3

Published by
THE UNIVERSITY OF WALES PRESS
6, Gwennyth Street, Cathays, Cardiff, CF2 4YD

Text set by Medwen Williams, Students' Union,
University College of North Wales, Bangor, and by
Jubal Multiwrite Ltd, London, SE13

Printed in Great Britain by
South Western Printers Ltd., Caerphilly, Mid Glamorgan

Contents

Introduction

The aim of this book is to examine the syntactic structures of Welsh and, to some extent, the meanings involved in those structures. We do not aim at an exhaustive treatment of the structure and meaning of Welsh, but at a selective description of the main syntactic and semantic characteristics of the language.

In the main, the treatment of any particular point follows the same procedure:

a statement of the superficial facts;
a statement of their meanings where possible;
a more abstract explanation intended to bring out further significant points; a formalised presentation of the analysis within the framework of a system of rules.

The description of Welsh presented in the following chapters is couched, though informally and selectively, in terms of transformational-generative grammar. Technical terminology in many instances has been retained, and the overall framework of the theory provides a basis for the presentation of the description. Although we do not introduce the details of formalisation, the approach is still relatively formal compared with traditional approaches, since transformational-generative grammar does not readily lend itself to informality.

Basic colloquial forms and spellings in the examples reflect generally recurring features of colloquial north Welsh, as evidenced in the speech of educated speakers (a fact which does not preclude the occurrence of sub-standard forms on occasion, and of some others of dubious acceptability).

We are essentially concerned with the expression of configurations of meanings which occur in all dialects of Welsh, and the choice of a north Welsh rendering serves only as illustration. The precise morphological realisation of any pattern may vary between varieties, of course, so that an example such as the northern *mi welith John Mair (John will see Mair)* can be discussed in exactly the same terms if written *fe weliff John Mair* to reflect southern usage.

However, there are variations (dialectal and stylistic) which involve different surface syntactic structuring, as with the dialectal variants:

mae John eisiau afal (northern)	*(John wants an apple)*
mae John ynmoyn afal (southern)	*(John wants an apple)*

or the stylistic variants:

gwneith John ganu	*(John will sing)*
canith John	*(John will sing)*

Variation involving syntactic differences is specifically **discussed**, and it should be borne in mind that the choice of a particular structure for exemplification (e.g. of forms employing the auxiliary *gwneith* + lexical verb as opposed to the inflected lexical verb *canith* in the second example above) does not reflect any difference in frequency of occurrence, or imply prestige; it is simply a convenience which arises from the greater separation of meaningful elements in surface structure which is afforded by one structure as compared with its correlates.

Though our aim is to provide an academically viable description of Welsh, it would please us if the book were to prove of interest to teachers and others whose interest might be less specialized. Accordingly, chapters I, II and IV, and short sections in some others contain informal and discursive discussions of elementary matters, to help in the orientation of the reader of less specialised interest.

Acknowledgements

This volume is the product of the research phase of the Schools Council project in Welsh as First Language at the Secondary Stage, based at University College of North Wales (1969–75), and I take this opportunity of recording my indebtedness to Morris Jones, my principal colleague both in research and in preparations for publication. We both acknowledge, too, our indebtedness to G.W. Roberts, who was with us in 1969 and 1970; Mrs E.M. Jones, who dealt with a lengthy and difficult typing task with patience, imagination and care, and Eric Evans, H.P. Hughes and Myrddin Jenkins, who made extensive and helpful comments on the text. We acknowledge with gratitude the encouragement and support of Professors Alan E. Sharp and J.R. Webster and the late Professor Melville Richards.

Some of the faults in this volume we can recognise without prompting — they stem largely from the selective nature of the text, and are natural hazards of all attempts to prepare material which might prove useful to a wide range of users. But there will be others, deriving from our theoretical and methodological prejudices, and perhaps some oddities of usage which stem from linguistic prejudices of a more familiar kind: for both, we remain unrepentant.

Alan R. Thomas
Department of Linguistics
University College of North Wales, Bangor

Abbreviations

The following are the main abbreviations used in the discussion:

ACT	Active
ADJ	Adjective
ASP	Aspect
AUX	Auxiliary
COMP	Comparative, complement
CONJ	Conjunction, conjunctive
COP	Copula
DET	Determiner
EMPH	Emphatic
EQ	Equative
FUT	Future
LOC	Locative
N	Noun
NEG	Negative
NP	Noun phrase
NUM	Numeral
P	Preposition
PASS	Passive
PLU	Plural
PP } PREP. PH }	Prepositional phrase
PRED. ADJ	Predicative adjective
PRED. PH	Predicate phrase
PRES	Present
PT	Pre-sentential particle
Q	Quantifier
REL	Relative
S	Sentence
SING	Singular
SUP	Superlative
V	Verb
VP	Verb phrase

I Welsh sentences

1 THE CONCEPT OF THE SENTENCE

1a The sentence as a basic category of linguistic description

The approach being followed here to the study of Welsh syntax adopts the concept of the SENTENCE as the most useful general category of linguistic description.[1] By this approach the Welsh language (like any other) can be defined in terms of the range of sentence types which it employs; and the native speaker's command over Welsh represents his control over the production and the understanding of these sentences. On this basis we can describe the nature and structure of the Welsh language by describing the nature and structure of Welsh sentences. This approach may be seemingly questioned by referring to the occurrences of utterances of one word or phrase such as *John* or *ar y gadair (on the chair)* but, as will be suggested in section 2, these utterances are regarded as being developed from sentences through the application of various operations.

1b The sentence and the word

Many traditional grammars discuss sentences last and begin their analyses by looking at the concept of the WORD.[2] The bulk of the chapters in such traditional grammars are concerned with *parts of speech* (or different types of words) such as *noun, verb, adjective*, etc. The approach to the structure of sentences is based upon a prior description of the words in the language and sentences are thought of as being made up of combinations of words:

(1)   SENTENCE
            ↑
        WORDS

This approach tends to give the impression that speakers of a language are equipped with a vocabulary of different types of words and that sentences are built up by joining the various words together in an appropriate order. The approach to the description of Welsh adopted here follows the reverse direction. We begin with sentences and work down to words:

(2)   SENTENCE
            ↓
        WORDS

This second approach has two advantages. Firstly, the sentence is a general unit of the syntax of a language while the word is a much more specific unit. By adopting the

1

most general unit we can make more general statements about the syntax of Welsh. Secondly, words are better discussed in relation to their occurrence in a sentence as it is this which tells us so much about their type and function. It helps, therefore, if we describe sentences before words. But, as all occurring sentences undoubtedly contain words, it may seem rather difficult to talk about sentences without referring to words. We find, however, that the variety of words which occur in a sentence can be represented by abstract *syntactic categories* such as *noun phrase* or *verb phrase* and, as will be shown in the following sections, it is these abstract syntactic categories that are used to discuss the syntax of sentences. The relationship between the sentence and the word is, therefore, not a direct one and can be illustrated in the following diagram:

(3)   SENTENCE
                  ↓
         SYNTACTIC CATEGORIES
                  ↓
         WORDS

This arrangement displays the way in which various syntactic categories (see section 3 below) mediate between sentence and word and, as such, play an important role in the description of sentences.

1c   Definitions of the sentence

The approach to the sentence adopted here does not follow the notional conception of the sentence found in some traditional writings. We do not define the sentence as 'a group of words which makes complete sense and expresses a complete thought' or by any other similar notional definition. (But we must emphasise that we are not rejecting a notional definition: we simply do not aim for one, as it does not help us to express what we want to say about sentences.) Even less helpful is the definition of a sentence as 'a structure which begins with a capital letter and ends with a full stop'. In the first place, such a definition is only relevant to the written language and, in the second place, it tells us nothing *about* sentences. In effect, we take the sentence for granted and rely initially upon our intuitive recognition of what is a sentence. Thus, given two examples:

(4)   mae John yn gweld Mair heno   *(John is seeing Mair tonight)*
       is   John in see   Mair tonight

(5)   *mae John gweld heno   *(*John is see tonight)*
        is   John see   tonight

we know intuitively that (4) is a sentence and that (5) is not.

2

It is implicit in traditional grammar that some sentences are more basic than others and the most familiar distinction in this respect is that between SIMPLE sentences and COMPLEX sentences. But before going on to this major distinction, various relationships of a sort of complexity can be seen amongst simple sentences.

Consider the following example:

(6)   *mae'r ceffyl wedi bwyta'r moron i gyd*   *(the horse has eaten all the carrots)*
       is the horse after eat the carrots all

Through the application of certain syntactic rules a number of slightly different variations of this sentence can be produced and two examples can be given as follows:

(7)   *'dydy   'r ceffyl ddim wedi bwyta'r moron i gyd (the horse hasn't eaten all*
       NEG is the horse NEG after eat the carrots all   *the carrots)*

(8)   *ydy'r ceffyl wedi bwyta'r moron i gyd?*   *(has the horse eaten all the*
       is the horse after eat the carrots all   *carrots?)*

Example (7) is traditionally known as a *negative (NEG) sentence* and represents a variation of (6) through application of the *negative operation* (see chapter IX, section 4). Example (8), by contrast, is an *interrogative sentence* and is produced by applying to the sentence in (6) the *interrogative operation* (see chapter IX, section 3). Traditionally, examples like (6) tend to be more basic[3] than (7) and (8) and the discussion of the former sorts of sentence usually precedes the discussion of sentences of the latter type. This procedure will be followed here, and the negative and interrogative features, along with other phenomena, are discussed later in chapter IX.

There is a different sort of complexity from that discussed above, which can be illustrated by the following example:

(9)   *mae'r ceffyl a wnaeth ddianc allan o'r cae wedi bwyta*   *(the horse that*
       is the horse REL did escape out of the field after eat   *escaped out of the*
                                                                                                  field has eaten the
       'r moron mae John wedi tyfu ar gyfer y sioe   *carrots that John*
       the carrots is John after grow on count the show   *has grown for*
                                                                                                  the show)

In traditional terms example (9) is explicitly labelled a 'complex' sentence. We will adopt the traditional distinction between a simple sentence like (6) and a complex sentence like (9).[4] But the important point is that complex sentences of this type are made up of *more than one* simple sentence modified in certain ways. In effect, example (9) is made up of three simple sentences:

(10) (i) *mae'r ceffyl wedi bwyta'r moron*   *(the horse has eaten the*
          is the horse after eat the carrots   *carrots)*

    (ii) *mi wnaeth y ceffyl ddianc allan o'r cae*   *(the horse escaped out of*
          PT. did the horse escape out of the field   *the field)*

    (iii) *mae John wedi tyfu moron ar gyfer y sioe* *(John has grown carrots*
          is John after grow carrots on count the show   *for the show)*

They are combined and modified to produce the complex sentence (9) (see chapter VII, section 5).

The apparent counter-examples to the assertion that sentences are the basic unit of language *(John* and *ar y gadair (on the chair)*, in the opening section 1a of this chapter) are viewed as being the remnants of a sentence which are produced by the operation of ellipsis (see chapter IX, section 5). For example, given questions such as *pwy sy'n cnocio ar y ffenestr? (who is knocking on the window?)* and *lle mae'r llyfrau? (where are the books?)*, full and detailed responses could involve *John sy'n cnocio ar y ffenestr (it's John who is knocking on the window)* and *mae'r llyfrau ar y gadair (the books are on the chair)*, but through the operation of ellipsis these sentences are reduced to *John* and *ar y gadair (on the chair).*

3   TWO ASPECTS OF THE DESCRIPTION OF SENTENCES : SYNTAX AND SEMANTICS

It is generally accepted that sentences can be described from two points of view. In traditional terminology, we can say that sentences can be described in terms of their 'form', and in terms of their 'meaning'. Another way of explaining this dual descriptive process is to use the words 'structure' and 'function'. In this work we will use the labels SYNTAX for 'form' or 'structure' and SEMANTICS for 'meaning' or 'function'.[5]

The following illustration will help to clarify the distinction we draw between the syntax of sentences and their semantics:

(11) *mi wnaeth y bachgen agor y drws*   *(the boy opened the door)*
     PT did the boy   open the door

(12) *mi wnaeth y bachgen baentio'r drws*   *(the boy painted the door)*
     PT did the boy   paint the door

By using the syntactic categories which are introduced in the following sections and the next chapter we can say that both these examples have the same syntax:

(13) | PARTICLE | AUXILIARY | NOUN PHRASE | VERB | NOUN PHRASE |
|---|---|---|---|---|
| *mi* | *wnaeth* | *y bachgen* | *agor* | *y drws* |
| *mi* | *wnaeth* | *y bachgen* | *baentio* | *y drws* |

4

At this level of syntactic description the two sentences are identical. But, in terms of a semantic analysis, the two sentences can be distinguished in certain respects. This can be illustrated by considering various *paraphrases* associated with each example. Example (11) is subject to the following paraphrase:

(14) *mi wnaeth y bachgen wneud i'r drws agor*   *(the boy made the door*
      PT did   the boy   make to the door open   *open)*

And, further, we can compare example (11) with:

(15) *mi wnaeth y drws agor*   *(the door opened)*
      PT did the door open

But these possibilities are not available for (12):

(16) **mi wnaeth y bachgen wneud i'r drws baentio*   *(*the boy made the*
      PT did the boy   make to the door paint   *door paint)*

(17) **mi wnaeth y drws baentio*   *(*the door painted)*
      PT did   the door paint

To use semantic terms which are discussed in greater detail in chapter X, we can say that Y BACHGEN (THE BOY) in both examples is the AGENT who engineers the action referred to by the verb. The two occurrences of Y DRWS (THE DOOR), however, have two different functions: in (11) it both suffers and performs the action of the verb, as examples (14) and (15) illustrate; while in (12) it only suffers the action of the verb and does not perform it, as examples (16) and (17) illustrate. Thus, we can say that in (11) Y DRWS (THE DOOR) is PATIENT/ACTOR while in (12) it is only PATIENT. This rather brief illustration not only displays the syntactic and semantic aspects of sentences but also demonstrates that similarity in one respect may involve differences in the other. We attempt to discuss both aspects of Welsh sentences.

Notes to chapter I

1. The clearest illustration of this approach from a transformational-generative point of view is seen in Chomsky (1957; 1965). Witness the same emphasis on the sentence in a more informal and simplified presentation in Jacobs and Rosenbaum (1967a, 1967b). Langendoen (1969; 1970), although representing a different approach, likewise uses the sentence as the basis of study.

2. See, for instance, Williams (1959), which is a good example of the use of the traditional 'parts of speech-to-sentence' model for the description of (mainly written) Welsh, as its contents page indicates.

3. Other terms used to describe such a sentence include *kernel* (Chomsky, 1957) although this latter term has no place in Chomsky's later work, and *elementary sentence* (Langendoen, 1970).

4. Recent work by Ross (1970) suggests that the term 'simple sentence' is only a surface structure term. A detailed analysis must allow for pre-verbs such as performatives. Thus example (13) is derived from a complex sentence:

> *'dwi'n datgan bod y ceffyl wedi bwyta'r moron*   *(I declare that the*
> *am I in declare be the horse after eat the carrots*   *horse has eaten the*
>   *carrots)*

For the sake of simplicity and presentation, we retain the traditional notion of a simple sentence.

5. In Chomsky (1965) the main emphasis in the description of language is on the syntactic aspect of sentences. The semantic component is viewed as an interpretive component which operates upon structures produced by the syntactic component. Since 1965, however, there has been a growing emphasis on the semantics of language and recent trends put forward the view that semantic information may be organised in such a way that syntactic structures are derived from their semantics (McCawley, 1968; Halliday, 1970; Lakoff, 1971). For our purposes, we treat the syntactic and semantic aspects separately. Such a procedure tends to create an impression of a dichotomy between the two which current research does not reveal, but to do otherwise would involve a presentation which could be too advanced for the aims of this book. The separation of syntax and semantics is one of convenience only, and interested readers are referred to the literature quoted immediately above for remarks on a composite presentation.

It must be pointed out that the study of (Welsh) syntax presented here, though based on transformational grammar, is much narrower than that undertaken by Chomsky (1965) in relation to English. For whereas Chomsky discusses categorial material, strict sub-categorisation features, selectional restrictions and transformational operations, this description of Welsh syntax is primarily concerned with categorial matters and transformational possibilities. Strict sub-categorisation features are implicit in the study of the verb phrase in chapter III and complex sentences in chapter VIII but no explicit formulation is offered, while selectional features are only briefly touched upon in chapter VII, section 2d, in the discussion of the noun.

It can also be borne in mind that two possible uses exist for semantics, one in terms of referential meaning (compare dictionary entries) and the other in terms of grammatical meaning. For example, in the discussion of examples (11) and (12) the referential analysis of the semantics of DRWS (DOOR) would be the same in its occurrence in both sentences but, as the discussion illustrated, its grammatical meaning is dependent upon its grammatical context and varies accordingly.

6

II   The syntax of simple sentences

1   CONSTITUENT STRUCTURE OF SIMPLE SENTENCES

1a   Segmentation, labelling and branching-diagrams

The sentences that we have looked at so far are, on the face of things, strings of words organised in succession:

> (1) *mi wnaeth y ceffyl fwyta'r moron i gyd*   *(the horse ate all the*
>   PT *did the horse eat the carrots all*   *carrots)*

An account which analyses sentences as sequences of individual words joined one to another like a succession of railway carriages after the following fashion *mi + wnaeth + y + ceffyl + fwyta + 'r + moron + i + gyd* does not provide a revealing description of their syntax. By contrast, it is more satisfactory to say that the syntax of sentences involves a structuring of *groups* or *clusters* of one or more words. The significant point at this stage is that it is possible to isolate these groups or clusters through a process of *segmentation* or division.[1] The segmentation itself is arrived at through an awareness of the various functions and interrelationships of the groups involved. This means that segmentation involves functional criteria; but for our purposes in this chapter we are only concerned with the segments that are produced.[2]

The first segmentation[3] involves splitting off the initial particle MI from the rest of the sentence, WNAETH Y CEFFYL FWYTA'R MORON I GYD. (The particle MI is extensively used in North Wales but in other parts of Wales FE and, less extensively, I occur and are analysed like MI.) The motivation for this division is an intuitive awareness of the fact that MI is an element which tells us something about the rest of the sentence as a whole. This can be made clearer by comparing example (1) with variations of the same sentence:

> (2) (i)   *mi*   *wnaeth y ceffyl fwyta'r moron i gyd*   *(the horse ate all*
>   PT   *did the horse eat the carrots all*   *the carrots)*
>
>   (ii)   *(a)*   *wnaeth y ceffyl fwyta'r moron i gyd?*   *(did the horse eat*
>   Q   *did the horse eat the carrots all*   *all the carrots?)*
>
>   (iii) *(ni)*   *wnaeth y ceffyl fwyta'r moron i gyd*   *(the horse didn't*
>   NEG   *did the horse eat the carrots all*   *eat all the carrots)*

By comparing the three sentences in (2), we can see that MI is a member of a set of items which convey something about the nature of sentences in which they occur. The item MI tells us that the sentence is positive (amongst other things); the item A tells us that the sentence is a question; while the item NI tells us that the sentence is negative. In view of their position we can refer to these items as PRE-SENTENTIAL PARTICLES.[4] In spontaneous speech only MI (FE or I) regularly occurs while A and NI are only consistently used in formal written Welsh — hence their enclosure in brackets in the above examples. Nevertheless, they provide a useful framework for explaining the function of MI. It should also be noted that MI (FE or I) does not always occur in speech and, in many circumstances it is left out. These particles are discussed in greater detail in chapter IX.

The second segmentation detaches the form WNAETH from the remainder, Y CEFFYL FWYTA'R MORON I GYD. The item WNAETH conveys information about *tense,* and can be isolated on these grounds alone. Items like WNAETH are traditionally known as auxiliary (or helping) verbs and, consequently, we can use the term AUXILIARY to label this particular segment. It can be seen from the function of WNAETH that the auxiliary is involved with tense or time reference. But this is not the only function of the auxiliary; other features may also be involved, as for example in:

(3) *mi wneith y ceffyl fwyta'r moron i gyd*   *(the horse will eat all the*
      PT   will the horse   eat   the carrots all   *carrots)*

The item WNEITH here involves a judgement about the likelihood of an event's happening.[5] The discussion of the auxiliary is a complicated question and is treated at length in chapter V. At this introductory stage we give a simplified account of the auxiliary in that we supply an actually occurring item, WNEITH, as an indication of the auxiliary constituent. Later, however, in chapter III, sections 2b and 2c, a distinction is made between an *auxiliary feature* (that is, a *verbal inflection*) and an *auxiliary carrier* (that is, the verb form which displays the inflection). At this point, however, such a distinction would complicate the introduction of the basic syntax of Welsh sentences and its discussion is postponed. During the introductory stages, auxiliary verbs will be used in the exemplification of the auxiliary but we must emphasise that auxiliary verbs are not themselves the auxiliary components despite the similarity of labelling.

The remaining part of the sentence, Y CEFFYL FWYTA'R MORON I GYD, can be thought of as the core[6] of the sentence in that it conveys the basic 'message'; it describes the event which actually occurred, namely, the horse's eating all the carrots. This part of the sentence consists of Y CEFFYL on the one hand and FWYTA'R MORON I GYD on the other hand. Since the 'major' word in the former is the noun CEFFYL, the whole segment can be labelled a NOUN PHRASE; and since the 'major' word in the latter is the verb FWYTA, the whole segment can be labelled a VERB PHRASE.

The segmentation of Welsh sentences in this manner can be illustrated by using a diagram of the following type:

8

(4)

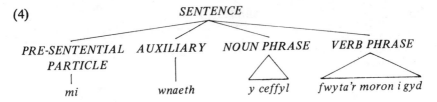

The diagram is basically a branching-diagram or tree-diagram involving *syntactic categories* such as AUXILIARY and NOUN PHRASE and items such as WNAETH and Y CEFFYL.[7] The diagram begins with the major syntactic unit of SENTENCE from which a number of branches extend. Each branch indicates the various labelled segments of the sentence in terms of further syntactic categories such as NOUN PHRASE and VERB PHRASE. The diagram terminates in the representations of the actual bits of the sentence itself.[8] Further segmentation of the segments of the sentence is possible, as in the case of the verb phrase and noun phrase, which are discussed in chapters III and VII. But where additional segmentation is possible but not illustrated, as in the case of these latter two categories, a triangular arrangement is used.

1b   Constituent structure and sentence variation

On the basis of the foregoing, a sentence can be thought of as being *constituted* of various segments. The segments can therefore be regarded as the *constituents in the structure of the sentence* and are accordingly labelled as CONSTITUENTS. Since the structure of sentences can be revealed in terms of constituents, it is useful to talk of the CONSTITUENT STRUCTURE of sentences.

The significant point is that all Welsh sentences have a constituent structure to the level of detail worked out in (4) above. Consider the following examples, which are superficially quite different from each other:

(5) *mae'r ci yn chwyrnu*   *(the dog is snoring)*
     is   the dog in snoring

(6) *mi wneith Gwil lwyddo*   *(Gwil will succeed)*
     PT will do Gwil succeed

(7) *mi ddaru   John ennill y gwpan* *(John won the cup)*
     PT happened John win   the cup

(8) *maen nhw'n gwrando ar y radio*   *(they're listening to the radio)*
     are they in listen on the radio

They can all be described by the same branching-diagram:

(9)

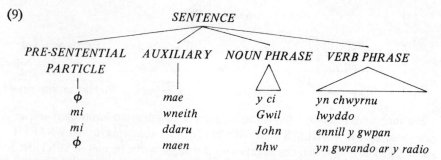

SENTENCE

PRE-SENTENTIAL PARTICLE   AUXILIARY   NOUN PHRASE   VERB PHRASE

PRE-SENTENTIAL PARTICLE	AUXILIARY	NOUN PHRASE	VERB PHRASE
φ	mae	y ci	yn chwyrnu
mi	wneith	Gwil	lwyddo
mi	ddaru	John	ennill y gwpan
φ	maen	nhw	yn gwrando ar y radio

The significance of this observation is that at this level of sentence constituency we need set up only one *general rule* which will partly account for all Welsh simple sentences. This rule is expressed in (9) above but can be presented in words as follows:

(10) *the syntactic structure of simple Welsh sentences is made up of a pre-sentential particle constituent, an auxiliary constituent, a noun phrase constituent and a verb phrase constituent.*

We can represent (10) by a shorter formula:

(11) *SENTENCE → PRE-SENTENTIAL   AUXILIARY   NOUN   VERB PARTICLE   PHRASE   PHRASE*

For the purposes of economy we can introduce abbreviations for the constituent labels so that SENTENCE is represented by S, PRE-SENTENTIAL PARTICLE by PT, AUXILIARY by AUX, NOUN PHRASE by NP and VERB PHRASE by VP. Rule (11) can thus be given as:

(12) *S → PT   AUX   NP   VP*

The arrow in (11) and (12) represents the relationship between the most general syntactic category, S, and the constituents of S, telling us that the structure of a sentence is made up of these various constituents. The rule in (12) will, in fact, be further developed in the final paragraph of this chapter to include a fifth constituent labelled as *adjunct*. It is omitted at this stage for the sake of simplicity.

So far we have reached a stage where we can account for the syntax of sentences in terms of one general rule. But a further brief glance at (9) will show that this one general rule encompasses a variety of possibilities within a sentence. For instance, with some auxiliary verbs like MAE or MAEN in examples (5) and (8) there is no pre-sentential particle and this is represented by the sign (φ) in the branching-diagram of (9). Again, while it is true that each sentence has the constituent 'auxiliary', under auxiliary, as (9) illustrates, there are a number of different items such as MAE, WNEITH, DDARU and MAEN. The verb phrase, too, is a general sentence constituent;

10

but it has a whole variety of possibilities, ranging from fairly complex examples such as ENNILL Y GWPAN (WIN THE CUP) or YN GWRANDO AR Y RADIO (LISTEN TO THE RADIO) to fairly simple examples such as LLWYDDO (SUCCEED). Obviously, then, if we want to develop our awareness of the structure of Welsh sentences we must proceed to consider the constituents themselves. This task is undertaken in the succeeding chapters.

In addition to the four sentence constituents so far established, there is a fifth which can be illustrated by the underlined material in the following example:

(13) *mi wneith y ceffyl fwyta'r moron i gyd* <u>*yn y nos*</u>   *(the horse will eat*
         PT   will the horse eat   the carrots all in the night   all the carrots in the
                                                                                      night)

The fifth constituent is labelled ADJUNCT; the re-writing rules can be extended as follows:

(14) *S → PT AUX NP VP ADJUNCT*

The adjunct is further discussed in chapter IV. It frequently involves a prepositional phrase as in the above example; therefore, since prepositional phrases can also be involved in the constituent structure of the verb phrase, distinctions must be made between the two. This point is discussed in chapter IV, section 1a.

Notes to chapter II

1. A process very similar to the process in traditional school grammar known as *parsing*.

2. As mentioned in note 5 to chapter I the fact that we discuss syntactic and semantic criteria separately for the purposes of presentation and discussion does not mean that there is no significant relationship between them.

3. The traditional parsing of Welsh sentences follows the classical model of *subject-predicate*, and then proceeds to analyse the predicate into *verb-rest of the predicate* (see, for instance, Anwyl, 1899: 82). Under this approach features which in this book are attributed to the auxiliary would be attributed to the verb. Indeed, it is this sort of analysis which provides the basis for Chomsky (1957:26, 38-42, 111):

(i)

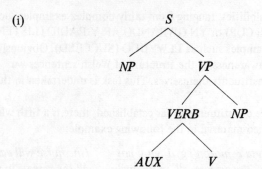

This approach in modified form is also seen in Chomsky (1965:102, 106-109, 129, 130,etc.):

(ii)

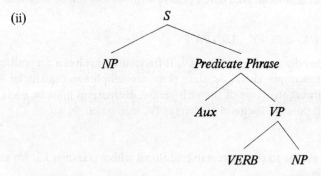

From (ii) it can be seen that the auxiliary and the verb phrase are treated differently, but we still have an essentially subject-predicate analysis. In the same work, however, there is also mention of a different approach (Chomsky, 1965: 65, 68-9, 85-6) whereby the sentence is initially analysed into noun phrase, auxiliary, verb phrase:

(iii)

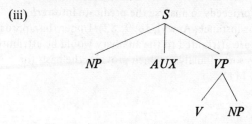

This analysis is later modified by inserting the predicate phrase to dominate the auxiliary and verb phrase as in (ii) above, thus returning to the traditional subject-predicate analysis. It is the approach in (iii) which is adopted as a basis for the description of the constituent structure of Welsh sentences here. The branching-diagrams for English, as in (iii), and Welsh sentences are quite different:

(iv) (a)

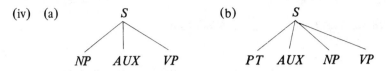

(b)

The particle appears to be an extra constituent but can compare with morphemes, like Q set up to account for interrogative sentences, in the work of Katz and Postal (1964). The fact that the AUX precedes the NP as opposed to following it merely reflects the order of these elements in the ultimate form of the sentence.

An alternative approach to sentence constituency is outlined in Fillmore (1968:21-5), who proposes a modality-proposition segmentation. Such an analysis is designed partly to bring out semantic features of the type discussed in chapter X. A variant of this approach is also seen in the predicate-arguments analysis of Langendoen (1969:96-127; 1970:46-51).

4. Frequently labelled in descriptions of Welsh as pre-verbal particles (Anwyl, 1899:178; Williams, 1959:192-9) or introducing words, 'rhageiriau' (Evans, 1960:233 ff.).

5. Chomsky (1965:106-7) establishes the auxiliary to include information about tense, modal verbs and aspect. In the present book the auxiliary refers only to information involved in verbal inflections, and modal verbs and aspect are handled in the verb phrase (see chapters III, section 2c, V and VI).

6. Compare Langendoen's (1970: 32 ff.) propositional core.

7. The properties of a branching-diagram are discussed in Chomsky (1965:64-8).

8. This branching-diagram involves an immediate division of the sentence into four segments (a fifth is added in chapter IV) based on a variant of the diagramming of Chomsky (1965) - see note 3. Given branching-diagrams of this general type, it may be that a more sophisticated diagramming of these segments which reveals their relationship to the sentence and to each other can be given as follows:

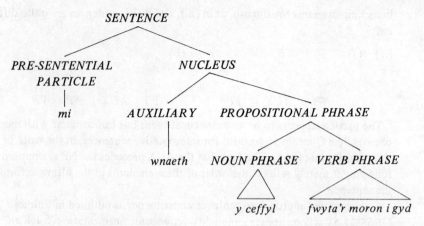

Although the use of a nucleus segment and a segment equivalent to a pre-sentential particle is attested in Katz and Postal (1964), the use of such a tree-diagram would involve terminological and conceptual innovations which would be outside the scope of this book. Consequently, the more general approach typified by the diagram in (4) will be used.

III The syntax of the verb phrase

1 INTRODUCTION

1a The constituent structure of the verb phrase

The verb phrase is itself subject to a constituent structure analysis as can be demonstrated by considering the example that has been used previously for illustration:

(1) *mi wnaeth   y   ceffyl fwyta'r moron i gyd*   *(the horse ate all*
     PT do + PAST the horse eat the carrots all   *the carrots)*

In this sentence we have a verb phrase FWYTA'R MORON I GYD (EAT ALL THE
CARROTS) which is divisible into two constituents — FWYTA (EAT) and 'R MORON
I GYD (ALL THE CARROTS). The first constituent, FWYTA (EAT), is a *verb*, so the
constituent label VERB, abbreviated to V, can be used. The second constituent, 'R
MORON I GYD (ALL THE CARROTS) is a noun phrase for the reasons outlined
in section 1a of chapter II. We can now incorporate these labelled constituents of
the verb phrase into the overall branching-diagram and develop it as follows:

(2)

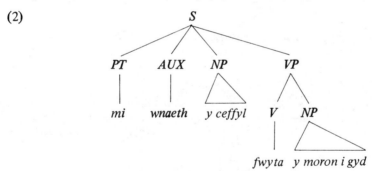

As can be seen from the triangular branching, the noun phrases are open to further
segmentation; the constituent structure of the noun phrase is discussed in some detail
in chapter VII.

1b Variations in the constituent structure of the verb phrase

It is found, however, that constituent structure analyses of various sentences reveal
different syntactic types of verb phrase. In addition to example (1) above consider,
for instance, the following examples:

(3) *mi wneith   y ceffyl edrych am y moron   i gyd (the horse will look for all*
     PT do + AUX the horse look for the carrots all   the carrots)

15

(4) *mi wneith   y ceffyl chwyrnu*   *(the horse will snore)*
     PT do + AUX the horse snore

The verb phrase in example (3) can be divided into EDRYCH (LOOK) and AM Y MORON I GYD (FOR ALL THE CARROTS). The first of these constituents is the same as before, namely, VERB. The second constituent is different because of the initial item AM (FOR): items like AM (FOR) are *prepositions* (compare, for instance, AR (ON), AT (TO), I (TO), WRTH (TO), etc.) and, consequently, the expression PREPOSITIONAL PHRASE, abbreviated to PP, can be used to label this particular constituent. In effect, however, the prepositional phrase is itself open to a constituent structure analysis with the two constituents of PREPOSITION, abbreviated to P, for AM (FOR), and NOUN PHRASE for Y MORON I GYD (ALL THE CARROTS), as is displayed in the branching-diagram in (5) below. The verb phrase in example (4) is distinctive in that it only has the one constituent of VERB. The two additional verb phrases can now be represented in the overall branching-diagram for the sentences:

(5)

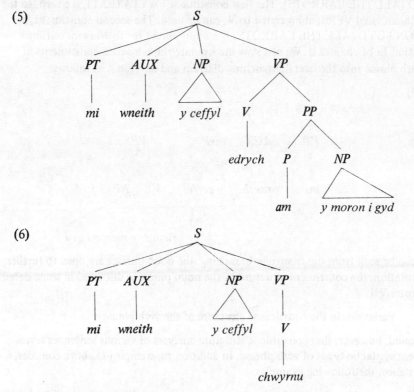

(6)

By comparing the three verb phrases in (2), (5) and (6), it can be seen that the

16

syntactic differences between them lie in the items that follow the verb: in (2) the verb is followed by a noun phrase, in (5) it is followed by a prepositional phrase and in (6) it is followed by nothing at all. It is, therefore, in this area of the verb phrase that we find the syntactic differences which enable us to distinguish various types.

1c   Verb types

Associated with the setting up of different verb phrase types is the fact that only certain verbs can occur in each of them, as can be demonstrated by considering the following *unacceptable* examples:

(7) *mi wneith   y ceffyl fwyta am y moron   (*the horse will eat for
     PT do + AUX the horse eat for the carrots   the carrots)

(8) *mi wneith   y ceffyl edrych y moron   (*the horse will look the
     PT do + AUX the horse look the carrots   carrots)

The verb BWYTA (EAT) usually occurs in a verb phrase type V NP, whereas in (7) above it occurs in a verb phrase type V PP. The verb EDRYCH (LOOK) is subject to the opposite restrictions. An acceptable verb phrase thus depends upon appropriate *syntactic co-occurrence relationships* between the verb and whatever follows in the verb phrase, and the phenomenon of *syntactic co-occurrence relationships* is therefore an important concept in analysing the verb phrase.[1] To further illustrate the point, note that CHWYRNU (SNORE) does not readily occur in either of these verb phrase types:

(9) *mi wneith   y ceffyl chwyrnu am y moron   (*the horse will snore
     PT do + AUX the horse snore for the carrots   for the carrots)

(10) *mi wneith   y ceffyl chwyrnu y freuddwyd   (*the horse will snore
     PT do + AUX the horse   snore   the dream   the dream)

In certain uses of language, such as literature or humour, it would be possible for such normally 'odd' patterns to occur but in order to make the fundamental point that verb types can be set up on the basis of their occurrences in verb phrases we have concentrated upon more 'normal' uses.

There are apparent examples of BWYTA (EAT) and EDRYCH (LOOK) occurring in verb phrases having the same structure as that in which CHWYRNU (SNORE) occurs, namely V:

(11) *mi wneith   y ceffyl fwyta   (the horse will eat)
     PT do + AUX the horse eat

(12) *mi wneith   y ceffyl edrych   (the horse will look)
     PT do + AUX the horse look

But we have to take account of the fact that examples such as these imply a 'covert' constituent of the verb phrase, which represents what is 'eaten' or 'looked at'. This type of apparent similarity is discussed intermittently below in section 3.

It thus emerges that the various verbs in the language can be sub-classified according to their potentiality of occurrence in the various syntactic verb phrase types: so far we have established three types in BWYTA (EAT), EDRYCH (LOOK) and CHWYRNU (SNORE). Such a classificatory technique is widely recognised by traditional grammar, where reference is made to *transitive* verbs like BWYTA (EAT) and *intransitive* verbs like CHWYRNU (SNORE). But it must be noted that such a classification will be complex, as many verbs can occur in more than one type. For instance, the verb GWEITHIO (WORK) can occur like BWYTA (EAT) or EDRYCH (LOOK):

(13) *mi wneith*   *John weithio'r peiriant*   *(John will work the*
     PT do + AUX John work the machine   *machine)*

(14) *mi wneith*   *John weithio ar y peiriant*   *(John will work on the*
     PT do + AUX John work on the machine   *machine)*

Finally, it must be added that it is not only constituent structure which controls the occurrence of verbs in various verb phrases. For instance, the verb BWYTA (EAT) occurs in an appropriate verb phrase in the following example but we do not have an acceptable sentence: **mi wneith y ceffyl fwyta'r llanw (*the horse will eat the tide).* It may be held that this type of unacceptability is not the concern of grammar but comes under our everyday knowledge of human experience in general: the tide is simply not eaten. But it has been suggested by some linguists that information of this type can be accounted for within grammar by giving verbs a type of semantic description which defines the sorts of nouns with which they can occur.[2] This book does not propose to pursue this point in greater detail than this brief introduction (apart from further remarks in the discussion of nouns in chapter VII) but merely seeks to draw attention to the importance of semantic factors in the use of verbs.

1d   The verb phrase and the adjunct constituent

It was pointed out at the end of section 1b above that the syntactic differences between verb phrases are located after the verb. But it is most important that the scope of the verb phrase in this direction is clearly marked. Consider, for instance, the following example:

(15) *mi wneith*   *y ceffyl edrych am y moron i gyd*   *(the horse will*
     PT do + AUX the horse look for the carrots all   *look for all the*
     yn y nos   *carrots in the*
     in the night   *night)*

Following the verb there are two prepositional phrases AM Y MORON I GYD (FOR

ALL THE CARROTS) and YN Y NOS (IN THE NIGHT). Although the second prepositional phrase occurs in a post-verbal position, it is not a constituent of the verb phrase. We can illustrate this point by showing that there is no close syntactic co-occurrence relationship between the verb and this particular prepositional phrase. A prepositional phrase like YN Y NOS (IN THE NIGHT) in this example can occur with all the three verb types so far introduced:

(16) *mi wneith   y ceffyl fwyta'r moron   i gyd yn y nos*   *(the horse will*
     PT do + AUX the horse eat   the carrots all in the night   *eat all the carrots*
                                                                  in the night)

(17) *mi wneith   y ceffyl chwyrnu yn y nos*   *(the horse will snore in*
     PT do + AUX the horse snore in the night   *the night)*

A prepositional phrase like YN Y NOS (IN THE NIGHT) in these examples is not syntactically part of the verb phrase constituent.[3] Rather, it supplies additional information about the sentence as a whole and, consequently, it can be labelled ADJUNCT.[4] The relationship between the prepositional phrases of the adjunct and those of the VP is further discussed in chapter IV, section 1a; further remarks will also be made about the adjunct in the course of the following sections of this chapter.

2   SURFACE STRUCTURE, DEEP STRUCTURE AND TRANSFORMATIONS

2a   Introduction

One of the most important contributions of the contemporary study of syntax is the principle that we cannot understand the nature and structure of sentences on the basis of the way they actually 'look'. Their shapes are only superficial ordering of the various constituents involved. In addition to their superficial structure there are much more significant relationships. In order, therefore, to distinguish between the superficial form of sentences and their deeper relationships, we introduce the concepts of SURFACE STRUCTURE to refer to the superficial appearance of sentences, and DEEP STRUCTURE to represent the more significant relationships involved.[5] In many instances, this distinction involves drawing branching-diagrams in a manner which does not directly correspond to the surface organisation of the forms in the sentence: this means that we do not simply segment sentences, but that we must very often analyse them in an abstract manner to bring out important internal relationships. On this basis the syntactic descriptions of the deep structure may be quite different from descriptions of the surface structure, and in order to match the two we apply certain operations to the syntax of the deep structure known as TRANSFORMATIONS. So far we have illustrated the structure of a sentence with an example where surface and deep structure are very similar, which does not raise any problems: but below we exemplify the setting up of slightly different deep structure analyses compared with the surface structures.

2b   Verbal inflections and auxiliary verbs

A good example of the way in which surface structure differs from deep structure is found in sentences containing inflected verbs. Consider, for instance, the following three examples:

(18) *mi balodd   John yr ardd*   *(John dug the garden)*
     PT dig + AUX John the garden

(19) *mi balith   John yr ardd*   *(John will dig the garden)*
     PT dig + AUX John the garden

(20) *mi balai   John yr ardd*   *(John would dig the garden)*
     PT dig + AUX John the garden

As they stand, not one of these examples is readily representable in terms of the general framework of constituent structure for Welsh sentences so far established:

(21)

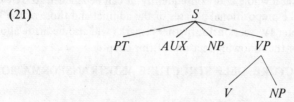

The examples with inflected verbs appear not to be segmentable in exactly these terms, as they differ from the branching-diagram in (21) in two respects. Firstly, the verb PALU (DIG) follows the particle and, secondly, it is inflected:

(22) *PT V + INFLECTION NP NP*

It can be argued, however, that the differences are superficial or surface and that, in terms of deep structure, examples with inflected verbs do indeed have the constituent structure represented in (21).

Firstly, the inflections -ODD, -ITH and -AI can be assigned to the constituent AUX. Secondly, although the verb PALU (DIG) in examples (18), (19) and (20) immediately follows the particle, it has the same syntactic co-occurrence relationships with the noun phrase object YR ARDD (THE GARDEN) as do verbs which immediately precede the noun phrase object. The verb PALU (DIG) is a verb which can occur in a verb phrase V NP but not in other verb phrases as the following illustrate:

(23) **mi ddylai John balu   i'r ardd*   *(*John should dig to the garden)*
     PT should John   dig to the garden

(24) **mi ddylai John balu yn athro*   *(*John should dig a teacher)*
     PT should   John dig   in teacher

20

Compare these non-occurring sentences with the use of RHEDEG (RUN) and MYND (GO) in the following:

(25) *mi ddylai   John redeg i'r ardd*   *(John should run to the garden)*
     PT should John   run to the garden

(26) *mi ddylai   John fynd yn athro*   *(John should become a teacher)*
     PT should John go in teacher

The important point is that exactly the same restrictions occur when the verb occurs in inflected form in initial position:

(27) **mi balith   John i'r ardd*   *(*John will dig to the garden)*
     PT dig + AUX John to the garden

(28) **mi balith   John yn athro*   *(*John will dig a teacher)*
     PT dig + AUX John in teacher

The fact that PALU (DIG) immediately follows the particle in the surface structure of examples (18), (19) and (20) should not be allowed to obscure the fact that the same relationships are involved.

We can bring out the relationships in examples (18), (19) and (20) by reorganising the examples in an abstract form. If we move the verb PALU (DIG) to a position before the noun phrase 'R ARDD (THE GARDEN) in deep structure and leave the inflection in its original position, the examples become exactly comparable with the general representation of constituent structure of Welsh sentences as represented in (21):

(29)   *MI* $\left\{\begin{array}{l} \textit{-ODD} \\ \textit{-ITH} \\ \textit{-AI} \end{array}\right.$ *JOHN BALU'R ARDD*

    PT   *AUX*   *NP*   *V*   *NP*

In these terms we can represent these sentences by the same branching-diagram:

(30)

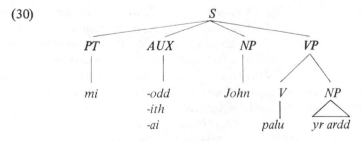

It is not really surprising that we should argue for an analysis like that in (30), where the verb is re-positioned and the inflection occurs initially, because there are many varieties of Welsh which use the auxiliary verb GWNEUD (DO, MAKE) to *carry* the inflection in a position following the particle and place the verb in the verb phrase:

(31) *mi wneith John balu'r ardd*   *(John will dig the garden)*
       PT do + AUX John dig the garden

Here the use of GWNEUD (MAKE, DO) preserves the deep structure organisation of the verb of the sentence, PALU (DIG).

However, the analysis in (30) gives us a sentence which does not actually occur:

(32) **mi -ith John balu'r ardd*
       PT AUX John dig the garden

The constituent structure analyses, as well as isolating syntactic categories (such as NP and VP) and the actual bits of language (such as *John* and *palu 'r ardd*), also concentrate upon the more significant relationships and word groupings involved rather than upon the superficial organisation of the forms in a sentence. Although they turn out to be more revealing in this sense, they are also abstract and removed from the actually occurring sentence itself. In order to develop deep structure analyses like (30) into surface structures like (19), operations are used which are known as TRANSFOR-MATIONS. Thus we can transform the abstract or deep sentence produced by (30) into the actual or surface sentence in (19) by moving the verb PALU (DIG) into the auxiliary so that it carries the inflection.[6] This particular transformation can be called the *auxiliary carrier* transformation; others are discussed in chapters VII and VIII.

The above treatment of inflected verbs introduces sufficient detail to facilitate discussion of the concept of the *subject* of a sentence. Referring back for a moment to the branching-diagram given in (2) above, it can be seen that a noun phrase constituent can occur as a direct constituent of the sentence, realised by Y CEFFYL (THE HORSE), or as a constituent of the verb phrase, realised by Y MORON I GYD (ALL THE CARROTS). The first of these is traditionally labelled as the subject of the sentence and this term will be used in our account to distinguish this particular noun phrase as the *subject noun phrase* (namely, the NP which is immediately dominated by S). In traditional grammar, the subject is individually highlighted in parsing in relation to the rest of the sentence (the predicate in traditional terms), and involves functional implications usually to the effect that the subject is the 'doer' of the sentence. The question of the subject is discussed in some detail in chapter X, section 3b; at this stage it suffices to make the point that the term 'subject' is used here merely in a positional sense to indicate that noun phrase which is immediately dominated by S, and involves no functional implications of a traditional character.

The positional definition of the subject given above is based upon its place and rela-tionships in a branching-diagram. The traditional definition depends upon linear charac-teristics of the surface structure of sentences and, traditionally, the subject is character-

22

ised as that item which follows the verb. The definition offered here is therefore quite different, as in all the branching-diagrams given so far the subject precedes the verb. The apparent contradiction can be resolved by a stricter definition of terms. In traditional Welsh grammar the inflected verbal form, such as WNAETH (DID) in (1) and (2) above, would be described as the 'verb' of the sentence while FWYTA (EAT) would be described as the 'verb-noun' occurring as object to the verb: in these terms the subject follows the 'verb'. Here however, we make a distinction between a verb and an auxiliary carrier. The latter can be an auxiliary verb such as GWNEUD (MAKE, DO) or DYLU (SHOULD), a verb such as BWYTA (EAT) or a form of the copula BOD (BE) as is discussed in the next section. In the linear organisation of surface structure, therefore, the subject always follows the inflected form which is the auxiliary carrier (the 'verb' of traditional grammar); but in terms of a deep structure branching-diagram the subject always precedes the verb.

It would also be relevant here to point out that the noun phrase of the verb phrase in the branching-diagram in (2) can be positionally identified by its traditional label of *object* as the *object noun phrase*. Again this term is used without the traditional functional implications and is discussed in detail from a functional or semantic view-point in chapter X. Further remarks can also be found in section 3b below.

2c Aspect

We also find a similar situation with examples like the following:

(33) *'roedd John yn edrych ar y teledu*   *(John was looking at the*
     was John in look on the television   *television)*

The important point here is that 'ROEDD (WAS) in initial position and YN (IN) in third position cannot occur without each other. Thus we cannot have:

(34) **'roedd John edrych ar y teledu*   *(*John was look at the*
     was John look on the television   *television)*

We have, then, a close relationship between 'ROEDD (WAS) and YN (IN). The use of the various forms of BOD, like 'ROEDD (WAS), and the prepositional form YN (IN) in this manner comes under the label of ASPECT, abbreviated to ASP, as is discussed in detail in chapter VI. Despite the fact that these forms are closely related as *aspect markers* they are separated in the surface structure by the interposing subject noun phrase; thus the surface structure tends to conceal the relationships involved. Consider now an example like the following:

(35) *mi ddylai John fod yn edrych ar y teledu*   *(John should be looking*
     PT should John be in look on the television   *at the television)*

Here we find YN (IN) occurring side by side with the BOD (BE) form. And just as it was impossible to have 'ROEDD (WAS) or YN (IN) occurring without each other, so it is impossible to have BOD (BE) and YN (IN) occurring without each other:

(36) *mi ddylai John   yn edrych ar y teledu   (*John should looking at
     PT should John   in look on the television   the television)

It thus emerges that the item YN as an aspect marker must always co-occur with a form of BOD.

In view of the relationship between the examples (33) and (35), it is desirable to relate 'ROEDD (WAS) in (33) with the BOD (BE) form of (35), as both are involved with the occurrence of YN (IN). As (35) clearly shows the relationships involved, we can reorganise (33) along similar lines:

(37) (i)   'R   JOHN OEDD YN EDRYCH AR Y TELEDU
     (ii) MI DDYLAI JOHN FOD YN EDRYCH AR Y TELEDU

By adopting an abstract, or deep structure, analysis in this manner we can produce a clearer representation of the relationships involved.

However, the form 'ROEDD (WAS) is involved in two functions, as a marker of aspect and of tense; whereas the BOD (BE) form in (35) is only a marker of aspect. We can distinguish the two functions of 'ROEDD by representing the tense element as -AI positioned in the auxiliary constituent, and by representing its aspectual function as BOD (BE) in the VP:

(38) (i)   'R -AI   JOHN BOD YN EDRYCH AR Y TELEDU (i.e. (33)
                                                          above)
     (ii) MI DDYLAI JOHN FOD YN EDRYCH AR Y TELEDU (i.e. (35)
                                                          above)

The occurrence of BOD + YN as a marker of aspect is now clearly shown.

The occurrence of BOD + YN can be assigned to the verb phrase constituent.7 We can thus represent sentences like (33) by the same generalised branching-diagram by introducing the aspect markers in the verb phrase:

(39)

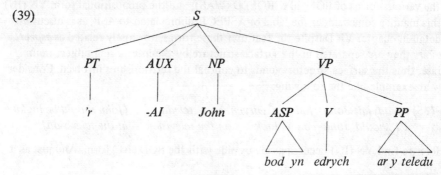

24

Again we have a difference between surface and deep structure. The auxiliary item -AI does not occur by itself and, in order to produce an acceptable sentence, we have to apply the auxiliary carrier transformation, this time to move the aspectual BOD (BE) form to the auxiliary position which, as a carrier of the auxiliary item -AI, becomes OEDD (WAS): this process compares with the moving of the verb to the front. We can say, therefore, that in the absence of a form of BOD (BE), the verb is moved to the front as a carrier of the auxiliary material; but if BOD (BE) is present as a marker of aspect, the BOD form is moved to the front as a carrier of the auxiliary features. There are other items besides YN (IN) which are involved in aspect and the BOD (BE) form can take other shapes besides 'ROEDD (WAS). These points are discussed in detail in chapter VI. At this stage we will simply note that like YN (IN) are AR (ON), WEDI (AFTER) and NEWYDD (NEW):

(40) 'roedd John ar fynd   *(John was about to go)*
     was   John   on go

(41) 'roedd John wedi edrych ar y teledu   *(John had looked at the*
     was   John   after look   on the television   *television)*

(42) 'roedd John newydd edrych ar y teledu   *(John had just looked at the*
     was   John   new   look   on the television   *television)*

We can also have combinations of these items. The important point is that where two of these items occur together each one has an accompanying form of BOD (BE):

(43) *mae John <u>wedi</u> <u>bod yn</u> edrych ar y teledu*   *(John has been looking at*
     is   John   after be in look   on the television   *the television)*

The fact that each of these prepositional items has an accompanying form of BOD (BE) is clearly seen with DYLAI (SHOULD), for instance:

(44) *mi ddylai John <u>fod wedi</u> <u>bod yn</u> edrych ar y teledu*   *(John should have*
     PT should John be after be in look   on the television   *been looking at*
                                                    the television)

But with sentences like (43) this can only be clearly shown by describing them in terms of their deep structure. Other forms like 'ROEDD (WAS) are MAE (IS), BU (WAS), BYDD (WILL BE), BYDDAI (USED TO, WOULD BE) and BUASAI (WOULD):

(45) *mae John yn edrych ar y teledu*   *(John is looking at the television)*
     is   John   in look   on the television

(46) *mi fuodd John yn edrych ar y teledu*   *(John was looking at the television)*
     PT was   John   in   look   on the television

(47) *mi fydd John yn edrych ar y teledu*   *(John will be looking at the*
     PT will be John in look   on the television   *television)*

(48) *mi fyddai John yn edrych ar y teledu*   *(John used to look at the*
     PT used to John in look on the television   *television)*

(49) *mi fuasai John yn edrych ar y teledu*   *(John would be looking at the*
     PT would be John in look on the television   *television)*

Each of these forms corresponds to different auxiliary features. They are discussed in chapter VI, section 3.

The discussion of aspect in this sub-section and of inflected verbs in the preceding sub-section have introduced the distinction between an auxiliary element (for our purposes, a verbal inflection such as -ITH, -AI and -ODD) and various verbal forms which can occur as carriers of the auxiliary element. Up to this point we have explicitly listed verbs like PALU (DIG), and the aspectual BOD (BE) as verbal forms which can occur as auxiliary carriers (for the copula BOD (BE), see section 4). It has also been suggested that they are best accounted for by being analysed as constituents of the verb phrase (even when, in surface structure, they occur in a position before the subject noun phrase) and that their occurrence in inflected form immediately before the subject is achieved by the application of the auxiliary carrier transformation. The class of auxiliary carriers also includes the auxiliary verbs (see chapter V) GWNEUD, DARFOD, CAEL, GALLU, MEDRU and DYLU as these, too, can occur in verbal inflected form in surface structure. To be consistent, therefore, we should also account for the auxiliary verbs in a manner similar to the other verbal forms which can occur as auxiliary carriers - treating them as deep structure constituents of the verb phrase that achieve their surface structure positions through the application of the auxiliary carrier transformation. For the purposes of this description, however, we will not attempt such a formulation for two reasons: firstly, such an approach would introduce an additional complexity which would burden our present aims; secondly, such a treatment would not adequately account for the complex semantics and relationships of the auxiliary verbs to the rest of the sentence. Consequently, whenever any one of these auxiliary verbs appears in a branching-diagram we adopt the expedient of placing it directly under the auxiliary constituent in inflected form — as has been done in example (4) of chapter II and examples (2), (5) and (6) of this chapter.

3   SYNTACTIC TYPES OF VERB PHRASE IN WELSH

3a   VP type : V

This type of verb phrase has already been introduced in section 1b. It involves only the one constituent, VERB. Such verbs are very familiar in traditional grammar where they are labelled INTRANSITIVE. Example (4) from section 1b can be re-introduced for illustration:

(50) *mi wneith y ceffyl chwyrnu*   *(the horse will snore)*
     PT do + AUX the horse snore

The branching-diagram for such a sentence is given in (6) of section 1b.

There are comparatively few true intransitive verbs and the number of verbs which occur in this type of verb phrase is small. The following can be listed as typical examples, however:

(51) *BLINO (tire)*   *DISGLEIRIO (shine)*
       CRYNU (shiver)   *MARW (die)*
       CHWYRNU (snore)   *PETRUSO (pause)*
       DIFLANNU (disappear)

There are a number of sentences which 'look like' intransitives but which, on further analysis, are found to be derived from other patterns:

(52) *mae Mair yn beirniadu*   *(Mair is adjudicating)*
       is Mair in adjudicate

(53) *mae John yn edrych*   *(John is looking)*
       is John in look

In both cases a further constituent of the verb phrase has been left out. Basically, we have:

(54) *mae Mair yn beirniadu RHYWUN/RHYWBETH*   *(Mair is adjudicating*
       is Mair in adjudicate someone/something   *SOMEONE/SOMETHING)*

(55) *mae John yn edrych AR RYWUN/RYWBETH*   *(John is looking at*
       is John in look on someone/something   *SOMEONE/SOMETHING)*

The omission of constituents in this manner is called ELLIPSIS and is discussed in chapter IX, section 5.

A special type of intransitive pattern occurs with verbs like YMOLCHI (WASH ONESELF):

(56) *mae John yn 'molchi*   *(John is washing (himself))*
       is John in wash oneself

Although intransitive in form in that the verb phrase consists of only one constituent, namely the verb YMOLCHI, in terms of implication this particular example compares with a sentence with a verb phrase of the type V NP, such as:

(57) *mae John yn golchi'r dillad*   *(John is washing the clothes)*
       is John in wash the clothes

In (57) the subject noun phrase JOHN performs the action of the verb upon the object noun phrase Y DILLAD (THE CLOTHES). Similarly in (56) JOHN performs the action of the verb but, in this case, upon himself. Both examples essentially convey the same relationship involving an object. Examples like (56) are traditionally called

27

REFLEXIVES and are frequently marked by placing the prefix YM- before the verb. The verb YMOLCHI (WASH ONESELF) gives classic illustration of a reflexive in form and function. But the use of this type of reflexive, apart from common examples like YMOLCHI (WASH ONESELF), tends to be a formal practice which is not productive in spontaneous speech. Examples of this latter type of reflexive can be listed as follows:

(58) *mae Mair yn <u>ymbaratoi</u>*   *(Mair is preparing (herself))*
     is Mair in prepare oneself

(59) *maen nhw 'n <u>ymbesgi</u>*   *(they are fattening up)*
     are they in fatten oneself

(60) *mae o 'n <u>ymddilladu</u>*   *(he's dressing (himself))*
     is he in dress oneself

(61) *mae hi 'n <u>ymesgusodi</u>*   *(she's excusing herself)*
     is she in excuse oneself

Many of these verbs are rare in everyday use and where they do occur the YM- prefix tends to be replaced by a reflexive pronoun occurring after the verb:

(62) *mae Mair yn paratoi ei hun*   *(Mair is preparing herself)*
     is Mair in prepare her self

(63) *mae hi 'n esgusodi ei hun*   *(she's excusing herself)*
     is she in excuse her self

Here we have a verb phrase of the type V NP which explicitly reveals the relation-ships in an intransitive pattern.

Reflexives in Welsh, however, are not always equivalent to a V NP verb phrase. Consider the following:

(64) *mae Mair yn 'madael*   *(Mair is leaving)*
     is Mair in leave

(65) *Mae'r afon yn ymchwyddo*   *(the river is swelling)*
     is the river in swell

The two verbs YMADAEL (ONESELF TO LEAVE) and YMCHWYDDO (ONESELF TO SWELL) are not equivalent to the use of reflexive pronouns after the verb:

(66) *mae Mair yn gadael ei hun*   *(Mair is leaving herself)*
     is Mair in leave her self

(67) *mae'r afon yn chwyddo ei hun*   *(the river is swelling itself)*
     is the river in swell   itself

In this instance the subject noun phrase is merely involved in the action of the verb without being affected by it. There are a number of reflexive verbs which have no equivalent transitive correlate; in addition to YMADAEL and YMCHWYDDO, we can list YMATEB (RESPOND), YMATAL (REFAIN), YMDEBYGU (RESEMBLE) and YMDDANGOS (ONESELF TO SHOW = APPEAR). In spontaneous speech note that YMADAEL and YMCHWYDDO can occur without the YM- prefix:

(68) *mae Mair yn gadael*   *(Mair is leaving)*
      is Mair   in leave

(69) *mae'r afon yn chwyddo*   *(the river is swelling)*
      is the river in swell

Again there is a formal 'educated' air about these verbs and only YMADAEL regularly occurs in spontaneous speech.

Another special type of intransitive exists with verbs like OERI (GO COLD) and TYWYLLU (DARKEN (light)):

(70) *mae'ch te chi 'n oeri*   *(your tea is going cold)*
      is your tea you in cold

(71) *mae'n tywyllu*   *(it's darkening/getting dark)*
      is in darken

In both cases paraphrases can be given as follows:

(72) *mae'ch te chi 'n mynd yn oer*   *(your tea is going cold)*
      is your tea you in go   in cold

(73) *mae'n mynd yn dywyll*   *(it's getting dark)*
      is in go in dark

This type of intransitive expresses a change in the state of the subject and is tradition-ally called INCHOATIVE. The paraphrases involve verbs like MYND (GO), DOD (COME) and TYFU (GROW) to represent the idea of changing, and adjectives like OER (COLD) and TYWYLL (DARK) to identify the state. Other verbs like OERI (GO COLD) and TYWYLLU (DARKEN) are:

(74) *CALEDU (harden)*   *GWLYCHU (get wet)*   *POETHI (get hot)*
      CRYFHAU (strengthen)   *GWYNNU (whiten)*   *SYCHU (get dry)*
      CYNHESU (warm)   *LLEIHAU (get less)*   *TEWHAU (get fat)*
      GOLEUO (lighten (colour))   *GWELLA (get better)*   *TRISTAU (get sad)*
      GWAETHYGU (worsen)   *MEDDALU (get soft)*   *YSGARNHAU (get light)*

Inchoatives are not restricted to intransitive types, as similar relationships are also found with certain transitive types (see section 3b below).

Finally, we can note the distinctive nature of intransitive verbs which typically end in -A, like CELWYDDA (LIE). They are subject to paraphrases involving a verb phrase of the type V NP:

(75) *mae hi 'n celwydda*   *(she is lying)*
     is she in lie

(76) *mae hi 'n dweud celwydd*   *(she's telling a lie)*
     is she in tell lie

Other verbs of this type include:

(77) *BRECWASTA (breakfast)* : *CAEL BRECWAST (have breakfast)*
     CNEUA (nut)   : *HEL CNAU (gather nuts)*
     COBLERA (cobble)   : *GWNEUD GWAITH COBLER*
                                 (do cobbler's work)

We can say that the intransitive pattern is a *synthetic* pattern while the use of the proposition NP VERB NP is an *analytic* pattern. In the main, the analytic (V NP) patterns are commoner than are the synthetic intransitive patterns.

3b   VP type : V NP

This type of verb phrase has been previously introduced in section 1a above. In traditional grammar this type of pattern goes under the label TRANSITIVE. Example (1) of section 1a above can be re-introduced for exemplification:

(78) *mi wnaeth   y ceffyl fwyta'r moron i gyd*   *(the horse ate all the*
     PT did   the horse   eat   the carrots all   *carrots)*

The branching-diagram for this type of sentence is given in (2) of the same sub-section.

The verbs which can occur in this pattern are very much greater in number than the intransitives discussed in the previous sub-section and typical examples can be given as follows:

(79) *ADNABOD (know (a*   *COPÏO (copy)*   *GWYNEBU (face)*
        person))   *DEALL (understand)*   *HOFFI (like)*
     ASTUDIO (study)   *DEFNYDDIO (use)*   *LICIO (like)*
     BWYTA (eat)   *GOLYGU (imply)*   *MWYNHAU (enjoy)*
     CANMOL (praise)   *GWASANAETHU*   *OFNI (fear)*
     CARIO (carry)   *(serve)*   *TREFNU (organise)*
     CEFNOGI (support)   *GWASGU (squeeze)*   *YSTYRIED (consider)*
     CLYWED (hear)   *GWELD (see)*   *YSGWYD (shake)*
     COFIO (remember)   *GWYBOD (know (a*
     COLLI (lose)   *fact))*

As with the intransitive patterns, we find a number of examples which 'look like' transitives but which further analysis reveals to be otherwise. Firstly, there are apparent transitives due to ellipsis:

(80) *mae John yn dweud y stori*   *(John is telling the story)*
    is John in tell   the story

(81) *mae Mair yn gwerthu ei char*   *(Mair is selling her car)*
    is Mair in   sell   her car

In both cases further constituents in the verb phrase have been left out:

(82) *mae John yn dweud y stori WRTH RYWUN*   *(John is telling the*
    is John in tell the story to someone   *story TO SOMEONE)*

(83) *mae Mair yn gwerthu ei char i RYWUN AM RYWFAINT*   *(Mair is selling*
    is Mair in   sell   her car to someone for so much   *her car TO*
                                                              SOMEONE
                                                              FOR SO MUCH)

The verb phrase types in (82) and (83) are discussed in sections 3e and 3f respectively. Secondly, there are examples involving verbs like AROS (STAY), CERDDED (WALK) and PWYSO (WEIGH):

(84) *mae'r ymwelwyr yn aros wythnos*   *(the visitors are staying a*
    is the visitors in stay week   *week)*

(85) *mae'r dynion wedi cerdded milltir*   *(the men have walked a mile)*
    is the men   after walk   mile

(86) *mae'r cerrig yn pwyso tunnell*   *(the stones weigh a ton)*
    is the stones in weigh ton

The surface structure of the verb phrase assumes a transitive form. But in each case it is also possible to have:

(87) *mae'r ymwelwyr yn aros tuag wythnos*   *(the visitors are staying*
    is the visitors in stay about week   *about a week)*

(88) *mae'r dynion wedi cerdded tua milltir* *(the men have walked about*
    is the men   after walk about a mile   *a mile)*

(89) *mae'r cerrig yn pwyso tua thunnell*   *(the stones weigh about a*
    is the stones in weigh about ton   *ton)*

And in the case of (84) and (85) it is also possible to have:

(90) *mae'r ymwelwyr yn aros   am wythnos*   *(the visitors are staying for a*
     is the visitors   in stay   for   week   *week)*

(91) *mae'r dynion yn cerdded am filltir*   *(the men are walking for a mile)*
     is   the men in walk   for mile

None of these variations is possible with transitives proper:

(92) **mi wnaeth y ceffyl fwyta tua 'r moron i gyd*   *(*the horse ate about*
     PT   did the horse   eat   about the carrots all   all the carrots)

(93) **mi wnaeth y ceffyl fwyta am y moron i gyd*   *(*the horse ate for*
     PT   did   the horse   eat   for the carrots all   all the carrots)

In examples (84) - (86) the noun phrase which follows the verb quantifies the activity referred to by the verb in terms of *time, distance* and *weight*. Thus (92) could be made acceptable as:

(94) *mi wnaeth y ceffyl fwyta tua hanner pwys o'r moron*   *(the horse ate*
     PT did the horse   eat about half pound of the carrots   *about half a*
                                                                    pound of
                                                                    carrots)

It happens in Welsh (as in English) that some verbs allow a quantifier to be expressed in a transitive-looking pattern.

The noun phrase which follows the verb in this type of verb phrase is traditionally labelled *object*. This term will be used to distinguish this particular noun phrase as *object noun phrase*. But, as pointed out in section 2b, the term object is not here used with the traditional functional implications. It is used merely to identify this particular noun phrase on positional grounds as the noun phrase which immediately follows the verb in the verb phrase. The term object is itself inadequate as a functional term for, as will be seen in chapter X, there are a variety of functions which can occur in object position - some of which, moreover, can occur in subject as well as object position.

There are some verbs which occur in both intransitive and transitive patterns. Typical examples are AGOR (OPEN), SYMUD (MOVE) and TORRI (BREAK):

(95) (i)   *mae John wedi agor y drws*   *(John has opened the door)*
           is   John after open the door

     (ii) *mae'r drws wedi agor*   *(the door has opened)*
           is the door after open

(96) (i)   *mae Mair wedi symud y gadair*   *(Mair has moved the chair)*
           is   Mair after move   the chair

32

(ii)	*mae'r gadair wedi symud*		*(the chair has moved)*
	is the chair after move		

(97) (i)   *mae'r ferch wedi torri'r gwpan*   *(the girl has broken the cup)*
        is the girl after break the cup

    (ii)   *mae'r gwpan wedi torri*   *(the cup has broken)*
         is the cup after break

They are discussed in more significant terms in chapter X.

3c   **VP type : V PP**

This type of verb phrase has already been discussed in section 1b and the example cited there can be re-introduced here:

(98) *mi wneith y ceffyl edrych am y moron i gyd*   *(the horse will look*
     PT will the horse look for the carrots all   *for all the carrots)*

This verb phrase involves a prepositional phrase following the verb and can be labelled as OBLIQUE TRANSITIVE. The noun of the prepositional phrase itself can be termed an OBLIQUE OBJECT. In traditional Welsh grammar, this pattern is usually treated under the heading 'verbs which are followed by a preposition'.

There are a variety of verbs that can occur in this type of verb phrase, but in listing them we must also bear in mind that there are various prepositions involved. By way of illustration the following prepositions and verbs can be put forward:

(99) *AM (for):*   *AROS (wait), CHWILIO (search), DISGWYL (wait),*
                 EDRYCH (look), GALW (call), GOFALU (care),
                 GWISGO (dress), POENI (worry)

     AR (on):   *BLINO (tire), CEFNU (forsake), DIBYNNU (depend),*
                 DYLANWADU (influence), EDRYCH (look),
                 GWENU (smile), GWRANDO (listen),
                 MANYLU (detail), SYLWI (notice), SBĨO (look)

     AT (towards): *APELIO (appeal), EDRYCH YMLAEN (look*
                 forward), SYNNU (surprise)

     AR ÔL (after): *EDRYCH (look)*

     Â ⎫
     GYDA ⎬ *:*   *ARFER (accustom), CYDWEITHIO (co-operate),*
     EFO ⎭   *CYFARFOD (meet)*

     I (to):   *ANUFUDDHAU (disobey), ADWEITHIO (react),*
                 ILDIO (yield), PERTHYN (belong),
                 UFUDDHAU (obey), YMATEB (respond),
                 YMROI (devote oneself)

     O (of):   *CYFRANOGI (partake)*

(99) RHAG (from):   GWYLIO (mind, guard), YMGROESI (beware, shun),
                     YMATAL (refrain)
      WRTH (to):   CENFIGENNU (envy), GLYNU (stick)
      YN/MEWN (in): ARBENIGO (specialise), CREDU (believe),
                     CYDIO (take hold), GAFAEL (grasp, get hold)
      YN ERBYN (against): PECHU (sin), TRAMGWYDDO (offend)

Some verbs can occur with one or more prepositions: this choice can be significant,
involving different semantics — as in the case of EDRYCH (LOOK), AM (FOR) or
AR (ON).

Again it must be borne in mind that there are sentences involving verb phrases
which look like oblique transitives but can be seen not to be so on further analysis:

(100) mae Mair yn sôn am y llyfr   (Mair is talking about the
       is Mair in talk about the book   book)

(101) mae John yn dweud wrth ei chwaer   (John is telling his sister)
       is John in tell   to his sister

The process of ellipsis has removed a further constituent, as basically we have:

(102) mae Mair yn sôn am y llyfr WRTH RYWUN   (Mair is talking about
       is Mair in talk about the book to someone   the book TO SOME-
                                                      ONE)

(103) mae John yn dweud RHYWBETH wrth ei chwaer   (John is telling
       is John in tell something to his sister   SOMETHING to his
                                                        sister)

Both these patterns are discussed in sections 3d and 3e respectively.

3d   VP type : V PP PP

This type of verb phrase has not been previously discussed; along with the verb
phrases in the remainder of this chapter it represents new material. This particular
verb phrase can be exemplified as follows:

(104) mi wneith   Mair sôn am y llyfr wrth John   (Mair will talk about
       PT do + AUX Mair talk about the book to John   the book to John)

Here we have a verb phrase SÔN AM Y LLYFR WRTH JOHN (TALK ABOUT THE
BOOK TO JOHN) which has three constituents: the first one is the verb SÔN (TALK)
and the second and third are the prepositional phrases AM Y LLYFR (ABOUT THE
BOOK) and WRTH JOHN (TO JOHN). The overall branching-diagram for such a
sentence is as follows:

34

(105)

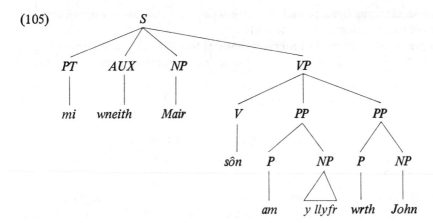

This type of verb phrase is not widely noted in traditional Welsh grammars; where it is touched upon it tends to be introduced under the heading of 'verbs which are followed by a preposition', one of the two prepositional phrases being neglected. A possible label based solely upon the characteristics of the verb phrase is DOUBLE OBLIQUE TRANSITIVE.

The example given above involves the verb SÔN (TALK) and two prepositional phrases involving the prepositions AM (ABOUT) and WRTH (TO). But there are numerous other verbs, many involving other prepositions:

(106) (i)   *ACHWYN (complain)*   *AM (about) . . . WRTH (to) . . .*
             CWYNO (complain)   *AM (about) . . . WRTH (to) . . .*
       (ii) *DARLITHIO (lecture)*   *AR (on)   . . . I (to)*   . . .
             PREGETHU (preach)   *AR (on)   . . . I (to)*   . . .
       (iii) *ANGHYTUNO (disagree)*   *AM (about) . . . EFO/GYDA/Â (with) . . .*
             ANGHYDWELD (disagree)   *AM (about) . . . EFO/GYDA/Â (with) . . .*
             CYDWELD (agree)   *AM (about) . . . EFO/GYDA/Â (with) . . .*
             CYTUNO (agree)   *AM (about) . . . EFO/GYDA/Â (with) . . .*
             DADLAU (argue)   *AM (about) . . . EFO/GYDA/Â (with) . . .*
             FFRAEO (quarrel)   *AM (about) . . . EFO/GYDA/Â (with) . . .*

The functions of the prepositions are discussed in chapter X. At this stage we can briefly observe the distinctive nature of the third type, as the following comparison illustrates:

(107) (i)   *mae John yn dadlau am   y llyfr efo Mair*   *(John is arguing*
             is John in argue about the book with Mair   *about the book*
                                                               with Mair)
       (ii) *mae John a Mair yn dadlau am y llyfr*   *(John and Mair are argu-*
             is John and Mair in argue about the book ing about the book)

35

Such paraphrasing is not possible with the other two types and the significance of this is discussed in chapter X, section 2h.

The prepositional phrases which are involved in this type of verb phrase must be distinguished from those which are not. For instance, we can have an example like:

(108)   *mae Mair yn chwyrnu ar y gwely yn y tywyllwch*   *(Mair is snoring*
        is Mair in snore on the bed in the dark   *on the bed in the*
                                                                dark)

The two prepositional phrases AR Y GWELY (ON THE BED) and YN Y TYWYLLWCH (IN THE DARK) are not in a close syntactic relationship with the verb CHWYRNU (SNORE). They can also occur with SÔN (TALK):

(109)   *mae Mair yn sôn am y llyfr wrth John*   *(Mair is talking about the*
        is Mair in talk about the book to John   *book to John on the bed*
                                                         in the dark)
        ar y gwely yn y tywyllwch
        on the bed in the dark

But we cannot say:

(110)   **mae Mair yn chwyrnu am y llyfr wrth*   *(*Mair is snoring about the*
        is   Mair in snore   about the book to   *book to John on the bed*
                                                          in the dark)
        John ar y gwely yn y tywyllwch
        John on the bed in the dark

As already pointed out earlier, prepositional phrases of this type are adjunctival and do not belong to the verb phrase. It is only those prepositional phrases that are syntactically related to the verb that are constituents of the verb phrase.

3e   **VP type : V NP PP**

The fifth type of verb phrase can be illustrated by an example such as the following:

(111)   *mi wneith John ddweud y stori wrth Mair*   *(John will tell the story*
        PT do + AUX John tell the story to Mair   *to Mair)*

The verb phrase in such an example is DDWEUD Y STORI WRTH MAIR (TELL THE STORY TO MAIR). It has the constituent structure of verb DDWEUD (SAY), noun phrase Y STORI (THE STORY) and prepositional phrase WRTH MAIR (TO MAIR). The overall branching-diagram for such a sentence is as follows:

(112)

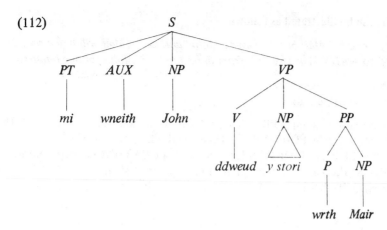

There is no traditional label for this pattern, but as a combination of transitive and oblique transitive it could be called TRANSITIVE - OBLIQUE TRANSITIVE. In some traditional Welsh grammars, due to the influence of the prepositional phrase constituent - but to the neglect of the noun phrase - examples of verbs occurring in this pattern, like the previous verb phrase type, also arise under the heading 'verbs which are followed by a preposition'.

There are a large number of verbs in addition to DWEUD (TELL) which can occur in this pattern, and the situation is complicated by the fact that different verbs require different prepositions in the prepositional phrase constituent. Since, unlike the double oblique transitive pattern, the list of verbs is not short, the following list merely exemplifies the type:

(113) *NP AR (on) + NP:*   *CADW (keep), LLWYTHO (load), TAFLU (throw),*
                           GALW (call), SEILIO (establish)
       NP WRTH (to) + NP: *ADDEF (promise), ADRODD (relate), CADWYNO*
                           (chain), CLYMU (tie), HOELIO (nail)
       NP I (to) + NP: *DREIFIO (drive), ANFON (send), CYFLWYNO*
                           (introduce), DANGOS (show), DYSGU (teach)
       NP Â/GYDA/EFO
            (with) + NP: *CYMHARU (compare), CYSYLLTU (connect),*
       NP O (of) + NP: *CYHUDDO (accuse), ATGOFFA (remind)*

At this stage we are concerned only with illustrating the constituent structure of this type of verb phrase, but it should be borne in mind that there are a variety of semantic relationships involved (some of which are discussed in chapter X).

3f   VP type : V NP PP PP

The sixth type of verb phrase is the most complicated in terms of the number of its constituents. It can be illustrated as follows:

(114) *mi wneith   Mair brynu car gan John am*   *(Mair will buy a car from*
      PT do + AUX Mair buy   car from John for   *John for one hundred*
                                      pounds)
      gant   o bunnoedd
      hundred of pounds

The verb phrase in this example PRYNU CAR GAN JOHN AM GANT O BUNNOEDD
(BUY A CAR FROM JOHN FOR ONE HUNDRED POUNDS) has a total of four
constituents: the verb PRYNU (BUY), object noun phrase CAR (CAR), prepositional
phrase GAN JOHN (FROM JOHN) and prepositional phrase AM GANT O BUNNOEDD
(FOR ONE HUNDRED POUNDS). The overall branching-diagram for such a sentence
is as follows:

(115)

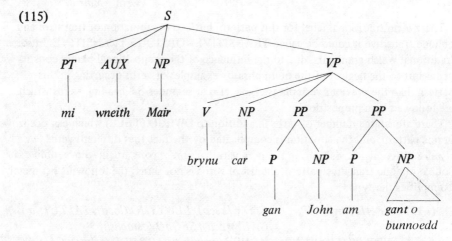

There is no traditional label for such a pattern in Welsh, but as it has an object noun
phrase with two prepositional phrases it could be labelled as TRANSITIVE - DOUBLE
PREPOSITIONAL PHRASE.

There are only a small number of verbs that can occur in this pattern; in addition to
PRYNU (BUY), verbs like GWERTHU (SELL), RHENTIO (RENT), HEIRIO (HIRE)
and, possibly, NEWID (CHANGE), CYFNEWID (EXCHANGE), ADDO (PROMISE),
CYNNIG (OFFER) can also be selected. As with the previous pattern in section
3e a variety of prepositions are involved but, in this instance, the variation appears to
be limited to the first prepositional phrase, as in the following exemplification:

(116) *mae John wedi gwerthu car i Mair am gant*   *(John has sold a car*
      is   John after   sell   car to Mair for hundred   *to Mair for one*
      o bunnoedd   *hundred pounds)*
      of pounds

(117) mae'r cwmni yn rhentio'r bws i'r ysgol *(the company is renting*
       is the company in rent   the bus to the school *the bus to the school*
                                                     for £1)
       am bunt
       for pound

(118) mae'r ysgol yn heirio'r bws gan y cwmni *(the school is hiring the*
       is the school in hire the bus from the company *bus from the company*
                                                     for nothing)
       am bunt
       for pound

(119) mae John wedi newid ei gitar efo Mair am lyfrau *(John has changed*
       is John after change his guitar with Mair for books *his guitar with*
                                                     Mair for books)

An interesting point here is that we have pairs of verbs like PRYNU (BUY) and
GWERTHU (SELL) or RHENTIO (RENT) and HEIRIO (HIRE) where each member
of the pair conveys the same activity as the other member but from an opposite view-
point. This, in part, accounts for the differences in preposition, and this point is
discussed in greater detail in chapter X. Notice that in the case of NEWID (CHANGE)
the same verb can be used to give the reverse view:

(120) mae Mair wedi newid ei llyfrau efo John am gitar *(Mair has*
       is Mair after change her books with John for guitar *changed her*
                                                     books with
                                                     John for a
                                                     guitar)

The preposition remains the same but the noun phrase object and noun phrase in
the AM (FOR) prepositional phrase change positions.[8]
It must be emphasised that the prepositional phrases are part of the verb phrase. In
the case of PRYNU (BUY), the process of buying involves buying 'something' from
'someone' for 'something'. There are examples which appear to be similar sentences:

(121) mae Mair wedi paentio'r tŷ efo John am bunt *(Mair has*
       is Mair after paint the house with John for pound (£) *painted the*
                                                     house with
                                                     John for £1)

But here the two prepositional phrases present additional facts, as it is not necessary
that 'painting something' involves a 'co-participant' (see chapter X, section 2h) or a
'reward'. In this type of sentence these prepositional phrases are not part of the verb
phrase.

VP type : V predicative phrase

The seventh type of verb phrase involves a constituent which is also seen in copula sentences as discussed in section 4b below. It can be exemplified as follows:

(122) *mae Mair yn mynd yn nyrs*   *(Mair is becoming a nurse)*
        is   Mair in   go   in nurse

(123) *mae John yn dod   yn well*   *(John is getting better)*
        is   John in come in better

(124) *mae'r goeden   yn tyfu 'n fawr*   *(the tree is growing big)*
        is the tree   in grow in bigger

The verb phrase in these examples involves a verb like MYND (GO), DOD (COME) or TYFU (GROW) and a constituent such as YN NYRS (IN NURSE), YN WELL (IN BETTER) or YN FAWR (IN BIG). This second constituent is characterised by the initial occurrence of the item YN (IN). The item YN (IN) has previously been encountered in relation to aspect (section 2c). In this environment, YN is traditionally referred to as predicative YN[9] and, consequently, the constituent can be referred to as the PREDICATIVE PHRASE [10](which can be abbreviated to PRED.PH). The overall branching-diagram for this type of sentence can be given as follows:

(125)

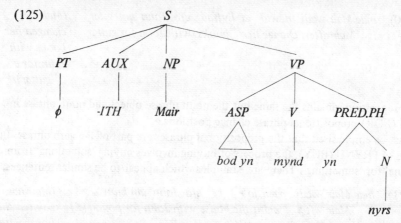

On the basis of the PRED.PH constituent, sentences containing this type of verb phrase could be labelled as PREDICATIVE sentences.

The predicative phrase of this type of verb phrase can involve either a noun as in example (122) or an adjective as in example (123). The noun is always indefinite; it is not possible to have a definite marker occurring before the noun:

(126) **mae Mair yn mynd yn y nyrs*   *(NO APPROPRIATE*
        is   Mair in   go   in the nurse   *TRANSLATION)*

However, it must be noted that a marker of definiteness does occur in genitive (or possessive) constructions as in the following example:

(127)   *mae Mair yn mynd yn nyrs y pentre'*   *(Mair is becoming*
         is   Mair in go   in nurse the village   *the village nurse)*

In this particular predicative phrase the noun NYRS (NURSE) is specific in reference. However, there is no formal marker of definiteness before the noun NYRS (NURSE) itself and to this extent the rule of indefiniteness is maintained.

Predicative sentences of this type are syntactically very similar to *copula predicative sentences* as discussed in section 4b below. If the branching-diagram in (125) above is compared with that in (142) of section 4b, it can be seen that both involve a predicative phrase in the verb phrase, the only difference being that predicative sentences involve verbs like MYND (GO), DOD (COME) and TYFU (GROW) while copula sentences involve BOD (BE). Both types of sentence could be handled together but, following the decision to adopt the traditional distinction between verbal and copula sentences (see note 11), predicative verbal sentences are discussed separately from predicative copula sentences. It is important, however, to bear in mind the syntactic similarities between the two.

It could be argued that verbs like MYND (GO), DOD (COME) and TYFU (GROW) are a sort of copula (like BOD (BE)). Consider the following comparison:

(128)   (i)   *mi eith   Mair yn nyrs*   *(Mair will become a nurse)*
               PT go + AUX Mair in nurse

        (ii)   *mi fydd   Mair yn nyrs*   *(Mair will be a nurse)*
               PT be + AUX Mair in nurse

(129)   (i)   *mi ddaeth   John yn well*   *(John got better)*
               PT come + AUX John in better

        (ii)   *'roedd   John yn well*   *(John was better)*
               be + AUX John   in better

Semantically, however, the verbs MYND (GO), DOD (COME) and TYFU (GROW) involve a change of characteristics or state while BOD (BE) involves actually being in a particular state or having particular characteristics. Traditionally, therefore, verbs like MYND (GO), DOD (COME) and TYFU (GROW) are labelled as INCHOATIVE verbs which signify a change or development to a different state.

Concerning inchoative verbs, it is relevant to point out that the three verbs listed above are *inchoative pro-verbs* which can be selected for use in a verb phrase which involves a predicative phrase. In other words, they can occur with predicative nouns or adjectives. But it is also the case that many adjectives occur in verbal form and the inchoative pro-verbs can then be dispensed with:

41

(130) (i)   *mae John yn mynd yn goch*   *(John is going red)*
             is   John in   go   in red

       (ii) *mae John yn cochi*   *(John is reddening)*
             is   John in redden

(131) (i)   *mae John yn dod   yn well*   *(John is getting better)*
             is   John in come in better

       (ii) *mae John yn gwella*   *(John is improving)*
             is John in improve

Thus it is possible to use an intransitive pattern involving an inchoative verb alone
and these are discussed in section 3a above, where further examples of inchoative
verbs are given in (74).

There are examples which are syntactically identical with predicative verbal
sentences:

(132) *mae Mair yn edrych yn goch*   *(Mair looks red)*
       is   Mair in   look   in red

(133) *mae John yn swnio 'n well*   *(John sounds better)*
       is   John in sound in better

But it is argued that sentences of this type are basically complex sentences and the
details are given in chapter VIII, section 5b.

4   **COPULA SENTENCES**

4a   **Introduction**

The verb phrases discussed in the previous section have contained the constituent
VERB realised by words like CYSGU (SLEEP), PAENTIO (PAINT), EDRYCH (LOOK),
SÔN (TALK), DWEUD (TELL) and many others. Each of these verbs has its own particular meaning: CYSGU (SLEEP) and PAENTIO (PAINT), for instance, have an
obvious meaning in that they refer to and convey a particular sort of activity. Sentences
which involve verbs in this manner can be collectively labelled as *verbal* sentences.

In addition, however, there are sentences which do not contain a verb of the type
listed above. They can best be introduced through exemplification:

(134) *mae John yn wirion*   *(John is silly)*
       is   John in silly

(135) *'roedden nhw 'n athrawon*   *(they were teachers)*
       were   they in teachers

42

(136) *Mair <u>fydd</u>   y   llywydd*   *(Mair will be the president)*
      Mair will be the president

(137) *<u>'roedd</u> yna gwpan ar y bwrdd*   *(there was a cup on the table)*
      was   there cup on the table

The significant item in each case is underlined: MAE (IS), 'ROEDDEN (WERE), FYDD (WILL BE) and 'ROEDD (WAS). Compared with verbs like CYSGU (SLEEP) and PAENTIO (PAINT) these items have no obvious meaning of their own. It will emerge in the discussion below that these items have a purely syntactic function: (i) to 'link' together the other constituents involved and (ii) sometimes to carry the auxiliary features. It is the first of these functions which has supplied the name traditionally given to items of this type, namely COPULA. Consequently, the sentences in which they occur can be labelled as *copula sentences*.[11]

Copula forms are a type of verb in that they can occur as auxiliary carriers, and despite the difference in labelling (copula as opposed to verb) they are here regarded as the verbal form of the verb phrase. Consequently, for the sake of generality, copula sentences will be assigned a verb phrase constituent which contains the copula as its verbal form, rather than a copula phrase constituent; in all instances, however, the copula form will be labelled as copula and not as verb. (See note 12 for further remarks on the labelling of verb and copula.)

There are a number of sub-types of copula sentence and each one will be outlined below. In the following discussion, however, functional factors are explicitly used in the treatment of syntactic material. The main aim will be to describe the syntax of all copula sentences within the framework of the account set up for verbal sentences. In this way, a characterisation can be established which is general enough to represent the syntax of all simple sentences.

4b   Descriptive or predicative copula sentences

The first type of copula sentence can be illustrated by the following examples:

(138) *mae Mair yn athrawes*   *(Mair is a teacher)*
      is Mair in teacher

(139) *'roedd y merched yn ddel*   *(the girls are pretty)*
      was   the girls   in pretty

(140) *mi fydd y dyn tal 'na yn blismon da*   *(that tall man will be a*
      PT will be the man tall there in policeman good   *good policeman)*

In terms of the surface structure of these sentences, a copula form such as MAE (IS), 'ROEDD (WAS) or FYDD (WILL BE) is followed by a noun phrase like MAIR, Y MERCHED (THE GIRLS), Y DYN TAL 'NA (THAT TALL MAN), which is finally followed by a predicative phrase constituent as described in section 3g above. The surface structure can thus be represented as:

(141)   *COPULA + NP + PRED.PH*

In addition to YN, the predicative phrase constituent involves a noun such as ATHRAWES (TEACHER (female)), an adjective such as DEL (PRETTY), or both as in PLISMON DA (GOOD POLICEMAN). The problem is to show that sentences with this type of surface structure fit in with the general rule of the syntax of Welsh sentences established in chapter II, section 1b.

In copula sentences like (138) - (140), the noun or adjective has the function of describing the noun in the noun phrase: thus, in (138) MAIR is described as a teacher. This function can be adopted as a label for the sentence and examples like (138) - (140) could be labelled as DESCRIPTIVE copula sentences. An alternative label is PREDICATIVE, on the basis of the predicative phrase constituent. In the descriptive relationship between the noun phrase and the predicative phrase, the copula form serves as a link. It is possible to bring out the linking function of the copula by placing it between the noun phrase and the predicative phrase in the deep structure.

Thus, the overall branching-diagram for a descriptive copula sentence like (118) can be given as:

(142)

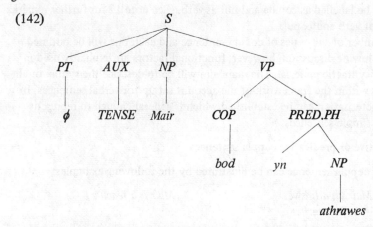

On this basis, descriptive copula sentences come under the same syntactic rules as predicative verbal sentences[12] (section 3g). However, in the actual surface structure the copula form occurs in a front position. It is possible to account for its occurrence here in terms of the second function of the copula as a carrier of the auxiliary features. Thus in (142) above the BOD (BE) form is moved by the auxiliary carrier transformation so that it carries the auxiliary feature and assumes the form MAE (IS). This is nothing new, for it was seen in section 2 above that either the verb or the aspectual BOD was moved to carry auxiliary features.

The copula form BOD (BE) is identical in shape with the aspectual BOD (BE) (section

44

2c and also chapter VI, section 1a). They can both operate as carriers of auxiliary features and they both assume the same forms in MAE (IS), 'ROEDD (WAS), BU (WAS), BYDD (WILL BE), BYDDAI (USED TO BE, WOULD BE) and BUASAI (WOULD BE). In addition, of course, the item YN is involved in occurrences of both predicative and aspectual BOD's. Occurrences of predicative YN can be distinguished from occurrences of aspectual YN in that the item which follows the former is subject to soft mutation. The following sentence illustrates the predicative and aspectual functions of BOD (BE) and YN (IN):

(143) *mae John yn bod yn wirion*   *(John is being silly)*
       is   John   in   be   in   silly

The various functions of the BOD and YN forms can be clearly displayed in the overall branching-diagram for such a sentence as follows:

(144)

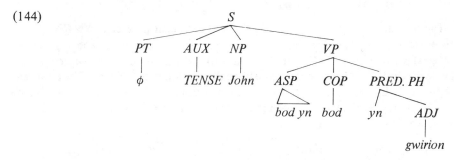

The left-most BOD is always taken as the auxiliary carrier and, in this case, that happens to be the aspectual BOD. In the absence of an aspectual BOD, the copula is used as in example (138).

Where a noun occurs in the predicative phrase in descriptive sentences, that noun is always a *generic*.noun: that is, a noun which represents a class of objects. The descriptive relationship is thus one of proposing that the noun of the subject noun phrase is a member of this particular class of objects: in (138) above, Mair is a member of that class known as teachers. Related to this point is the restriction that the noun of the predicative phrase is always indefinite. The following unacceptable examples illustrate that it is impossible for a noun which is accompanied by a marker of definiteness (such as the article) to occur:

(145) **mae Mair yn yr athrawes*   *(NOT EQUIVALENTLY*
       is   Mair in the teacher   *TRANSLATABLE)*

(146) **mi fydd   y   dyn tal 'na   yn*   *(NOT EQUIVALENTLY*
       PT   will be the man tall there in   *TRANSLATABLE)*

       y   plismon   da
       the policeman good

This restriction is also discussed in relation to predicative verbal sentences in section 3g above. The same point can be made in relation to copula sentences as was made in relation to these latter sentences: namely, that *specificness* is allowable — *mae Mair yn nyrs y pentre' (Mair is the village nurse)* — but the predicative noun itself — *nyrs (nurse)* — is not subject to definiteness. The second type of copula sentence, discussed in the next sub-section, is the pattern which must be adopted when the predicative noun is definite.

While discussing copula descriptive or predicative sentences, it is convenient to discuss the occurrence of FEL (LIKE, AS) phrases. Compare the following examples:

(147)   *mae Mair yn athrawes*   *(Mair is a teacher)*
        is   Mair in teacher

(148)   *mae Mair fel athrawes*   *(Mair is like a teacher)*
        is   Mair like teacher

The comparison suggests that FEL (LIKE, AS) can occur in place of YN (IN) in a predicative phrase. The meaning of the two examples is very similar and any difference(s) between them can be attributed to FEL, which can be said to suggest an approximate description rather than an unqualified description with YN (IN). The occurrence of FEL (LIKE, AS) in predicate phrases is much more restricted than that of YN (IN). Firstly, it only occurs where a noun is involved (as in (148) above) and never where an adjective alone occurs:

(149)   *mae Mair yn ddel*   *(Mair is pretty)*
        is   Mair in pretty

(150)   **mae Mair fel del*   *(*Mair is like pretty)*
        is   Mair like pretty

It can, of course, occur with an adjective which modifies a noun as in *mae Mair fel athrawes dda (Mair is like a good teacher)* but here the presence of the noun allows its occurrence. Secondly, it is limited to copula sentences and does not occur in verbal predicative sentences involving inchoative pro-verbs (as discussed in section 3g) even though a noun occurs:

(151)   *mae Mair yn mynd yn nyrs*   *(Mair is becoming a nurse)*
        is   Mair in go   in nurse

(152)   **mae Mair yn mynd fel nyrs*   *(*Mair is becoming like a nurse)*
        is   Mair in go   like nurse

This latter example could be accepted with a different interpretation which attributes a different function to FEL (LIKE, AS), as is briefly mentioned below.

The predicative phrase constituent thus has two possibilities, one involving YN (IN), the other involving FEL (LIKE, AS). This information can be represented by the following rule:

(153) $\quad PRED.\ PH \rightarrow \left\{ \begin{matrix} YN \\ FEL \end{matrix} \right\} \left\{ \begin{matrix} NP \\ ADJ \end{matrix} \right\}$

There is, of course, the additional restriction that the FEL phrases only occur with the copula, and not with verbal predicative sentences, and only where a noun occurs in the predicative phrase. This information can be represented by introducing a contextual restriction on the introduction of FEL in the form of FEL/COP__NP:

(154)
$$PRED.\ PH \rightarrow \left\{ \begin{matrix} YN \left\{ \begin{matrix} NP \\ ADJ \end{matrix} \right\} \\ FEL/COP\_\_NP \end{matrix} \right\}$$

Such a formulation states that the FEL phrase only occurs if (i) the copula occurs and (ii) that a noun at least is involved in the predicative phrase.

The item FEL (LIKE, AS) also occurs in a variety of other environments, some of which can be illustrated as follows:

(155) *mae Mair, fel John, yn anghytuno efo 'r awgrym*   *(Mair, like John,*
     is Mair like John in disagree   with the suggestion   disagrees with the
     suggestion)

(156) *mae o 'n chwifio ei freichiau fel melin wynt*   *(he waves his arms*
     is he in   wave his arms   like mill   wind   like a windmill)

(157) *mi fydd hon yn flwyddyn bwysig i ni fel teulu*   *(this will be an*
     PT will be this in   year important for us as family   important year
     for us as a family)

(158) *mae Mair yn mynd fel nyrs*   *(Mair is going as a*
     is Mair in go   like nurse   nurse)

(159) *mae hi 'n canu 'r gân yma fel cân brotest*   *(she sings this song*
     is she in sing the song here as song protest   as a protest song)

In these examples there is no ready association of the FEL phrase with predicative phrases involving YN (IN). Particularly interesting is example (158), which contrasts with the unacceptable example involving MYND (GO) in (152) above. But in this case, MYND (GO) is literally a verb of movement and the item FEL indicates the capacity in which Mair is going (to some place or event).

4c   Identificatory copula sentences

The second type of copula sentence can be introduced through the following examples:

(160) y dyn tal 'na ydy'r plismon   *(that tall man is the*
      the man tall there is the policeman   *policeman)*

(161) *Mair oedd yr athrawes*   *(Mair was the teacher)*
      Mair   was the teacher

In terms of its surface structure, this type of copula sentence is made up of two noun phrases with a copula placed between them:

(162) *NP + COP + NP*

In this type of sentence, one of the noun phrases is identified in terms of the other noun phrase: in (160) Y DYN TAL 'NA (THAT TALL MAN) is identified as Y PLISMON (THE POLICEMAN). The relationship between the noun phrases is not one of description in terms of class membership: the two noun phrases are equated. In view of the identificatory function, this type of copula sentence can be labelled as an IDENTIFICATORY copula sentence.

The overall branching-diagram for such sentences can be given as follows:

(163)

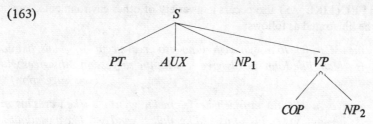

The noun phrases are numbered only for convenience in the discussion which follows. The copula again has a linking function and an auxiliary carrier function. This latter function would however produce:

(164) *COP + AUX NP$_1$ NP$_2$*

which is not the appropriate sequential order for an identificatory sentence. A further transformation is necessary which moves one of the noun phrases to initial position. An indication as to which noun phrase is moved can be gained by considering a descriptive sentence. An example like (138) above can assume a surface structure very similar to an identificatory sentence by *inverting* (see chapter IX, section 2) the noun in the predicative phrase:

(165) (i)   *mae Mair yn athrawes*   *(Mair is a teacher)*
          is   Mair in teacher

→ (ii)   *athrawes ydy Mair*   *(a teacher is Mair)*
          teacher   is   Mair

48

The inversion of the subject noun phrase produces a different configuration:

(165) (iii) *Mair sydd yn athrawes*   *(it is Mair who is a teacher)*
          Mair   is   in   teacher

On the basis of (165) (ii) it can be suggested that identificatory sentences compulsorily invert the noun phrase in the verb phrase. Thus (164) becomes:

(166) NP_2 $COP + AUX$ NP_1

In this syntactic environment the BOD form which carries the auxiliary feature
becomes YDY or YW as opposed to the MAE of normal descriptive sentences as in
(165) (ii), or the SYDD of subject inverted descriptive sentences as in (165) (iii). But
with other auxiliary features the same form occurs in *all* copula sentences; for example
consider OEDD (WAS):

(167) (i) *'roedd Mair yn athrawes*   *(Mair was a teacher)*
          was   Mair in teacher

    (ii) *Mair oedd yn athrawes*   *(it was Mair who was a*
          Mair was in teacher   *teacher)*

    (iii) *athrawes oedd Mair*   *(a teacher was Mair)*
           teacher   was Mair

(168) *Mair oedd yr athrawes*   *(Mair was the teacher)*
      Mair was the teacher

The distinctiveness of the copula form in identificatory copula sentences thus only
applies to the MAE (IS) paradigm.

Unlike the descriptive copula sentences discussed in the previous sub-section,
identificatory copula sentences can involve a marker of definiteness in the noun phrase
of the verb phrase. That is, both noun phrases can occur with the definite article. The
situation seems to be that the subject noun phrase, that is, the noun phrase which
follows the copula form in surface structure, is invariably marked for definiteness.
But the same does not apply to the noun phrase which occurs initially in surface structure as we find examples such as *rhaff ydy 'r ateb (a rope is the answer)* which contain
an initial noun phrase which is indefinite. Such an example is superficially similar to
an inverted descriptive sentence such as (165) (ii) above. However, we do not find the
non-inverted variety **mae 'r ateb yn rhaff (the answer is a rope)* and the above example
is quite clearly an identificatory copula sentence with an initial indefinite noun phrase.

4d   Copula sentences involving locatives

There are a variety of copula sentences which all involve a locative of some kind:

(169) (i) *mae 'r gwpan ar y bwrdd*   *(the cup is on the table)*
         is the   cup   on the table

(ii) (a) *mae cwpan ar y bwrdd* *(a cup is on the table)*
         is   cup   on the table

     (b) *mae yna gwpan ar y bwrdd* *(there is a cup on the table)*
         is there cup   on the table

(170) (i) *mae goriad gan/gyda John* *(John has a key)*
          is   key   LOC   John

      (ii) *mae gan (/gyda) John oriad* *(John has a key)*
           is LOC   John key

(171) (i) *mae eisiau afal ar Mair* *(Mair wants an apple)*
          is want   apple on Mair

      (ii) *mae gan Mair eisiau afal* *(Mair wants an apple)*
           is LOC Mair   want apple

There are three major sub-types involving slightly different relationships. But in each sub-type a locative marker plays a basic role in the expression of the particular relationship involved. It will be seen that the locative marker involves not only obvious locatival prepositions like AR (ON), but also prepositions like GAN (WITH) and GYDA (WITH), as in (170).

The surface structures of the sentences in (169) involve a copula form followed by a noun phrase which is followed by a locatival prepositional phrase:

(172) *COPULA + NP + PP*

These sentences can be divided into two groups according to the definiteness of the noun phrase. In (169) (i) the noun phrase is definite, whereas in (169) (ii) it is indefinite. In the case of the MAE (IS) form of the copula this distinction is formally marked in negatives and interrogatives: the definite type has YW/YDY (similar, of course, to identificatory sentences discussed above) while the indefinite has OES, for example:

(173) (i) *ydy 'r gwpan ar y bwrdd?* *(is the cup on the table?)*
          is the   cup   on the table

      (ii) (a) *oes cwpan ar y bwrdd?* *(is a cup on the table?)*
               is cup   on the table

           (b) *oes yna gwpan ar y bwrdd?* *(is there a cup on the table?)*
               is there cup   on the table

The indefinite type can be further sub-classified according to the occurrence of a locative particle YNA (THERE) immediately after the auxiliary carrier. Where YNA

(THERE) occurs in this manner, the noun phrase is always subject to soft mutation as in examples (169) (ii) (b) and (173) (ii) (b).

The sub-types in (169) can all be locatival proper: that is, they can propose that a certain object is located in a particular place. As such, they have two formal characteristics. Firstly, the locative marker cannot be deleted:

(174)   (i)   *mae'r gwpan   (*the cup is)
                 is the cup

       (ii)   *mae cwpan   (*a cup is)
                 is   cup

       (iii)   *mae yna gwpan   (*there is a cup)
                 is   there cup

Secondly, the progressive aspect does not occur:

(175)   (i)   *mae'r gwpan yn bod ar y bwrdd   (NOT EQUIVALENTLY
                 is the cup   in be   on the table   TRANSLATABLE)

       (ii)   *mae cwpan yn bod ar y bwrdd   (NOT EQUIVALENTLY
                 is   cup in   be on the table   TRANSLATABLE)

       (iii)   *mae yna gwpan yn bod ar y bwrdd   (NOT EQUIVALENTLY
                 is   there cup   in be   on the table   TRANSLATABLE)

The locatival relationship proposed by this type of sentence is a *dimensional* one: that is, location is proposed in terms of the spatial relationship of one object to another - whether it is 'on' the other object (giving AR (ON)), 'in' it (giving YN (IN)) or 'above' it etc. (giving UWCHBEN (ABOVE),etc.). The significance of this distinction will become clearer when example (170) (i) is discussed below.

The indefinite examples can also have another function,which can be illustrated by sentences such as:

(176)   (i)   mae bleiddiau yn Rwsia   (there are wolves in Russia)
                 is   wolves   in Russia

       (ii)   mae yna fleiddiau yn Rwsia   (there are wolves in Russia)
                 is there wolves   in Russia

Examples of this type can occur without a locative marker and the progressive aspect can also occur:

(177)   (i)   mae bleiddiau   (there are wolves)
                 is   wolves

       (ii)   mae yna   fleiddiau   (there are wolves)
                 is   there wolves

(178) (i) *mae bleiddiau yn bod (yn Rwsia)*   *(= wolves exist)*
            is   wolves   in be (in Russia)

       (ii) *mae yna fleiddiau yn bod (yn Rwsia)*   *(=there exist wolves)*
            is   there wolves   in be (in Russia)

It is possible to argue that the main function of examples like (176) is to propose the *existence* of a particular object as opposed to its location, even though its existence occurs at a particular place and in a particular time. Existence, however, is not restric-. ted to indefinite noun phrases; in some instances it is also possible to propose the existence of a definite noun phrase, but in so doing the progressive is *compulsory*:

(179) (i) *mae'r problemau 'ma yn bod*   *(= these problems exist)*
            is the problems   here in be

       (ii) **mae'r problemau*   *(= *these problems are)*
            is the problems

It is interesting to note in this respect that the verb BYW (LIVE) also occurs in the progressive.

(180) *'roedd Llywelyn Fawr yn byw yn y 13edd ganrif*   *(Llywelyn*
       was   Llewelyn Great in live in the 13th century   *the Great*
                                                               lived in the
                                                               13th century)

The use of the progressive in this manner is further discussed in chapter VI, section 3b. Up to this point two functions have been assigned in a definable manner to the examples in (169). A third can be added by the following examples:

(181) (i)   *'roedd y ddamwain neithiwr*   *(the accident was last night)*
                was   the accident last night

       (ii) (a) *'roedd damwain neithiwr*   *(an accident was last night)*
                was   accident last night

            (b) *'roedd yna ddamwain neithiwr*   *(there was an accident last*
                was   there accident last night   *night)*

(182) (i)   *'roedd y cyfarfod neithiwr*   *(the meeting was last night)*
                was   the meeting last night

       (ii) (a) *'roedd cyfarfod neithiwr*   *(a meeting was last night)*
                was meeting   last night

            (b) *'roedd yna gyfarfod neithiwr*   *(there was a meeting last*
                was   there meeting last night   *night)*

52

The significant factor in these sentences is the nature of the noun in the noun phrase: they all involve *events* of some sort as opposed to the locative and existential sentences which involve *entities*. As can be seen by the above examples, they can occur without the locative marker; but progressive cannot occur, as can be demonstrated by (181) (ii) (b) and (182) (ii) (b):

(183) *'roedd yna ddamwain yn bod neithiwr   (= *an accident existed
          was   there accident in be last night   last night)

(184) *'roedd yna gyfarfod yn bod neithiwr   (= *there existed a
          was   there meeting in be   last night   meeting last night)

Existential statements concerning entitles generally involve a *durative* period of time while statements concerning events involve a *punctual* time marker. Event statements, however, can themselves be divided into two types. In (181) the event concerned is *fortuitous* but that in (182) is an event *designed* by various agents. Fortuitous events can also be expressed by DIGWYDD (HAPPEN, OCCUR) while designed events can be expressed by CYNNAL (HOLD) but not vice versa:

(185) (i)   mi ddigwyddodd y ddamwain neithiwr   (the accident happened
              PT happened   the accident last night   last night)

     (ii)   (a)   mi ddigwyddodd damwain neithiwr   (an accident happened
                   PT happened   accident last night   last night)

          (b)   mi ddigwyddodd yna ddamwain neithiwr   (there happened
                   PT happened   there accident last night   an accident last
                                              night)

(186) (i)   *mi gynhaliwyd y ddamwain neithiwr   (*the accident was
              PT was held the accident last night   held last night)

     (ii)   (a)   *mi gynhaliwyd damwain neithiwr   (*an accident was held
                   PT was held accident last night   last night)

          (b)   *mi gynhaliwyd yna ddamwain neithiwr   (*there was held
                   PT was held there accident last night   an accident last
                                               night)

(187) (i)   mi gynhaliwyd y cyfarfod neithiwr   (the meeting was held
              PT was held the meeting last night   last night)

     (ii)   (a)   mi gynhaliwyd cyfarfod neithiwr·   (a meeting was held
                   PT was held meeting last night   last night)

          (b)   mi gynhaliwyd yna gyfarfod neithiwr   (there was held
                   PT was held there meeting last night   a meeting last
                                             night)

(188) (i) *mi ddigwyddodd y cyfarfod neithiwr   (*the meeting
            PT happened   the meeting last night   happened last night)

       (ii) (a) *mi ddigwyddodd cyfarfod neithiwr (*a meeting hap-
                  PT happened   meeting last night pened last night)

             (b) *mi ddigwyddodd yna gyfarfod neithiwr (*there happened
                  PT happened   there meeting last night a meeting last
                                                                night)

The verb CYNNAL (HOLD) occurs in the *passive* (chapter VIII, section 6) and, consequently, implies an *agent,* someone who is involved in the meeting. With fortuitous events, participants can also be involved but they are not the agents; rather they suffer the event. An additional point is that the verb CAEL (HAVE, RECEIVE) can be used to show that participants are involved without implying that they are agents or otherwise. As such, CAEL (HAVE, RECEIVE) can occur in both *fortuitous* events and *designed* events, being neutral to the question of agency:

(189) mi gawson nhw ddamwain   (they had an accident)
       PT had   they accident

(190) mi gawson nhw gyfarfod   (they had a meeting)
       PT had   they meeting

Whereas, therefore, DIGWYDD (HAPPEN) is confined to *fortuitous* events and CYNNAL (HOLD) is confined to *designed* events, CAEL (HAVE) is not as restricted.

On the basis of the foregoing discussion of examples like those in (169), it can be concluded that such sentences, under certain conditions, can involve locatival, existential and event propositions.[13]

The surface structures of the examples in (170) contain a copula form, a noun phrase and a prepositional phrase involving either the preposition GAN (WITH) or the preposition GYDA (WITH). As can be seen by comparing (170) (i) with (170) (ii), there are two sequential varieties: either the noun phrase precedes the prepositional phrase or vice versa. The surface structure can thus be represented as:

(191) (i)   COP + NP   + PREP. PH

       (ii) COP + PREP. PH + NP

The sequential variation plays a significant part in this type of copula sentence.

The examples in (170) are traditionally labelled as 'possessive' sentences: that is, that the referent of the noun in the prepositional phrase possesses the referent of the noun in the noun phrase (John possesses a key, etc.). But possession is only one of a number of relationships involved and is, furthermore, dependent upon the sequential ordering.

The sequence in (170) (i) where the noun phrase precedes the prepositional phrase is basically *locatival*. Syntactically, such a sentence is identical with the locatival sentences in (169) and, indeed, it is possible to have:

(192) (i)   *mae'r goriad gan/gyda John*   *(John has the key)*
            is the key   LOC   John

        (ii) (a)   *mae goriad gan/gyda John*   *(John has a key)*
                   is   key   LOC   John

              (b)   *mae yna oriad gan/gyda John*   *(John has a key)*
                   is there key   LOC   John

There is no necessary constraint that John actually possesses the key; it may simply be that the key is temporarily in John's safekeeping and is then to be found with John. And, indeed, in North Wales EFO (WITH) can be used:

(193) *mae'r goriad efo John*   *(the key is with John)*
       is the   key with John

John is thus the location for the key. But it is a location which is not expressible in dimensional terms and in these circumstances the preposition GAN (WITH) or GYDA (WITH) is used as opposed to AR (ON) or YN (IN),etc.

The second sequential possibility can involve a variety of relationships, including possession:

(194) *mae gan y   bwrdd goesau hir*   *(the table has long legs)*
       is LOC the table legs   long

(195) *mae gan John deimlad drwg*   *(John has (got) an awful feeling)*
       is LOC John feeling   bad

(196) *mae gan John bres*   *(John has (got) some money)*
       is LOC John money

In each case something is being said about a location in terms of what is located at that location. In (194) the table is characterised as having long legs, in (195) John is associated with a particular feeling, while in (196) we have the traditional relationship of possession. It is this latter relationship which has been over-generalised to all occurrences of this type of sentence, but it must be emphasised that neither this type of pattern nor its sequential variation is always concerned with possession.

The third type of sentence (171) involves a copula form, a noun phrase and a prepositional phrase. There are two sequential possibilities which reflect dialectal and and stylistic factors:

(197) (i)   *COP + NP   + PREP. PH*

        (ii)   *COP + PREP.PH + NP*

With each sequence a particular preposition occurs. Thus (197) (i) occurs in the speech of South Wales and in written Welsh and the preposition AR (ON) is used. The sequence in (197) (ii) occurs in speech in North Wales and GAN (WITH) is the preposition selected.

This type of copula sentence is very similar to (195) above in that a certain feeling is associated with a person through a locatival pattern: Mair, for instance, is associated with the want of an apple. In view of these semantic factors it follows that North Walian speakers, in fact, use one sequential variety of the so-called 'possessive' pattern.

The distinctive feature in these sentences is the nature of the noun phrase. It contains nouns like (EISIAU (WANT), OFN (FEAR), CHWANT (DESIRE) and AWYDD (DESIRE). By using a compound noun phrase, these various feelings expressing wants, fears and desires are focussed upon a particular object: EISIAU AFAL (WANT AN APPLE), OFN DWR (FEAR OF WATER), AWYDD CREMPOG (DESIRE FOR PANCAKES). The outstanding characteristic of such sentences, however, is the fact that they can be paraphrased by a copula sentence of the following type:

(198) *mae Mair eisiau/mo(f)yn afal*   *(northern/southern)*   *(Mair wants*
      is Mair   want   apple   *an apple)*

(199) *mae John ofn dwr*   *(northern)*   *(John fears*
      is John fear water   *water)*

(200) *'dwi awydd crempog*   *(northern)*   *(I want a*
      am I desire   pancake   *pancake)*

Another item which can occur in this type of sentence is HIRAETH (LONGING (nostalgia)). But when it occurs in the locatival pattern it is always followed by the preposition AM (FOR):

(201) (i) *mae hiraeth am gartre' arna' i*   *(I long for home)*
          is nostalgia for home   on I

      (ii) *mae gan i hiraeth am gartre'*   *(I long for home)*
          is LOC I nostalgia for home

Moreover, it is not certain whether it can occur in a pattern like that in (198) to (200) or whether it must assume a verbal form (a possibility which is also open to OFN and MO(F)YN):

(202) (i) *'dwi hiraeth am gartre'*   *(northern)*   *(I long for home)*
          am I nostalgia for home

      (ii) *'dwi'n hiraethu am gartre'*   *(I long for home)*
          am I in   long   for home

The various types of locatival copula sentence studied in this sub-section can be

56

characterised by one syntactic type of werb phrase which directly represents the copula sentence in (169) (i) and can be given as:

(203)

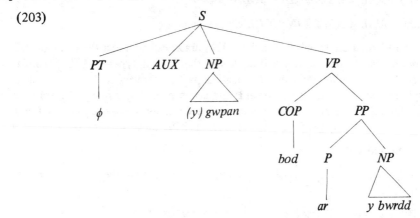

As it stands, this branching-diagram accounts for the types of locatival sentence in (169) (ii) (a), (170) (i) and (171) (i) in addition to (169) (i). But in the case of (169) (ii) (b), the occurrence of the locative item YNA (THERE) is not allowed for and in the case of (170) (ii) and (171) (ii) the noun phrase and prepositional phrase are in reverse positions.

The item YNA (THERE) may always, but not necessarily, accompany an indefinite noun phrase. It can, therefore, be suggested that, when the noun phrase is indefinite, an optional transformation inserts YNA (THERE) before the noun phrase subject. This transformation can be illustrated as follows:

(204) *AUX   CWPAN BOD AR Y BWRDD*

(205) *AUX YNA CWPAN BOD AR Y BWRDD*

(206) *MAE YNA CWPAN   AR Y BWRDD*

The deep structure is given in (204), the YNA (THERE) insertion is given in (205) and the auxiliary carrier transformation is given in (206) which moves the BOD form to auxiliary position where it occurs as MAE (IS). This transformation which inserts YNA (THERE) can be labelled the *YNA (THERE) insertion* transformation. It is also accompanied by a rule which says that if YNA (THERE) is inserted, the initial consonant of the following noun phrase is soft mutated.

Turning to the sub-types in (170) (ii) and (171) (ii), it is suggested that both are derived from a deep structure like that in (203) by inverting the prepositional phrase and the noun phrase (so that the prepositional phrase occurs in more prominent subject position). The transformational processes involved can be illustrated in respect of example (170) (ii):

(207) *TENSE GORIAD BOD GAN JOHN*

(208) *MAE GORIAD GAN JOHN*

(209) *MAE GAN JOHN GORIAD*

This transformation, which moves the GAN phrase, can go under the name of the *GAN phrase movement* transformation. Notice that the sub-types in (170) (ii) and (171) (ii) basically follow on from the locatival pattern as given in (208) above. The GAN phrase movement transformation is also accompanied by a rule which soft-mutates the initial consonant of the noun phrase which essentially follows the GAN phrase. This rule finally produces (170) (ii) from (209) above.

5   SUMMARY

The survey of the syntax of Welsh simple sentences began with the rule given in chapter II, 0.2:

(210) $S \rightarrow PT$ *AUX*   *NP*   *VP*   *ADJUNCT*

Sections 3 and 4 above have examined the syntax of the verb phrase and a total of ten syntactic types of verb phrase have been given. On this basis, it is possible to set up a further ten rules which contain the details of the syntax of the verb phrase:

(211)
(i)	$VP \rightarrow$	*(ASP)*	*V*			
(ii)	$VP \rightarrow$	*(ASP)*	*V*	*NP*		
(iii)	$VP \rightarrow$	*(ASP)*	*V*	*PP*		
(iv)	$VP \rightarrow$	*(ASP)*	*V*	*PP*	*PP*	
(v)	$VP \rightarrow$	*(ASP)*	*V*	*NP*	*PP*	
(vi)	$VP \rightarrow$	*(ASP)*	*V*	*NP*	*PP*	*PP*
(vii)	$VP \rightarrow$	*(ASP)*	*V*	*PRED. PH*		
(viii)	$VP \rightarrow$	*(ASP)*	*COP*	*PRED. PH*		
(ix)	$VP \rightarrow$		*COP*	*NP*		
(x)	$VP \rightarrow$	*(ASP)*	*COP*	*PP*		

The brackets enclosing ASP indicate that it can be either selected or not selected; in the case of identificatory copula sentences in (211) (ix) aspect is not involved. These ten rules account for all the verb phrase types given in sections 3a through to 4d. As they stand, however, these rules contain a considerable amount of repetition. Substantial abbreviation is possible if we introduce brackets and braces to generalise these formulae. A more economical and compact representation of the details in (211) can then be given as follows:

(212)

$$V \rightarrow (ASP) \left\{ \begin{array}{l} V \left\{ \begin{array}{l} (NP)\ (PP)\ (PP) \\ (PRED.\ PH) \end{array} \right\} \\ COP \left\{ \begin{array}{l} PRED.\ PH \\ NP \\ PP \end{array} \right\} \end{array} \right\}$$

58

The rule in (212) states that a verb phrase can either involve or not involve aspect. In addition the verb phrase can be either verbal or copular. If it is verbal, the verb phrase can take one of seven forms as listed in (211) (i) to (211) (vii). The syntactic categories involved in addition to V include NP, PP and PRED.PH in various combinations, and all this information is summarised in abbreviated form in (212). A copula sentence involves a predicative phrase or noun phrase or prepositional phrase and this choice, too, is indicated in (212).

In the course of the preceding sections, details of the constituent structure of a prepositional phrase (section 1b) and predicative phrase sections 3g and 4b were also introduced. Additional rules can summarize this information:

(213) $PP \rightarrow P\ NP$

(214)
$$PRED.PH \rightarrow \left\{ \begin{array}{l} YN \left\{ \begin{array}{c} NP \\ ADJ \end{array} \right\} \\ FEL/COP \underline{\quad} NP \end{array} \right\}$$

The three rules in (212), (213) and (214) now give all the details about the constituent structure of the verb phrase which have been introduced in this chapter.

By combining the rules given in (210), (212), (213) and (214) we can now summarise all the information about the syntax of Welsh sentences given in chapters II and III, as follows:

(215) (i) $S \rightarrow PT\ AUX\ NP\ VP\ ADJUNCT$

(ii)
$$VP \rightarrow (ASP) \left\{ \begin{array}{l} V \left\{ \begin{array}{l} (NP) \quad (PP) \quad (PP) \\ (PRED.PH) \end{array} \right\} \\ COP \left\{ \begin{array}{l} PRED.PH \\ NP \\ PP \end{array} \right\} \end{array} \right\}$$

(iii) $PP \rightarrow P\ NP$

(iv)
$$PRED.PH \rightarrow \left\{ \begin{array}{l} YN \left\{ \begin{array}{c} NP \\ ADJ \end{array} \right\} \\ FEL\ /\ COP \underline{\quad} NP \end{array} \right\}$$

In addition to the above rules we also require four *transformational rules* which produce the surface structures of sentences. Firstly, the *auxiliary carrier* transformation (chapter III, section 2b) applies to all deep structures produced by the above rules and moves aspectual BOD (BE) if selected, or the verb or copula BOD (BE) (if the aspectual BOD (BE) does not occur), to the place of the auxiliary constituent in order to carry the auxiliary features in various inflected forms. Secondly, the *identificatory noun phrase inversion* transformation (chapter III, section 4c) compulsorily moves the object noun phrase of identificatory copula sentences to initial position. Thirdly, the *YNA (THERE) insertion* transformation (chapter III, section 4d) optionally applies to insert YNA (THERE) immediately after the auxiliary carrier in the case of locative sentences involving an indefinite subject noun phrase. Fourthly, the *GAN movement* transformation (chapter III, section 4d) applies to locative sentences involving GAN and interchanges the GAN phrase with the subject noun phrase.

The significant point is that all simple Welsh sentences as discussed in chapters II and III are accounted for by the set of re-write rules given in (215) and the appropriate application of the four transformational rules. [14] Even more significant is the fact that *all* Welsh sentences, simple or otherwise, can be seen as based upon this set of re-write and transformational rules and any additional complex types are produced by re-applying these rules or by performing operations on the sentences produced by these rules. The re-application of these rules and the carious operations are discussed in chapters VIII and IX.

Notes to chapter III

1. Labelled and discussed by Chomsky (1965 : 90-106) as *strict sub-categorisation* features.

22. Labelled and discussed by Chomsky (1965 : 90-106) as *selectional* features.

3. This distinction is sometimes referred to in terms of *nuclear* and *extra-nuclear* (see Lyons,1969 : 334, bearing in mind that he is illustrating the subject-predicate approach).

4. The employment of the term *adjunct* is here based upon its use in Halliday (1961) and Lyons (1969 : 334, 345). Chomsky (1965 : 101-3) discusses this type of phenomenon but does not introduce an overall 'cover' constituent like *adjunct* for the various types of features involved.

5. The concept of deep structure was first explicitly formalised by Chomsky (1957). It was considerably modified in Chomsky (1965) where it is used to relate surface structures to deep structures without producing changes in meaning. It is this sense that deep structure and surface structure are used in this book, but it is pointed out that the nature of deep structure itself and its relationship with surface structure is nowadays a controversial issue, (see, for instance, various papers in the *Linguistics* section in Steinberg and Jakobovits, 1971).

6. This is a highly *ad hoc* formulation of the application of a transformation. It is not primarily the aim of this work to work out the precise mechanics of a transformation. Where a transformation which has been formulated in the general linguistics literature is introduced, brief discussion will be supplied with details of the reference in the notes. In all other cases an *ad hoc* verbalisation only will be given. Whereas it is acknowledged that a loose consideration of the details of a transformation may lead to a re-assessment of the analysis, the view adopted here is that an awareness of the function of a transformation in general terms will suffice to achieve our aims without a precise formulation of the operation.

7. In Chomsky (1965), *aspect* is assigned to the AUX along with *tense* and *modality*. Such an approach does not account for an occurrence of aspect in Welsh. Fillmore (1968 : 23), in a footnote, suggests that aspect may be a feature of the verb in the *proposition* (as used by Fillmore). Although the simple linear presentation presented in (39) is naïve, it does capture some characteristics of aspect and will suffice for our descriptive purposes.

8. In the case of ADDO (PROMISE) and CYNNIG (OFFER), reversing the appropriate elements requires the introduction of CAEL (HAVE):

> *mae John wedi cynnig ei gar i Mair am bunt* *(John has offered his car to Mair for £1)*

> → *mae Mair wedi cael cynnig ei gar gan John an bunt* *(Mair has had the offer of his car from John for £1)*

9. The remarks on the distribution of YN are merely surface observations. A significant analysis would have to consider the possibility of a generalisation over its various uses. There is, for instance, syntactic similarity between aspectual and predicative YN:

   (i)   *mae'r merched yn ddel*   *(the girls are pretty)*
           is the girls in pretty

   (ii) *mae'r merched yn canu*   *(the girls are singing)*
           is the girls in sing

The mutation difference is offset by a greater balance of syntactic context. In other uses, YN can also occur as a locative preposition and with manner adverbs:

   (iii) *mae'r merched yn yr ardd*   *(the girls are in the garden)*
           is the girls in the garden

   (iv) *mae'r merched yn canu yn uchel* *(the girls are singing loudly)*
           is the girls in sing in high

61

For our purposes, the distributional distinctions will be maintained giving an *aspectual YN* as in (i), a *predicative YN* as in (ii), a *locative YN* as in (iii), and an *adverbial YN* as in (iv). For translation into English in the detailed grammatical glosses, however, the locative interpretation is used in each case.

10. The label predicative phrase is here used as a constituent of the verb phrase and not as in Chomsky (1965 : e.g. 106-7) as a constituent of the sentence which itself includes the verb phrase. See diagram (ii) of note 3 to chapter II.

11. Traditional grammars of Welsh reserve the term copula for examples like (136) above, and all the other examples would be described as 'verbal'. The motivation for the traditional label may be due to the distinctive surface syntax of examples like (136) as is described in section 4c. This book thus represents a departure from the labelling of traditional Welsh grammar in that all four types in (134) to (137) are described as copula. Related to this point is the fact that traditional grammars also attribute to the 'verbal' BOD the semantics of 'existence' where BOD is equivalent to BODOLI (EXIST).

12. Some writers (e.g. Ross,1969) argue that the copula can be treated in the same categorial terms as verbs and accounted for under the category V as opposed to COP. We follow the more conventional labelling as in Chomsky (1965 :e.g. 106-7).

13. A great deal of this material is discussed by Lyons (1969 : 345-9. 388-90) in relation to English sentences.

14. It would be more accurate to say that these rules supply a basis for handling all Welsh simple sentences as, in some respects, they need extending to account for some sentence types which have not been discussed. This is the case with descriptive copula sentences, for instance, where certain adjectives and nouns can be followed by prepositional phrases:

    (i)   *mae John yn hoff o Mair*   *(John is fond of Mair)*
              is   John in   fond of Mair

    (ii)   *'roedd Mair yn flin am y damwain*   *(Mair was angry about*
             was   Mair in angry about the accident   the accident)

    (iii) *mae dwr yn dda i ti*   *(water is good for you)*
             is   water in good for you

    (iv)   *mae Mair yn ffrind i John*   *(Mair is a friend to John)*
             is   Mair in   friend to John

In order to cater for examples of this type the rules relating to descriptive copula sentences would have to be developed to account for the prepositional phrases.

IV The syntax and semantics of the adjunct constituent

1 INTRODUCTION

Verb phrase and adjunct

In addition to the four major sentence constituents of PT, AUX, NP and VP there is a fifth, which has been given the label of ADJUNCT. The following examples illustrate sentences which have no adjunct constituent:

(1) *mae John yn cysgu*   *(John is sleeping)*
     is John in sleep

(2) *mae John yn torri coed*   *(John is cutting wood)*
     is John in cut   wood

(3) *mae John yn edrych ar y   teledu*   *(John is looking at the*
     is John in look   on the television   *television)*

There are restrictions on the kinds of constituent (s) which can occur with particular verbs as the post-verbal constituent (s) in the verb phrase — thus a noun phrase like COED (TREES, WOOD) can occur with TORRI (CUT) but not with the other verbs. But we can take an expression like YN Y PARLWR (IN THE PARLOUR) and add it unrestrictedly to all three:

(4) *mae John yn cysgu yn y parlwr*   *(John is sleeping in the*
     is John in sleep in the parlour   *parlour)*

(5) *mae John yn torri coed yn y   parlwr*   *(John is cutting wood in*
     is John in cut   wood in the parlour   *the parlour)*

(6) *mae John yn edrych ar y teledu   yn y   parlwr* *(John is looking at the*
     is John in   look on the television in the parlour *television in the parlour)*

An expression like YN Y PARLWR (IN THE PARLOUR) applies to the sentence as a whole, and can occur with any one of the sentence patterns so far established; it is an adjunct supplying additional information, in this case the *location* of the activity.

It is thus possible to develop the overall tree-diagram of the major sentence constituents to include ADJUNCT:

(7)

$$S$$

PT   AUX   NP   VP   ADJUNCT

We find, however, that there are a variety of adjunct types. The following sections are therefore devoted to an illustration of some, but not all, adjunct possibilities in Welsh.

2 TIME WHEN, DURATION AND FREQUENCY

A number of adjunct types are involved with 'time' in its most general sense. Consider the three following examples, in which the adjuncts are underlined:

(8)   'roedd John yn palu'r ardd   <u>ddoe</u>   *(John was digging the*
     was   John in   dig the garden yesterday   *garden yesterday)*

(9)   'roedd John yn palu'r ardd   <u>am awr</u>   *(John was digging the*
     was   John in   dig the garden for hour   *garden for an hour)*

(10)   'roedd John yn palu'r ardd   <u>bob nos</u>   *(John was digging the*
     was   John in   dig the garden every night   *garden every night)*

The first type, illustrated by DDOE (YESTERDAY), establishes the 'time when' the event occurred. It is always associated with the PRYD (WHEN) interrogative type, and we can label this type of adjunct as a TIME WHEN adjunct. Other examples in addition to DDOE (YESTERDAY) are:

(11)

HEDDIW	*DDOE*	*YFORY*
(today)	*(yesterday)*	*(tomorrow)*
Y BORE 'MA	*BORE DDOE*	*NOS YFORY*
(this morning)	*(yesterday morning)*	*(tomorrow night)*
YR WYTHNOS YMA	*NEITHIWR*	*YR WYTHNOS NESA'*
(this week)	*(last night)*	*(next week)*
Y MIS YMA	*YR WYTHNOS DIWETHA'*	*Y MIS NESA'*
(this month)	*(last week)*	*(next month)*
Y FLWYDDYN	*Y MIS DIWETHA'*	*Y FLWYDDYN NESA'*
YMA/ELENI	*(last month)*	*(next year)*
(this year)	*Y FLWYDDYN*	*YN Y BORE,*
HENO	*DDIWETHA'/*	*PNAWN, etc.*
(tonight)	*Y LLYNEDD*	*(in the morning,*
NAWR/RŴAN	*(last year)*	*afternoon, etc.)*
(now)	*ECHDOE*	*GYDA'R NOS*
Y FUNUD YMA	*(day before yesterday)*	*(in the evening)*
(this minute)	*FLYNYDDOEDD YN ÔL*	*AR ÔL TE, etc.*
	(years ago)	*(after tea, etc.)*

There are many more examples, the list in (11) being merely illustrative.

The second type, AM AWR (FOR AN HOUR), establishes the duration of the activity of the proposition and is associated with the interrogative type AM (BA) FAINT (FOR (HOW) MUCH) or PA MOR HIR (HOW LONG). It is accordingly labelled DURATIVE. Other durative items like AM AWR (FOR AN HOUR) are:

(12)

AM (Y) BORE	*TRWY ('R) BORE*
(for a (the) morning)	*(through a (the) morning)*
AM (Y) P'NAWN	*TRWY ('R) P'NAWN*
(for a (the) afternoon)	*(through a (the) afternoon)*
AM (Y) DYDD/DIWRNOD	*TRWY ('R) DYDD*
(for a (the) day)	*(through a (the) day)*
AM (YR) WYTHNOS	*TRWY ('R) WYTHNOS*
(for a (the) week)	*(through a (the) week)*
AM (Y) FLWYDDYN	*TRWY ('R) FLWYDDYN*
(for a (the) year)	*(through a (the) year)*

We find that durative adjuncts frequently occur as prepositional phrases beginning with either AM (FOR) or TRWY (THROUGH) followed by a noun signifying a temporal period. The AM (FOR) types have the characteristic that AM (FOR) can be omitted:

(13) *mae hi wedi gweithio (am) wythnos*   *(she's worked (for) a week)*
      is she after work (for) week

(14) *mae hi 'n aros (am) y nos efo ni*   *(she's staying (for)*
      is she in stay (for) the night with us   *the night with us)*

(15) *mae hi wedi byw yn Llundain (am) blwyddyn*   *(she's lived in*
      is she after live in London (for) year   *London (for) a year)*

In (13), (14) and (15) we have an apparent noun phrase, e.g. WYTHNOS (WEEK), following the verb. We have then a pattern which looks like a transitive pattern. But, as the discussion in chapter III, 3b showed, the resemblance is only superficial, since we have the possibility of inserting AM (FOR): it just happens that duration adjuncts can assume a 'reduced' noun phrase form as well as a 'full' prepositional phrase form.

As a final point on duration, we can add that very often adjuncts of duration compare very closely with markers of distance. This is particularly common where the verb involves movement:

(16) *mae hi wedi cerdded am filltir*   *(she has walked a mile)*
      is she after walk for mile

The phrase AM FILLTIR (FOR A MILE) measures the distance of walking. But distance is closely associated with time, as we can measure the walking of a mile in terms of the time it takes:

(17) *mae hi wedi cerdded am hanner awr*   *(she has walked for half*
      is she after walk for half hour   *an hour)*

It is significant in this respect to note that phrases of duration and phrases of distance

65

in such contexts are mutually exclusive: thus we do not find examples such as *mae hi wedi cerdded am filltir am awr (she's walked for a mile for an hour).* Consequently, we could think of phrases like AM FILLTIR as durative-type phrases in terms of distance. We can also bear in mind that the answer to the question PA MOR BELL (HOW FAR) is often given in terms of time, and it is also common to measure journeys in terms of time - three-hour ride to Cardiff, three-day cruise to Rome, five-minutes' walk, etc.

The third type establishes the frequency of the action and is associated with the interrogative type PA MOR AML (HOW OFTEN). This type of adjunct can accordingly go under the label FREQUENCY. Adjuncts of the frequency type quite commonly take the form of BOB (EVERY) (to indicate the frequency) followed by a nominal to indicate a temporal period, like BOB NOS (EVERY NIGHT) as in (10) above. Other instances can be given as follows:

(18) *BOB DYDD (every day)*   *BOB BLWYDDYN (every year)*
     BOB BORE (every morning)   *BOB DYDD IAU (every Thursday)*
     BOB WYTHNOS (every week)   *BOB HAF (every summer)*
     BOB MIS (every month)   *BOB PASG (every Easter)*

But, although noun phrases beginning with BOB are very common as frequency adjuncts, there are also other possibilities. For instance, we can use:

(19) *YN AML IAWN (very often)*
     PRYD BYNNAG (whenever) . . . . . *(e.g. pryd bynnag dwi'n ei weld o)*
                                        (whenever I see him)

In addition to (10), therefore, we could also have:

(20) *'roedd o 'n palu'r ardd yn aml iawn*   *(he was digging the garden*
     was he in dig the garden in often very   *very often)*

(21) *'roedd o 'n palu'r ardd pryd bynnag welwn i o* *(he was digging the*
     was he in dig the garden whenever saw I him *garden whenever I*
                                                      saw him)

It is possible to find *time when, duration* and *frequency* types occurring together:

(22) *'roeddwn i 'n palu'r ardd bob nos*   *(I was digging the garden*
     was   I in dig the garden every night   *every night for an hour*
                                                   last year)
     am awr llynedd
     for hour last year

It is noticeable that when a frequency adjunct co-occurs with a time adjunct, the length of the time period must be big enough to contain the frequency adjunct. Thus we can say *bob nos (every night) llynedd (last year)* but we cannot say:

(23) *'roeddwn i'n palu'r ardd bob nos neithiwr(*I was digging the
was   I in dig the garden every night last night   garden every night last
                                                     night)

(24) *'roeddwn i 'n palu'r ardd bob mis   (*I was digging the
was   I in dig the garden every month   garden every month
                                             last week).
wythnos diwetha'
week   last

3   BENEFICIARY, PRINCIPAL AND GOAL

The underlined items in the following examples illustrate a number of roles which can
be discussed together for convenience:

(25) mae o 'n 'sgrifennu'r llyfr 'ma ar gyfer plant ysgol   (he's writ-
is   he in   write the book here on count children school ing this
                                                            book for
                                                            school
                                                            children)

(26) mae o 'n prynu'r llyfr 'ma dros John   (he's buying this book
is   he in buy the book here over John   for John)

(27) mae o 'n prynu'r llyfr 'ma i John   (he's buying this book
is   he in buy the book here to John   for John)

In the first of these, AR GYFER (ON COUNT = FOR) shows that the work is being
done for the benefit of school children and, consequently, the role that it marks can
be described as *beneficiary*. In the second example, (DROS (OVER = FOR) is used to
mark that person on whose behalf the book is bought: thus, JOHN in example (26)
can be said to be the *principal*. In example (27), we have a sentence similar to (26).
But in (27) there is no necessity that the NP in subject position is acting on John's
instructions. The book could be a present for John, the action being done without
his knowledge. In this sense, JOHN can be described as the *goal* and this role is marked
by the preposition I (TO = FOR).

4   REWARD

The role of *reward* can be illustrated as follows:

(28) mae John yn golchi'r car am bunt   (John is washing the car
is   John in   wash the car for pound   for a pound)

In example (28) the phrase AM BUNT (FOR A POUND) signifies the *reward* of the
activity. The preposition AM (FOR), as we have seen, can convey duration:

(29) *mae hi 'n aros am yr wythnos*   *(she's staying for the week)*
     is she in stay for the week

It is fairly easy to distinguish these two functions of AM (FOR). For instance, AM duration is associated with the interrogative AM FAINT or PA MOR HIR, whereas AM (FOR) reward is associated with an interrogative such as AM BETH (FOR WHAT).

5   REASON

Another type of adjunct can be illustrated as follows:

(30) *mae hi 'n gadael oherwydd y sŵn*   *(she's leaving because of*
     is she in leave because the noise   *the noise)*

(31) *mae hi 'n licio John oherwydd ei wallt o* *(she likesJohn because of*
     is she in like John because his hair he   *his hair)*

In these examples we have phrases beginning with OHERWYDD (BECAUSE). Their function is to give a reason for the action involved and they are associated with the interrogative type PAM (WHY). They are accordingly labelled as REASON.

6   PLACE

A very common type of adjunct can be illustrated as follows:

(32) *mae John yn chwarae gitâr yn yr ardd*   *(John plays a guitar in*
     is John in play   guitar in the garden   *the garden)*

Quite simply, YN YR ARDD (IN THE GARDEN) locates the action of John's playing the guitar. It is associated with LLE (WHERE) interrogatives and can accordingly be labelled as PLACE.

7   CONCLUDING REMARKS

7a   The adjunct and verb phrase again

It must be emphasised that an adjunct cannot necessarily be identified by the semantics and syntactic form of the adjunct constituent itself. It is not the case, for instance, that every prepositional phrase which indicates place is an adjunct. It happens that prepositional phrases of place can occur both as an adjunct constituent and also as a post-verbal constituent of the verb phrase, as the following examples illustrate:

(33) *mi ganodd John gân ar y gadair*   *(John sang a song on the*
     PT sang John song on the chair   *chair)*

(34) *mi eisteddodd John ar y gadair*   *(John sat on the chair)*
     PT sat   John on the chair

The respective branching-diagram for these two examples can be given as follows:

(35)

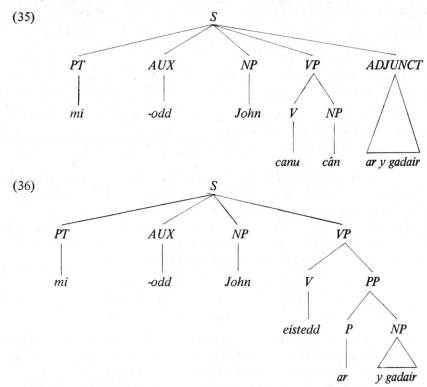

(36)

It can be seen that in (35) the prepositional phrase is a place adjunct while in (36) it is a prepositional object to the verb. The differences can be further illustrated by the types of interrogatives associated with each one:

(37) *lle   gannodd John gan?*   *(where did John sing a song?)*
     where sang John   song

(38) *ar beth eisteddodd John?*   *(on what did John sit?)*
     on thing sat   John

The adjunctival prepositional phrase locates the whole of the action of the sentence whereas the prepositional object can be said to 'suffer' the action of the verb — and, of course, it can be further located adjunctively as in *yn y llofft (in the bedroom)*.

The same type of distinction can also be made in respect of reward, as the following examples illustrate:

(39) *mae John yn golchi'r car am bunt*   *(John is washing the car*
    is John in wash the car for pound   *for a pound)*

(40) *mae John yn gwerthu'r car am bunt i Mair*   *(John is selling the car*
    is John in sell the car for pound to Mair   *for one pound to Mair)*

In (39) *am bunt* is not a necessary constituent, whereas in (40) the same phrase *is* a necessary constituent of the verb phrase.

7b   Problems of the constituent structure of the adjunct

The characterisation of the adjunct constituent in terms of a branching-diagram relies upon functional rather than syntactic criteria. The noun phrase and verb phrase, for example, are characterised by the presence of a noun and verb in the structure of the phrase. The label adjunct, however, cannot be related to any such syntactic characteristic. There are problems in obtaining a syntactic label for the adjunct. It seems to involve a variety of syntactic possibilities, as the following list illustrates:

(41) (i)   *prepositional phrases:* *am wythnos (for a week)*
     (ii) *noun phrases:*   *bob wythnos (every week)*
     (iii) *adverbs:*   *yn aml iawn (very often)*

It can be argued that noun phrases are in fact derived from prepositional phrases. It was shown in section 2 of this chapter that noun phrases functioning as adjuncts can involve a deleted preposition and, on this basis, it can be suggested that noun phrases like *bob wythnos (every week)* involve the compulsory deletion of a deep structure preposition. In this way, the prepositional phrase can be set up as a general adjunct constituent which also accounts for noun phrases. The problem, however, is to account for the adverbs. In the case of *yn aml iawn (very often)* it is clearly difficult to set up an account in terms of prepositional phrases. Other traditional adverbs include HEDDIW (TODAY), ELENI (THIS YEAR), HENO (TONIGHT), RWAN (NOW), DDOE (YESTERDAY), NEITHIWR (LAST NIGHT), LLYNEDD (LAST YEAR), ECHDOE (DAY BEFORE YESTERDAY), YFORY (TOMORROW). But it could be argued that these are nouns and, furthermore, examples with an occurring preposition are readily found:

(42) *rydan ni wedi gwneud digon (am) heddiw/heno /rŵan*   *(we have done*
    are we after do enough for today /tonight /now   *enough for*
                                              today/tonight/
                                              now)

Consequently, noun forms like HEDDIW (TODAY), etc. could be derived from prepositional phrases through the deletion of the preposition. The real problem, then, is to account for the *yn*-types like *yn aml iawn (very often)*.

For the sake of simplicity, however, we will use the term adjunct as a label for the material under discussion in this chapter.

V The syntax and semantics of the auxiliary

1   INTRODUCTION

1a   The AUXILIARY and auxiliary verbs

The AUXILIARY is taken to involve a *verbal inflection,* as in the following examples:

(1)   (i)   *mi welodd   Mair y   ddamwain*   *(Mair saw the accident)*
            PT see + AUX   Mair the accident

      (ii) *mi atebith   hi cyn bo hir*   *(she will answer before*
            PT answer + AUX she before long   *long)*

      (iii) *mi brynai   hi 'r cwbl lot*   *(she would buy the whole*
            PT buy + AUX she   the whole lot   *lot)*

As discussed in chapter III, section 2c, the auxiliary verb is not handled here under the constituent AUXILIARY. The verbal inflections are concerned with a variety of semantic features, as are the auxiliary verbs; the occurrence of an auxiliary verb can involve both its own semantic features and those of the AUXILIARY. That is, as the following examples demonstrate, an auxiliary verb can carry an AUXILIARY feature in the form of a verbal inflection just like a lexical verb:

(2)   (i)   *mi wnaeth   hi wrthod*   *(she refused)*
            PT do + AUX she refuse

      (ii) *mi allai   John weld Mair*   *(John could see Mair)*
            PT can + AUX John see Mair

      (iii) *mi ddylen nhw fod wedi bod yn gweithio* *(they should have*
            PT should they be after be in work   *been working)*

It will be shown below that the auxiliary verbs GWNEUD (DO) and DARFOD (etymologically HAPPEN) do not enjoy semantic distinctiveness in the same way as other auxiliary verbs; and their relationship with the AUXILIARY is slightly different too. But, in the main, we have two distinct phenomena of AUXILIARY features and auxiliary verb features, both of which involve a variety of syntactic and semantic features, and it is the aim of this chapter to explore the factors involved in both.[1]

In terms of a branching-diagram for Welsh sentences, the verbal inflections might best appear under the AUX constituent while the auxiliary verbs could be assigned a position in the VP. In effect, the auxiliary verbs might be thought of in some respects

72

as being like lexical verbs, and they can be particularly linked with the catenative verbs outlined in the discussion of sentence complexity in section 4 of chapter VIII. The branching-diagram for example (2) (ii) could therefore be given as follows:

(3)

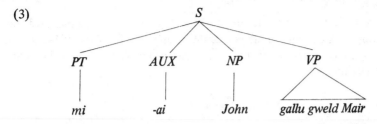

The configuration above shows the inflection occurring in the AUX and the auxiliary verb GALLU (CAN) as a verb in the verb phrase, followed by an infinitival phrase *gweld Mair (see Mair)*. However, as stated in chapter III, section 2c, this approach will not be formally worked out because of the complexity and additional detail that this would introduce. Consequently, in branching-diagrams representing sentences which involve auxiliary verbs, the auxiliary verb is located under the AUXILIARY constituent for convenience of statement. It must, however, be emphasised that this is not the most expressive representation of their syntax. The auxiliary verbs could be reasonably discussed in chapter VIII along with catenative verbs. But, as illustrated below, they are syntactically distinct from the catenatives and this point, together with the traditional linking of the auxiliary verbs and the AUXILIARY constituent, has determined their discussion here.[2]

1b Auxiliary verbs

Traditionally, auxiliary verbs are regarded as 'helping' verbs which contribute to or modify the verb of the sentence in a variety of ways. In Welsh the following can be listed as auxiliary verbs:

(4) (i)   *GWNEUD (DO)*
     (ii) *DARFOD (etymologically HAPPEN)*
     (iii) *CAEL (RECEIVE)*
     (iv) *GALLU (CAN)*
     (v)   *MEDRU (CAN)*
     (vi) *DYLU (SHOULD, OUGHT)*

They are listed above in their uninflected forms and, as such, DARFOD and DYLU are 'artificial' forms, in that they occur only in inflected·form (in spoken Welsh, at least); they are listed in this form for convenience of reference. There is another group of auxiliary verbs which are traditionally known as the BOD (BE) auxiliaries. They involve the various paradigms MAE (IS), OEDD (WAS), BYDD (WILL BE), etc. All these forms as auxiliary verbs are involved in the occurrence of aspect markers.

Consequently, they can be labelled as ASPECTUAL AUXILIARIES and are discussed in chapter VI, section 3. Other grammarians (for example Rowland 1876:75) include MYNNU (WISH, WILL) as an auxiliary verb, although it is rejected as such in this presentation (see below).

Auxiliary verbs occur in an environment where they themselves are inflected and are followed by the noun phrase subject, as the examples in (2) above illustrate. The surface structure characteristics of their occurrence can be illustrated by the following branching-diagram:

(5)

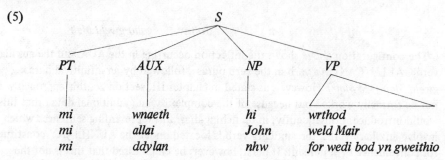

PT	AUX	NP	VP
mi	wnaeth	hi	wrthod
mi	allai	John	weld Mair
mi	ddylan	nhw	for wedi bod yn gweithio

(It is emphasised again, however, that auxiliary verbs, despite their traditional name, are not produced under the auxiliary but only occur there in surface structure because they carry verbal inflections. In deep structure, auxiliary verbs can be said to occur in the verb phrase and are moved to auxiliary position by the auxiliary carrier transformation.[3]) But, as shown in the discussion of complex sentences (chapter VIII, section 4), there are many verbs which can occur in the same environment as auxiliary verbs, as the following examples illustrate:

(6) mi *benderfynith* Mair aros efo ni   *(Mair will decide to stay with us)*
PT *decide* + AUX   Mair *stay with us*

(7) mi *ddewisith*   Mair aros efo ni   *(Mair will choose to stay with us)*
PT *choose* + AUX   Mair *stay with us*

(8) mi *driith*   Mair aros efo ni   *(Mair will try to stay with us)*
PT *try* + AUX Mair *stay with us*

(9) mi *wrthodith*   Mair aros efo ni   *(Mair will refuse to stay with us)*
PT *refuse* + AUX Mair *stay with us*

(10) mi *gytunith*   Mair aros efo ni   *(Mair will agree to stay with us)*
PT *agree* + AUX Mair *stay with us*

However, the verbs listed in (4) are syntactically different on two related points.

Firstly, auxiliary verbs can occur as the *tag* in a tag question (see chapter IX, section 3b) and, secondly, they can occur as answer words to yes-no interrogatives (see chapter

74

IX, section 3b), for example:

(11) (i)   mi all John ei gweld hi,   *(John can see her, can't he - yes)*
        PT can John her see her,

        yn gall − gall
        Q NEG − can

  (ii)   all John ddim ei gweld hi,   *(John can't see her, can he - no)*
        can John NEG her see she,

        na all - na all
        NEG can NEG can

(12) (i)   mi ddylem nhw fod wedi bod yn gweithio   *(they should have*
        PT should they be after be in work   *been working,*
                                                    shouldn't they
        yn   dylan - dylan   *- yes)*
        Q + NEG should - should

  (ii)   ddylen nhw ddim fod wedi bod yn gweithio, *(they shoudn't*
        should they NEG be after be in work   *have been work-*
                                                      ing, should they -
        na ddylan - na ddylan   *no)*
        NEG should - NEG should

Verbs like those listed in examples (6) to (10) do not occur in similar contexts; for example:

(13) (i)   *mi benderfynith Mair aros efo ni,*   *(*Mair will decide*
        PT decide + AUX Mair stay with us,   *to stay with us,*
                                                  will deciden't she
        yn   penderfynith - penderfynith   *will decide (= yes))*
        Q + NEG decide + AUX - decide + AUX

  (ii)   *benderfynith   Mair ddim aros efo ni,*   *(*Mair will not*
        decide + AUX Mair NEG   stay with us *decide to stay with*
                                                  us, will decide she -
        na benderfynith - na benderfynith   *will not decide*
        NEG decide + AUX- NEG decide + AUX   *(= no))*

(14) (i)   *mi ddewisith Mair aros efo ni,*   *(Mair will choose*
        PT choose + AUX Mair stay with us,   *to stay with us,*
                                                  will choosen't she -
        yn   dewisith   - dewisith   *will choose (= yes))*
        Q + NEG decide + AUX - decide + AUX

(ii) *ddewisith   *Mair* *ddim*   *aros efo ni*   *(Mair will not choose*
     decide + AUX *Mair* NEG   stay with us   *to stay with us,*

     na *ddewisith*   -   *na* *ddewisith*   *will decide she -*
     NEG decide + AUX - NEG decide + AUX   *will not decide (=*
                                          no))

Verbs of this type are called *catenative* verbs and are discussed in chapter VIII, section 4; they share the same syntactic environment as auxiliary verbs but do not occur as tags or answer words.

The verb MYNNU (WILL, WISH), mentioned earlier as a traditional member of the class of auxiliary verbs, can be seen not to be an auxiliary by these two criteria. It occurs neither as part of a tag nor as an answer word, *fynni di ddim aros yma, na fynni? - na fynnaf*. Where a tag or answer word is required for a sentence containing a catenative verb, a *pro-verb* is used, namely the auxiliary verb GWNEUD; for example:

(15) (i)   *mi benderfynith*   *Mair aros efo ni,*   *(Mair will decide to*
       PT decide + AUX *Mair* stay with us   *stay with us, won't*

       yn   *gwneith*   -   *gwneith*   *she - yes)*
       Q + NEG do + AUX -   do + AUX

    (ii)   *phenderfynith* *Mair* *ddim* *aros efo ni,*   *(Mair will not decide*
       decide + AUX   *Mair* NEG   stay with us   *to stay with us,*

       na *wneith*   - *na wneith*   *will she - no)*
       NEG do + AUX - NEG do + AUX

(16) (i)   *mi ddewisith*   *Mair aros efo ni*   *(Mair will choose*
       PT choose + AUX *Mair* stay with us   *to stay with us,*

       yn   *gwneith*   -   *gwneith*   *won't she - yes)*
       Q + NEG do + AUX -   do + AUX

    (ii)   *ddewisith*   *Mair* *ddim* *aros efo ni,*   *(Mair will not choose*
       choose + AUX *Mair* NEG   stay with us,   *to stay with us,*

       na *wneith*   -   *na* *wneith*   *will she - no)*
       NEG do + AUX   -   NEG   do   + AUX

There is a rule in traditional grammar of Welsh (Anwyl, 1898:70) which says that yes-no questions are answered by using an appropriate form of the inflected verb in the question (Williams 1959:197 briefly mentions use of GWNEUD). But, as examples (9) to (14) above suggest, this is the case in contemporary spontaneous spoken Welsh only for auxiliary verbs. The only lexical verbs which illustrate the traditional rule are found in a small group which includes CAEL (RECEIVE) and GWNEUD (MAKE, DO) occurring as lexical verbs and MYND (GO), DOD (COME) and GWELD (SEE);

76

for example:

(17) (i)   *mi ddaw   hi r̂wan, yn   daw*   *(she'll come now,*
          PT come + AUX   she now Q + NEG come + AUX won't she - yes)

           -    *daw*
           - *come + AUX*

      (ii)   *ddaw   hi ddim r̂wan na   ddaw*   *(she won't come now,*
           come + AUX she NEG now   NEG come + AUX   will she - no)

           - *na ddaw*
           - *NEG come + AUX*

(18) (i)   *mi geith   hi fraw,*   *(she'll have a fright,*
          PT receive + AUX she fright   *won't she - yes)*

          yn   ceith   - ceith
          Q + NEG receive + AUX - receive + AUX

      (ii)   *cheith   hi ddim   braw,*   *(she won't have a*
          receive + AUX she NEG   fright   *fright, will she - no)*

          na cheith   - na cheith
          NEG receive + AUX - NEG receive + AUX

But even here there is the possibility of using the auxiliary verb GWNEUD as a tag and answer word. The only real exception is GWELD (SEE) when used in a non-modal sense (see section 2b below):

(19) *weli   di 'r   tŷ   acw   - gwelaf*   *(can/do you see*
      see + AUX you the house yonder - see + AUX   *that house - yes)*

Here it is inappropriate to use *gwnaf* as an answer, as the semantics of the question and the answer word are not compatible.

As a final remark on the comparison of auxiliary and lexical (particularly catenative) verbs, it should be noted that all inflected verbs behave in the same way when the inflection involves the -ODD paradigm in that the tags and answer words involve DO and NADDO:

(20) (i)   *mi wnaeth   hi wrthod,   yndo   -do*   *(she refused, didn't*
          PT do + AUX   she refused   Q + NEG yes - yes   she   - yes)

      (ii)   *wnaeth   hi ddim   gwrthod, naddo - naddo* *(she didn't refuse*
          do + AUX she NEG   refuse   NEG yes - NEG yes   did she - no)

(21) (i) *mi benderfynodd Mair aros efo ni, yndo*   *-do (Mair decided*
        PT decide + AUX Mair stay with us, Q + NEG yes - yes to stay with
                                              us, didn't
                                              she - yes)

(ii) *phenderfynodd Mair ddim aros efo ni,*   *(Mair didn't*
       decide + AUX Mair NEG stay with us,   *decide to stay*
                                         with us, did
       naddo - naddo   *she - no)*
       NEG yes - NEG yes

In this respect a difficulty arises when accounting for DARFOD (HAPPEN), which is always equivalent to the -ODD (PAST) inflection and has DO (YES) and NADDO (NO) as tags and answer words. But it is interpreted as an auxiliary verb because it lacks any semantic content itself and occurs solely as a carrier of verbal inflections, as discussed below.

The auxiliary verbs listed in (4) above can be divided into two groups. One group includes GWNEUD (DO) and DARFOD (HAPPEN); in the main, they have no meaning themselves apart from their inflections. Consequently, they serve only to *carry* the verbal inflections, and can be labelled as the CARRIER AUXILIARIES. The second group is made up of CAEL (RECEIVE), GALLU (CAN), MEDRU (CAN) and DYLU (SHOULD); they have semantic content in themselves (in addition to the inflections) and convey a variety of different meanings. They can be labelled as the SEMANTIC or LEXICAL AUXILIARIES. Along with the aspectual auxiliaries mentioned earlier and discussed in chapter VI, section 3, there are thus three classes of auxiliary verb classess in Welsh.

2   THE AUXILIARY AND THE CARRIER AUXILIARY VERBS GWNEUD (DO) AND DARFOD (HAPPEN)

2a   Introduction

The significant point about GWNEUD (DO) and DARFOD (HAPPEN) is that they can be used as alternative auxiliary carriers in place of the verb. Thus, it is possible to compare the following:

(22) *mi ganith   Mair heno*   *(Mair will sing tonight)*
       PT sing + AUX Mair tonight

(23) *mi wneith   Mair ganu heno*   *(Mair will sing tonight)*
       PT do + AUX Mair sing tonight

In example (22) the -ITH paradigm of the auxiliary is carried by the verb CANU (SING), but in (23) the same inflection is carried by the auxiliary verb GWNEUD (DO) while the verb is uninflected. Since there is no perceptible semantic difference between the two examples, the auxiliary verb GWNEUD (DO) can be regarded as a carrier auxiliary, the function of which is to carry inflections which are otherwise carried by the verb.

Traditional grammars of Welsh (for example John Morris-Jones (1913: 317-18)) list eleven distinct inflectional paradigms for the majority of verbs:

(24)

	Present		Imperfect		Aorist		Pluperfect	
	Active	Passive	Active	Passive	Active	Passive	Active	Passive
Ind.	CÂR	CERIR	CARAI	CERID	CARODD	CARWYD	CARASAI	CARASID
Subj.	CARO	CARER	CARAI	CERID	-	-	-	-
Imp.	CARED	CARER	-	-	-	-	-	-

The classical taxonomic framework of the description of the inflected verb is based mainly upon the grammatical categories of *mood* (indicative, subjunctive, imperative), *voice* (active, passive) and *tense* (present, imperfect, aorist and pluperfect). Some of the possible combinations are filled out by duplicating various of the eleven inflected paradigms as illustrated in (24), and Welsh grammars differ according to the extent of duplication (see, for instance, Anwyl, 1898:47, who does not duplicate the indicative imperfect as the subjunctive imperfect; or Rowland, 1876:75-6, who proceeds in the other direction and has an indicative future-perfect and a subjunctive pluperfect). In spontaneous spoken Welsh there are only three complete and contrastive paradigms which are regularly used. These are:

(25) (i) *-ITH paradigm: compare the traditional present (and/or future)*
indicative;

(ii) *-AI paradigm: compare the traditional imperfect indicative;*

(iii) *-ODD paradigm: compare the traditional aorist indicative.*

They can be illustrated as follows:

(26) (i) mi ganith   Mair heno   *(Mair will sing tonight)*
PT sing + AUX Mair tonight

(ii) fe ganai   Mair heno petae   hi 'n iawn   *(Mair would*
PT sing + AUX Mair tonight if COND she in all right *sing tonight*
if she were all
right)

(iii) mi ganodd   Mair neithiwr   *(Mair sang last night)*
PT sing + PAST Mair last night

The traditional practice of giving the various paradigms tense-labels will not be followed. As is illustrated below, a variety of meanings are involved in their use, and the traditional labellings are both unrevealing and inadequate; consequently, formal labels are employed, as in (25) above.

The traditional pluperfect occurs in some areas as a variant of the -AI paradigm:

(27) *fe gansai   Mair heno   petasai   hi 'n iawn*   *(Mair would sing*
PT sing + AUX Mair tonight if COND she in all right   *tonight if she were*
all right)

There is no functional difference between the -AI and -ASAI paradigm (for the pluperfect *petasai* see chapter VI, section 3e), and they can be regarded as variant realisations of the same auxiliary feature. The impersonal forms -IR, -ID, -WYD, -ASID and -ER are not as frequent in speech as the -ITH, -AI and -ODD paradigms. They are at their most productive in formal situations, and occur with high frequency in news bulletins and formal written uses of the language. Even in these situations, however, -ASID rarely occurs. The impersonal inflections will be discussed with the passive in chapter VIII, section 6. But two points should be noted here: the impersonal inflections are not carried by the carrier auxiliaries, and the semantics of -ITH and -IR are not always comparable. The imperative occurs mainly in respect of the second person and is thus a depleted paradigm - it is discussed below and also more fully in chapter IX, section 6. There are some dialects, however, which make restricted use of a third singular imperative form as in *eled e! (let him go!)*, and which in other dialects can relate to an expression involving the verb GADAEL (LEAVE) in the second person as in *gadewch iddo fo fynd! (let him go!)*. The subjunctive occurs in spontaneous speech only in set expressions such as CYN BO HIR (BEFORE (IT MAY BE) LONG), DA BO CHI (GOOD MAY YOU BE = GOODBYE), WNELO A (DO WITH, CONNECTED WITH) and is otherwise restricted to formal written Welsh.

In this chapter the discussion will concentrate upon the three paradigms -ITH, -AI/ -ASAI and -ODD, and the auxiliary can be thought of as involving these three verbal inflections. On this basis the re-write rules which characterise Welsh simple sentences, as listed in chapter III, section 5, can now be further developed by re-writing the AUX constituent in terms of these three inflections:

(28) (i) $S \rightarrow$ PT AUX NP VP ADJUNCT

(ii) $AUX \rightarrow \begin{Bmatrix} \text{-ITH} \\ \text{-AI} \\ \text{-ODD} \end{Bmatrix}$

(iii) $VP \rightarrow$ (ASP) $\begin{Bmatrix} V \begin{Bmatrix} (NP) & (PP) & (PP) \\ (PRED\ PH) \end{Bmatrix} \\ COP \begin{Bmatrix} PRED\ PH \\ NP \\ PP \end{Bmatrix} \end{Bmatrix}$

80

(iv) $PP \longrightarrow P\ NP$

(v) $PRED.PH \rightarrow \begin{Bmatrix} YN \\ FEL/COP\_NP \end{Bmatrix} \begin{Bmatrix} NP \\ ADJ \end{Bmatrix}$

The re-writing of the AUX in (28) (ii) uses braces { } around the three inflections to indicate that only one is selected. Such a characterisation of the auxiliary in terms of the inflectional paradigms which occur is basically very simple. In contrast to this approach, one must also bear in mind that the inflections possess their own semantics, and the auxiliary would be characterised in terms of semantic features rather than by the representations -ITH, -AI and -ODD of the inflectional paradigms that occur.[4]
The traditional semantic analysis of the inflections is based mainly upon the category of *tense,* involving time relations: thus, in (22) above, -ITH would be described as a present (or future) tense, -AI as an imperfect tense and -ODD as an aorist or past tense. But in the analysis of the semantics of the inflections presented below, tense is given only as a partial explanation of the inflections and the main emphasis falls upon various other meanings that are involved.

The carrier auxiliary GWNEUD regularly carries the -ITH and -ODD inflection:

(29) (i)   *mi ganith   Mair heno*   *(Mair will sing tonight)*
         PT sing + AUX Mair tonight

(ii)   *mi wneith   Mair ganu heno*   *(Mair will sing tonight)*
         PT do + AUX Mair sing tonight

(30) (i)   *mi ganodd   Mair neithiwr*   *(Mair sang last night)*
         PT sing + PAST Mair last night

(ii)   *mi wnaeth   Mair ganu neithiwr*   *(Mair sang last night)*
         PT do + PAST Mair sing last night

Its function as a carrier of the -AI paradigm, however, depends upon the semantics involved and, in some instances; it is replaced by the aspectual auxiliary BUASAI/BYDDAI (WOULD BE) (see chapter VI, section 3e). The auxiliary carrier DARFOD (HAPPEN) only occurs as an equivalent of the -ODD (PAST) inflection. Thus (30) (i) could also be expressed as:

(31) *mi ddaru   Mair ganu neithiwr*   *(Mair sang last night)*
      PT happen + PAST Mair sing last night

It is also distinctive in the fact that, unlike the other auxiliary verbs, it only occurs in the form *ddaru* [ðarɨ] *(happen + PAST)*, being otherwise uninflected.

The various occurrences can be summarised as follows:

(32) (i)   *-ITH*   *mi ganith*   *mi wneith ... ganu*
                        PT sing + AUX   PT do + AUX sing

     (ii) *-AI/-ASAI* *mi ganai*   *mi wnai ... ganu; mi fuasai/fyddai ...*
                        PT sing + AUX   PT do + AUX sing PT would be

                        yn canu
                        in sing

     (iii) *-ODD*   *mi ganodd*   *mi wnaeth ... ganu; mi ddaru ...*
                        PT sing + PAST PT do + PAST sing PT happen + PAST

                        ganu
                        sing

The occurrence of any particular pattern is dependent upon stylistic and regional considerations. Inflected verbs are traditionally used in formal written Welsh in sentences of normal order and it is unusual to find a periphrastic pattern involving GWNEUD (DO) or DARFOD (HAPPEN). In spontaneous Welsh, however, both patterns occur, depending upon regional influences; an accurate statement of the regional distribution of the patterns would require research beyond the bounds of this work, but an impressionistic judgement could suggest that, on the whole, the inflected patterns are more frequent in South Wales while the periphrastic patterns are used extensively in North Wales.

2b   The -ITH paradigm

In formal written Welsh the -ITH paradigm sometimes has a function which is similar to the use of MAE .. YN .. (IS .. IN ..) (see chapter VI, section 3b) in spontaneous speech. Consider the following examples:

(33) *ysgrifennaf   atoch i holi   am   y   swydd   (I'm writing/I write to you*
     write + AUX to you to enquire about the post   to enquire about the post)

In spontaneous speech such an example would be rendered as:

(34) *'dwi 'n 'sgrifennu atoch chi i holi am   y swydd   (I'm writing*
     am I in   write   to you you to enquire about the post   to you to
                                                                enquire about
                                                                the post)

On the basis of this comparison it can be seen that in formal written Welsh the -ITH paradigm can be used to make *factual* statements: we will refer to factual reference as *non-modal* reference. This is a very rare use of the inflection in speech, and only occurs with lexical auxiliaries (see section 3f below) and a limited number of lexical verbs such as GWELD (SEE) and CLYWED (HEAR), especially in interrogatives:

(35) *weli   di 'r   tŷ   acw?*   *(can/do you see that house?)*
     see + AUX you the house yonder

This use of the -ITH inflection, paraphrased by MAE . . YN . . (IS . . IN . .) is thus restricted.

In spontaneous speech at least three uses of the -ITH paradigm can be distinguished: (i) *prediction*, (ii) *volition*, (iii) *imperative*. Not only are these three uses notionally distinguishable but, more important, they have their own formal characteristics, each one behaving differently in relation to aspect contrasts and past time reference.

It is common for the -ITH paradigm to be used to refer to a future event:

(36) (i)   *mi gyrhaeddith   y   bws am ddeg heno*   *(the bus will arrive*
           PT arrive + AUX the bus at   ten tonight   *at ten tonight)*

     (ii) *mi wneith   y   bws gyrraedd am ddeg heno* *(the bus will arrive*
           PT do + AUX the bus arrive   at   ten tonight *at ten tonight)*

Traditionally, this use of -ITH is referred to as a 'future tense'. While this paradigm is undoubtedly used to refer to events seen as occurring in the future, it must also be borne in mind that there are other auxiliary verbs which can refer to future events:

(37) *mi ddylai 'r bws gyrraedd am ddeg heno*   *(the bus should arrive*
     PT should the bus arrive   at   ten tonight   *at ten tonight)*

(38) *mae' r bws yn cyrraedd am ddeg heno*   *(the bus arrives/is*
     is the bus   in arrive   at   ten tonight   *arriving at ten tonight)*

Reference to future events is not a function which is unique to -ITH, and the significant point is that other differences of meaning are involved in the selection of a particular form. The auxiliary DYLU is discussed in section 3d below and for the moment illustration of this point will centre upon comparison of (36) and (38). The selection of MAE (IS) depends upon the occurrence of the future event being a *present fact*. This becomes clear by showing that there are certain events which, in normal circumstances, are not expressed by MAE (IS):

(39) **mae 'n glawio yfory*   *(*it's raining tomorrow)*
     is   in rain   tomorrow

(40) **mae Mair yn ennill y gwpan yfory*   *(*Mair wins/is winning the*
     is   Mair in win   the cup   tomorrow   *cup tomorrow)*

These events are not assessable as facts at the present moment. But it is possible to express them by using -ITH:

(41) (i)   *mi lawith   yfory*   *(it will rain tomorrow)*
        PT rain + AUX tomorrow

(ii)   *mi wneith   hi lawio yfory*   *(it will rain tomorrow)*
        PT do + AUX she rain tomorrow

(42) (i)   *mi enillith   Mair y   gwpan*   *(Mair will win the cup)*
        PT win + AUX Mair the cup

(ii)   *mi wneith   Mair ennill y gwpan* *(Mair will win the cup)*
        PT do + AUX   Mair win the cup

It is possible to suggest, therefore, that part of the function of -ITH is to refer to future events that it is thought will occur on the basis of the speaker's own personal beliefs and judgement, rather than of fact. More specifically, we can say that -ITH is used to *predict* the occurrence of an event.

It is a characteristic of the predictive use of -ITH that it can occur in the *progressive aspect* (see chapter VI, section 1 by using BYDD . . YN . . (WILL BE . . IN . . = WILL BE -ING). Thus examples (36), (41) and (42) could be expressed as:

(43) *mi fydd   y   bws yn cyrraedd am ddeg heno* *(the bus will be*
      PT will be the bus in arrive   at   ten   tonight *arriving at ten*
                                                     tonight)

(44) *mi fydd   hi 'n glawio   yfory*   *(it will be raining*
      PT will be she in   rain   tomorrow   *tomorrow)*

(45) *mi fydd   Mair yn ennill y   gwpan yfory*   *(Mair will be winning*
      PT will be Mair in   win the cup   tomorrow   *the cup tomorrow)*

Examples (43) to (45) likewise predict an event and differ from (36), (41) and (42) only in respect of aspect features. Another characteristic of predictive -ITH is that the -AI paradigm occurs as an equivalent, to predict past events which are considered to be habitual (that is, -AI is the past tense of -ITH predicative for habitual events):

(46) *mi ai   Mair am dro bob nos*   *(Mair would go for a*
      PT go + AUX Mair for walk every night   *walk every night)*

(47) *mi wnai   Mair fynd am dro   bob   nos* *(Mair would go for a*
      PT do + AUX Mair   go for   walk every night   *walk every night)*

In this respect there is the possibility of using BUASAI/BYDDAI (WOULD BE . . IN . . = WOULD BE -ING) as a past time pattern of prediction:

(48) *mi fuasai/fyddai Mair yn mynd am dro bob nos* *(Mair would go for*
   PT would be   Mair in   go for walk every night   a walk every night)

However, if the event is an episode as opposed to a habitual activity, the *perfect aspect* pattern (see chapter VI, section 1) involving BYDD . . WEDI . . (WILL BE . . AFTER . . = WILL HAVE -EN) occurs:

(49) *mi fydd   Mair wedi paratoi bwyd neithiwr* *(Mair will have prepared*
   PT will be Mair after prepare food last night   *food last night)*

Past time reference involving prediction is thus rather complicated, depending upon whether the activity is habitual or episodic.

The -ITH paradigm can be used to convey *willingness* or *volition*. This is clearly seen with polite requests but also occurs with statements, particularly negative statements:

(50) (i) *agorwch   chi'r drws i mi?* *(will you open the door*
      open + AUX you the door for me   *for me?)*

   (ii) *wnewch   chi agor y drws i mi?* *(will you open the door*
      do + AUX you open the door for me   *for me?)*

(51) (i) *mi helpith   Mair ni* *(Mair will help us)*
      PT help + AUX Mair us

   (ii) *mi wneith Mair ein helpu ni* *(Mair will help us)*
      PT do + AUX Mair our help us

(52) (i) *arhosith   Mair ddim efo ni* *(Mair will not stay with us)*
      stay + AUX Mair NEG with us

   (ii) *wneith   Mair ddim aros efo ni* *(Mair will not stay with us)*
      do + AUX Mair NEG stay with us

It is typical of volitional -ITH that it involves and event which will occur in the future. But such sentences are more concerned with the presence or absence of the subject's willingness to partake in the event than with any temporal reference. In example (52), for instance, it is possible to supply an interpretation which involves knowing for a fact that Mair has voiced her refusal to stay. As such, we are clearly referring to her lack of willingness.

More significant in establishing volition as a separate use of -ITH is the fact that this use has quite different formal characteristics. It is never possible to express volition statements in the progressive aspect by using BYDD . . YN . . Thus examples (50) to (52) above are not equivalent to the following:

(53) *fyddwch chi 'n agor y drws i mi?* *(will you be opening*
   will be   you in open the door for me   *the door for me?)*

(54) *mi fydd*   *Mair yn ein helpu ni*   *(Mair will be helping us)*
     PT will be   Mair in our help us

(55) *fydd Mair   ddim yn aros efo ni*   *(Mair won't be staying with*
     will be Mair NEG in stay with us   *us)*

Examples (53) to (55) are all predictive and not volitional. In the vast majority of cases, volition always occurs with the non-progressive, and it is only rarely that we may have:

(56) *wnei   di fod yn sefyll yma mewn hanner awr?*   *(will you be standing*
     do + AUX you be in stand here in   half   hour   *here in half an hour?)*

As far as past time is concerned, the -AI paradigm is used, and this is clearly seen when the sentence is negative; but BUASAI/BYDDAI . . YN . . (WOULD BE . . IN . . = WOULD BE -ING) is inappropriate:

(57) (i) *arhosai*   *Mair ddim efo ni neithiwr*   *(Mair wouldn't stay*
        stay + AUX Mair NEG with us last night   *with us last night)*

     (ii) *wnai*   *Mair ddim aros efo ni neithiwr*   *(Mair wouldn't stay*
        do + AUX Mair NEG stay with us last night   *with us last night)*

(58) **fuasai/fyddai Mair yn aros efo ni neithiwr*   *(NO APPROPRIATE*
     would be   Mair in stay with us last night   *TRANSLATION)*

And even though such sentences could refer to an episodic event, BYDD . . WEDI . . (WILL BE . . AFTER . . = WILL HAVE -EN) could never occur to express past volition:

(59) **fydd   Mair ddim wedi aros efo ni neithiwr*   *(*Mair won't have*
     will be Mair NEG after stay with us last night   *stayed with us last*
                                                   night)

The method of past time reference involving -ITH volition is thus quite different from that involving -ITH prediction. A third distinctive characteristic of -ITH volition is that it is possible to use a paraphrase for negative (or lack of) volition involving (NA) CÁU (REFUSE) (northern), PALLU (southern), PEIDIO (general) in either past or present; for example:

(60) *mae Mair yn 'cau aros efo ni*   *(Mair won't stay with us)*
     is   Mair in refuse stay with us

Note that the selection of MAE (IS) in the paraphrase of (52) in (60) using 'CAU clearly indicates that we are concerned with the present (lack of) volition and not the futurity of the event itself.

All the above examples have involved animate subjects. Very similar are negative sentences which involve inanimates:

(61) (i)   *chychwynnith   'nghar i ddim*   *(my car won't start)*
              start + AUX my   car   I   NEG

       (ii)   *wneith   'nghar i ddim cychwyn*   *(my car won't start)*
              do + AUX my car   I   NEG start

(62) (i)   *agorith   y drws ddim*   *(the door won't open)*
              open + AUX the door NEG

       (ii)   *wneith   y drws ddim agor*   *(the door won't open)*
              do + AUX the door NEG open

It is inappropriate to speak of volition when an inanimate is involved. And yet, such statements are formally identical with the characteristics of volition statements; for example:

(63) **fydd   'nghar i ddim yn cychwyn*   *(*my car won't be starting)*
       will be my car I NEG in start

(64) (i)   *chychwynnai   'nghar i ddim neithiwr*   *(my car wouldn't start*
              start + AUX my car I   NEG last night *last night)*

       (ii)   *wnai   'nghar i ddim cychwyn neithiwr*   *(my car wouldn't*
              do + AUX my car I NEG start   last night   *start last night)*

(65) **fuasai/fyddai 'nghar i ddim yn cychwyn neithiwr* *(NO APPROPRIATE*
       would be   my car I   NEG in start   last night   *TRANSLATION)*

(66) **fydd   'nghar i ddim wedi cychwyn neithiwr* *(*my car will not*
       will be my car I NEG after   start   last night   *have started last*
                                                            night)

(67) *mae 'nghar i yn 'cau cychwyn*   *(my car won't start)*
       is my car I in refuse start

Although it is odd to attribute qualities of volition to inanimate objects, the similarity in the grammar of the use of -ITH with animates and inanimates does suggest that the two should be handled together.

The -ITH inflection can also be used with *imperative* force, and such an interpretation can be applied to the following examples:

(68) (i)   *mi arhosi   di yma tan amser cinio*   *(you will stay here*
              PT stay + AUX you here until time dinner   *until dinner time)*

       (ii)   *mi wnei   di aros yma tan amser cinio*   *(you will stay here*
              PT do + AUX you stay here until time dinner   *until dinner time)*

These examples can compare very closely with an imperative sentence:

(69) *aros yma tan amser cinio*   *(stay here until*
      stay here until time dinner   *dinner time)*

As pointed out in the survey of contemporary inflectional paradigms, the imperative paradigm mainly involves the second person in spontaneous speech. By using -ITH, commands can be given in third person form:

(70) (i)   *mi godith y gynulleidfa*   *(the congregation will rise)*
          PT rise + AUX the congregation

     (ii)   *mi wneith y gynulleidfa godi*   *(the congregation will rise)*
          PT do + AUX the congregation rise

The direct speaker-addressee relationship is here 'softened' by introducing third person address.

As with -ITH predictive, the equivalent progressive aspect pattern BYDD . . YN . . (WILL BE . . IN . . = WILL BE -ING) can also be used to convey imperative force:

(71) *mi fyddi di 'n aros yma tan amser cinio*   *(you will be staying here*
      PT will be you in stay here until time dinner   *until dinner time)*

But, unlike the previous two uses, there is no possibility of past time reference; an imperative can only refer to a future event. Thus, it is not possible to have:

(72) (i)   **mi arhoset ti yna nes ddois i 'n ôl*   *(*you would*
          PT stay + AUX you there until come + AUX I in back stay there
                                                          until I
                                                          came back)

     (ii)   **mi wnaet ti aros yna nes ddois i 'n ôl*   *(*you would*
          PT do + AUX you stay there until come + AUX I in back stay there
                                                         until I came
                                                          back)

(73) **mi fuaset/fyddet ti 'n aros yna nes*   *(NO APPROPRIATE*
      PT would be + AUX you in stay there until   *TRANSLATION)*

      ddois i 'n ôl
      come + AUX I in back

The imperative use of -ITH is most distinctive in terms of its temporal restrictions.

The formal characteristics of the three uses of -ITH noted above, *prediction, volition* and *imperative,* represent the grammar of each use. The operation of aspectual and past time reference over these uses is summarised in the following table:

	BYDD . . YN		PAST TIME REFERENCE		
	-AI	GWNEUD + -AI	-AI	BYDD . . WEDI	BUASAI/BYDDAI . . YN
Prediction	+	+	+	+	+
Volition	−	+	+	−	−
Imperative	+	−	−	−	−

In addition to the above, -ITH volition in negative sentences also has the characteristic of a paraphrase involving (NA) CAU, etc. (REFUSE). Note also the fourth use equivalent to MAE . . YN . ., which is stylistically marked as a characteristic of formal Welsh (apart from a small number of verbs) as discussed above.

2c   The -AI paradigm

In formal written Welsh the -AI paradigm can be used to convey a durative activity in past time:

(75) gorweddwn   yn fy ngwely yn meddwl am   y   broblem
     lie + AUX   in my bed   in think about the problem

(I was lying in bed thinking about the problem)

The use of the -AI paradigm here emphasises the durative character of the activity. In spontaneous spoken Welsh it is equivalent to OEDD . . YN . . (WAS . . IN . . = WAS -ING):

(76) 'roeddwn   i'n   gorwedd yn   'y   'ngwely
     was   I in lie   in   my bed

     yn meddwl am y broblem
     in think about the problem

(I was lying in bed thinking about the problem)

This comparison illustrates that -AI is here being used as a past tense for statements of fact where the durational character of an activity is emphasised. In traditional Welsh grammar this use is labelled as the imperfect tense.

The above use of the -AI paradigm in contemporary Welsh is confined to formal written Welsh and in spontaneous speech it has quite different uses. A total of four can be distinguished: (i) *past tense* for prediction about habitual events in past time; (ii) *past tense* to refer to past time volition; (iii) *hypothetical* statements in the non-past; and (iv) *tentative* statements in the non-past.

The first two uses have already been introduced in the discussion of the -ITH paradigm. As a past tense for predictive habitual sentences, -AI can be illustrated as follows:

(77) (i) mi alwai   hi i 'n gweld ni bron
          PT call + AUX she to our see us almost

          bob nos
          every night

(she would call to see us nearly every night)

(ii) *mi wnai   hi alw i 'n gweld ni bron*   *(she would call*
PT do + AUX she call to our see   us almost   *to see us nearly*
every night)

bob nos
every night

But a frequently occurring pattern in this use involves BUASAI/BYDDAI . . YN . . (WOULD BE . . IN . . = WOULD BE -ING):

(78) *mi fuasai/fyddai hi yn galw i 'n gweld ni*   *(she would call to see*
PT would be   she in call to our see us   *us nearly every night)*

bron   bob nos
almost every night

In this use -AI is restricted to habitual events, and in the case of an episodic event BYDD . . WEDI . . (WILL . . AFTER . . = WILL HAVE -EN) is used:

(79) *mi fydd   hi wedi galw i 'n gweld ni neithiwr* *(she will have called to*
PT will be she after call to our see   us last night see us last night)

In the case of volitional statements, however, only -AI occurs and it is not restricted to a habitual activity:

(80) (i) *symudai   hi ddim*   *(she wouldn't move)*
move + AUX she NEG

(ii) *wnai   hi ddim symud*   *(she wouldn't move)*
do + AUX she NEG move

The use of BUASAI/BYDDAI (WOULD BE) is not possible here, as noted above. The third use of -AI, to make hypothetical statements, can be illustrated as follows:

(81) *mi ganai   Mair i ni heno*   *(Mair would sing for us tonight)*
PT sing + AUX Mair for us tonight

The occurrence of GWNEUD (DO) as a carrier of -AI in this use is not very frequent. In example (81) above, the event referred to is not proposed as a 'real' event but is expressed in 'unreal' terms.

Compared with the two previous uses of -AI as a past tense for predictive and volitional statements, the 'unreal' use of -AI is distinctive in that it refers to events in the *non-past* period and not in the past period. Another characteristic, however, is that it can occur with a PE (hypothetical IF) clause:

(82) *mi ganai   Mair i ni heno*   *(Mair would sing for us tonight*
PT sing + AUX Mair for us tonight   *if she was/were all right)*

petai   hi 'n iawn
if COND she in all right

90

The PE (IF) clause states the 'unreal' condition which, if it were to occur, would allow the event to take place. In Welsh, conditional clauses have two clause conjunctions: PE for 'unreal' conditions, as in (82) above, and OS for 'real' conditions, as in the following examples:[5]

(83) *mi ganith   Mair heno os bydd   hi 'n iawn*   *(Mair will sing*
     PT sing + AUX Mair tonight if will be she in all right)   tonight if she is
                                                                   all right)

Many speakers prefer to use BUASAI/BYDDAI .. YN .. (WOULD BE .. IN .. = WOULD BE -ING) for 'unreal' statements, and in place of (81) or (82) it is possible to have:

(84) *mi fuasai/fyddai Mair yn canu (petai   hi 'n iawn)   (Mair would sing*
     PT would be   Mair in sing   if COND she in all right (if she was/were
                                                               all right))

Many northern speakers use only this pattern for conditional statements and no aspectual contract is possible. The use of BUASAI/BYDDAI (WOULD BE), is however, really significant as far as 'unreal' events in the past are concerned. In these circumstances BUASAI/BYDDAI .. WEDI .. (WOULD BE .. AFTER .. = WOULD HAVE -EN) is the only possible pattern, and the past time equivalent of (81) or (82) is:

(85) *mi fuasai/fyddai Mair wedi canu neithiwr   (Mair would have sung*
     PT would be   Mair after sing last night   last night if she had been
                                                       all right)

     (petai   hi wedi bod yn iawn)
     if COND she after be   in all right

The items BUASAI/BYDDAI (WOULD BE) are discussed in detail in chapter VI, section 3e.

The fourth use of -AI is not as common, perhaps, as the other uses. There are examples of -AI being used in a statement where the event is not viewed as being 'unreal' and, furthermore, where an OS (IF) clause can occur with a 'real' as opposed to 'unreal' reference:

(86) *?os wnei   di adael r̂wan, mi gyrrhaeddet ti   (if you leave now, you*
     if do + AUX you leave now   PT arrive + AUX you   would arrive in London
                                                          by ten)

     Llundain erbyn deg
     London   by   ten

In this use -AI is being used to make a tentative statement and its outstanding characteristic is the occurrence of the -ITH inflection in the co-occurring OS (IF) clause.

Where **this use** of -AI is extended to polite requests involving volitional -ITH, the result is that the request is more polite. Consider the following:

(87) (i) basi   di'r   halen?   *(will you pass the salt?)*
      pass + AUX   you the salt

(ii) wnei   di basio'r halen?   *(will you pass the salt?)*
     do + AUX you pass the salt

(88) alli   di basio'r   halen?   *(can you pass the salt?)*
    can + AUX you pass the salt

These are already polite requests, but by using the -AI inflection they become even more polite:

(89) (i) basiet   ti 'r halen?   *(would you pass the salt?)*
      pass + AUX you the salt

(ii) wnaet   ti basio 'r halen?   *(would you pass the salt?)*
     do + AUX   you   pass the salt

(90) allet   ti basio 'r halen   *(could you pass the salt?)*
    can + AUX   you pass the salt

More frequent for many speakers as a politer form would be BUASAI/BYDDAI, giving sentences like:

(91) fuaset/fyddet ti 'n pasio'r halen?   *(would you pass the salt?)*
    would be   you in pass the salt

The four uses of -AI along with the formal characteristics can be summarised in the following table:

(92)

		Time reference		Conditional clauses	
		Non-past	Past	PE	OS
(i)	*Past prediction*	*(-ITH)*	+ *(BUASAI/BYDDAI . . YN . .)*	-	+
(ii)	*Past volition*	*(-ITH)*	+	-	+
(iii)	*Hypothetical*	+	*(BUASAI/BYDDAI . . WEDI . .)*	+	-
(iv)	*Tentativity*	+	*(BUASAI/BYDDAI . . WEDI . .)*	+	+

The main differences are found in the temporal features, distinguishing the occurrences of -AI as a past tense for prediction and volition from its occurrences to convey hypotheticalness and tentativity in the non-past. Within this major differentia-tion, prediction is distinguished from volition by the possibility of BUASAI/BYDDAI .. YN .. for the former; and hypotheticalness is distinguished from tentativity accord-ing to the nature of the co-occurring conditional clause.

2d   The -ODD paradigm

The -ODD (PAST) paradigm is much simpler to discuss than either the -ITH paradigm or the -AI paradigm. Firstly, it is confined to past time, as the following examples illustrate:

(93) (i)   *mi ganodd   Mair neithiwr*   *(Mair sang last night)*
               PT sing + PAST   Mair   last night

       (ii)   *mi wnaeth/ddaru*   *(Mair sang last night)*
               PT do + PAST   happen + PAST

               Mair ganu   neithiwr
               Mair sing   last night

(94) (i)   **mi ganodd   Mair yfory*   *(*Mair sang tomorrow)*
               PT sing + PAST   Mair tomorrow

       (ii)   **mi wnaeth/ddaru*   *(*Mair sang tomorrow)*
               PT do + PAST happen + PAST

               Mair   ganu   yfory
               Mair   sing   tomorrow

As a past time form, -ODD compares with OEDD .. YN .. (WAS .. IN .. = WAS -ING):

(95) *'roedd Mair yn canu neithiwr*   *(Mair was singing last night)*
      was   Mair in sing   last night

More will be said about this relationship in chapter VI, sections 3a and 3b.

Secondly, in terms of its semantics the inflectional paradigm -ODD has only one meaning, which can be characterised as *factual*: it tells us nothing about the attitude or beliefs of the speaker but is involved only with making statements about the occurrence of a particular activity on the basis of *fact*. Thus, in (93) above, it is known for a fact that Mair sang. As such, the -ODD paradigm has no equivalent non-past inflection in the manner that -AI past prediction or volition can be represented in the non-past by -ITH. Factual statements in the non-past are made by using a periphrastic pattern involving MAE (IS), discussed more fully in sections 3a and 3b of chapter VI.

2e   Summary and conclusion

The auxiliary has been discussed in the foregoing sub-sections by taking each inflection and listing its range of associated uses. Basically, each inflection involves both a semantic feature and a tense feature in combination. For example, the -ITH inflection can refer to *non-past volition*. The various semantic and tense features involved can be summarised in the following list:

(96) (i)   *-ITH:*   (a)   *prediction non-past;*
             (b)   *volition non-past;*
             (c)   *imperative non-past;*

   (ii)   *-AI:*   (a)   *prediction past;*
             (b)   *volition past;*
             (c)   *hypothetical non-past;*
             (d)   *tentative non-past.*

   (iii)   *-ODD:*   *fact past.*

There are, however, certain useful distinctions that can be made by looking at the auxiliary from the point of view of its semantic and tense features, as in the next paragraph.

The following table can serve to illustrate the manner in which the various uses either share the same inflectional characteristics or involve different inflectional characteristics:

(97)

			Non-past	Past
(i)	(a)	Prediction	-ITH	-AI
	(b)	Volition	-ITH	-AI
(ii)		Imperative	-ITH	–
(iii)	(a)	Conditional	-AI	see chapter VI, section 3e
	(b)	Tentative	-AI	see chapter VI, section 3e
(iv)		Fact	see chaper VI section 3b	-ODD

In terms of inflectional characteristics, *prediction* and *volition* fall together, both having -ITH for non-past and -AI for past; imperative, too, has -ITH for non-past but has no past expression; conditional and tentative fall together in that -AI and not -ITH is used for non-past while special provisions involving aspect (see section 2c above) are involved for past reference; finally, -ODD is quite distinct in that it is used for factual statements in the past.[6]

A significant point is that, whereas -ITH and -AI are related tense forms in terms of prediction and volition, the -ODD inflection bears no relation in terms of semantics to either -AI or -ITH. As is seen in section 3f below and chapter VI, section 4, an entirely different situation arises with the lexical auxiliaries, where -ITH, -AI and -ODD can fall together as tense forms with the same semantic feature.

3 THE LEXICAL AUXILIARIES CAEL, GALLU, MEDRU AND DYLU

3a Introduction

Unlike GWNEUD (DO) and DARFOD (HAPPEN), the lexical auxiliaries have their own semantic content so that their function involves more than that of carrying an inflection. In the following sub-sections the discussion will explore the sorts of meanings that these four verbs involve. Formal criteria will again be used to support the setting up of various uses, and reference will be made to (i) the type of temporal reference in the non-past period, (ii) the use of inflections for tense contrasts, and (iii) various other criteria, particularly paraphrase. Significant distinctions can also be made by referring to aspectual possibilities, but such a discussion is best left until aspect has been treated (see chapter VI, section 2b).

3b CAEL

The verb CAEL (RECEIVE) has at least three uses which can be listed as follows: (i) *permission*, (ii) *obtainment*, (iii) *suggestion*.

The following example illustrates CAEL being used to convey *permission:*

(98) *mi gei   di fenthyg ei lyfr o*   *(you may/can borrow*
   PT CAEL + AUX you borrow his book he   *his book)*

In this particular example CAEL (RECEIVE) occurs in a declarative sentence and conveys the information that the subject of the sentence has permission to borrow the speaker's book. The speaker, in fact, can be regarded as giving the permission and the whole sentence compares with:

(99) *dwi   'n caniatau i   ti fenthyg yn llyfr i*   *(I permit you to borrow*
   am I in   permit for you borrow my book I   *my book)*

This use of CAEL frequently occurs in questions where the element of permission is clearly present:

(100) *ga'   i fenthyg dy lyfr di?*   *(can/may I borrow your*
    CAEL + AUX I borrow your book you   book)*

The paraphrase involving CANIATAU (PERMIT) is a fairly clear indication of the *permission* use of CAEL. In terms of its temporal reference with -ITH, CAEL *permission*

95

always refers to a future event, that is, an event which follows the moment of speaking; in addition, it can refer to past time events with either the -AI or the -ODD paradigm:

(101) mi gawn   i aros yn lle John   (I'd be allowed to stay
       PT CAEL + AUX I stay in place John   in John's place)

(102) mi gefais   i aros yn lle John   (I was allowed to stay
       PT CAEL + AUX I stay in place John   in John's place)

The following example illustrates the second use of CAEL, *obtainment:*

(103) (i)   mi gei   di wybod yfory   (you'll know tomorrow)
             PT CAEL + AUX you know tomorrow

       (ii) mi geith   o fynd i fyny 'r Wyddfa   (he'll get to go up
             PT CAEL + AUX he go up the Snowdon   Snowdon this
                                                         summer)
             yr ha' 'ma
             the summer here

The use of CAEL here establishes that the event referred to will come about as a matter of course. In (103) (i), for instance, the subject will eventually obtain the knowledge while in (103) (ii) the subject will get to go up Snowdon. As such, CAEL is here being used in its more general sense of 'to receive'. This use of CAEL commonly occurs with verbs of the senses like GWYBOD (KNOW), GWELD (SEE) and CLYWED (HEAR); but it also occurs with other verbs such as MYND (GO), as in (103) (ii). On the basis of this distinction it could be argued that there are two uses of CAEL. But it seems that any difference arises because of the different verbs involved, and in this account both types are handled under the same heading of obtainment. In terms of temporal reference, CAEL *obtainment* is very like CAEL *permission*. With -ITH it always refers to a future event, and -AI and -ODD can be used for the past time:

(104) (i)   mi gawn   i wybod yn y   diwedd   (I would get to know
             PT CAEL + AUX I know in the end   in the end)

       (ii) mi gefais   i wybod wedyn   (I got to know afterwards)
             PT CAEL + AUX I know after

(105) (i)   mi gawn   i fynd i fyny 'r Wyddfa (I'd get to go up
             PT CAEL + AUX I go up   the Snowdon   Snowdon)

       (ii) mi gefais   i fynd i fyny 'r Wyddfa (I got to go up Snowdon)
             PT CAEL + AUX I go up   the Snowdon

The possibilities of paraphrase, however, clearly distinguish *obtainment* from *permission.*

The following example illustrates the *suggestion* use of CAEL:

(106) *mi gei*   *di osod y bwrdd*   *(you can lay the table)*
       PT CAEL + AUX you lay the table

In (106) the speaker is suggesting to the subject of the sentence that he goes ahead and performs the action referred to. The sentence compares with:

(107) *'dwi 'n awgrymu dy fod ti 'n gosod y bwrdd*   *(I suggest that*
       am I in suggest your be you in lay the table   *you lay the table)*

This use of CAEL is not limited to second person subjects and further examples can be given:

(108) (i) *mi geith*   *hi helpu John*   *(she can help John)*
            PT CAEL + AUX she help John

       (ii) *dwi 'n awgrymu ei bod hi 'n helpu John*   *(I suggest that*
            am I in suggest her be she in help John   *she helps John)*

(109) (i) *mi ga'*   *i olchi'r llestri*   *(I can wash the dishes)*
            PT CAEL + AUX I wash the dishes

       (ii) *dwi 'n awgrymu 'mod   i' n golchi'r llestri*   *(I suggest that I*
            am I in suggest my + be I in wash the dishes   *wash the dishes)*

The -ITH paradigm can here only refer to an event which follows the moment of speaking and is therefore a future event. Other than this, suggestion is like imperative (see section 2b above) as it does not refer to any event in the past period with either -AI or -ODD:

(110) **mi gaet*   *ti osod y bwrdd*   *(*you could lay the table)*
       PT CAEL + AUX you lay the table

(111) **mi gefaist*   *ti osod y bwrdd*   *(*you could lay the table)*
       PT CAEL + AUX you lay the table

In terms of temporal reference, therefore, CAEL *suggestion* can be clearly distinguished from either *permission* or *obtainment*.

3c MEDRU and GALLU

The verbs MEDRU and GALLU have three uses in common and can be discussed together: (i) *ability*, (ii) *physical possibility*, (iii) *disposition*. There are also three other uses of GALLU, sharing one in a restricted manner with MEDRU: (i) *possibility*, (ii) *permission*, (iii) *perception*.

The following example illustrates a familiar use of GALLU/MEDRU which is extensively quoted in traditional grammars, namely *ability:*

(112) *mi fedr/all*   John   ddreifio   car   *(John can drive a car)*
       PT can   John   drive   car

This example states that John has the ability to drive a car. Although the -ITH paradigm occurs with MEDRU/GALLU *ability,* it never refers to a specific future event and it is not possible to have:

(113) **mi fedr/all   John   ddreifio   car   yfory*   *(*John can drive a car*
       PT can   John   drive   car   tomorrow   *tomorrow)*

The use of *ability* to refer to a future event can be achieved, however, by using the aspectual auxiliary BYDD . . YN . . (WILL BE . . IN . . = WILL BE -ING) (but see chapter VI, section 3c):

(114) *mi fydd   John   yn   medru/gallu   dreifio   car   yfory*   *(John will be able*
       PT will be John   in   ABILITY   drive   car   tomorrow   *to drive a car*
                                                                        tomorrow)

In terms of past time, either -AI or -ODD can occur:

(115) *mi allai/fedrai   John   ddreifio   car*   *(John could drive a car)*
       PT could   John   drive   car

(116) *mi allodd/fedrodd John   ddreifio   car   neithiwr*   *(John was able to*
       PT was able   John   drive   car   last night   *drive a car last night)*

By contrast, the following example refers to *physical possibility* and states that there is no physical impediment or hindrance which will prevent the activity involved:

(117) *mi fedr/all   John   fynd   trwy   Bethesda*   *(John can go*
       PT can   John   go   through Bethesda   *through Bethesda)*

The distinctive characteristic of this use is that GALLU/MEDRU can be paraphrased as follows:

(118) *mae'n   bosib   i   John   fynd   trwy   Bethesda*   *(it is possible for*
       is in   possible for John   go   through Bethesda   *John to go through*
                                                                   Bethesda)

In terms of time reference, GALLU/MEDRU *physical possibility* can use -ITH to refer to a specified future event and -AI and -ODD can be used for past time:

(119) *mi all/fedr   John   fynd   trwy   Bethesda   yfory*   *(John can go through*
       PT can   John   go   through Bethesda   tomorrow   *Bethesda tomorrow)*

(120) *mi allai/fedrai   John   fynd   trwy   Bethesda*   *(John could go*
       PT could   John   go   through Bethesda   *through Bethesda)*

98

(121) *mi allodd/fedrodd John fynd trwy Bethesda*   *(John was able to*
       PT could   John go through Bethesda   *go through Bethesda)*

In the following example, MEDRU/GALLU is used in a polite request and appeals to the subject's *disposition* or, perhaps, willingness to perform the action referred to:

(122) *fedri/alli di basio'r halen?*   *(can you pass the salt?)*
       can   you pass the salt

This use compares with -ITH *volition* discussed in section 2b above:

(123) *wnei   di basio'r halen?*   *(will you pass the salt?)*
       do + AUX you pass the salt

The difference between the two seems to be that -ITH requests the subject of the sentence actually to perform the action while MEDRU/GALLU enquires about the subject's willingness or disposition towards performing the action. There is a comparable use of MEDRU/GALLU in negative statements:

(124) *fedra'/alla' i ddim gwrthod*   *(I can't refuse)*
       can   I NEG refuse

(125) *fedra'/alla' i ddim cymryd y près gynno fo*   *(I can't take the*
       can   I NEG take the money from his   *money from him)*

These examples convey the subject's disposition or attitude towards the event rather than his actually going ahead and performing the action. This use of GALLU/MEDRU is quite distinctive in terms of time reference. It can refer to a specific future event:

(126) *alli/fedri di 'n helpu ni yfory?*   *(can you help us tomorrow?)*
       can   you our help us tomorrow

Furthermore, in terms of past time reference it only seems to occur in the negative and only with the -AI paradigm.

(127) *allwn/fedrwn i ddim gwrthod*   *(I couldn't refuse)*
       can + AUX I NEG refuse

(128) **allais/fedrais i ddim gwrthod*   *(*I wasn't able to refuse)*
       can + AUX I NEG refuse

The verb GALLU is one of the most heavily loaded items in the Welsh language. The first of its additional uses, *possibility*, can be illustrated as follows:

(129) *efallai*   *bod Mair yn gweithio(maybe Mair is working)*
       it + PT + GALLU + AUX be Mair in work

The item EFALLAI (COULD) is described as an adverb by some writers. However,

99

it is directly related to GALLU and is the result of an earlier historical pattern EFE + A + ALLAI, giving EFALLAI. In speech it occurs as 'FALLAI (pronounced (va⁊e) or (va⁊a)) or ALLAI (pronounced (a⁊a) or (a⁊ε)). The function of GALLU here is to provide the semantic basis or *modal* feature for making the proposition BOD MAIR YN GWEITHIO (THAT MAIR IS WORKING). In effect, it establishes that the proposition is put forward as a possibility or, in alternative terms, that the occurrence of a particular event is possible. As such, it is subject to the following paraphrases:

(130) mae'n bosib bod Mair yn gweithio   *(it's possible that Mair*
        is in possible be Mair in work   *is working)*

(131) hwyrach bod Mair yn gweithio   *(perhaps Mair is working)*
        perhaps be   Mair in work

The paraphrase involving POSIB (POSSIBLE) clearly reveals the semantics of the sentence and contrasts with the physical possibility use of GALLU described above. It is inappropriate to paraphrase (129) as:

(132) mae'n bosib i Mair weithio   *(it's possible for Mair*
        is in possible for Mair work   *to work)*

The surface structure characteristics alone of the occurrence of GALLU in (129) are sufficient to distinguish it from other uses. In addition, in this particular syntactic environment GALLU only occurs with the -AI paradigm; -ITH and -ODD do not occur:

(133) *efallith   bod Mair yn gweithio *(NO APPROPRIATE*
        it + PT + GALLU + ITH be Mair in work   *TRANSLATION)*

(134) *efallodd   bod Mair yn gweithio *(NO APPROPRIATE*
        it + PT + GALLU + ODD be Mair in work   *TRANSLATION)*

The surface structure configuration of (129) is a typical one for a modal feature in Welsh but is quite different from the normal syntactic environment of an auxiliary verb. However, when occurring in relative clauses, GALLU *possibility* behaves like an auxiliary verb. Compare the following examples:

(135) efallai   y gwneith   y ceffyl   *(maybe this horse*
        it + PT + GALLU + AI PT do + AUX the horse *will win)*

        'ma ennill
        here win

(136) dyma   'r ceffyl a allai   ennill   *(here is the horse*
        here is the horse PT GALLU + AUX win   *that might win)*

Moreover, only in this environment can GALLU occur with the -ITH paradigm:

(137) *dyma 'r   ceffyl   a   all   ennill*   *(here's the horse*
       here is the   horse   PT GALLU + ITH win   *that may win)*

And, finally, in this environment there is also the possibility of using MEDRU:

(138) *dyma 'r   ceffyl   a   fedr/fedrai   ennill*   *(here's the horse that*
       here is the   horse PT   MEDRU + AUX   win   *may/might win)*

Modal features are discussed in chapter VIII, section 2f.
Some speakers use GALLU, like CAEL, to convey *permission:*

(139) *mi alli   di   fenthyg ei   lyfr   o*   *(you can/may borrow*
       PT GALLU + AUX   you   borrow his   book he   *his book)*

(140) *alla'   i fenthyg dy   lyfr di?*   *(can I borrow you book?)*
       GALLU + AUX   I   borrow your book you

In this use GALLU *permission* has the characteristics of CAEL *permission.*
   There is also a special use of GALLU which is evident when it accompanies verbs
of perception like GWELD (SEE), CLYWED (HEAR) and TEIMLO (FEEL):

(141) *mi alla'   i weld y mynyddoedd*   *(I can see the mountains)*
       PT GALLU + AUX   I see   the mountains

(142) *mi alla'   i deimlo rhywbeth yn rhedeg*   *(I can feel some-*
       PT GALLU + AUX I feel   something in   run   *thing running*
                                                            down my back)
       i lawr 'y   'nghefn
       down my   back

In these examples GALLU emphasises the perceptive process involved in the verbs
and in this particular context its function can be labelled as *perception.* The verbs
involved, however, are inherently perceptive and it would be possible to produce the
sentences without GALLU. Many speakers, especially in North Wales, in fact do this
and perceptive verbs occur by themselves:

(143) *dwi   'n gweld y mynyddoedd*   *(I see the mountains)*
       am I in   see   the mountains

(144) *dwi 'n teimlo rhywbeth   yn rhedeg*   *(I feel something running*
       am I in feel   something   in run   *down my back)*
       i lawr 'y   'nghefn
       down   my + back

The outstanding characteristic of the perceptive use of GALLU is that when it
occurs with the -ITH paradigm it can describe an activity which is present contemporaneous in time reference; that is, actually occurring at the moment of speaking. Thus,

101

in example (141) above, actually seeing the mountains accompanies the moment of revealing the fact. As far as past time is concerned, there is some uncertainty. It is true that both -AI and -ODD are possible:

(145) (i)   *mi allwn*   *I weld y mynyddoedd*   *(I could see the*
               PT GALLU + AUX I see the mountains   *mountains)*

(ii)   *mi allwn*   *i deimlo rhywbeth yn*   *(I could feel*
               PT GALLU + AUX I feel   something in   *something running*
                                                       down my back)
               rhedeg i lawr 'y 'nghefn
               run   down my + back

(146) (i)   *mi allais*   *I weld y mynyddoed*   *(I was able to see*
               PT GALLU + AUX I see the mountains   *the mountains)*

(ii)   *mi allais*   *i deimlo rhywbeth yn*   *(I was able to feel*
               PT GALLU + AUX I feel   something in   *something running*
                                                       down my back)
               rhedeg i lawr 'y 'nghefn
               run   down my + back

It is problematic whether these examples are equivalent to present *perceptive* examples or whether they involve *physical possibility*, especially in the case of the -ODD inflection in (146) (to which some speakers may in any case feel some resistance). A similar problem exists where the -ITH paradigm refers to a future event, for example:

(147)   *mi alla'*   *i weld y lleuad heno*   *(I can see the moon*
        PT GALLU + ITH I see the moon tonight   *tonight)*

Here it seems fairly certain that physical possibility is involved, and on this basis GALLU *perception* in the non-past period appears to be restricted to a present contemporaneous reference.

3d   DYLU

The auxiliary verb DYLU is traditionally called a defective verb as it has a limited inflectional range, occurring only with the -AI paradigm. Moreover, it does not occur in uninflected form and the use of the artificial form DYLU here is no more than a labelling convenience. There are two uses of DYLU which have been observed so far: (i) *likelihood*, (ii) *unfulfilment*.

The verb DYLU is frequently used to supply the semantic basis or modal feature of a sentence in the form of *likelihood*. As such, there are two possible surface structure configurations:

(148) *mi ddylai fod y bws yn cyrraedd erbyn deg*   *(the bus should*
       PT should be the bus in arrive   by   ten   *arrive by ten)*

(149) *mi ddylai 'r bws gyrraedd erbyn deg*   *(the bus should*
       PT should the bus arrive   by   ten   *arrive by ten)*

In both instances the event is proposed on the basis of what the speaker thinks is likely. The surface structure configuration in example (148) is that of a surface complex sentence and is discussed in chapter VIII, section 2f. The surface structure in (149) involves the typical syntactic environment of an auxiliary verb. Both patterns can be used when the viability of the event is discernible in the present time situation. But where the future event is not related to present factors, the second is used. Compare:

(150) **mi ddylai bod hi 'n bwrw yfory*   *(*it should be that*
       PT should be she in rain tomorrow   *it rains tomorrow)*

(151) *mi ddylai hi fwrw yfory*   *(it should rain tomorrow)*
       PT should she rain tomorrow

This distinction reflects the factual-predictive contrast discussed in relation to examples (39) to (42) above.

The second use of DYLU can be illustrated as follows:

(152) *mi ddylai Mair ymddiheuro*   *(Mair should apologise)*
       PT should Mair apologise

(153) *mi ddylai pawb   anfon y llyfrau 'n ôl*   *(everyone should send*
       PT should everyone send the books   back   *the books back)*

This use traditionally goes under the heading of 'obligation'; that is, the speaker claims that the subject of the sentence has a sense of obligation or duty to perform the action referred to. In effect, however, this is probably a circumstantial explanation governed by the animacy of the subjects involved. The characteristic which distinguishes this use of DYLU from its *likelihood* use is suggestive of a more general account of the concepts involved. Examples like (152) and (153) can be contradicted, for example:

(154) *mi ddylai Mair ymddiheuro - ond wneith   hi ddim*   *(Mair should*
       PT should Mair apologise   - but do + AUX she NEG   *apologise - but*
                                                                she won't)

This is not possible with a *likelihood* example like those in (148) to (151). This use of DYLU thus allows *non-occurring* events to be proposed; as in the case, for instance, of approaching an empty shelf where one expects to find books:

(155) *mi ddylai 'r llyfrau fod yn fan hyn*   *(the books should*
       PT should the books be in place this   be here)

On this basis it is possible to suggest that DYLU is used to allow for *unfulfilment*. There is, therefore, an element of 'unreality' or hypotheticalness about it, and perhaps that is why only the -AI paradigm occurs (see section 2c above). It is this factor of unfulfilment which makes DYLU particularly useful for expressing 'obligation'. It is interesting to compare DYLU with RHAID (NECESSARY) and GORFOD (BE OBLIGED):

(156) *mae rhaid   i Mair ymddiheuro*   *(Mair must apologise)*
       is NECESSARY for Mair apologise

(157) *mae Mair yn gorfod   ymddiheuro*   *(Mair has (got) to apologise)*
       is Mair in BE OBLIGED apologise

But DYLU's allowance for unfulfilment clearly distinguishes it from RHAID (NECESSARY) and GORFOD (BE OBLIGED TO), as neither of the latter can be contradicted:

(158) **mae rhaid   i Mair ymddiheuro -*   *(*Mair must apologise*
       is NECESSARY for Mair apologise   -   - but she won't)

       ond wneith   hi ddim
       but do + AUX   she NEG

       *mae Mair yn gorfod   ymddiheuro -   *(*Mair has (got) to*
       is   Mair in BE OBLIGED apologise   -   apologise - but she
                                                    won't)
       ond wneith   hi ddim
       but do + AUX she NEG

We can suggest, therefore, that DYLU allows for *unfulfilment* whereas RHAID (NECESSARY) and GORFOD (BE OBLIGED TO) do not; to this extent, DYLU is 'weaker' in terms of 'obligation' than either of the other two.

3e   Summary of the uses of the lexical auxiliaries

A considerable amount of detail has been introduced in this sub-section and a brief summary can be tabled as follows:

		Tense			Time ref. with -ITH		Other criteria
		-ITH	-AI	-ODD	PRES.	FUT.	
CAEL	permission	+	+	+	−	+	CANIATAU
	obtainment	+	+	+	−	+	
	suggestion	+	−	−	−	+	AWGTYMU
MEDRU/GALLU							
	ability	+	+	+	−	−	
	phys. possibility	+	+	+	−	+	...POSIB I...
	disposition	+	+	−	−	+	
GALLU	possibility	(+)	+	−	(AI)	-AI	...POSIB + S...
	permission	+	+	+	−	+	
	perception	+	?	?	+	−	
DYLU	likelihood	−	+	−	(AI)	-AI	
	unfulfilment	−	+	−	(AI)	-AI	CONTRADICTION

The brackets around the positive entry for the occurrence of the -ITH inflection indicate the syntactic restriction of relative clause occurrence. Note that the present reference for DYLU and GALLU/MEDRU *possibility* are likewise enclosed in brackets as such a reference is only possible if the progressive aspect occurs as discussed in chapter VI, section 2b.

3f   The lexical auxiliaries and the AUXILIARY

Sections 3 b − 3e above have discussed and explored the semantics of the lexical auxiliaries, and only in connection with this aim has reference been made to the relationship between the lexical auxiliaries and the AUXILIARY features outlined in sections 2b − 2d and summarised in section 2e above. In this sub-section the aim is to examine the manner in which the lexical auxiliaries relate to the three inflectional paradigms -ITH, -AI, and -ODD, to the various semantic features of *prediction, volition, imperative, conditional, tentative* and *fact* and to the tense features *non-past* and *past*.

The lexical auxiliaries as a class are characterised by the following properties.

    (i)   Of the three uses of -ITH, only *prediction* is involved.

   (ii) -ITH in this sense with lexical auxiliaries is carried by:

        (a)   the copula BOD (BE) in a progressive pattern, or

        (b)   the carrier auxiliary GWNEUD (DO), which may be a less likely pattern;

when -ITH is directly carried by a lexical auxiliary, it does not convey *prediction*.

(iii) *Prediction* in this manner only occurs with certain uses of certain auxiliaries.

The first two points can be illustrated by the following examples involving CAEL *permission*, GALLU/MEDRU *ability*, and GALLU/MEDRU *physical possibility*:

(161) (i) *mi gei di aros efo ni*   *(you can stay with us)*
       PT *may you stay with us*

    (ii) *mi fyddi di 'n cael aros efo ni*   *(you will be allowed to stay*
        PT *will be you in PERM stay with us*   *with us)*

    (iii) *?mi wnei di gael aros efo ni*   *(you'll be allowed to*
        PT *will you PERM stay with us*   *stay with us)*

(162) (i) *mi all/fedr John ddreifio car*   *(John can drive a car)*
       PT *can John drive car*

    (ii) *mi fydd John yn gallu/medru dreifio car*   *(John will be*
        PT *will be John in ABILITY drive car*   *able to drive a*
                                                   car)

    (iii) *?mi wneith John allu/fedru dreifio car*   *(John will be able*
        PT *will John ABILITY drive car*   *to drive a car)*

(163) (i) *mi alli/fedri di fynd trwy Bethesda*   *(you can go through*
       PT *can you go through Bethesda*   *Bethesda)*

    (ii) *mi fyddi di 'n gallu/medru mynd*   *(you will be able*
        PT *will be you in PHYS POSS go*   *to go through*
                                                 Bethesda)
        trwy Bethesda
        through Bethesda

    (iii) *?mi wnei di allu/fedru mynd trwy*   *(you'll be able to*
        PT *will you PHYS POSS go through go through Bethesda)*
        Bethesda
        Bethesda

In (i) of each example the lexical auxiliary carries the inflection -ITH but in no case does the -ITH inflection convey prediction. In effect, the -ITH inflection with the lexical auxiliaries conveys a statement of *fact*: it is a *fact* that *permission* is given in (161) (i), that the *ability* exists in (162) (i) and that the *physical possibility* exists in (163) (i). The semantics of -ITH with the lexical auxiliaries are not, therefore, the same as its semantics with lexical verbs, as the following comparison illustrates:

(164) (i) *mi ganith   Mair*   *(Mair will sing)*
            PT   will sing   Mair

       (ii) *mi fydd   Mair   yn canu*   *(Mair will be singing)*
            PT will be   Mair   in sing

       (iii) *mi wneith Mair ganu*   *(Mair will sing)*
             PT   will   Mair sing

(165) (i) *mi geith   Mair   ganu*   *(Mair may/can sing)*
            PT   may   Mair   sing

       (ii) *mi all/fedr Mair ganu*   *(Mair can sing)*
            PT   can   Mair sing

In (164), whether carried by the lexical verb as in (i) or by the other patterns in (ii) and (iii), the -ITH inflection can involve *prediction*. But in (165), with the lexical auxiliaries, the -ITH inflection involves *fact*. In the event of the feature *prediction* being required, the alternative patterns given above are compulsorily selected. By comparing (i) and (ii) of examples (161) to (163), the distinction between non-predictive and predictive statements involving the lexical auxiliaries is readily discernible.

The third point can be detailed as follows. The feature occurs with CAEL *permission*, MEDRU/GALLU *ability, physical possibility* and *disposition,* and GALLU *permission,* some of which are illustrated above. But *prediction* is excluded with CAEL *suggestion* and GALLU *possibility* and *perception:*

(166) (i) **mi fyddi di 'n cael gwybod*   *(NO EQUIVALENT PATTERN)*
            PT   will be you in get   know

       (ii) **mi wnei di gael gwybod*   *(NO EQUIVALENT PATTERN)*
            PT   will you get   know

  c.f. (iii) *mi gei   di wybod*   *(you'll get to know)*
             PT will get you know

(167) (i) **dyma'r ceffyl a fydd yn gallu ennill*   *(NO EQUIVALENT*
            here is the horse PT will be in POSS win   *TRANSLATION)*

       (ii) **dyma   'r ceffyl a wneith   allu ennill*   *(*here is the horse*
            here is the horse PT do + AUX POSS win   *that will/may win)*

  c.f. (iii) *dyma'r   ceffyl a all   ennill*   *(here is the horse*
             here is the horse PT may+ AUX win   *that may win)*

107

(168) (i) *mi fydda'   i'n gallu   gweld y lleuad   *(NO EQUIVALENT*
        PT will be   I in PERCEPT see the moon   *PATTERN)*

    (ii) *mi wna 'i allu   gweld y lleuad   *(NO EQUIVALENT*
         PT will I PERCEPT   see   the moon   *PATTERN)*

c.f. (iii) *mi alla 'i weld y lleuad   (I can see the moon)*
           PT can I   see the moon

The example in (168) (i) is acceptable if reinterpreted as *physical possibility* but it is not acceptable in terms of *perception*. The auxiliary verb DYLU is excluded from *prediction* in both its uses simply because the -ITH paradigm is not carried by DYLU in any case.

The -AI inflection is used to carry both the conditional feature and the tentative feature by all the uses of the lexical auxiliaries with four exceptions. The acceptable occurrences can be illustrated by CAEL *permission* and GALLU *physical possibility* and *disposition,* in relation to conditional statements:

(169) *mi gaet   ti   aros efo   ni*   *(you could stay with us)*
      PT would you stay with us

(170) *mi allet ti fynd trwy   Bethesda*   *(you could go through*
      PT could you go through Bethesda   *Bethesda)*

(171) *allwn   i   ddim gwrthod 'tasa*   *(I couldn't refuse if he asked)*
      could I NEG   refuse   if + would be

      fo 'n gofyn
      he in ask

Three uses, namely, GALLU *possibility* and DYLU *likelihood* and *unfulfilment,* always occur with the -AI inflection, apart from GALLU in relative clauses, and a conditional/non-conditional contrast is not formally marked. It is also problematic to what extent the *perception* use of GALLU can involve *conditionality*. Examples such as the following:

(172) *mi allwn   i weld y   lleuad*   *(I could see the moon if that*
      PT could I see the   moon   *cloud were not there)*

      petae'r   cwmwl yna ddim yna
      if + would be cloud there NEG there

suggest *physical possibility* rather than *perception*.

As far as tense is concerned, the significant and interesting point in connection with the lexical auxiliaries is that for some uses there are three possible tense contrasts. The situation is complicated by the fact that not all speakers use all three tenses; and, moreover, some speakers use aspectual patterns. To simplify the situation, the tense contrasts will be discussed here, and the aspectual patterns in chapter VI, section 3g.

All the lexical auxiliary verbs involve the -ITH paradigm apart from DYLU, and the exceptional nature of this latter auxiliary is discussed below. As discussed above, the -ITH paradigm has the same general tense feature of *non-past* as it does with lexical verbs, although within the general time period of non-past a number of distinctions can be made. Firstly, the *perception* use of GALLU is rather special in that -ITH can be used to report a contemporaneous present event, one taking place at the time of speaking:

(173)   *mi   alla'   y glywed Mair yn canu*   *(I can hear Mair singing)*
        PT GALLU + AUX I hear   Mair in   sing

Secondly, there are a number of uses which are restricted to a future event within the non-past period and these include CAEL *permission, obtainment* and *suggestion*, MEDRU/GALLU *possibility*, GALLU *permission* and DYLU *likelihood* and *unfulfilment*:

(174)   *mi gei   di fynd yfory*   *(you can/may go tomorrow)*
        PT CAEL + AUX you go   tomorrow

(175)   *mi gei   di wybod yfory*   *(you will know tomorrow)*
        PT CAEL + AUX you know   tomorrow

(176)   *mi gei   di olchi'r car   yfory*   *(you can wash the car*
        PT CAEL + AUX you wash the car tomorrow   *tomorrow)*

(177)   *mi elli   di fynd yfory*   *(you can/may go tomorrow)*
        PT GALLU + AUX you go   tomorrow

(178)   *mi ddylet ti   ymddiheuro yfory*   *(you should apologise*
        PT should you   apologise   tomorrow   *tomorrow)*

Although it is possible for *rŵan (now)* to occur with these examples, the event is still future, as it can only follow the moment of speaking. Thirdly, there are a number of uses which neither allow the occurrence of a future time adverb nor refer to a present contemporaneous event. Such uses refer to a state which continues throughout a period of time, and include MEDRU/GALLU *ability* and *disposition:*

(179)   **mi fedr John godi 'r gadair 'na yfory*   *(*John can lift that*
        PT can   John lift the chair there tomorrow   *chair tomorrow)*

(180)   **fedra' i ddim gwrthod yfory*   *(*I can't refuse tomorrow)*
        can   I NEG   refuse   tomorrow

As discussed earlier, such uses can only refer to a future event with the modal feature prediction when the aspectual auxiliary BYDD .. YN .. (WILL BE .. IN .. = WILL BE -ING (but see also chapter VI, section 4d) occurs:

(181)   *mi fydda*   *John yn medru codi 'r*   *(John will be able to*
           PT will be John in ABILITY lift the   *lift that chair tomorrow)*

           gadair 'na yfory
           chair there tomorrow

(182)   *fydda' i   ddim yn medru gwrthod yfory*   *(I won't be able to*
           will be I   NEG in DISP   refuse   tomorrow   *refuse tomorrow)*

When the lexical auxiliaries in these functions directly carry -ITH, it is most unusual for them to involve a time adverb, thus locating the event in time; their normal reference is that of a continuing state of ability, physical possibility or disposition. It can be mentioned at this point that a number of uses which are restricted to future events in examples (174) to (178) above can refer to present contemporaneous events if the progressive aspect occurs, and to past events if the perfect aspect occurs. But these points are left for discussion until the introduction of aspect in chapter VI.

The selection of the -AI paradigm as a past tense has two possible uses. Firstly, the -AI paradigm can express the meaning of the auxiliary verb as a *state* which endures over a period of time. As such, it can occur with time-when adjuncts which signify a long period of time:

(183)   *mi allai*   *John godi 'r gadair 'na*   *(John could lift that*
           PT GALLU + AUX John lift the chair there   *chair when he was*
                                              young)

           pan oedd o'n ifanc
           when he   was young

The use of GALLU here involves *ability*. But this example does not necessarily refer to the actual realisation of that ability; rather, it states that the ability to lift the chair, if required, was always available. This contrasts with the second use of -AI, which refers to one single episode which involves actually realising the meaning of the auxiliary verb. As such, an episodic temporal adverb can be used:

(184)   *mi allai*   *John godi 'r gadair 'na*   *(John could lift that*
           PT GALLU+AUX John lift the chair there   *chair last night even*
           neithiwr er   ei fod o 'n methu rŵan   *though he can't now)*
           last night though his be he in fail   now

This example necessarily involves actually performing the action referred to. This use of the -AI paradigm can be referred to as the *episodic* tense.

In the discussion of the inflections -ITH, -AI and -ODD in relation to lexical verbs in sections 2b - 2e above, it was pointed out that, whereas -ITH and -AI are related tense forms in some of their uses, the inflection -ODD is a completely unrelated tense form which is involved with an entirely different use of factual reference. But, as we have already seen in this sub-section, the -ITH paradigm and, consequently, its related tense form -AI are not involved with modal reference in regard to the lexical auxiliaries, having by contrast a non-modal reference. This now aligns -ITH, -AI and -ODD together. Consequently, the -ODD paradigm exists as a possible alternative to the -AI paradigm as a past tense form, although the -ODD paradigm seems to be limited to an episodic reference and, unlike -AI, cannot occur as a stative tense:

(185) *mi allodd*   *John godi 'r gadair*   *(John was able to lift*
       PT GALLU + AUX John lift the chair   *that chair last night)*

       'na **neithiwr**
       there **last night**

(186) *?? mi allodd*   *John godi'r gadair 'na*   *(NO APPROPRIATE*
             PT GALLU + AUX John lift the chair there   *TRANSLATION)*

       pan oedd o'n ifanc
       when was he in young

The selection of -ODD thus involves the event occurring and the meaning of the auxiliary verb actually manifesting itself.

The stative-episodic contrast is typical of the lexical auxiliaries. Even here, however, it is not total and there are four exceptions. Firstly, CAEL *suggestion* is limited to the non-past period and does not refer to a past event with either -AI or -ODD:

(187) (i)   *mi gei*   *di osod y bwrdd*   *(you can lay the table)*
             PT CAEL + AUX you lay the table

       (ii) **mi gaet*   *ti osod y bwrdd pan*   *(*you could lay the*
             PT CAEL + AUX you lay the table when   *table when you were*
                                                                 young)
             oeddet   ti 'n ifanc
             was   you in young

       (iii) **mi gefaist*   *ti osod y bwrdd neithiwr*   *(*you could lay*
             PT CAEL + AUX you lay the table last night   *the table last*
                                                                         night)

In terms of temporal restriction, CAEL *suggestion* is thus similar to -ITH *imperative* (see section 2b above). Secondly, as noted in section 3c above, GALLU *perception* only seems to function with present contemporaneous reference, and like CAEL *suggestion* does not occur with past time reference. Thirdly, MEDRU/GALLU *disposition* only has -AI for past time and not -ODD, for example:

(188)	(i)	*fedra'*	*i ddim*	*gwrthod*	*(I can't refuse)*
		MEDRU + AUX I NEG		refuse	
	(ii)	*fedrwn*	*i ddim*	*gwrthod*	*(I couldn't refuse)*
		MEDRU + AUX I NEG		refuse	
	(iii)	**fedrais*	*i ddim*	*gwrthod*	*(NO APPROPRIATE*
		MEDRU + AUX I NEG		refuse	*TRANSLATION)*

Moreover, there is no necessary constraint that this use of MEDRU/GALLU must occur in a stative context. In the above example, NEITHIWR (LAST NIGHT) could easily occur. The significant point seems to be that no action is actually realised and hence -AI is more appropriate than -ODD. This links up with the use of -AI as a past tense for -ITH *willingness* discussed earlier (sections 2b and 2c above). Fourthly, GALLU *possibility* is a quite different use, which only occurs with -AI unless in a relative clause and is limited to the non-past period.

Notes to chapter V

1. The treatment of AUX as far as English is concerned in the standard theory of transformational grammar involves *tense, modal verbs* and *aspect,* characterised by the re-write rule:

    (i) *AUX → Tense (M) (Aspect)*

    Here the AUX for Welsh is considered to involve only those phenomena involved with verbal inflections. AUX is re-written as:

    (ii) *AUX → Verbal inflections*

    The auxiliary verbs and aspect are thus not regarded as constituents of AUX.

2. This treatment of the auxiliary verbs is an over-simplified account of their categorial status, as their characterisation depends not upon their characteristics as a class but on their individual semantic features.

3. Example (2) (i), for instance, is derived from a deep structure of the following type:

    (i)

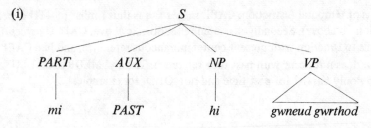

112

The transformations from deep to surface structure can be given as follows:

(ii) (a)   *mi PAST hi gwneud gwrthod*
            PT   she do   refuse

    (b)   *mi gwneud + PAST hi gwrthod*
            PT do   she refuse

    (c)   *mi gwnaeth hi gwrthod*
            PT did   she refuse

    (d)   *mi wnaeth hi wrthod*
            PT did   she refuse

Many varieties of Welsh delete the deep structure *gwneud* and use the main verb as auxiliary carrier, eventually giving the equivalent:

(iii)   *mi wrthododd hi*
      PT refused   she

4.   The semantic features are listed in the discussion.
5.   Some (particularly southern) speakers also use OS in a conditional clause *along with* the conditional inflection -AI. A typical instance involves BUASAI (WOULD BE) in an example such as the following:

*os buasai   Mair yn mynd, mi fuaswn   i 'n mynd   (if Mair went, I
if would be Mair in go,   PT would be I in go   would go)*

For our purposes, however, the PE : OS dichotomy will be used for simplicity.

6.   In this account, the three features *prediction, volition* and *imperative* are all handled together under one heading. Distinctions could be made involving *prediction* as an *epistemic modal, volition* as a *non-epistemic modal* and *imperative* as an illocutionary feature involving *mood.* This latter distinction would allow for the tense restrictions on imperative. Further, conditionality can contrast with non-conditionality, but this point has not been incorporated in order to avoid over-complexity.

VI The syntax and semantics of aspect

1   ASPECT MARKERS

1a   Introduction

The category of aspect[1] refers to a number of items that can occur in periphrastic verbal expressions. These items include three prepositional forms, YN (IN), WEDI (AFTER), AR (ON) and one adjectival form, NEWYDD (NEW). Thus, a periphrastic verbal expression such as that in example (1) can be modified by the addition of the above aspect markers as in (2) to (5):

(1) *mi ddylai John gychwyn*   *(John should start)*
    PT should John   start

(2) *mi ddylai John fod yn cychwyn*   *(John should be starting)*
    PT should John be   in   start

(3) *mi ddylai John fod wedi cychwyn*   *(John should have started)*
    PT should John be after   start

(4) *mi ddylai John fod ar gychwyn*   *(John should be about to*
    PT should John be on start   *start)*

(5) *mi ddylai John fod newydd gychwyn*   *(John should have just*
    PT should John be   new   start   *started)*

Examples (2) to (5) show that these items occur immediately before the verb of the verb phrase, and it can also be observed that the two items AR (ON) and NEWYDD (NEW) are distinctive in that the following verb is soft-mutated where appropriate. The function of the aspect markers is to modify the activity involved in a certain definable manner; but before going on to discuss their functions, further remarks are necessary on their syntax.

As pointed out and discussed in chapter III, section 2c, aspect involves more than the occurrence of the items YN (IN), WEDI (AFTER), AR (ON) and NEWYDD (NEW). In examples (2) to (5) these items are always accompanied by a form of BOD (BE). It is impossible for the four items to occur without BOD (BE), as the following unacceptable examples demonstrate:

(6) **mi ddylai John yn cychwyn*   *(cf. *John should starting)*
    PT   should John in   start

114

(7) *mi ddylai John wedi cychwyn   (cf. *John should started)
      PT should John after start

(8) *mi ddylai John ar gychwyn   (cf. *John should about to
      PT should John on start   start)

(9) *mi ddylai John newydd gychwyn (cf. *John should just started)
      PT should John new start

Aspect in Welsh, therefore, involves a form of BOD plus an aspect marker, giving four aspectual systems which we can represent here as BOD + YN, BOD + WEDI, BOD + AR and BOD + NEWYDD.

In addition to the four items listed above, HEB (WITHOUT) and AM (FOR) can also be considered in relation to aspect. Like the other items, these two cannot occur without an accompanying form of BOD (BE):

(10) (i)   mi ddylai John fod heb gyrraedd   (John should not have
           PT should John be without arrive   arrived)

      (ii) *mi ddylai John heb gyrraedd   (cf. *John should not
           PT should John without arrive   arrived)

(11) (i)   mi ddylai John fod am fynd   (John should be for
           PT should John be for go   going)

      (ii) *mi ddylai John am fynd   (cf. *John should for
           PT should John for go   going)

There are, however, significant differences. Firstly, the item HEB (WITHOUT) involves a negative feature and is the negative equivalent of WEDI (AFTER). Example (10) (i) is thus equivalent to:

(12) ddylai John ddim bod wedi cyrraedd   (John should not have
      should John NEG be after arrive   arrived)

The item HEB (WITHOUT) involves both aspect and negation and is discussed in the treatment of negation in chapter IX, section 4. Secondly, the item AM (FOR) is quite different in that it can be followed by other items besides a verb:

(13) mi ddylai John fod am goffi   (John should be for
      PT should John be for coffee   coffee)

(14) mi ddylai John fod am i 'r merched ddod (John should be for the
      PT should John be for for the girls come   girls' coming)

From these examples it can be suggested that AM is essentially concerned with conveying the subject's attitude towards a particular concept. Semantically, AM (FOR) is thus to be distinguished from the aspect markers and is closer to nouns like EISIAU (WANT), AWYDD (WANT) and CHWANT (DESIRE), which are discussed in chapter III, section 4d. It is significant, too, that these latter items cannot occur without a form of BOD (BE):

(15) (i)   *mi ddylai John fod eisiau/awydd/chwant coffi*   *(John should*
           PT should John be   want/want /desire   coffee   *want, etc.*
                                                    coffee)

           *mi ddylai John eisiau/awydd/chwant coffi   *(NO*
           PT should John   want/want/desire   coffee   *APPROPRIATE*
                                                    TRANSLATION)

These items, like AM, form a semantic and syntactic system quite distinct from the aspect markers.

A third item to be considered as an aspect marker is BRON Â (NEARLY WITH). Not previously listed in the literature as a possible aspect marker, it is given special consideration in section 1d below.

1b   Semantics of the aspect markers

The BOD + YN^2 pattern traditionally goes under the heading of 'continuous' or 'progressive'. We will use the latter label and call this pattern the PROGRESSIVE aspect.

The progressive aspect pattern is perhaps the most difficult to characterise but it can be regarded as emphasising the *durative* nature of a particular activity. Compare the following examples:

(16) *mi geith Mair olchi'r llestri*   *(Mair shall wash the dishes)*
      PT can Mair   wash the dishes

(17) *mi geith Mair fod yn golchi'r llestri*   *(Mair shall be washing*
      PT can Mair be   in   wash the dishes   *the dishes)*

(18) *mi ddylai John weithio bob nos yr wythnos yma*   *(John should work*
      PT should John work   every night the week here   *every night this week)*

(19) *mi ddylai John fod yn gweithio bob nos*   *(John should be*
      PT should John be   in   work   every night   *working every night*
                                                  this week).
      yr wythnos yma
      the week here

(20) *mi all John balu'r ardd nos yfory*   *(John can dig the garden*
      PT can John dig the garden night tomorrow   *tomorrow night)*

(21) *mi all John fod yn palu'r ardd   nos yfory*   *(John can be*
      PT can John be in dig the garden night tomorrow   *digging the garden*
                                                  tomorrow night)

116

It must be emphasised that the occurrence of the non-progressive aspect in examples (16), (18) and (20) does not imply that the activity has no duration. Indeed, it is true to say that the activities in each case inherently involve duration. The significant point is that the selection of the progressive, as in (17), (19) and (21) *explicitly* conveys the fact that duration is involved. A significant use of the durative nature of the progressive aspect is seen with the aspectual auxiliaries as outlined in section 3b below.

An interesting consequence of the function of the progressive aspect arises when a time-when adjunct (specifying a particular point of time) occurs:

(22) *mi ddylai John weithio pan ddaw y bws*   *(John should work*
    PT *should John work when comes the bus*   *when the bus comes)*

(23) *mi ddylai John fod yn gweithio pan ddaw y bws*   *(John should be*
    PT *should John be in work when comes the bus*   *working when the*
    bus comes)

When the non-progressive aspect occurs, as in (22), the activity referred to *succeeds* the point of time conveyed by the time-when adjunct. But in the case of the progressive aspect the activity *overlaps* that point of time. In these circumstances the non-progressive/progressive contrast can represent a succeeding/overlapping contrast.

As a consequence of the 'overlapping' character of the progressive aspect, it is found that the progressive is necessary to refer to a present contemporaneous activity. Compare the following:

(24) *mi ddylai John fod yn gweithio rŵan*   *(John should be*
    PT *should John be in work now*   *working now)*

(25) *mi ddylai John weithio*   *(John should work)*
    PT *should John work*

(26) *mi all John fod yn palu'r ardd rŵan*   *(John can be digging*
    PT *can John be in dig the garden now*   *the garden now)*

(27) *mi all John balu'r ardd*   *(John can dig the*
    PT *can John dig the garden*   *garden)*

The present contemporaneous situation is essentially one overlapping the moment of speaking. Consequently, the progressive aspect is chosen to refer to such events as those in examples (24) and (26). The equivalent non-progressive patterns, as in (25) and (27), suggest succeeding activity, following the moment of speaking. However, there are a few instances where references to present contemporaneous activity is possible without the progressive aspect. As illustrated in sections 3c and 3f of chapter V, GALLU *perception* occurs in the non-progressive to convey present contemporaneous perception:

(28) *mi alla' i weld y lleuad*   *(I can see the moon)*
     PT *can I see the moon*

The stative verb GWYBOD (KNOW) is a similar example:

(29) *mi ddylai John wybod ei henw hi*   *(John should know*
     PT *should John know her name she*   *her name)*

John's revealing of the name may follow the moment of speaking, but his actually
knowing the name is a relatively permanent state which applies at the moment of
speaking.

The progressive aspect is further discussed in the treatment of the aspectual
auxiliaries in section 3 below.

The semantics of BOD + AR are relatively easy to explain. Consider the following
example:

(30) *mi ddylai John fod ar weithio*   *(John should be about*
     PT *should John be on work*   *to work)*

The selection of BOD + AR has the effect of suggesting that the event is *imminent*,
that is, about to happen. Consequently, this type of aspect can be labelled as
IMMINENT aspect.

The selection of the imminent aspect demands that the event should occur relatively
close to another preceding point of time. It is odd to have a temporal adverb which is
relatively distant in time, as in the following example:

(31) *mi ddylai John fod ar weithio nos yfory*   *(John should be about*
     PT *should John be on work night tomorrow*   *to work tomorrow night)*

There is too big a gap between 'now' and 'tomorrow' and a point of time must be
introduced which is much nearer to the occurrence of the event, as:

(32) *mi ddylai John fod ar weithio*   *(John should be about to*
     PT *should John be on work*   *work this time tomorrow*
                                                  night)
     yr amser yma nos yfory
     the time here night tomorrow

With examples like (30), where no temporal adverb is given, the related point of
time is the moment of speaking itself.

It is sometimes claimed that imminent aspect refers to future events. This is not an
adequate explanation, and it is more satisfactory to say that imminent aspect refers
to an event which is yet to happen in a relatively short time but, as such, can occur
in past or non-past time on the condition that the event is imminent in relation to an
immediate point of time:

118

(33) mi ddylai John fod wedi bod ar gychwyn   (John should have been
     PT should John be after be on start   about to start this time
                                                    last night)
     yr amser yma neithiwr
     the time here last night

(34) mi ddylai John fod ar gychwyn rŵan   (John should be about
     PT should John be on start now   to start now)

(35) mi ddylai John fod ar gychwyn   (John should be about
     PT should John be on start   to start this time
                                                    tomorrow night)
     yr amser yma nos yfory
     the time here night tomorrow

The function of imminent aspect is thus to refer to imminent events, irrespective of
the period of time in which they occur.

The BOD + WEDI aspect pattern is traditionally given the name 'perfect' and likewise
can be labelled here the PERFECT aspect. The function of the perfect aspect can best
be introduced by comparing the following examples:

(36) mi ddylai John weld Mair heno   (John should see Mair
     PT should John see Mair tonight   tonight)

(37) *mi ddylai John weld Mair neithiwr   (*John should see
     PT should John see Mair last night   Mair last night)

(38) mi all John balu'r ardd heno   (John can dig the
     PT can John dig the garden tonight   garden tonight)

(39) *mi all John balu'r ardd neithiwr   (*John can dig the
     PT can John dig the garden last night   garden last night)

As these examples stand, they cannot refer to events in past time. But such a temporal
reference is possible for these ostensibly non-past verbal forms if the perfect aspect
is selected:

(40) mi ddylai John fod wedi gweld Mair neithiwr   (John should have seen
     PT should John be after see Mair last night   Mair last night)

(41) mi all John fod wedi palu'r ardd neithiwr   (John can have dug
     PT can John be after dig the garden last night the garden last night)

119

Perfect aspect is not a sort of past tense, however, as it can also refer to events which have their occurrence in the future:

(42) mi   ddylai John fod wedi gweld Mair
     PT should John be after see   Mair   *(John should have seen Mair by this time tomorrow)*

erbyn yr amser yma yfory
against the time here tomorrow

(43) mi all John fod wedi palu'r   ardd
     PT can John be after dig the garden   *(John can have dug the garden by this time tomorrow)*

erbyn yr amser yma yfory
against the time here tomorrow

On the basis of a consideration of the above examples, it can be suggested that perfect aspect has a *retrospective* function: it can look back from a given point of time and temporally locate a particular action as being prior to that given point of time. Very often, as in examples (40) and (41), this point of time is given by the moment of speaking and the perfect aspect looks back into the past from the present. But, as in the case of examples (42) and (43), it can also look back from a given point of time in the future to a previous event. To complete the picture, it is also possible to retrospect from a past point of time further into the past:

(44) mi ddylai John fod wedi gweld Mair
     PT should John be after see   Mair   *(John should have seen Mair before eight last night)*

cyn   wyth neithiwr
before eight last + night

The retrospective possibilities can thus be represented in diagrammatic form as follows:

(45)   *PAST*   *PRESENT*   *FUTURE*

In this light we must be critical of any claim that the perfect aspect refers to past time. As we have seen, it retrospects from a given or implied point in any period of time, and past reference is thus only one consequence of a more general function. The situation in this respect is similar to the range of temporal periods in which imminent aspect can occur.

Although the label *perfect* aspect is used, it must be emphasised that this type of aspectual modification does not necessarily involve 'completion' of an event. Consider the following example:

120

(46) *mi ddylai John fod wedi cysgu am awr rŵan*   *(John should have*
     PT should John   be after sleep   for   hour   now   *slept for an hour now)*

There is no necessary constraint that John has finished sleeping and that the activity will not continue into the future. The function of the perfect is to retrospect back into the previous hour, and it does not necessarily establish that the event or activity is completed.

The function of BOD + NEWYDD is so similar to that of BOD + WEDI that it can be treated under the same general heading as the former. Compare the following:

(47) *mi ddylai John fod   wedi gweld Mair*   *(John should have seen Mair)*
     PT should John be   after see   Mair

(48) *mi ddylai John fod   newydd weld Mair*   *(John should have just*
     PT should John be   new   see   Mair   *seen Mair)*

They are both retrospective and both can come under the heading of perfect aspect. But NEWYDD (NEW) establishes that the event referred to is very recent to the point of time from which the retrospection takes place. Consequently, BOD + NEWYDD can be distinguished by a labelling of *recent* perfect or possibly *marked* perfect. (See note 3 for further remarks on NEWYDD.)

1c   Aspect marker co-occurrence

In addition to individual occurrences, the aspect markers can also co-occur with each other in certain definable ways. Firstly, the perfect markers BOD + WEDI and BOD + NEWYDD tend not to occur with each other.[3] Moreover, as they are functionally similar they can be regarded as members of the same system, which can be represented by the use of braces as follows:

(49) *mi ddylai John* {*fod wedi*} *stopio*   *(John should* {*have*} {*stopped)*
     PT should   John {be   after} stop   {have just}
                      {fod newydd}
                      {be new}

Secondly, the aspect markers BOD + YN and BOD + AR likewise tend not to occur with each other:

(50) *?? mi ddylai John fod ar   fod yn gweithio*   *(John should be about*
        PT should John be   on   be   in   work   *to be working)*

But, because they are functionally distinct, they are regarded as two independent but non-co-occurring systems, even though for our purposes the choice between them is again represented by braces:

(51) *mi ddylai John* $\left\{\begin{array}{l}\textit{fod ar} \\ \textit{be on} \\ \textit{fod yn} \\ \textit{be in}\end{array}\right.$ *stopio (John should* $\left\{\begin{array}{l}\textit{be about·to} \\ \textit{be}\end{array}\right\}$ *stop (ing))*
　　　PT should John　　　　*stop*

Thirdly, given the three aspect systems of perfective, progressive and imminent, we find that both perfects can co-occur with either progressive or imminent aspect:

(52) (i)　*mi ddylai John fod wedi bod yn gweithio*　　*(John should have*
　　　　　PT should John be after be in work　　　*been working)*

　　(ii)　*mi ddylai John fod wedi bod ar weithio*　　*(John should have*
　　　　　PT should John be after be on work　　　*been about to work)*

　　(iii)　*mi ddylai John fod newydd fod yn gweithio*　*(John should just have*
　　　　　PT should John be new   be in   work　　*been working)*

　　(iv)　*mi ddylai John fod newydd fod ar weithio*　*(John should just have*
　　　　　PT should John be new   be on work　　*been about to work)*

Some of the patterns may seem odd out of context but they are grammatically possible and their oddness is purely contextual.

The aspect co-occurrences are mainly responsible for the complexity of patterning in verbal expressions. Using DYLU as an illustration, the aspectual possibilities can be exemplified as follows:

(53) (i)　*mi ddylai John*　　　　　　　　　　　*weithio*
　　　　　PT should John　　　　　　　　　　　*work*

　　(ii)　*mi ddylai John*　　　　　　　*fod yn gweithio*
　　　　　PT should John　　　　　　　*be in   work*

　　(iii)　*mi ddylai John*　　　*fod ar*　　　*weithio*
　　　　　PT should John　　　*be on*　　　*work*

　　(iv)　*mi ddylai John fod wedi*　　　　　*gweithio*
　　　　　PT should John be after　　　　　*work*

　　(v)　*mi ddylai John fod wedi*　　*bod yn gweithio*
　　　　　PT should John be after　　*be in   work*

　　(vi)　*mi ddylai John fod wedi bod ar*　*weithio*
　　　　　PT should John be after be on　*work*

　　(vii)　*mi ddylai John fod newydd*　　　*weithio*
　　　　　PT should John be new　　　　*work*

(53) (viii)   *mi ddylai John fod newydd*   *fod yn   gweithio*
                PT should John be   new   *be in   work*

    (ix)   *mi ddylai John fod newydd fod ar*   *weithio*
                PT should John be   new   be on   *work*

In Welsh, therefore, there are nine aspectual contrasts. They range from non-perfect, non-imminent, non-progressive as in (53) (i) to perfect, non-imminent, progressive as in (53) (v).

In the light of the co-occurrences listed in (53) above the ASP constituent can be rewritten as any one of the following:

(54) (i)   *ASP* → $\emptyset$
     (ii)   *ASP* →   *bod yn*
    (iii)   *ASP* →   *bod ar*
    (iv)   *ASP* →   *bod wedi*
     (v)   *ASP* →   *bod newydd*
    (vi)   *ASP* →   *bod wedi*   *bod yn*
    (vii) *ASP* →   *bod wedi*   *bod ar*
   (viii) *ASP* →   *bod newydd* *bod yn*
    (ix)   *ASP* →   *bod newydd* *bod ar*

The rules in (54) (ii) and (iii) are mutually exclusive, as YN and AR do not co-occur. These two rules can therefore be conflated:

(55)   *ASP* → $\begin{Bmatrix} bod\ yn \\ bod\ ar \end{Bmatrix}$

The same applies to rules (54) (iv) and (v) involving WEDI and NEWYDD:

(56)   *ASP* → $\begin{Bmatrix} bod\ wedi \\ bod\ newydd \end{Bmatrix}$

The remaining rules in (54) (vi) to (ix) are concerned in effect with the occurrence of the two aspects in (55) with the two aspects in (56). The four rules (54) (vi) to (54) (ix) can be conveyed by combining the two modified rules in (55) (i) and (ii) as follows:

(57)   *ASP* → $\begin{Bmatrix} bod\ wedi \\ bod\ newydd \end{Bmatrix}$ *and/or* $\begin{Bmatrix} bod\ yn \\ bod\ ar \end{Bmatrix}$

The rule in (57) needs additional explanation: it is intended to represent a situation where either one aspectual pattern can be selected (perfect or recent perfect or progressive or imminent) or a combination of aspectual features can be selected as already described - hence the use of the convention and/or between pairs of braces. The rule in (57) could also be expressed by using the aspect labels in place of the formal markers concerned:

$$(58) \quad ASP \rightarrow \begin{Bmatrix} perfect \\ recent\ perfect \end{Bmatrix} \quad and/or \quad \begin{Bmatrix} progressive \\ imminent \end{Bmatrix}$$

Additional rules would then be necessary to state how the aspect systems are marked by the various formal items concerned, and they could be given as follows:

(59) (i)   *perfect*   →   *bod wedi*
    (ii) *recent perfect* →   *bod newydd*
    (iii) *progressive*   →   *bod yn*
    (iv) *imminent*   →   *bod ar*

The overall re-writing rules for simple sentences can now be further developed by incorporating the information about aspect as follows (the constituent ADJUNCT will be omitted here, and in succeeding formalisations of these rules where its external structure is not under discussion):

(60) (i) $S \quad \rightarrow \quad PT \quad AUX \quad NP \quad VP$

    (ii)
$$AUX \rightarrow \begin{Bmatrix} \text{-}ITH \\ \text{-}AI \\ \text{-}ODD \end{Bmatrix}$$

    (iii)
$$VP \rightarrow (ASP) \begin{Bmatrix} V \begin{Bmatrix} (NP) \quad (PP) \quad (PP) \\ (PRED\ PH) \end{Bmatrix} \\ COP \begin{Bmatrix} PRED\ PH \\ NP \\ PP \end{Bmatrix} \end{Bmatrix}$$

    (iv)
$$ASP \rightarrow \begin{Bmatrix} PERFECT \\ RECENT\ PERFECT \end{Bmatrix} and/or \begin{Bmatrix} PROGRESSIVE \\ IMMINENT \end{Bmatrix}$$

    (v) $PP \quad \rightarrow \quad P \quad NP$

    (vi)
$$PRED\ PH \rightarrow \begin{Bmatrix} YN \begin{Bmatrix} NP \\ ADJ \end{Bmatrix} \\ FEL/COP - NP \end{Bmatrix}$$

Rules for the formal marking of aspect contrasts can be given in a different part of the grammar (along with similar rules relating to other constituents).

1d   The status of BRON (Â) (NEARLY (WITH))

On the grounds that BRON (Â) (NEARLY (WITH)) does not occur without a form of BOD (BE), it can be argued that it is an aspect marker:

(61) *mi ddylai John fod bron (â) gorffen*   *(John should be nearly finished)*
    PT should John be nearly   finished

(62) **mi ddylai John bron (â) gorffen*   *(cf. *John should nearly finished)*
    PT should John nearly   finish

Moreover, it has other similarities with the aspect markers. Firstly, it is limited to their syntactic environment, co-occurring only with verbs and not with nouns or any other structures:

(63) **mi ddylai John fod bron â choffi*   *(*John should nearly coffee)*
    PT should John be nearly coffee

(64) **mi ddylai John fod bron â i 'r merched ddod*   *(*John should nearly*
    PT should John be nearly for the girls come   *for the girls to come)*

Secondly, it is semantically similar to perfect and imminent aspect in that a temporal feature may be detected which, although different, compares in general terms with recent perfect or imminence.

There are, however, formal differences between BRON (Â) and the four listed aspect markers. Firstly, BRON (Â) (NEARLY) can occur with another aspect marker without another occurring form of BOD (BE):

(65) *mae o bron wedi gorffen*   *(he has nearly finished)*
    is he nearly after finish

In traditional written Welsh, examples are found which show BRON (Â) (NEARLY (WITH)) in this context occurring with an extra BOD: *mae ef bron â bod wedi gorffen (he has nearly finished)*. On this basis, therefore, it could be suggested that the spoken pattern involves a deletion of the uninflected BOD. Although this possibility seems to be restricted to the co-occurrence of BRON (Â) with WEDI (AFTER), it is not a possibility which is regularly shared amongst the other four aspect markers (but see remarks on NEWYDD (NEW) in note 3). Secondly and more revealingly, however, BRON (Â) (NEARLY) can be moved to a post-verbal position:

(66) *mae Mair yn crio bron*   *(Mair is crying nearly)*
    is Mair in cry nearly

(67) *mae John wedi gorffen bron*   *(John has finished almost)*
    is John after finish nearly

Such a shift of position is not possible with any of the four aspect markers. Thirdly, the most significant difference is semantic. Compare the following two examples:

(68) *mae Mair bron â chrio*   *(Mair is nearly crying)*
     is   Mair nearly   cry

(69) *mae John bron â gorffen*   *(John has nearly finished)*
     is   John nearly   finish

In (68) BRON (Â) (NEARLY) marks the *inception* of an activity while in (69) with
GORFFEN (FINISH) it marks the approaching *completion* of a process. It would
fragment the analysis to establish two uses of BRON (Â) along these lines. However,
the difficulty can be overcome by interpreting BRON (Â) as a modifier of the aspectual possibilities. This can be achieved by deriving (68) from (66) and (69) from (67).
By adopting this suggestion, BRON (Â) has one meaning of 'nearness' and the apparent
differences between 'nearness of inception' and 'nearness of completion' are due to
progressive and perfect aspect respectively. Thus, it can be suggested that the basic
position of BRON (Â) is post-verbal; and when it is shifted to a pre-verbal position,
the aspect markers are usually deleted.

2   ASPECT AND THE AUXILIARY VERBS

2a   Introduction

Of the six auxiliary verbs, only the lexical auxiliaries *in some of their uses* occur with
positive aspect marking. For the carrier auxiliaries, positive aspect marking is not
common and they usually occur without aspect markers, for example:

(70) (i)   *mi wneith   John aros*   *(John will stay)*
           PT do + ITH   John stay

     (ii) *?mi wneith   John fod yn/ar/wedi/newydd aros*   *(NO APPRO-*
           PT do + ITH   John be in/on/after/new   stay *PRIATE*
                                                             TRANSLATION)

(71) (i)   *mi wnaeth   John aros*   *(John stayed)*
           PT do + ODD   John stay

     (ii) *?mi wnaeth   John fod yn/ar/wedi/newydd aros*   *(NO*
           PT do + ODD John be in/on/after/new   stay   *APPROPRIATE*
                                                             TRANSLATION)

(72) (i)   *mi ddaru   John aros*   *(John stayed)*
           PT happen + AUX John stay

     (ii) *?mi ddaru   John fod yn/ar/wedi/newydd aros*   *(NO*
           PT happen + AUX John be in/on/after/new   stay   *APPROPRIATE*
                                                                TRANSLATION)

126

There is one possible occurrence of an aspect marker with GWNEUD (DO + ITH in the sense of volition:

(73) *wnei   di fod yn aros yn fan hyn*   *(will you be waiting*
     do + ITH you be in stay in   place this   *in this place when the*
                                                     bus comes?)
     pan ddaw y bws?
     when comes the bus

Example (73) requires the volition to be involved in an overlapping activity. But it is as well to note that (73) could be more likely realised as:

(74) *fuaset ti 'n meindio aros yn fan hyn*   *(would you mind*
     would you in mind   stay in place this   *waiting in this place*
                                                     when the bus comes?)
     pan   ddaw y bws?
     when comes the bus

In effect, then it can be suggested that the carrier auxiliaries and the inflected verb are always negatively marked for aspect.

2b   The lexical auxiliaries

Aspect marking of the verb of the sentence only occurs with certain uses of the lexical auxiliaries, namely CAEL *permission* and *suggestion,* MEDRU/GALLU *physical possibility* and DYLU *likelihood* and *unfulfillability.* This leaves CAEL *obtainment,* MEDRU/GALLU *ability* and GALLU *perception* not occurring with positive aspect marking of the verb.

The distinctiveness of these last three uses does reveal something about their nature. The ability use of MEDRU/GALLU, for instance, is not really involved with the action of the verb as such, but only with the subject's ability to perform it. The use of GALLU *perception* can be viewed in the same terms. The third exception, CAEL *obtainment,* is probably less significant and the lack of aspect contrasts may be contextual rather than to do with the nature of the use.

Of the eight uses which occur with aspect marking of the verb, the significant factor is the possibility of temporal reference with the progressive or perfect when the auxiliary verb has a non-past inflection. Four uses, namely CAEL *permission* and *suggestion,* GALLU/MEDRU *disposition* and GALLU *permission* are restricted to *future events.* CAEL *permission* and *suggestion* can both be exemplified by the same (ambiguous) example:

127

(75) (i) *mi gei*   *di fod yn darllen pan ddaw y dynion*   *(you can be*
        PT CAEL + ITH you be in   read   when come the men   *reading when*
                                                             the men come)

(ii) *mi gei*   *di fod wedi darllen pan ddaw y dynion* *(you can have*
       PT CAEL + ITH you be after   read   when come the men   *read when*
                                                               the men come)

GALLU/MEDRU *disposition* and GALLU *permission* can be respectively illustrated as follows:

(76) (i) *elli/fedri*   *di fod yn darllen pan ddaw y bos?*   *(can you be*
        can + ITH you be   in   read   when comes the boss   *reading when*
                                                              the boss comes?)

(ii) *elli/fedri*   *di fod wedi darllen pan ddaw y bos?* *(can you have*
       can + ITH you be after   read   when comes the boss *read when the*
                                                             boss comes?)

(77) (i) *mi elli*   *di fod yn darllen*   *(you can be reading)*
        PT can + ITH   you be   in   read

(ii) *mi elli*   *di fod wedi darllen*   *(you can have read)*
       PT can + ITH   you be after   read

The four remaining uses, GALLU/MEDRU *physical possibility*, GALLU *possibility* and DYLU *likelihood* and *unfulfillability*, in addition to future time events, can also refer to present contempraneous events with the progressive, and to past time events with the perfect:

(78) (i) *mi all John fod yn gweithio rŵan*   *(John can be working now)*
        PT can John be in   work   now

(ii) *mi all John fod wedi gweithio neithiwr* *(John can have worked*
       PT can John be   after work   last night   *last night)*

(79) (i) *efallai*   *bod John yn gweithio rŵan*   *(maybe John is*
        PT + GALLU + AI be John in   work   now   *working now)*

(ii) *efallai*   *bod John wedi gweithio neithiwr*   *(maybe John*
       PT + GALLU + AI be John after   work last night   *has worked*
                                                              last night)

(80) (i) *mi ddylai*   *'r bws fod yn cyrraedd rŵan*   *(the bus should be*
        PT should the bus be   in   arrive   now   *arriving now)*

(ii)   *mi ddylai 'r bws fod wedi cyrraedd neithiwr*   *(the bus should have*
       PT should the bus be after arrive   last night   arrived last night)

(81) (i)   *mi ddylai Mair fod yn gweithio rŵan*   *(Mair should be*
        PT should Mair be in   work   now   working now)

(ii)   *mi ddylai Mair fod wedi gweithio neithiwr*   *(Mair should have*
       PT should Mair be after   work   last night   worked last night)

The different temporal ranges of the two groups correlate with a very significant semantic difference. In the main, the second group involves semantic features which provide the basis for the fundamental message (or proposition) of the sentence (see also chapter VIII, section 2f) and they can therefore relate to events in the past, present and future. In this light, it is understandable why the various aspect markings can involve different temporal references. The first group, by contrast, is not concerned with features of this sort and hence is limited to future time events.

2c   The carrier auxiliaries

The discussion of the carrier auxiliaries and the inflected verbs is best carried out in section 3.

3   ASPECTUAL AUXILIARIES

3a   Introduction

It has been suggested above that the carrier auxiliaries seldom occur with aspect marking while an inflected verb never occurs with aspect marking. Related to this point is the significant fact that there are verbal expressions involving aspect which correspond to a simple verbal expression. These aspectual equivalences are produced by using the BOD (BE) form involved in aspect as a carrier of the AUXILIARY features. For example, compare the following:

(82) *mi wnaeth / ddaru   John ganu; mi ganodd   John   (John*
      PT do + ODD / happen + ODD John sing; PT sing + PAST John   sang)

(83) *'roedd John yn canu*   *(John was singing)*
      was   John in sing

Example (83) is the progressive aspect equivalent of example (82). There is a syntactic parallel between (82) and (83) in that just as the former occurs *without* an aspect marker, the latter obligatorily occurs *with* an aspect marker:

(84) **'roedd John canu*   *(cf. *John was sing)*
      was   John sing

The restrictions dovetail into each other and there is a complementary relationship between the carrier and the aspectual auxiliaries.

In all, there are six aspectual auxiliaries: MAE (IS), OEDD (WAS), BU (WAS), BYDDAI (USED TO BE), BYDD (WILL BE) and BUASAI/BYDDAI (WOULD BE). Basically we see here the BOD (BE) form that is involved in aspectual occurrences of the lexical auxiliaries. But, in the absence of any other item, the BOD form is used to carry AUXILIARY features and thus assumes the forms of the various paradigms listed above. Traditionally, the patterns involving the aspectual auxiliaries are called 'compound tenses'. Whereas tense and other features are involved, as will be shown below, the BOD forms are also aspectual, and this can be seen by the contrast of succeeding and overlapping activity produced when a point of time adjunct occurs:

(85) *mi wnaeth / ddaru   John ganu pan gyrhaeddais i*   *(John sang*
    PT do + ODD / happen + ODD John sing when arrived   I   when I
    arrived)

(86) *'roedd John yn canu pan gyrhaeddais i*   *(John was singing when*
    was John in sing when arrived   I   *I arrived)*

In (85) John's singing follows the arrival while in (86) it overlaps the arrival. The tense and other features of the auxiliary remain the same.

Of the six aspectual auxiliaries, two do not occur with perfect aspect, namely BU (WAS) and BYDDAI (USED TO BE):

(87) (i)   *mi fu(odd) John yn gweithio*   *(John was working)*
        PT was   John in work

    (ii)   *mi fu(odd) John ar weithio*   *(John was about to work)*
        PT was   John on work

    (iii)   **mi fu(odd) John wedi gweithio*   *(NO APPROPRIATE*
        PT   was   John after work   *TRANSLATION)*

    (iv)   **mi fu(odd) John newydd weithio*   *(NO APPROPRIATE*
        PT   was   John new   work   *TRANSLATION)*

(88) (i)   *mi fyddai   John yn gweithio*   *(John used to work)*
        PT used to be John in   work

    (ii)   *mi fyddai   John ar weithio*   *(John used to be about*
        PT used to be John on work   *to work)*

    (iii)   **mi fyddai   John wedi gweithio*   *(NO APPROPRIATE*
        PT used to be John after work   *TRANSLATION)*

    (iv)   **mi fyddai   John newydd weithio*   *(NO APPROPRIATE*
        PT used to be John new   work   *TRANSLATION)*

This aspectual restriction is also shared by the habitual use of BYDD (see section 3c below). In other respects the aspectual occurences are as outlined above, and any special conditions will be mentioned in the following sub-sections.

The relationships of the aspectual auxiliaries with the carrier auxiliaries and inflected verbs can be illustrated in the following arrangement:

(89)	(i)	*MAE . . YN/AR/WEDI/NEWYDD . .* *is in /on /after /new*	—
	(ii)	*OEDD . . YN/AR/WEDI/NEWYDD . .* *was in /on / after /new*	*-ODD/WNAETH/DDARU* *PAST/do + /happen +* * -ODD -ODD*
	(iii)	*BU . . YN/AR . .* *was in /on*	—
	(iv)	*BYDDAI . . YN/AR . .* *used to be in /on*	—
	(v)	*BYDD . . YN/AR/WEDI/NEWYDD . .* *will be in /on /after /new*	*-ITH/WNEITH* *will /do + 'will'*
	(vi)	*BYDDAI/BUASAI . .* *would be* *YN/AR/WEDI/NEWYDD . .* *in /on /after /new*	*-AI /WNAI* *would/do + 'would'*

It can be seen from (89) that MAE (IS), BU (WAS) and BYDDAI (USED TO BE) have no equivalent simple expressions. This is also true of the habitual use of BYDD - a use which also has the aspectual restrictions of BU (WAS) and BYDDAI (USED TO BE).

3b The MAE (IS), OEDD (WAS) and BU (WAS) paradigms

The MAE (IS) paradigm is involved in making statements of *fact* in the *non-past* period. Traditionally, it is accounted for as a 'present tense', that is, used to describe activities going on at the present time. However, MAE (IS) can be used to refer to any event where the occurrence is *factually verifiable by present time circumstances:*

(90) *mae John yn gweithio ers amser cinio*   *(John has been working*
    is John in work   since time dinner   *since dinner time)*

(91) *mae John yn gweithio rŵan*   *(John is working now)*
    is John in work   now

(92) *mae John yn gweithio yfory*   *(John is working tomorrow)*
    is John in work   tomorrow

Example (90) includes past time, example (91) involves a present contemporaneous event and example (92) involves future time. Thus we have a range of temporal events as follows:

(93)

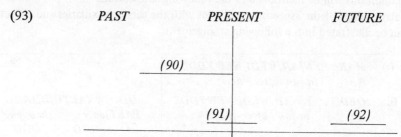

But the common factor in each case is that the actual occurrences of the events are *factually assertable by present time circumstances.* All past time events are excluded from the reference of MAE (IS):

(94) *mae John yn gweithio neithiwr*   *(*John is working last night)*
    is   John in work   last night

The factual basis for this event lies outside present time and MAE (IS) is inappropriate. The use of MAE (IS) to refer to past time events must be based upon present time features. This is the case with example (90) above and also controls the use of MAE (IS) with perfect aspect; compare the following for instance:

(95) *mae John wedi bod yn canu heddiw*   *(John has been singing today)*
    is John after be in sing today

(96) *mae John wedi bod yn canu ddoe*   *(*John has been singing*
    is   John after be in   sing yesterday   yesterday)

In example (95) the event comes within present time while in (96) it lies outside:

(97)

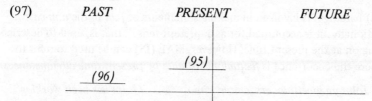

Further remarks are made below about example (90).

The factual basis of the MAE (IS) paradigm can be made clearer by considering certain future events which cannot be factually proposed:

(98) *mae 'n bwrw glaw yfory   *(*it's raining tomorrow)*
       is   in   rain   tomorrow

(99) *mae 'r adar yn canu yfory   *(*the birds are singing*
       is the   birds in   sing tomorrow   *tomorrow)*

(100)   *mae 'r   haul   yn disgleirio yfory   *(*the sun is shining*
          is   the   sun   in   shine   tomorrow   *tomorrow)*

These events cannot be referred to by MAE (IS), not because they are future but because they are non-factual. They could be expressed by any one of the other modal features, such as BYDD (WILL BE), which is discussed below in section 3c.

Example (90) is interesting in that the ERS (SINCE) phrase also occurs with perfect aspect:

(101)   *mae John wedi bod yn gweithio ers amser cinio*   *(John has been*
       is   John after be   in   work   since time dinner   *working since dinner*
                                                                     time)

The difference between (90) and (101) seems to be that the perfect retrospects back into the past and does not allow for future developments - whereas the non-perfect allows backward and forward reference:

(102)   *PAST*   *PRESENT*   *FUTURE*

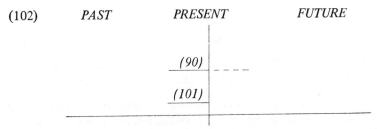

The non-perfect essentially gives the past point of inception of action that is still going on at the present time. It must be emphasised that the perfect in (101) does not imply that the activity will not continue into the future - it simply concentrates upon prior occurrence;

The MAE (IS) paradigm is distinctive in that it has no simple equivalent (see (89) above). Thus, it can be used to refer to all events that are factually verifiable in present time irrespective of episodic or habitual features:

(103)   *mae John yn gweithio yfory*   *(John is working tomorrow)*
       is   John in   work   tomorrow

(104)   *mae John yn gweithio yfory*   *fel arfer*   *(John works tomorrow as*
       is   John in   work   tomorrow as use   *usual)*

Other aspectual paradigms allow contrasts of progressive : non-progressive, as will be illustrated below.

The OEDD (WAS) paradigm is the past time equivalent of MAE (IS). It can convey the same type of factual statement, but the factual knowledge is based upon past conditions:

(105)   'roedd John yn gweithio neithiwr   *(John was working last*
        was John in work last night   night)*

As such, the reference of OEDD (WAS) is limited to past time events that are temporally distinct from the present moment.

There is an apparent exception to this explanation in examples like:

(106)   'roedd John yn gweithio yfory   *(John was working tomorrow)*
        was John in work tomorrow

An example like (106) can be interpreted such that it proposes John's intention to work tomorrow. But it essentially refers to a past intention or plan in regard to future time:

(107)   *PAST*   *PRESENT*   *FUTURE*

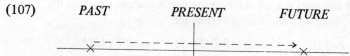

It is just as possible to convey a past intention in relation to a later date in the past:

(108)   'roedd o 'n gweithio 'r diwrnod wedyn   *(he was working the*
        was he in work the day after   next day)*

Example (108) above is ambiguous. It may be a direct reference to an event which took place or, after the fashion of the use being studied here, it can refer to an intention:

(109)   *PAST*   *PRESENT*   *FUTURE*

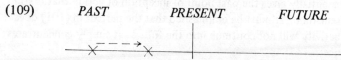

In effect, then, example (106) is not an exception; it is past in that it refers to a past intention. As will be seen below, reference to past intention is confined to the occurrence of the progressive and cannot be conveyed by the equivalent non-progressive pattern.

The contrast of the progressive pattern OEDD . . YN . . (WAS . . IN . . = WAS -ING) with the simple expression is of particular interest. There are two contexts in which OEDD . . YN . . (WAS . . IN . . = WAS -ING) can be used. Firstly, it can convey an habitual or durative activity or state over a long period of time; secondly, it can convey an episodic activity with durative emphasis. Both contexts can be illustrated respectively

134

as follows:

(110)   *'roedd John yn gweithio yn y   coleg*   *(John worked in the college*
          was   John in   work   in the college   *in those days)*

          yn y   dyddiau   'na
          in the   days   there

(111)   *'roedd John yn gweithio yn y coleg neithiwr*   *(John was working in*
          was   John in   work   in the college last night   *the college last night)*

In (110) a habitual state of affairs is being referred to while in (111) the reference is to one episode only. Given these two contexts, the simple expression is found to be untypical in a habitual or durative context but quite normal where required in an episodic context:

(112) (i)   *?mi wnaeth / ddaru   John weithio*   *(John worked in*
            PT do + ODD happen + ODD John   work   *the college in*
                                             those days)
            yn y coleg yn y dyddiau   'na
            in the college in the days   there

     (ii)   *?mi weithiodd   John yn y coleg*   *(John worked in*
            PT work +   ODD John in the college   *the college in*
                                            those days)
            yn y   dyddiau 'na
            in the   days   there

(113) (i)   *mi wnaeth / ddaru   John weithio*   *(John worked in*
            PT do + ODD   happen + ODD John work   *the college last*
                                           night)
            yn y   coleg neithiwr
            in the college last night

     (ii)   *mi weithiodd   John yn y coleg neithiwr*   *(John worked in*
            PT work + ODD John   in the college last night   *the college last*
                                                      night)

In a habitual or durative context, the progressive is far more normal in occurrence than the non-progressive.

There are a number of verbs which can inherently involve a durative feature and they occur more frequently in the progressive than the non-progressive. Common examples include BYW (LIVE), LICIO/HOFFI (LIKE) and GOBEITHIO (HOPE); the contrast with the non-progressive can be seen from comparing the following:

(114)   (i)   *'roedd o 'n byw yn Llundain*   *(he lived in London)*
             was he in live in London

       (ii)   *mi fywodd   o yn Llundain*   *(NO APPROPRIATE*
             PT live + ODD   he in London   *TRANSLATION)*

(115)   (i)   *'roedd Mair yn licio/hoffi'r   lle*   *(Mair liked the place)*
             was Mair in like   the place

       (ii)   *mi wnaeth   Mair licio/hoffi'r lle*   *(NO APPROPRIATE*
             PT do + ODD   Mair like   the place   TRANSLATION)

(116)   (i)   *'roedd John yn gobeithio y   buasai*   *(John hoped Mair*
             was John in hope   PT would   *would come)*

             Mair yn dod
             Mair in come

       (ii)   *mi wnaeth   John obeithio y buasai*   *(NO APPROPRIATE*
             PT do + ODD John   hope PT would   TRANSLATION)

             Mair yn dod
             Mair in come

Verbs of this type are labelled as *stative* verbs. Certain statives can occur in the non-progressive in some instances. The verbs GWYBOD (KNOW a fact) and ADNABOD (in the sense of KNOW a person) are typically stative:

(117)   (i)   *'roedd hi 'n gwybod hynny*   *(she knew that)*
             was she in know   that

       (ii)   **mi wybyddodd   hi hynny*   *(NO APPROPRIATE*
             PT know + ODD   she that   *TRANSLATION)*

(118)   (i)   *'roedd hi 'n adnabodd John*   *(she knew John)*
             was she in know   John

       (ii)   **mi adnabyddodd hı John*   *(NO APPROPRIATE*
             PT know + ODD she John   *TRANSLATION)*

But there are contexts in which a non-stative reference is possible, particularly where the moment or inception of the 'knowing process' is pin-pointed:

(119)   *mi wnaeth   hi wybod yr ateb yn syth*   *(she knew the answer*
          PT do + ODD she knew the answer in straight   straight away)

(120)   *mi wnaeth   hi adnabod John yn syth*   *(she knew John*
          PT do + ODD she know   John in straight   straight away)

The occurrence of the progressive with the stative verb is typical of its durative function and it is extended into other non-progressive : progressive contrasts. Thus we can contrast:

(121)   *mi fydd   Mair yn gwybod*   *(Mair will know)*
            PT will be Mair in know

(122)   *mi wneith   Mair wybod yn syth*   *(Mair will know straight*
            PT do + ITH Mair know in straight   *away)*

In (121) the state of Mair's knowing is *predicted* (see below) while in (122) the inception of her knowing is predicted. However, where a modal feature other than prediction occurs and an aspectual auxiliary is not used to carry auxiliary features, the same situation does not occur. Thus, with DYLU, the equivalent of (121) and (122) would both be non-progressive:

(123)   *mi ddylai Mair wybod (yn syth)*   *(Mair should know straight*
            PT should Mair know in straight   *away)*

The possibility of progressiveness in stative verbs is not maintained with DYLU.

The aspectual auxiliary BU (WAS) only occurs with progressive and imminent aspect and never with perfect aspect:

(124)   *mi fu (odd) John yn gweithio*   *(John was working)*
            PT was   John in work

(125)   *mi fu (odd) John ar gychwyn*   *(John was about to start)*
            PT was   John on start

(126)   **mi fu (odd) John wedi gweithio*   *(NO APPROPRIATE*
            PT was   John after work   *TRANSLATION)*

(127)   **mi fu (odd) John newydd weithio*   *(NO APPROPRIATE*
            PT was   John new   work   *TRANSLATION)*

The aspectual restrictions on the occurrence of perfect aspect are related to the function of BU (WAS) as a rather special past tense. As a tense form, BU (WAS) refers to events in the past and compares with OEDD (WAS); but it can be distinguished from OEDD (WAS) by its co-occurrence possibilities with time adjuncts. The aspectual auxiliary OEDD (WAS) is the unmarked past tense form in that it can refer to any event in the past, including overlapping or simultaneous events. But BU (WAS) is not so wide-ranging, as it cannot co-occur with an overlapping or simultaneous event:

(128) 'roedd John yn gweithio pan gyrrhaeddais i   (John was working
       was John in work when arrived I   when I arrived)

(129) *mi fu (odd) John yn gweithio pan gyrrhaeddais i   (NO APPRO-
       PT was   John in work when arrived I   PRIATE
                                                  TRANSLATION)

The aspectual auxiliary BU (WAS) always refers to a pre-occurring rather than a simultaneous event and can be designated as 'past-in-the-past' or 'past-past'.

The three aspectual auxiliaries MAE (IS), OEDD (WAS) and BU (WAS) thus have the following tense contrasts:

(130)

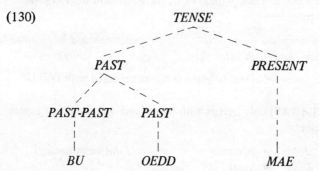

The past-past function of BU (WAS) compares with the retrospective function of perfect aspect in that they both look back. This can serve to explain the non-occurrence of perfect aspect with BU (WAS). It can also be noted that many traditional accounts label BU as a 'perfect tense'.

3c The BYDD (WILL BE) paradigm

The aspectual auxiliary BYDD (WILL BE) is traditionally described as a future tense auxiliary, and there is no doubt that it can indeed refer to future time events:

(131) mi fydd   John yn gweld Mair heno   (John will be seeing
       PT will be John in see   Mair tonight   Mair tonight)

The significant point is that it can also refer to present contemporaneous events and past time events:

(132) mi fydd John yn gweld Mair rŵan   (John will be seeing
       PT will be John in see   Mair now   Mair now)

(133) mi fydd   John wedi gweld Mair neithiwr   (John will have seen
       PT will be John after see   Mair last night   Mair last night)

As these examples suggest, there is more to BYDD (WILL BE) than a function as future tense. A key to its function is supplied by the fact that it serves as the progressive equivalent of the -ITH inflection in two of its functions, namely, *prediction* and *imperative:*

(134) (i) *mi wneith   hi fwrw glaw yfory*   *(it 'll rain tomorrow)*
            PT do + ITH she   rain   tomorrow

       (ii) *mi fydd   hi 'n bwrw glaw yfory*   *(it 'll be raining*
            PT will be she in   rain   tomorrow   *tomorrow)*

(135) (i) *mi wnei   di aros yma tan ddo'*   *(you 'll stay here*
            PT do +   ITH you stay here until come   *until I come back)*

            i yn ôl
            I back

       (ii) *mi fyddi   di 'n aros yma tan ddo'*   *(you 'll be staying*
            PT will be you in   stay here until come   *here until I come*
                                                               back)
            i yn ôl
            I back

The aspectual auxiliary BYDD (WILL BE), then, conveys two meanings - prediction and imperative. Future events, being by nature uncertain and speculative, are fittingly referred to by BYDD (WILL BE). Thus, it is entirely appropriate that BYDD (WILL BE) can be used to convey the non-factual statements which cannot be expressed by MAE (IS), as illustrated in examples (98) to (100) above:

(136) *mi fydd   hi 'n bwrw glaw yfory*   *(it will be raining tomorrow)*
       PT will be she in   rain   tomorrow

(137) *mi fydd   yr adar yn canu yfory*   *(the birds will be singing*
       PT will be the birds in sing tomorrow   *tomorrow)*

(138) *mi fydd   yr haul yn disgleirio yfory* *(the sun will be shining*
       PT will be the sun in shine   tomorrow   *tomorrow)*

But, as we have seen, it can also refer predictively to present and past events.

In its relationship with the -ITH paradigm, it must be emphasised that BYDD (WILL BE) does not convey volition. Thus, we do not have:

(139) (i) *wnei   di agor y   drws i mi?*   *(will you open the door*
            do + ITH you open the door for me   *for me?)*

       (ii) **fyddi   di 'n agor y drws i mi?* *(*will you be opening*
            will   be you in open the door for me   *the door for me?)*

The selection of BYDD (WILL BE) in (139) (ii) could only be interpreted in its predictive sense and not as a marker of volition.

There is also another function of BYDD (WILL BE) which is traditionally noted in most grammars; namely, as a marker of habitual actions. This use of BYDD can be illustrated as follows:

(140) *fyddi di 'n mynd i 'r pictiwrs bob wythnos?*   *(do you go to the*
       HAB *you in go   to the pictures every week   pictures every week?)*

In this use BYDD only occurs with progressive and imminent aspect and never with perfect aspect, and refers to habitual events in the non-past period.

3d   The BYDDAI (USED TO BE) paradigm

The equivalent habitual events in the past period to (140) above are conveyed by BYDDAI (USED TO BE), acting as a past tense of BYDD *habitual:*

(141) *fyddet   ti 'n mynd i 'r pictiwrs bob wythnos?*   *(did you go to*
       used to be you in go   to the pictures every week   the pictures
                                                                 every week?)

As far as habitual actions are concerned, therefore, the tense situation is as follows:

(142)

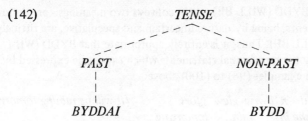

It must be noted, however, that not all speakers use BYDD and BYDDAI (USED TO) in this sense and for many speakers MAE (IS) and OEDD (WAS) serve as markers of habituality.

3e   The BUASAI/BYDDAI (WOULD BE) paradigm

The aspectual auxiliaries BUASAI (WOULD BE) and BYDDAI (WOULD BE) are variants of the same functions. In effect, they can convey the meanings of the -AI paradigm (see chapter V, section 2c) and the first of these, *'unreality'*, can be illustrated as follows:

(143) *mi fuasai/fyddai Mair yn canu petai   hi 'n iawn   (Mair would*
       PT   *would be   Mair in sing if COND she in all right sing if she*
                                                               were all right)

The aspectual auxiliaries MAE (IS) and BYDD (WILL BE) always refer to an event

140

in 'real' terms, as fact or prediction respectively: the BUASAI/BYDDAI auxiliaries exist as their 'unreal' counterparts. The distinguishing feature of BUASAI/BYDDAI is that they can occur with PE (IF) conditional clauses, as in example (143) above. But 'real' statements always have OS (IF) and cannot co-occur with PE (IF):

(144)　(i)　*mae / mi fydd*　　*Mair yn canu*　　*(Mair is/will be singing*
　　　　　　is / PT will be　　Mair in sing　　if she is/will be all right)

　　　　　　os ydy/bydd hi 'n iawn
　　　　　　if is / will be she in all right

　　(ii)　**mae/mi fydd*　　*Mair yn canu petai*　　*(Mair is/will be*
　　　　　　is / PT will　be　Mair in sing if COND　singing if she were
　　　　　　　　　　　　　　　　　　　　　　　　　　　all right)
　　　　　　hi 'n iawn
　　　　　　she in all right

In so far as past events are concerned, however, 'unreal' statements have no past tense form but modify the verb with perfect aspect:

(145)　*mi fuasai/fyddai Mair wedi canu petai*　　*(Mair would have sung*
　　　　PT would be　　　Mair after sing if COND　if she had been all right)

　　　　hi wedi bod yn iawn
　　　　she after be in all right

In addition to their 'unreal' use, BUASAI and BYDDAI (WOULD BE) have the second related function of *tentativity:*

(146)　*mi fuasai/fyddai John yn cyrraedd Llundain*　　*(John would reach*
　　　　PT would be　　　John in reach　　London　　London by ten)

　　　　erbyn　deg
　　　　against ten

A confident statement about John's time of arrival could be made as a fact by MAE (IS) or a prediction by BYDD (WILL BE). By selecting BUASAI/BYDDAI (WOULD BE), the statement can be made less positive, or tentative. The tentative nature of BUASAI/BYDDAI (WOULD BE) allows polite requests to be made even more polite:

(147)　*fuaset/fyddet ti 'n pasio'r halen, os gweli di'n dda?*　　*(would you pass*
　　　　would be　you in pass the salt, please　　　　　　the salt, please?)*

(148)　*wnei　　di basio'r halen, os gweli di'n dda?*　　*(would you pass*
　　　　do + ITH you pass the salt,　please　　　　　　the salt, please?)*

A comparison of these two examples shows how the normal polite request in (148) becomes more polite through the use of BUASAI/BYDDAI in (147).

A third function of BUASAI/BYDDAI (WOULD BE) occurs when they are used to make predictive statements about habitual activities in the past:

(149) mi fuasai/fyddai Mair yn mynd am dro bob nos   (Mair would go
       PT would be   Mair in go for turn every night for a walk every
                                                            night)

This use can be clearly distinguished from their 'unreal' or tentative use in the past by observing the absence of the perfect aspect, which is necessary for past by observing the absence of the perfect aspect, which is necessary for past time statements involving the other two uses. It must be noted that this is the only use of BUASAI/BYDDAI (WOULD BE) as a past tense which compares with -AI; but it does not occur as past volition:

(150) *fuasai/fyddai John ddim yn ein helpu ni neithiwr   (*John wouldn't
        would be   John NEG in our help we last night   help us last night)

Only the -AI paradigm carried by an inflected verb or the auxiliary carrier GWNEUD (DO) can occur here.

There is the possibility of a progressive : non-progressive contrast between BUASAI/BYDDAI . . YN (WOULD BE . . IN = WOULD BE -ING) and the -AI paradigm. For example, compare the following:

(151) petaet   ti 'n gweld Mair rŵan mi   (if you saw Mair now,
       if COND you in see   Mair now PT   she would be working)

       fuasai/fyddai hi'n gweithio
       would be she in work

(152) petaet   ti 'n gweld Mair rŵan mi   (if you saw Mair now,
       if COND you in see   Mair now PT   she would work)

       weithiai   hi
       work + AI   she

But many speakers only use BUASAI/BYDDAI for hypothetical statements and the possibilities of a formal contrast do not exist. To that extent BUASAI/BYDDAI (WOULD BE) is, like MAE (IS), fact in that there is no progressive aspect contrast.

The three uses of BUASAI/BYDDAI (WOULD BE) can be listed and distinguished as follows:

(153)

		PE clauses	Past events
(i)	'Unreal'	+	+ WEDI
(ii)	Tentativity	−	+ WEDI
(iii)	Past prediction (habitual)	−	− WEDI

3f   The aspectual auxiliaries and the AUXILIARY features

Sections 3b - 3e above have taken each aspectual paradigm and examined the semantic and tense features that are discernible in their occurrences. Such an approach, however, conceals the similarities or differences in how the aspectual auxiliaries relate to the auxiliary features, as compared with the lexical verbs discussed in chapter V, sections 2b - 2e, or the lexical auxiliaries discussed in chapter V, section 3f.

The following table shows how the auxiliary features are realised by the aspectual auxiliaries:

(154)

		Non-past	Past	Past-past
(i)	*Prediction*	*BYDD*	*BYDDAI/BUASAI*	–
(ii)	*Volition*	–	–	–
(iii)	*Imperative*	*BYDD*	–	–
(iv)	*'Unreal'*	*BYDDAI/BUASAI*	*See section 3e*	–
(v)	*Tentative*	*BYDDAI/BUASAI*	*See section 3e*	–
(vi)	*Fact*	*MAE*	*OEDD*	*BU*
(vii)	*Fact habitual*	*BYDD*	*BYDDAI*	–

From this table it can be seen that BOD + *prediction* involves the -ITH paradigm in the non-past, giving BYDD, and the -AI paradigm in the past, giving BYDDAI/ BUASAI (compare with lexical verbs). Similarly, BOD + *imperative* involves the -ITH paradigm, giving BYDD again for the non-past, but there is no associated past expression. Unlike the lexical verbs, the aspectual auxiliary does not convey *volition*. Like the lexical verbs and lexical auxiliaries, BOD + *'unreal'* and *tentative* involves the -AI paradigm in the non-past with special arrangements for past reference involving aspect. The realisation of the auxiliary feature *fact* is the most distinctive feature of the aspectual auxiliary BOD. Lexical verbs convey *fact* only in the past, by using -ODD, while lexical auxiliaries use the -ITH paradigm in the non-past. But BOD has three tense realisations of *fact* in the *non-past, past* and *past-past* periods. The aspectual auxiliary BOD + *fact* in the *non-past* is realised by an idiosyncratic paradigm MAE (IS) which is not readily identifiable in terms of any one of the inflections. In the past period BOD + *fact* involves the -AI paradigm like the lexical auxiliaries, giving OEDD (WAS). Unlike any other auxiliary carriers, however, aspectual BOD has an extra temporal contrast in the past, namely the *past-past*, which involves the -ODD inflection and gives BU.[4]

3g   The aspectual auxiliaries and the lexical auxiliaries
Some uses of the lexical auxiliaries can be expressed by using an aspectual auxiliary pattern. Compare the following occurrences of GALLU *ability:*

(155)   *mi all John ddreifio car*   *(John can drive a car)*
              PT can John drive   car

(156)   *mae John yn gallu   dreifio car*   *(John can drive a car)*
              is   John in ABILITY drive car

In (155) GALLU occurs as the inflected verb of the sentence, while in (156) it occurs uninflected in the presence of an aspectual auxiliary. The lexical auxiliaries which can occur in this manner are CAEL *permission* and *obtainment*, MEDRU/GALLU *ability* and *physical possibility* and GALLU *permission*.

All of the aspectual auxiliaries can occur with these lexical auxiliaries and of particular interest are the following contrasts:

(157)   (i)   *mi all John ddreifio*   *(John can drive)*
                  PT can John drive

        (ii) *mae John yn gallu   dreifio*   *(John can drive)*
                  is   John in ABILITY drive

(158)   (i)   *mi wneith   John allu   ei wneud o* *(John will be able*
                  PT do + ITH John ABILITY its do   it   *to do it)*

        (ii) *mi fydd   John yn gallu   ei wneud o* *(John will be able*
                  PT will be John in ABILITY its do   it   *to do it)*

(159)   (i)   *mi allai   John ddreifio*   *(John could drive)*
                  PT can + AI John   drive

        (ii) *'roedd John yn gallu   dreifio*   *(John could drive)*
                  was   John in ABILITY drive

(160)   (i)   *mi allai   John ddreifio heno*   *(John could drive tonight)*
                  PT can + AI John   drive   tonight

        (ii) *mi fuasai/fyddai John yn gallu   dreifio heno* *(John could*
                  PT would be   John in   ABILITY drive   tonight *drive tonight)*

In the first three instances it is possible to achieve a durative: episodic contrast, whereby the meaning of the lexical auxiliary can be expressed as a durative feature as well as with one particular episode in mind. However, it must be noted that ROEDD .. YN (WAS .. IN = WAS -ING) can be used for both durative and episodic events and that it can occur as an equivalent of -ODD (PAST):

(161)   *'roedd o yn gallu   ei wneud o neithiwr* *(he was able to do it*
             was   he in ABILITY its do   it last night   *last night)*

Moreover, as far as BUASAI/BYDDAI are concerned, many speakers prefer an aspectual pattern for 'unreal' and tentative statements rather than the -AI paradigm. In these circumstances durative : episodic contrasts lose a formal marking, as BUASAI/BYDDAI (WOULD BE) are used for both.

4   TENSE IN WELSH

4a   Introduction

Having discussed the verbal inflections and carrier auxiliaries, the lexical auxiliaries, and the aspectual auxiliaries, some attempt can now be made to present a generalised account of tense in Welsh. A fairly complex situation arises which involves three different tense systems, although the systems share various common features. The tense systems are identified by the various contrasts that are possible and the following can be established:

    (i)   one-term system: non-past only;
   (ii)   two-term system: non-past and past;
  (iii)   three-term system: non-past, past and past-past.

In effect, there are three tenses in Welsh - non-past, past and past-past. But various forms relate to these terms in various ways. The past tense of the three-term system also allows further distinctions, as will be demonstrated below. The treatment of tense in this account is quite different from the traditional approach in Welsh grammars, and it is found that the classification presented here cuts across the formal distinctions made in Welsh grammars. For instance, whereas the traditional account treats all the BOD forms as related tense forms, here they are variously differentiated and occur in different tense systems.

4b   The one-term tense system

The non-past tense reference is the one tense feature that is common to the three systems and that all forms take. But the one-term tense system itself is realised by the -AI paradigm:

(162) *mi ddylai John aros adre*   *(John should stay at home)*
        PT should John stay home

(163) *mi fuaswn   i'n gwrthod mynd*   *(I would refuse to go)*
        PT would be I in refuse   go

(164) *mi ganai   Mair heno*   *(Mair would sing tonight)*
        PT sing + AI Mair tonight

This particular tense system exists with the *'unreal'* and *tentative* use discussed in chapter V, section 2c, and chapter VI, section 3e; it is illustrated by examples (163) and (164) above. As indicated by example (162), this tense system also occurs with

DYLU in both its uses. Also relevant here is the *possibility* use of GALLU:

(165) efallai   bod John yn gweithio   *(maybe John is*
       it + PT + GALLU + AI   be   John in   work   *working)*

In all cases no other tense contrast is possible by inflection, and temporal distinctions are made through aspectual modification. Consider DYLU in example (162) above; aspectual contrasts allow the following temporal references:

(166) (i)   mi ddylai John weithio   yfory   *(John should work tomorrow)*
             PT should John work   tomorrow

       (ii) mi ddylai John fod yn gweithio yfory   *(John should be*
             PT should John be in   work   tomorrow   *working tomorrow)*

(167) mi ddylai John fod yn gweithio rŵan   *(John should be*
       PT should John be in   work   now   *working now)*

(168) mi ddylai John fod wedi gweithio neithiwr   *(John should have*
       PT should John be after work   last night   *worked last night)*

Reference to a future event is possible with both non-progressive and progressive, but reference to a present contemporaneous event compulsorily occurs with the progressive while reference to the past compulsorily occurs with perfect aspect.

4c   The two-term tense system

The two-term tense system involves the non-past and past and is realised by the -ITH paradigm for the non-past and the -AI paradigm for the past. This particular tense system involves the *prediction* and *volition* uses of -ITH discussed in chapter V, section 2b, and the *prediction* and *habitual* uses of BYDD (WILL BE) discussed in chapter VI, section 3c. The various possibilities can be illustrated as follows:

(169) (i)   mi ganith   Mair bob   nos   *(Mair will sing every night)*
             PT sing + ITH   Mair every night

       (ii) mi ganai   Mair bob nos   *(Mair would sing every*
             PT sing + AI   Mair every night   *night when she was young)*

             pan oedd hi 'n ifanc
             when was she in young

(170) (i)   chanith   Mair ddim heno   *(Mair will not sing tonight)*
             sing + ITH   Mair   NEG tonight

       (ii) chanai   Mair ddim neithiwr   *(Mair would not sing last*
             sing + AI   Mair   NEG last night   *night)*

(171) (i) *mi fydd   John yn gweithio rŵan*   *(John will be working*
            PT will be John in   work   now   *now)*

       (ii) *mi fuasai John yn gweithio yr amser yna* *(John would be*
             PT would be John in   work   the time there *working at that time)*

(172) (i) *mi fydda' i 'n mynd i 'r pictiwrs*   *(I go to the pictures*
            PT will be I in go   to the pictures   *every night)*

            bob   nos
            every night

       (ii) *mi fyddwn   i 'n mynd i'r   pictiwrs*   *(I went (used to go)*
             PT would be I in   go to the pictures   *to the pictures*
                                                         every night)
             bob   nos
             every night

There are restrictions on the use of the two-term system involving -ITH and -AI.
Firstly, -AI typically occurs as past equivalent of -ITH *prediction* only for habitual
events in the past and episodic events are predicted by BYDD . . WEDI (WILL BE . .
AFTER = WILL HAVE -EN):

(173) *mi fydd   Mair wedi canu   neithiwr*   *(Mair will have sung*
       PT will be Mair after sing last night   *last night)*

With -ITH *volition*, -AI typically occurs as past equivalent only with negatives, and
a positive occurrence of -AI in this sense is rare. The use of BUASAI/BYDDAI (WOULD
BE) as a past tense for BYDD (WILL BE) *prediction* is characterised by the distinctive
occurrence of the progressive. The most common past equivalent for BYDD (WILL BE)
prediction involves BYDD . . WEDI (WILL BE . . AFTER = WILL HAVE -EN), and
(171) (ii) could be expressed as:

(174) *mi fydd   John wedi bod yn gweithio yr amser yna*   *(John will*
       PT will be John after be in work   the time there *have been*
                                                              working at
                                                              that time)

The habitual use of BYDD (WILL BE) and BYDDAI (USED TO BE) remains as the
only regular occurrence of the two-term tense system.

We can also include here those uses of auxiliary verbs which operate only in the
non-past with the -ITH paradigm, such as the *imperative* function of -ITH and the
suggestion function of CAEL. Although they have only one temporal feature - i.e.
non-past - there exists the formal possibility of an inflectional contrast to provide
past reference by using -AI. These uses, however, are confined to non-past reference
and never assume the second contrast of -AI with past reference. As members of the

two-term system, they relate only partially to the possibilities of tense contrast.

4d   The three-term tense system

The three-term tense system involves the two previous tense features, *non-past* and *past,* and also has an additional one of *past-past.* Just as the realisations of the one-term and two-term systems are different, the three-term system likewise displays further differences. Moreover, it is possible to distinguish two types of three-term system.

Firstly, a three-term system can be illustrated by the non-modal use discussed in section 3b above:

(175)   *mae John yn gweithio*   *(John is working)*
   is John in work

(176)   (i) *'roedd John yn gweithio*   *(John was working)*
    was John in work

   (ii) *mi weithiodd John*   *(John worked)*
     PT work + ODD John

(177)   *mi fuodd John yn gweithio*   *(John was working)*
   PT was John in work

As can be seen from the above examples, this particular three term system primarily involves aspectual auxiliaries with MAE .. YN (IS .. IN = IS -ING) operating for non-past, OEDD .. YN (WAS .. IN – WAS -ING) operating for past and BU .. YN (WAS .. IN = WAS -ING) operating for past-past. This system is further characterised by a non-progressive past realised by the -ODD paradigm or one of the carrier auxiliaries GWNEUD (DO) or DARFOD (HAPPEN), as discussed in section 3a.

It is interesting here, of course, to compare MAE .. YN (IS .. IN = IS -ING) with the -ITH paradigm or BYDD .. YN (WILL BE .. IN = WILL BE -ING). Traditionally, the former is interpreted as a present tense while the latter two are interpreted as future tenses. But, as outlined in sections 3b and 3c above, the two are distinguished by their semantics and, within the semantic framework, have similar temporal possibilities. The compulsory occurrence of the progressive in the case of MAE .. YN (IS .. IN = IS -ING), however, allows both future and present contemporaneous reference; in the case of -ITH and BYDD .. YN (WILL BE .. IN = WILL BE -ING), only the latter has these possibilities, -ITH being confined to future events:

(178)   *mae John yn gweithio rŵan/yfory*   *(John is working now/*
   is John in work now / tomorrow   *tomorrow)*

(179)   (i) *mi weithith John yfory*   *(John will work tomorrow)*
    PT work + ITH John tomorrow

(ii) *mi fydd   John yn gweithio rŵan/yfory   (John will be*
      PT will be John   in   work   now/tomorrow   *working now/*
                                                     tomorrow)

The restrictions on -ITH, however, are entirely aspectual and the label non-past can be preserved.

The second three-term tense system involves the lexical auxiliaries but retains the three contrasts of non-past, past and past-past. Its significant characteristics are the realisations of the non-past and the possibilities of contrast in the case of past. The past-past remains the same as in the non-modal system. The various possibilities can be illustrated with MEDRU/GALLU *ability:*

(180) (i)   *mi fedr   John ddreifio*   *(John can drive)*
             PT can + ITH John drive

       (ii) *mae John yn medru   dreifio*   *(John can drive)*
             is   John in ABILITY drive

(181) (i)   *'roedd John yn medru   dreifio*   *(John could drive)*
             was   John in ABILITY drive

       (ii) *mi fedrai   John ddreifio*   *(John could drive)*
             PT can + AI   John drive

       (iii) *mi fedrodd   John ddreifio*   *(John could/was able to*
             PT can + ODD John drive   drive)*

(182) *mi fu (odd) John yn medru   dreifio*   *(John was able to drive)*
       PT was   John in ABILITY drive

It can be seen from the above examples that the three-term system for the lexical auxiliaries involves a mixture of the resources of the inflections and the aspectual auxiliaries, and that within the non-past and past features various contrasts are possible.

The non-past feature can involve either -ITH or MAE . . YN (IS . . IN = IS -ING) as illustrated by (180). As discussed in section 3g above, this can give an episodic reference in the case of -ITH and a durative reference in the case of MAE . . YN (IS . . IN = IS -ING). It is interesting, however, to compare the occurrence of -ITH with the lexical auxiliaries and lexical verbs respectively:

(183) *mi fedr   Mair ganu*   *(Mair can sing)*
       PT can + ITH Mair sing

(184) *mi ganith   Mair*   *(Mair will sing)*
       PT sing + ITH Mair

149

The occurrence of -ITH with a lexical auxiliary lacks the predictive force of its occurrence with a lexical verb; where prediction is required for a lexical auxiliary, either a carrier auxiliary or (questionably) BYDD . . YN (WILL BE . . IN = WILL BE -ING) is chosen:

(185) ?mi   wneith   Mair fedru   canu   (Mair will be able to sing)
       PT do + ITH Mair ABILITY   sing

(186) mi fydd   Mair yn medru   canu   (Mair will be able to sing)
       PT will be   Mair in ABILITY   sing

Since this point relates to the semantics of -ITH and not to its temporal reference, the label non-past can be retained.

The past feature presents an area of some complexity, largely because of the extent of dialectal variation and also because of variation within any particular idiolect. In theory, as outlined in chapter V, section 3f, there exists the choice of a durative or dispositional past tense with -AI, and an episodic past tense with -ODD. However, only -ODD constantly maintains its function as an episodic past tense, and compares with the use of -ODD with lexical verbs in the non-modal three term system.'ROEDD . . YN (WAS . . IN = WAS -ING) and the -AI paradigm, as well as occurring as a durative past tense, can also occur with episodic reference. The possibilities can be represented as follows:

(187) (i)   'roedd John yn medru   dreifio pan   (John could drive
             was   John in ABILITY   drive   when   when he was young)

             oedd o 'n ifanc
             was he in young

       (ii) mi fedrai   John ddreifio pan oedd   (John could drive
             PT can + AI John   drive   when was   when he was young)

             o 'n ifanc
             he in young

(188) (i)   'roedd John yn medru   ei wneud o neithıwr   (John could do
             was   John in ABILITY its do   it last night   it last night

       (ii) mi fedrai   John ei wneud o neithiwr   (John could do it
             PT can + AI John its do   it last night   last night)

       (iii) mi fedrodd   John ei wneud o neithiwr   (John could do it
             PT can + ODD John its do   it last night   last night)

Some speakers may prefer -AI to -ODD as the episodic past tense and contrast this with OEDD . . YN (WAS . . IN = WAS -ING) as the durative or dispositional past tense

150

(with the possibility of -AI sharing this function with OEDD .. YN, too).

The past-past reference with lexical auxiliaries is quite straightforward and, like the lexical verbs, merely involves the occurrence of the aspectual auxiliary BU .. YN (WAS .. IN = WAS -ING).

4e   Summary

The outline of tense in Welsh as given above can be summarised as follows:

(189)

	One-term	Two-term	Three-term	
			Non-modal	Lexical auxiliaries (e.g. MEDRU)
Non-past	-AI	-ITH; BYDD (PRED.); BYDD (HAB.)	MAE	(i) MEDR (-ITH) (ii) MAE .. YN MEDRU
Past	–	-AI; BUASAI/BYDDAI; BYDDAI	(i) OEDD (ii) -ODD	(i) OEDD .. YN MEDRU (ii) MEDRODD (iii) MEDRAI
Past-past	–	–	BU	BU .. YN MEDRU

The lexical auxiliaries thus emerge as distinctive because of their characteristics of contrast in non-past time, and also their use of both -AI and -ODD as well as OEDD .. YN in past time. The above table and most of the discussion in the foregoing sub-sections concentrate upon the temporal features of the auxiliary carriers. It must also be noted that aspect has temporal consequences, in that the progressive aspect is widely used for present contemporaneous reference and the perfect can be used for past reference. The latter is compulsory with the one-term system but supplies an additional variety of past time reference with the non-modal three-term system.

Notes to chapter VI

1. The discussion of aspect is here framed in taxonomic terms where one category, namely *aspect* itself, acts as a cover-label for various items. In a significant analysis, aspect would be best handled in terms of a framework which relates aspect to the rest of the sentence. The taxonomic approach is adopted here for its simplicity.
2. See note 8 to chapter III for distributional characteristics of the preposition YN.

3. The item NEWYDD (NEW) can be considered along the same general lines as BRON Â (NEARLY WITH) in section 1d:

    (i)   *mae John wedi mynd yn newydd*
    (ii)   *mae John wedi newydd fynd*
    (iii) *mae John newydd fynd*

    Some writers claim that NEWYDD (NEW) is a medially occurring adverb and, moreover, the type of pattern in (ii) above is listed by Richards (1938 : 19). This is a credible line of thought as it allows NEWYDD to be viewed as an adverbial modifier of the perfect aspect, as indeed it seems to be. But for our purposes the surface structure distributional relationships will be maintained, and NEWYDD (NEW) will be regarded as an aspect marker.

4. The relationship of BOD to the AUXILIARY inflections -ITH, -AI and -ODD cannot be accurately expressed without reference to the semantic and tense features of the AUXILIARY. The -AI paradigm, for instance, can be realised as OEDD *past fact,* BYDDAI *past fact habitual* and BYDDAI/BUASAI *non-past conditional/tentative.* In order to predict the occurrence of the various copula paradigms, therefore, the auxiliary would have to be re-written in terms of semantic and tense features rather than inflectional symbols. The former approach involves substantial complexity so the latter approach, although inadequate, is retained for simplicity here. The conditions under which each copula paradigm does occur, however, can be extracted from the discussion of their uses given in this chapter.

VII The noun phrase

1 INTRODUCTION

1a Scope of the material

The noun phrase constituent in surface structure can be a constituent of considerable complexity. The extent of its complexity can be illustrated by the following unlikely, but syntactically acceptable, example:

(1) ddaeth dim ond ychydig o'r   cant   o'r   *(only a few of those*
came NEG but   few   of the hundred of the   *hundred respectable*

hen   bobl   barchus acw   a   oedd   wedi bod   *old people who had*
old   people polite   there PT were   after be   *been worrying about*
                                              the proposal came
yn poeni am y cynnig   i'r   cyfarfod   *to the meeting)*
in   worry   about the proposal to the   meeting

In this discussion no attempt will be made to give a comprehensive account of the possibilities of structure in the noun phrase and, furthermore, we will concentrate on surface structure ordering only. The aim will be to examine the more commonly occurring elements and their arrangements in respect of each other. But example (1) can serve as a reminder that there is more to the discussion of the noun phrase than is given here.

1b The head word or noun

The following sentences illustrate some typical noun phrases:

(2) mae llawer o ddynion ifanc wedi   gwrthod   *(many young men*
is   many of men   young after   refuse   *have refused)*

(3) 'roedd yr hogiau o'r   pentref yn canu   *(the village boys were*
was   the boys   of the village in sing   *singing)*

(4) 'dwi ddim yn licio'r   ferch   a oedd   *(I don't like the girl*
am I NEG in like the girl   PT   was   *who was talking with*
                                              Mair)
yn siarad efo Mair
in   talk   with Mair

In each case the noun phrase contains one item which is more central to its structure than other items. A common way of illustrating this more central item is to ask which item in the noun phrase can stand by itself and still convey a similar sort of message.

In example (2), for instance, DYNION (MEN) is the central item in these terms and can stand by itself:

(5) *mae dynion wedi gwrthod*　　　　　　*(men have refused)*
　　is　men　after　refuse

Note, however, that it is also possible to have:

(6) *mae llawer wedi gwrthod*　　　　　　*(many have refused)*
　　is　many　after　refuse

But LLAWER (MANY) is not notionally central and is dependent upon DYNION (MEN). Example (6) is understood in terms of (2) and if (6) were uttered out of context without any previous introduction the reaction would be to ask the question 'llawer o beth?' (many what?) - which specifically requests information about the central item. In examples (3) and (4) there are no complications, and the only possible independent items in the noun phrases are HOGIAU (BOYS, LADS) and MERCH (GIRL):

(7) *'roedd hogiau yn canu*　　　　　　*(boys were singing)*
　　was　boys　in　sing

(8) *'dwi ddim yn licio'r ferch*　　　　　　*(I don't like the girl)*
　　am I NEG in　like the girl

The sentences in (7) and (8) are grammatically acceptable, although now different from (3) and (4). Note that in (8) the definite article in this case must be retained in order to maintain the specific reference which was established by the relative clause.

The items which can stand alone, like DYNION (MEN), HOGIAU (BOYS, LADS) and MERCH (GIRL), signify the HEAD of the noun phrase. In traditional terms, DYNION, HOGIAU and MERCH are each known as a NOUN, hence the label NOUN PHRASE.

1c　General structure of the noun phrase

The noun phrases in examples (2) to (4) involve more than the head nouns. In each case there are other items which *modify* the head in various ways. Compare, for instance, examples (2), (3) and (4) with (5), (7) and (8); it can be seen that the modifying items make the reference of the head nouns more specific. The modifying items can occur either before the head noun, like LLAWER O . . . in (2), or after the head noun, like . . . 'R PENTREF in (3). Consequently, it is possible to speak of PRE—MODIFICATION and POST—MODIFICATION. As an initial introduction to the structure of the noun phrase, we can say that the following is involved:

(9) *(PRE-MODIFICATION)*　　*N*　　*(POST-MODIFICATION)*

For the remainder of this chapter we will examine the concept of the head noun and some of the items that can occur in pre-modifying and post-modifying positions.

154

2 THE NOUN

2a Introduction

The noun is traditionally discussed in terms of GENDER, NUMBER and semantic
TYPE. The approach here will be to comment upon some aspects of these categories.

2b Gender

It is a fact familiar from traditional grammar that the noun in Welsh has two GENDERS,
which can be illustrated by DRWS (DOOR) and CADAIR (CHAIR). We can list five
features which reveal DRWS (DOOR) and CADAIR (CHAIR) to be different:

(10)

(i)	*mutation after the definite article*	DRWS - Y DRWS : CADAIR - Y GADAIR
(ii)	*adjective mutation after*	
	singular nouns	DRWS MAWR : CADAIR FAWR
(iii)	*numeral distinctions*	DAU DDRWS : DWY GADAIR
(iv)	*demonstrative distinctions*	Y DRWS HWN : Y GADAIR HON
(v)	*pronominal distinctions*	DRWS = FO/FE : CADAIR = HI

On the basis of these five criteria, two sub-classes of Welsh noun can be established;
one sub-class behaves like DRWS (DOOR) and the other like CADAIR (CHAIR).

Traditionally, these two sub-classes are given the names *masculine* (for nouns like
DRWS) and *feminine* (for nouns like CADAIR). There is an obvious relationship
between these terms and the sex-distinction terms *male* and *female*. And, as far as
animate objects are concerned, there are many cases of a male object being grammatically masculine and a female object being grammatically feminine:

(11)

(i)	*DYN (MAN)*	- *y dyn*	*DYNES*	- *y ddynes*
(ii)	*GWR (MAN)*	- *y gwr*	*GWRAIG*	- *y wraig*
(iii)	*HOGYN (LAD)*	- *dau hogyn*	*HOGEN*	- *dwy hogen*
(iv)	*BACHGEN (BOY)*	- *y bachgen*	*MERCH*	- *y ferch*
(v)	*BRAWD (BROTHER)*	*dau frawd*	*CHWAER*	- *dwy chwaer*
(vi)	*BRENIN (KING)*	- *y brenin*	*BRENHINES*	- *y frenhines*
(vii)	*TARW (BULL)*	- *y tarw*	*BUWCH*	- *y fuwch*
(viii)	*CEFFYL (HORSE)*	- *y ceffyl*	*CASEG*	- *y gaseg*
(ix)	*MOCHYN (PIG)*	- *dau fochyn*	*HWCH*	- *dwy hwch*
(x)	*MAHAREN (RAM)*	- *y maharen*	*DAFAD*	- *y ddafad*

But problems arise when this relationship between the grammatical concept of
gender and the biological concept of sex is extended to include inanimate objects
which are 'sexless'. Compare the following grammatically masculine and feminine

155

nouns:

(12)

(i)	DRÔR (drawer)	- y drôr	DESG (desk)	- y ddesg
(ii)	GWELY (bed)	- y gwely	CADAIR (chair)	- y gadair
(iii)	BOCS (box)	- y bocs	POTEL (bottle)	- y botel
(iv)	DRWS (door(	- dau ddrws	FFENESTR (window)	- dwy ffenestr
(v)	BLODYN (flower)	- y blodyn	COEDEN (tree)	- y goeden
(vi)	CAE (field)	- y cae	GARDD (garden)	- yr ardd

There seems to be no obvious reason why DROR (DRAWER) should be masculine and DESG (DESK) feminine, or CAE (FIELD) masculine and GARDD (GARDEN) feminine. Certainly it is inadequate to look for an explanation by using sex criteria. There have been attempts by older grammars to look for male and females characteristics in masculine and feminine nouns, and Rowland (1816:34) supplies a classic illustration worth quoting at length:

> '133. *Nouns are either of the masculine or feminine gender.*
> *The Welsh language does not recognize what is called the*
> *"neuter gender"; hence all inanimate things, which are*
> *classed as neuter in English, are considered either as*
> *masculine or feminine in our language; and "this is done*
> *by conceiving their properties to bear some resemblance*
> *to the qualities that are characteristic of sex in animated beings".'*

Rowland was a follower of the controversial grammarian W. O. Pughe, and he goes on further to explain this view of gender by quoting from the latter:

> ' "*Thus the masculine gender is given to substantives,*
> *which are conspicuous for the attributes of energy, and*
> *of acting upon and communicating to others. To such*
> *substantives as seem to denote the passive attributes of*
> *bearing, containing or bringing forth, we give the*
> *feminine gender.*" - *Dr. Pughe's Grammar, p. 30.*'

If one tries to apply such an explanation to the inanimates in (12), it is found that Dr. Pughe's criteria are hardly satisfactory. The nouns DRÔR (DRAWER), GWELY (BED) and BOCS (BOX) can 'bear' and 'contain' but are masculine. What is the difference between CAE (FIELD) and GARDD (GARDEN) in these terms? The concepts of grammatical gender (masculine and feminine) and biological sex (male and female) are clearly quite different as far as inanimate objects are concerned. Even with animate objects, moreover, there is no consistent one-to-one relationship between gender and sex. There are many collective nouns (see section 2c below) which refer to both male and female objects and are yet grammatically of one gender or the

156

other. There is the curious fact that a collective noun like POBL (PEOPLE) is feminine *(y bobl)* and yet a collective noun like CWMNI (COMPANY) is masculine *(y cwmni),* even though both may include male and female objects in their reference. A similar example is seen with masculine PLENTYN (CHILD) *(y plentyn)* which may refer to a boy or a girl. It is also interesting to note that the masculine numeral DAU (TWO) has the feminine characteristic of soft mutation after the definite article even when referring to male objects: *mae 'r ddau (frawd) yn dod (the two (brothers) are coming).* More striking still is the noun BYDDIN (ARMY) which is feminine: *y fyddin (the army).* Even with animate objects that refer directly to either male or female, it is important to note that the distinction is not asserted by gender alone but by either a change in word (BRAWD - CHWAER) or a change in word formation (DYN - DYNES). If there were a direct link between gender and sex, it would be sufficient to have Y DYN (MAN) and *Y DDYN (*WOMAN). But this is not the case, as sex-distinctions are conveyed by the choice of different words; it just happens that sex-distinctions tend to coincide with the grammatical distinction of gender. It is safe to conclude that gender is a grammatical concept which is not consistently concerned with sex-distinctions.

2c   Number

The concept of NUMBER basically involves the enumerating of objects. The enumeration involves *singular* for 'one' of a particular object and *plural* for 'more than one'. The discussion of number in Welsh usually concentrates upon the details of forming the plural in terms of addition, deletion, and internal change in the word, or of various combinations of these operations. In this account we will not be concerned with the details of plural formation; by contrast, we will concentrate upon the manner in which different nouns relate to the concept of number.

Firstly, it is possible to identify nouns which illustrate (i) straightforward number *contrast* in terms of singular and plural, where the plural is formed from the singular, and (ii) number *concord,* as with pronouns. The noun AFAL (APPLE) is a good illustration of this type:

(13) (i) *lle   mae 'r afal?* - *mae o ar y bwrdd*   *(where's the apple?-*
            where is the apple   is he on the table   *it's on the table)*

      (ii) *lle   mae 'r afalau?* - *maen nhw ar y bwrdd*   *(where are the*
            where is the apples   are they on the table   *apples?- they're*
                                                                on the table)

In these examples we have a singular form AFAL (APPLE) which concords with a singular pronoun (F) O/(F) E, and a plural form AFALAU (APPLES) which concords with the plural pronoun NHW (THEY, THEM). Nouns of this type invariably refer to concepts, like apples, that can be counted. Consequently, they are known as COUNT nouns. The majority of nouns in Welsh are count nouns; in addition to AFAL (APPLE), we can list:

(14)

		SING	*PLURAL*
(i)	*CADAIR (CHAIR)*	*cadair*	*cadeiriau*
(ii)	*BARDD (POET)*	*bardd*	*beirdd*
(iii)	*DRWS (DOOR)*	*drws*	*drysau*
(iv)	*DRÔR (DRAWER)*	*dror*	*droriau*
(v)	*DYN (MAN)*	*dyn*	*dynion*
(vi)	*GARDD (GARDEN)*	*gardd*	*gerddi*
(vii)	*LAMP (LAMP)*	*lamp*	*lampiau*
(viii)	*MERCH (GIRL)*	*merch*	*merched*
(ix)	*PEN (HEAD)*	*pen*	*pennau*
(x)	*TON (WAVE)*	*ton*	*tonnau*

As can be seen from a survey of the list in (14), there are a variety of ways of actually forming the plural.

However, there are special types of count noun which are characterised by a unique method of number contrast. Instead of forming the plural from the singular like AFAL (APPLE) — AFALAU, the singular is formed from the plural. This can be illustrated by ADAR (BIRDS) — ADERYN. Apart from the direction of change, such nouns are otherwise count nouns, exhibiting number contrast and concord:

(15) (i) *lle   mae'r adar? - mae nhw ar y   wal*   *(where are the birds?*
          where is the birds   is they on the wall   *- they're on the wall)*

     (ii) *lle   mae'r aderyn? - mae o ar y   wal*   *(where is the bird?*
          where is the bird   is he on the wall   *- it's on the wall)*

As far as number formation is concerned, the base form is the plural and not the singular, the latter being derived by the addition of the suffix -YN to the plural form. The -YN (feminine -EN) suffix thus emerges as a characteristic of this type of noun. There are two arguments for this view of number formation of plural to singular. Firstly, there are obviously plural forms like CNAU (NUTS) and BLODAU (FLOWERS) which are made singular by adding -YN/-EN, giving CNEUEN and BLODEUYN (with variant BLODYN). Secondly, internal changes are seen in the root form, as in PLANT (CHILDREN) → PLENTYN and CACWN (WASPS) → CACYNEN, and the normal procedure for such changes is that they are conditioned by addition rather than deletion. Given, then, that the plural is the base form rather than the singular, there is initial emphasis upon plural number or a group of objects. Consequently, this type will be given the label GROUP nouns. Examples can be given as follows:

158

(16)

		SING	PLURAL
(i)	*PLU (FEATHERS)*	*plu*	*pluen*
(ii)	*MOCH (PIGS)*	*moch*	*mochyn*
(iii)	*PYSGOD (FISH)*	*pysgod*	*pysgodyn*
(iv)	*GWELLT (GRASS)*	*gwellt*	*gwelltyn*
(v)	*SÊR (STARS)*	*sêr*	*seren*
(vi)	*PLANT (CHILDREN)*	*plant*	*plentyn*
(vii)	*CACWN (WASPS)*	*cacwn*	*cacynen*
(viii)	*CNAU (NUTS)*	*cnau*	*cneuen*
(ix)	*COED (TREES)*	*coed*	*coeden*
(x)	*CYLL (HAZEL TREES)*	*cyll*	*collen*

As can be seen, group nouns in fact commonly represent objects that regularly occur in groups like SÊR (STARS) and CNAU (NUTS). But the factual implications of this relationship cannot be pushed too far, as there are examples of ordinary count nouns like AFAL (APPLE) which also regularly occur in groups, and group nouns like PLANT (CHILDREN) where the object need not necessarily occur in groups. One point about the group noun pattern is that it has been applied to items borrowed from English. In effect, the English plural has been borrowed and the plural forms are made singular by adding -YN/-EN. Thus, from the borrowing of *bricks* and *peas* we have Welsh *brics - bricsen* and *pys - pysen*. This is an interesting example of the Cymricising of English-like items.

The outline of ordinary count nouns and group count nouns presented above can be represented as follows:

(17)

	COUNT NOUNS			
	PLURAL	SINGULAR		PLURAL
		(a)	(b)	
Ordinary	–	–	AFAL——→AFALAU	
Group	ADAR ——→ADERYN	–	–	

The situation is somewhat complicated, however, by count nouns that are a mixture of ordinary and group. We find nouns like CWNINGEN (RABBIT), for instance, that show the characteristic singular ending -EN of a singular group noun, but in fact form the plural something like an ordinary count noun, replacing -EN by a plural ending giving CWNINGOD (RABBITS). This type can be labelled as the MIXED count noun and other examples are:

(18)

		SING	PLURAL
(i)	CERDYN (CARD)	cerdyn	cardiau
(ii)	CERPYN (RAG)	cerpyn	carpiau
(iii)	DIFERYN (DROP)	diferyn	diferion
(iv)	MIEREN (BRIAR)	mieren	mieri
(v)	TECLYN (TOOL)	teclyn	taclau
(vi)	TATEN (POTATO)	taten	tatws
(vii)	MATSEN (MATCH)	matsen	matsys
(viii)	DEIGRYN (TEAR)	deigryn	dagrau
(ix)	ERFYN (TOOL)	erfyn	arfau
(x)	SLEISEN (SLICE)	sleisen	sleisys

As far as count nouns are concerned, then, the situation can be represented as follows:

(19)

	COUNT NOUNS			
	PLURAL	SINGULAR		PLURAL
		(a)	(b)	
Ordinary	–	–	AFAL——→AFALAU	
Group	ADAR——→ADERYN	–		–
Mixed	–	CWNINGEN————→ CWNINGOD		

As a class, count nouns are distinguished by their singular and plural forms and the appropriate number concord with each. The sub-groupings do not upset the basic characteristics but rest on the methods of plural or singular *formation*.

A second class of noun as far as number is concerned contains nouns like LLYWODRAETH (GOVERNMENT). Such nouns exhibit singular and plural contrast like count nouns:

(20) (i) mae llywodraeth Prydain yn cytuno   *(the government of*
        is   government Britain   in   agree   *Britain agrees with*

           efo   llywodraeth Luxemburg   *the government of*
           with government Luxemburg   *Luxemburg)*

     (ii) mae llywodraethau y byd yn cytuno   *(the governments of*
        is   governments the world in   agree   *the world agree)*

But the distinctive characteristic of nouns like LLYWODRAETH (GOVERNMENT) is that in their *singular* form they tend to have *plural* concord rather than singular concord:

(21)   beth mae'r   llywodraeth yn mynd i wneud? *(what's the government*
       what is the   government   in   go   to do   *going to do? - they're*
                                                          going to raise taxes)
       - maen nhw 'n mynd i godi trethi
         are   they in go   to raise taxes

Nouns like LLYWODRAETH (GOVERNMENT) typically refer to one single body made up of a number of people or other objects. As a body they are singular, but in terms of their membership they are plural. They are consequently labelled as COLLECTIVE nouns, and other examples are:

(22)

		SING	*PLURAL*
(i)	PWYLLGOR (COMMITTEE)	pwyllgor	pwyllgorau
(ii)	CYNGOR (COUNCIL)	cyngor	cynghorau
(iii)	POBL (PEOPLE)	pobl	pobloedd
(iv)	ADRAN (DEPARTMENT)	adran	adrannau
(v)	TÎM (TEAM)	tîm	tîmau

Although they have plural forms, their distinctive characteristic is plural concord with singular forms.

A third type of noun is exemplified by 'MENYN (BUTTER). This type of noun is distinctive, as nouns of this class do not normally have number contrast and have only singular concord. Generally speaking, they refer to a mass or substance of a particular commodity without signifying any countable characteristics. Consequently, they can be labelled as MASS nouns. Other nouns like 'MENYN (BUTTER) are:

(23)   (i)   GLO (COAL)   (vi)   MÊL (HONEY)
       (ii)   GWAED (BLOOD)   (vii)   PRÊS (MONEY)
       (iii) LLAFUR (LABOUR)   (viii) PRIDD (SOIL)
       (iv)   LLEFRITH (MILK)   (ix)   SIWGR (SUGAR)
       (v)   LLWCH (DUST)   (x)   TYWYDD (WEATHER)

It is also a common characteristic of mass nouns that they can co-occur with the mass determiner PETH (see below):

(24)   'dach chi eisiau (peth) siwgr?   *(do you want some sugar?)*
       are   you want   some   sugar

But those mass nouns that involve more abstract or less substantial concepts like TYWYDD (WEATHER), FFYDD (FAITH) or TRISTWCH (SADNESS) do not readily

161

accept this co-occurrence:

(25)   *?'dan ni 'n mynd i gael peth tywydd ofnadwy*   *(we are going to*
      are   we in   go to have some weather awful   *have some awful*
                                                                       weather)

(26)   *?oes gynnoch chi beth ffydd?*   *(have you any*
      is   LOC   you some faith   *faith?)*

Moreover, it must also be added that the concept of 'mass-ness' can also extend to count nouns. That is, a count noun can be used in a mass-like manner to indicate the substance that it refers to without introducing the question of countability. A good example is seen with the count noun AFAL (APPLE), for instance, where the singular form can be used to denote the substance and, as such, can occur with PETH:

(27)   *'dach chi eisiau peth afal?*   *(do you want some apple?)*
      are you want some apple

Example (27) could relate to apple sauce, for instance! An interesting point here is that in the case of ordinary count nouns, the singular form occurs to convey a mass reference, as with AFAL (APPLE) in the above example. But in the case of group count nouns, it is the plural form that occurs, giving *'dach chi eisiau pysgod/coed? (do you want some fish/wood?)*. The common factor seems to be that the uninflected form (that is, singular ordinary and plural group) is used for mass reference. In the case of the mixed count noun involving a change of inflectional ending, the practice seems to vary; thus we find the singular form *cwningen* as in *'dach chi'n licio cwningen?(do you like rabbit?)* but the plural form *tatws* as in *'dach chi'n licio tatws? (do you like potatoes?)*.

Fourthly, and finally, there are those nouns which only occur in the plural, either in form and concord, or in concord alone:

(28)   (i) *GWARTHEG (CATTLE)*   (ii) *RHIENI (PARENTS)*
      (iii) *TELERAU (TERMS)*   (iv) *TRIGOLION (INHABITANTS)*
      (v) *GLAFOERION (DRIVEL)*   (vi) *TYLWYTH TEG (FAIRIES)*
      (vii) *YMYSGAROEDD (BOWELS)* (viii) *YSGYFAINT (LUNGS)*

Many of these nouns, like TELERAU (TERMS), are obviously plural in form while others, like GWARTHEG (CATTLE), cannot be so distinguished. The significant point in each case, however, is that plural concord is involved:

(29)   *lle   mae'r gwartheg? maen nhw yn y coed*   *(where are* the cattle?
      where is the cattle   are they in the wood   *-they're in the wood)*

By the criteria of concord, therefore, a fourth group of PLURAL ONLY nouns can be established.

To summarise, number establishes four types of noun in Welsh:

(30)	(i)	COUNT	ordinary group mixed	AFAL (APPLE) ADAR (BIRDS) CWNINGEN (RABBIT)
	(ii)	COLLECTIVE		LLYWODRAETH (GOVERNMENT)
	(iii)	MASS		'MENYN (BUTTER)
	(iv)	PLURAL ONLY		GWARTHEG (CATTLE)

These four types, with sub-groupings in the case of count nouns, are distinguished by their different formal behaviour in the grammar of the Welsh language.

2d   Semantic features

Traditional grammars classify nouns into notional categories like *animate* or *inanimate, abstract* or *concrete*. The advantage of such a classification is that it can be used to explain why some nouns can occur with certain other nouns or verbs, while other nouns or verbs are excluded. For instance, consider the following examples:

(31) 'roedd y ferch yn crio   *(the girl was crying)*
      was   the girl   in cry

(32) *'roedd y garreg yn crio   *(*the stone was crying)*
      was the stone in cry

It is acceptable for MERCH (GIRL) to co-occur with CRIO (CRY) but not acceptable for CARREG (STONE) to do so. We might try to explain these facts by suggesting that CRIO (CRY) is a verb which only co-occurs with *animate* nouns like MERCH (GIRL) and not with inanimate nouns like CARREG (STONE). By analysing nouns in terms of their inherent features, some understanding can be gained of the relationships between nouns and other words. Common categories involve the following:

(33)	(i)	COMMON	v.	PROPER
	(ii)	ABSTRACT	v.	CONCRETE
	(iii)	ANIMATE	v.	INANIMATE
	(iv)	HUMAN	v.	NON-HUMAN

Each of these categories represents a choice - either COMMON or PROPER, for instance. This choice can therefore be represented in positive and negative terms where +COMMON = COMMON and —COMMON = PROPER.

The various categories can be organised in regard to each other. If a noun is +ABSTRACT, for instance, the category of 'animateness' will not apply; and if a noun is —ANIMATE the category of 'human-ness' will not apply. We can exemplify each of the categories and their relationships:

(34)

	COMMON	ABSTRACT	ANIMATE	HUMAN
JOHN (name for person)	−	−	+	+
PERO (name for dog)	−	−	+	−
FFRANC (FRANC)	−	−	−	0
BACHGEN (BOY)	+	−	+	+
CI (DOG)	+	−	+	−
LLYFR (BOOK)	+	−	−	0
SYNIAD (IDEA)	+	+	0	0

Such a classification is not only useful for explaining sentences but also serves to explicate striking effects that speakers sometimes achieve. Consider the following sentence:

(35)   mae'r pwyllgor wedi gwrthod y syniad   *(the committee have*
       is the committee after refuse the idea   *rejected the idea)*

This can be made more 'forceful' as follows:

(36)   mae'r pwyllgor wedi taflu'r syniad   *(the committee have*
       is the committee after throw the idea   *thrown the idea to*
                                     the four winds)
       i'r   pedwar gwynt
       to the four   winds

The verb TAFLU (THROW) normally co-occurs with concrete nouns rather than abstract nouns like SYNIAD (IDEA). But by treating SYNIAD (IDEA) like a concrete noun, the strength of the committee's opposition to the idea is emphasised. This type of sub-classification and the light that it throws upon word co-occurrences is useful for the discussion of literature. Many of the effects of imagery produced in poetry or prose can be associated with the word choices involved.

There are other possible sub-classifications of nouns in terms of semantic features, and the four categories suggested so far apply only to a limited number of nouns. Consider the following sentences:

(37)   (i)   mae John wedi llyncu'r papur   *(John has swallowed the*
           is John after swallow the paper   *paper)*

      (ii)   mae John wedi llyncu 'r te   *(John has swallowed the*
           is John after swallow the tea   *tea)*

(38)   (i)   *mae John wedi yfed y papur   (*John has drunk the*
           is John after drink the paper   *paper)*

    (ii)   *mae John wedi yfed y te*   *(John has drunk the tea)*
          is John after drink the tea

Both PAPUR (PAPER) and TE (TEA) are —ABSTRACT nouns but only TE (TEA) can occur with YFED (DRINK) while both can occur with LLYNCU (SWALLOW). It is necessary to add further characterising features of —ABSTRACT nouns in terms of LIQUID and SOLID, and it is then possible to suggest that YFED (DRINK) is a verb which only occurs with LIQUID while LLYNCU (SWALLOW) can occur with both. Again, it is now possible to explain certain 'odd' effects:

    (39)   *mae pawb wedi llyncu ei stori o*   *(everyone has swallowed*
          is everyone after swallow his story he   *his story)*

There are two interpretations of STORI (STORY). Firstly, as a —ABSTRACT SOLID noun, in the sense of a piece of paper or a book; this is unlikely, as people do not normally swallow books, etc. Secondly, as a +ABSTRACT noun in the sense of the contents of the story. Usually one would use CREDU (BELIEVE) in the sense of (39) but the selection of LLYNCU (SWALLOW) associates acceptance of the story with gullibility and suggests that the story has been accepted without careful thought.

3   DETERMINERS

3a   Introduction

A very common class of items in the pre-modification of a noun phrase is that of items which can be called DETERMINERS. Their occurrence can be illustrated as follows:

    (40)   (i)   *. . . y car newydd*   *(the new car)*
               the car new

         (ii) *. . . ei gar newydd*   *(his new car)*
               his car new

        (iii) *. . . pob car newydd*   *(every new car)*
               every car new

        (iv) *. . . rhyw gar newydd*   *(some new car)*
               some car new

         (v) *. . . unrhyw gar newydd*   *(any new car)*
               any car new

        (vi) *. . . dim car newydd*   *(no new car)*
               no car new

       (vii) *. . . ambell i gar newydd*   *(an occasional new car)*
               occasional to car new

ıne first two items, Y (THE) and EI (HIS) can be separated from the others for special attention, as they have certain relationships with post-modifying items which the others lack (as will be outlined below). These two items are named ARTICLE in the case of Y (THE) and POSSESSIVE PRONOUN in the case of EI (HIS).

3b   The article (and demonstratives)

In Welsh the use of the article compares with its absence for a definite-indefinite contrast:

(41)   (i)   *mae'r   dynion   wedi   cyrraedd*   *(the men have arrived)*
                is the   men   after   arrive

        (ii)   *mae   dynion   wedi   cyrraedd*   *(men have arrived)*
                is   men   after   arrive

In many cases the use of the article demands previous identification of the objects to which the noun is referring. Thus, in (41) (i) DYNION (MEN) refers to certain men that the speaker and possibly the hearer already know about, while in (42) (ii) the men referred to are not previously known. The absence of the article can involve at least two different references. Consider the following:

(42)   *mae   dyn   yn   medru   cyrraedd   y   lleuad*   *(man can reach the moon)*
         is   man   in   can   arrive   the   moon

In this example the unspecified singular noun DYN·(MAN) refers to the race of man as a whole. It can be said to have a GENERIC reference, referring to man as a class. Significantly, it does not compare with:

(43)   *mae   yna   ddyn   sy 'n   medru   cyrraedd   y   lleuad*   *(there is a man who*
         is   there   man   is in   can   arrive   the   moon   *is able to reach the*
                                                                             moon)

The example in (43) refers to one particular, but unidentified, man. Singular nouns may also occur without the article as follows:

(44)   *mae   dyn   yn   cerdded   i   lawr   y   ffordd*   *(a man is walking down*
         is   man   in   walk   down   the road   *the road)*

This can compare with:

(45)   *mae   yna   ddyn   yn   cerdded   i   lawr   y   ffordd*   *(there's a man walking*
         is   there   man   in   walk   down   the road   *down the road)*

The reference here is again to one particular but unidentified man, and it is characteristic of such a reference that a paraphrase like that in (45) is possible.

The occurrence of the article can be linked with certain post-modifying items.

166

Consider the following:

(46)   (i)   *'dwi 'n licio 'r ferch*   *(I like the girl)*
                    am I in like the girl

       (ii)   *'dwi 'n licio'r ferch <u>yma/yna/acw</u>*   *(I like this/that/that*
                    am I in like the girl here/there/yonder   *(yonder) girl)*

       (iii)   *'dwi 'n licio'r ferch <u>hon/honno</u>*   *(I like this/that girl)*
                    am I in like the girl this/that

In (46) (i) the article occurs alone. But in (46) (ii) and (iii) the reference of the
article is further specified by post-modifying items which go under the name of
DEMONSTRATIVES. In spontaneous spoken Welsh the demonstratives are YMA
(HERE), YNA (THERE) and ACW(YONDER). The traditional demonstratives
involving distinctions of animateness and gender - HWN (THIS), HWNNW (THAT),
HON (THIS) HONNO (THAT), HYN (THIS) and HYNNY (THAT) - rarely occur as
demonstratives in spoken Welsh except with certain nouns such as in Y FLWYDDYN
HONNO (THAT YEAR). Their function is now mainly *pronominal* (see section 8e
below), as in:

(47)   *pwy ydy hon?*   *(who is this?)*
        who is   she

In spoken Welsh the post-modifying demonstratives YMA (HERE), YNA (THERE),
ACW(YONDER) are very much simpler in view of the absence of any distinctions
of animateness and gender.

The demonstratives are used in two ways and in both cases they are *derived from
relative clauses*. Firstly, they can be used to refer to something which can actually
be seen:

(48)   *'dach chi 'n gweld y tŷ   'ma/'na/'cw?*   *(do you see this/that/*
        are you in see   the house here/there/yonder   *that (yonder) house?)*

There is *spatial reference* in each case and it is interesting to note how Welsh uses
locatival terms for demonstrative reference. In effect, they are derived from relative
clauses (see section 5 below):

(49)   *'dach chi 'n gweld y tŷ sydd yma/yna/acw?*   *(do you see the*
        are you in see the house is here/there/yonder   *house which is here/*
                                                there/yonder?)

Example (49) compares with:

(50)   *'dach chi 'n gweld y tŷ sydd ar y   bryn?*   *(do you see the house*
        are you in see the house is on the hill   *which is on the hill?)*

In both cases the relative clause can be *reduced,* producing (48) in the case of YMA/YNA/ACW or, in the case of (50), the following:

(51)   *'dach chi 'n gweld y ty ar y bryn?*   *(do you see the house*
       are you in see the house on the hill   *on the hill?)*

Secondly, in addition to spatial reference, there also exists the possibility of non-spatial reference, as:

(52)   *'dwi ddim yn licio'r ty   yma/yna*   *(I don't like this/that*
       am I NEG in like the house here/there   *house)*

The noun TY (HOUSE) in (52) can be interpreted as denoting an object not spatially visible but referred to *anaphorically.*

With this type of reference YNA (THERE) is more frequent than YMA (HERE), and ACW (YONDER) rarely occurs, being primarily spatial.

The discussion so far has concentrated upon a discontinuous co-occurrence relationship of the article and demonstrative forms: *article - noun - demonstrative.* Normally it is not possible for the demonstrative forms to occur in this position without the article. Thus, we do not find examples such as **dach chi'n gweld tŷ 'ma/'na/'cw? (*do you see house here/there/yonder?).* There are, however, two exceptions. The first relates to an idiosyncratic use of the temporal nouns BORE (MORNING) and P'NAWN (AFTERNOON), which can occur with demonstratives without the article: *mi wela'i Mair bore 'ma/p'nawn 'ma (I'll see Mair this morning/afternoon).* The second exception is syntactically conditioned rather than governed by the idiosyncratic behaviour of certain items. In a genitive structure (see section 7 below) the first noun can be followed by a demonstrative item without a preceding article: *pen yma'r stryd (this end of the street)* and *ochr yma'r tŷ (this side of the house).* As is outlined in the discussion of the genitive below, definiteness is always marked by the second noun of the genitive structure and not the first - in these circumstances the demonstrative item occurs without a definite article preceding the noun.

3c   **Possessive pronouns (and personal pronouns)**

Unlike the article, POSSESSIVE PRONOUNS involve a number of items depending upon *person* and *number.* In traditional written Welsh the following occur:

(53)

	PERSON		
	FIRST	*SECOND*	*THIRD*
SINGULAR	FY[və]	DY[də]	EI[ei]
PLURAL	EIN[ein]	EICH[eix]	EU[ei]

But in spontaneous spoken Welsh we have the following:

	PERSON		
	FIRST	*SECOND*	*THIRD*
SINGULAR	YN[ən]	DY[də]	I[iː]
PLURAL	YN[ən]	YCH[əx]	I[iː]

It can be seen that only DY is the same in both formal and spontaneous Welsh. In spoken Welsh, moreover, the singular and plural of the first and third persons are identical and are distinguished only by mutation. The third singular pronoun, both written EI and spoken I, is subject to gender contrasts which are governed by the possessor. Thus, if the possessor has masculine gender, the possessive pronoun likewise adopts masculine gender, and the same applies to feminine possessors. The shape of the possessive pronoun does not itself convey the gender features. They are realised by mutation on the possessed item, as the following examples illustrate:

(55) (i) *mae John wedi colli ei gar*   *(John has lost his car)*
           is John after lose his car

      (ii) *mae Mair wedi colli ei char*   *(Mair has lost her car)*
           is Mair after lose her car

(56) (i) *'dydy John ddim yn licio ei frawd*   *(John does not like*
           NEG is John NEG in like his brother   *his brother)*

      (ii) *'dydy Mair ddim yn licio ei brawd*   *(Mair does not like*
           NEG is Mair NEG in like her brother   *her brother)*

(57) (i) *mae John yn licio ei chwaer*   *(John likes his sister)*
           is John in like his sister

      (ii) *mae Mair yn licio ei chwaer*   *(Mair likes her sister)*
           is Mair in like her sister

Where mutation is appropriate, masculine EI or I softens the initial consonant of the possessed item, whereas feminine EI or I imposes the aspirate mutation. The third person plural possessive pronoun does not mutate the following possessed item.

The number contrasts of the second person are not necessarily concerned with singular and plural numbers. Both the singular and plural can refer to one person, in which case the singular conveys an *intimate* reference while the plural is more formal. The plural form, however, can also refer to more than one person and thus also occurs as a plural form proper.

Traditional formal Welsh has a special set of possessive pronouns which are used to follow vowel sounds, as:

(58)   *mae Mair yn siarad a'm   brawd*   *(Mair is talking with*
        is   Mair in   talk   with my brother   *my brother)*

These forms are:

(59)

	PERSON		
	FIRST	*SECOND*	*THIRD*
SINGULAR	*'M* [m]	*'TH* [θ]	*'I* [iː] / *'W* [u]
PLURAL	*'N* [n]	*'CH* [x]	*'U* [iː] / *'W* [u]

But in spontaneous Welsh the situation is very much simpler. Where a possessive pronoun begins with a vowel, that vowel is simply dropped. The pronoun DY remains the same and only the third person types are exceptional:

(60)

	PERSON		
	FIRST	*SECOND*	*THIRD*
SINGULAR	*'N* [n]	*DY* [də]	*I* [iː] / *'W* [u]
PLURAL	*'N* [n]	*'CH* [x]	*I* [iː] / *'W* [u]

The third person types remain as I after all vowels except after the preposition I (TO, FOR), when 'W occurs. Compare the following pairs:

(61)   (i)   *mae Mair yn siarad efo   'i brawd*   *(Mair is talking with*
            is   Mair in   talk   with her brother   *her brother)*

       (ii)   *maen nhw 'n aros efo   'i perthnasau*   *(they're staying with*
           are   they in   stay with their relations   *their relations)*

(62)   (i)   *mae Mair wedi   rhoi pres   i'w   brawd*   *(Mair has given money*
            is   Mair after   give money to her brother   *to her brother)*

       (ii)   *maen nhw wedi anfon llythyr i'w perthnasau*   *(they've sent a*
           are   they after   send   letter to their relations   letter to their
                                                relations)

In some southern areas, I (TO, FOR) in this environment sees the production of a following voiced fricative [ð] *dd,* so that the examples in (62) can be represented as follows: *mae Mair wedi rhoi pres idd'i brawd* and *maen nhw wedi anfon llythyr idd'i perthnasau.*

Like the article, the possessive pronouns can relate to various post-modifying items. Consider the following:

(63) (i)   'dwi wedi colli <u>yn</u> llyfr   *(I've lost my book)*
            am I after lose my book

      (ii) 'dwi wedi colli <u>yn</u> llyfr yn hun/yn hunan   *(I've lost my own*
            am I after lose my book REFLEXIVE   *book)*

      (iii) mae o wedi colli <u>yn</u> llyfr <u>i</u>   *(he's lost my book)*
            is he after lose my book <u>I</u>

The noun can be further specified either by a REFLEXIVE PRONOUN, as in (63)
(ii), or by a PERSONAL PRONOUN, as in (63) (iii). The selection of the post-modifying pronoun is partly involved with *contrastive emphasis.* In (63) (i) the subject
of the sentence and the possessor are identical and there is no need of a post-modifying
pronoun. In (63) (ii) the subject and the possessor are again identical but emphasis is
required, and in this situation a reflexive is chosen. In (63) (iii) the subject and
possessor are not identical and the possessor is accordingly supported by a possessive
pronoun. The pattern exemplified in (63) (iii) can also occur with similar emphatic
reinforcement to that of (63) (ii) where the subject is the same as the possessor.
Thus:

(64)   'dwi wedi colli'n llyfr <u>i</u>   *(I've lost my book)*
      am I after lose my book I

In this case a simple personal pronoun, as opposed to a reflexive pronoun, provides
the emphatic element. A fourth possibility also exists which involves a combination
of the patterns in (63) (ii) and (iii). That is, the pre-occurring possessive pronoun is
related both to a personal pronoun and to a reflexive pronoun in post-modifying
position, giving examples such as *yn syniad i fy hun (my own idea), dy bres di dy hun
(your own money)* and *'i gar o ei hun (his own car).*
A problematic pattern for possessives is one which can be illustrated as follows: ·

(65)   syniad <u>fi</u> oedd o   *(it was my idea)*
      idea   <u>I</u> was he

As seen above, the normal possessive pattern involves a pre-modifying possessive
pronoun with the post-modifying simple or reflexive pronoun being conditioned by
anaphoric features. But, in this instance, the possessive pattern is supplied by a
post-modifying simple pronoun only. Such a pattern compares syntactically with the
genitive construction (see section 7 below), where the possessor immediately follows
the possessed item:

(66)   syniad <u>John</u> oedd o   *(it was John's idea)*
      idea   John   was he

But it is problematic whether a pattern like that in (65) occurs to any great extent, and it is certainly sub-standard (though it is one of a number of sub-standard forms which seem to have a disturbingly high frequency in the speech of young children).

The discussion of articles and possessive pronouns can be concluded with the observation that they never occur together. Sentences like the following are not found:

(67)   (i)   *'dwi ddim yn licio <u>y</u> <u>ei</u> gar   (*I don't like the
            am I NEG in   like the his car   his car)

       (ii) *'dwi ddim yn licio <u>ei</u> gar o <u>yma</u>   (*I don't like his
            am I   NEG in   like his car he here   car here)

There thus exists a situation which can be summarised as follows:

(68) $\begin{bmatrix} ARTICLE \\ POSSESSIVE\ PRONOUN \end{bmatrix}$ NOUN $\begin{bmatrix} (DEMONSTRATIVE) \\ \begin{Bmatrix} (PERSONAL\ PRONOUN) \\ (REFLEXIVE\ PRONOUN) \end{Bmatrix} \end{bmatrix}$

In (68) we have a representation of the situation where the article can co-occur with the demonstrative or by itself, and the possessive pronoun can co-occur with either a personal pronoun or a reflexive pronoun or by itself.

3d   The remaining determiners

The remaining determiners are distinctive because they do not relate to any post-modifying item. It can be seen from the examples in (40) above that AMBELL (OCCASIONAL) is unique in that when it precedes the head of the noun phrase it is followed by the preposition I (TO, FOR). This particular set of determiners can be divided into two, according to their potentiality to occur with both singular and plural nouns:

(69)   (i)   ... pob car/*ceir ...   (... every car/*cars ...)
             every car/cars

      (ii) ... ambell i   gar/*geir ...   (... an occasional car/*cars ..)
             occasional car/cars

     (iii) ...   rhyw gar/geir   (... some car/cars ...)
             some car/cars

     (iv) ... unrhyw gar/geir ...   (... any car/cars ...)
             any   car/cars ...

      (v) ... dim car/ceir ...   (... no car/cars ...)
             no   car/cars ...

The items POB and AMBELL (I) thus emerge as the only two which are restricted

172

to co-occurrence with singular nouns.

The determiners RHYW (SOME) and UNRHYW (ANY) can theoretically avail the Welsh speaker of a specific (RHYW): non-specific (UNRHYW) contrast. But, as also discussed in chapter IX, section 4h, many Welsh speakers will use RHYW for both specific and non-specific reference:

(70)   *'rydach chi 'n cael y   rhain o*   *(you get these from*
       are   you in have the these from   *some special shop in*
                                         London)
       ryw siop arbennig yn Llundain
       some shop special   in   London

(71)   *'rydach chi 'n cael y   rhain o*   *(you get these from*
       are   you in have the these from   *any shop in the country)*
       ryw/unrhyw   siop yn y wlad
       any   shop in the country

In example (70) the determiner RHYW refers to one specific shop and this reference is not shared by UNRHYW. As example (71) demonstrates, however, RHYW can also be used like UNRHYW for non-specific reference. The item RHYW (SOME) also has a special function of modifying numerals so that the quantification is approximate only:

(72)   *mae yna ryw   gant   yno*   *(there are some hundred*
       is   there some hundred there   *there)*

This function is not shared by UNRHYW.

4   QUANTIFIERS

4a   Introduction

The items which are to be discussed in this section represent a complex area of Welsh grammar but their treatment here will be kept to the simplest form possible. The following examples illustrate that, in addition to the determiners, other items can occur in a pre-modifying position:

(73)   (i)   ... *lot o lyfrau*   *(lot of books)*
               lot of books

      (ii) ... *llawer o lyfrau*   *(many books)*
               many of books

      (iii) ... *digon o lyfrau*   *(enough books)*
               enough of books

(73)	(iv)	... *mwy o lyfrau* more of books	*(more books)*
	(v)	... *mwya' o 'r llyfrau* most of the books	*(most of the books)*
	(vi)	... *rhai o 'r llyfrau* some of the books	*(some of the books)*
	(vii)	... *nifer o lyfrau* number of books	*(number of the books)*
	(viii)	... *mwyafrif o 'r llyfrau* majority of the books	*(majority of the books)*
	(ix)	... *amryw o 'r llyfrau* several of the books	*(several of the books)*
	(x)	... *rhan fwyaf o 'r llyfrau* part most of the books	*(greatest part of the books)*
	(xi)	... *peth o 'r siwgr* some of the sugar	*(some of the sugar)*

Two distinguishing characteristics of these items can be mentioned here. Firstly, they typically occur in a partitive construction (see section 7c below) involving the occurrence of the preposition O (OF) before the head noun. This syntactic point correlates with the semantic function of these items: the partitive structure is used to indicate the quantitative relationship of a part to a whole and all these items quantify the head noun. They can thus be conveniently labelled as QUANTIFIERS. Certain of these items, namely RHAI (SOME), AMRYW (SEVERAL, VARIOUS), PETH (SOME), MWYAFRIF (MAJORITY) and RHAN FWYA' (GREATEST PART) can also occur without the preposition O (OF), as in the following structures: *rhai llyfrau (some books), amryw lyfrau (various books), peth siwgr (some sugar), mwyafrif y llyfrau (majority of the books)* and *rhan fwya'r llyfrau (greatest part of the books)*. In the case of RHAI (SOME) and AMRYW (SEVERAL, VARIOUS), it is suggested that the two structures involve two different functions: when occurring in the partitive structure with O (OF), as in (73) (vi) and (ix) above, both occur as quantifiers referring to an unspecific number from a set of books; but without O (OF) both items occur as determiners with non-specific reference and are not concerned with quantity. The item PETH (SOME) is clearly a quantifier when occurring in the partitive structure but the problem is whether PETH in a determiner environment is a determiner or quantifier. No attempt will be made to resolve this problem here and the analysis will stop at a statement of the descriptive facts. In the case of the remaining two items, MWYAFRIF (MAJORITY) and RHAN FWYA' (GREATEST PART), we have the change from a partitive structure as in (73) (viii) and (x) to a genitive structure (see section 7 below). There do not appear to be any semantic consequences of the sort discussed above, and it is suggested that here we merely have a syntactic choice.

Secondly, quantifiers can be used in co-occurrence with a determiner (as some of the above examples indicate), so that we can have sentences such as:

(74) (i) mae yna <u>lot</u> o '<u>r</u> llyfrau ar y bwrdd   *(there are a lot*
        is   there lot of the books   on the table   *of the books on*
                                                                     the table)

     (ii) mae yna <u>ddigon</u> o '<u>n</u> llyfrau i ar   *(there are enough*
         is   there enough of my   books I on   *of my books on*
                                                                  the table)
         y   bwrdd
         the   table

Positionally, therefore, the quantifiers occur to the left of the determiners in the pre-modification part of the noun phrase.

4b   Sub-types of quantifier

The sub-classification of quantifiers is a complex topic which could be pursued in relation to a number of criteria. For instance, we could take into account the relationship of the quantifier with the definite article when the latter occurs either before the quantifier itself - as with *y mwya'* (the most) and *y rhan fwya'* (the greatest part) but not with *digon* (enough) or *peth* (some), for example; or before the head noun - compare, for instance, the optionality of an article in *lot o'r llyfrau* (lot of the books) but its necessity in *rhai o'r llyfrau* (some of the books) and *peth o'r siwgr* (some of the sugar). This could provide an absorbing study of quantifiers in Welsh. In the present discussion, however, we will limit out remarks on quantifier sub-classification to their relationship with the number features of the head noun.

An interesting situation is found in relation to *mass* and *count* nouns. Of the eleven quantifiers listed in (73) above, only seven can occur with *mass* nouns such as 'MENYN (BUTTER) and EIRA (SNOW):

(75) (i) 'dan ni wedi cael <u>lot</u> o eira   *(we've had a lot of snow)*
        are we after have lot of snow

     (ii) 'dan ni wedi cael <u>llawer</u> o eira   *(we've had much snow)*
         are we after have   much of snow

     (iii) 'dan ni wedi cael <u>digon</u> o eira   *(we've had enough snow)*
          are we after have enough of snow

(75) (iv) *'dan ni wedi cael mwy o eira*   *(we've had more snow)*
        are we after have more of snow

      (v) *'dan ni wedi cael y mwya' o 'r eira*   *(we've had most*
        are we after have the most of the snow   *of the snow)*

     (vi) *'dan ni wedi cael y rhan fwya' o 'r eira* *(we've had the greatest*
        are we after have the part most of the snow   *part of the snow)*

   (vii) *'dan ni wedi cael peth o 'r menyn*   *(we've had some of*
        are we after have some of the butter   *the butter)*

The remaining four - RHAI (SOME), NIFER (NUMBER), MWYAFRIF (MAJORITY) and AMRYW (SEVERAL) - cannot be used with mass nouns: **rhai o 'r eira (*some of the snow), *mwyafrif o 'r eira (*majority of the snow)* and **amryw o 'r eira (*several of the snow). Count* nouns are best discussed in terms of plural and singular nouns separately. As far as plural count nouns are concerned, all of the quantifiers, allowing for dialectal variation in the case of PETH (SOME), can occur: this is demonstrated by (73) (i) - (x) above. In certain (particularly northern) areas the quantifier PETH (SOME) cannot be used with a plural count noun and we do not find examples such as **peth o 'r llyfrau (*some of the books).* But such a use of PETH (SOME) is possible in some southern areas.

Up to this point, therefore, we can distinguish three sub-types of quantifier for northern areas: (i) count quantifiers which occur with plural count nouns - RHAI (SOME), NIFER (NUMBER), MWYAFRIF (MAJORITY), AMRYW (SEVERAL); (ii) mass quantifiers which occur with mass nouns - PETH (SOME) only: (iii) those quantifiers which occur both with plural count nouns and with m. ss nouns - LOT (LOT), LLAWER (MANY, MUCH), DIGON (ENOUGH), MWY (MORE), MWYA' (MOST) and RHAN FWYA' (GREATEST PART). Some southern areas have only two sub-types combining (ii) and (iii) above.

The occurrence of quantifiers with singular count nouns is problematic in certain respects. Firstly, the singular noun must be capable of quantification. Such a noun is STORI (STORY), and it is found that the quantifiers which can occur with STORI (STORY) are those which can occur with mass nouns, i.e. those in (ii) and (iii) above:

(76) (i) *mae yna lot o 'r stori i ddod eto*   *(there's a lot of the*
        is   there lot of the story to come yet   *story to come yet)*

     (ii) *mae yna lawer o 'r stori i ddod eto*   *(there's much of the*
        is there   much of the story to come yet   *story to come yet)*

    (iii) *mae yna ddigon o 'r stori i ddod eto* *(there's enough of the*
        is there enough of the story to come yet *story to come yet)*

(iv)	*mae yna <u>fwy</u> o 'r stori i ddod eto*	*(there's more of the*
	is there more of the story to come yet	story to come yet)

(v)	*mae'r <u>rhan fwya'</u> o 'r stori i ddod eto*	*(the greatest part*
	is the part most of the story to come yet	of the story is to
		come yet)

(vi)	*'roeddwn i 'n licio <u>peth</u> o 'r stori*	*(I liked some of*
	was I in like some of the story	the story)

The problem here is that these quantifiers are not operating with a count function and the occurrence of PETH (SOME), particularly in view of its mass-only usage in some areas, suggests that we have here some sort of mass function. Secondly, the above examples do not include MWYA' (MOST) which is also classed as a count-and-mass quantifier. There may be some difficulty in contextualising occurrences of MWYA' (MOST) with a singular count noun, as a comparison of the following examples suggests:

(77)	*'dan ni wedi cael y <u>mwya'</u> o 'r stori*	*(we've had most of*
	are we after have the most of the story	the story)

(78)	*??mae'r <u>mwya'</u> o 'r stori i ddod eto*	*(most of the story*
	is the most of the story to come yet	is to come yet)

While example (77) may be acceptable, example (78) is far more problematic. We will not pursue these points; for our purpose the sub-categorisation of quantifiers into mass-only, count-only, and mass-and-count — or count-only and mass-and-count, depending upon dialectal usage — will suffice.

5   RELATIVE CLAUSES

5a   Relative clauses and recursivness

In the post-modification of nouns, the most important factor is the occurrence of RELATIVE CLAUSES. Consider the following example:

(79)	*mae John wedi gweld y <u>mwncïod</u>*	*(John has seen the*
	is John after see the monkeys	monkeys which have
	<u>sydd wedi dianc o 'r sŵ</u>	escaped from the zoo)
	is after escape from the zoo	

Example (79) contains a noun phrase, Y MWNCÏOD SYDD WEDI DIANC O'R SŴ, with noun MWNCÏOD and relative clause SYDD WEDI DIANC O'R SŴ. A relative clause is basically a sentence which occurs after a noun: relative clauses are thus another instance of the recursive nature of language. Example (79) can be analysed as containing two elementary sentences.

(80)   (i)   *mae John wedi gweld y mwncïod*   *(John has seen the*
           is   John after see   the monkeys   monkeys)

(ii)   *mae'r   mwncïod wedi dianc o'r sŵ* *(the monkeys have*
           is   the   monkeys after escape from the zoo escaped from the
                                                                             zoo)

Their combined co-occurrences can be illustrated by the branching-diagram in example (81) on page 179.

As (81) stands, it would eventually produce a sentence as follows:

(82)   *MAE JOHN WEDI GWELD Y MWNCÏOD MAE'R MWNCÏOD*
       IS   JOHN AFTER   SEE THE MONKEYS IS THE MONKEYS

      WEDI DIANC   O'R   SŴ
      AFTER ESCAPE FROM THE ZOO

Such a structure does not represent an acceptable sentence, and a *relativisation transformation* is necessary; this deletes the second identical occurrence of Y MWNCÏOD, and in the case of MAE the copula form is altered to SYDD, producing the sentence in example (79).

5b   Relative particles

Formal written Welsh commonly has the relative particles A or Y(R) following the head noun of the noun phrase when this is relativised:

(83)   *gwelodd John y mwncïod a   oedd wedi*   *(John saw the monkeys*
       saw   John the monkeys PT was after   *which had escaped*
                                                from the zoo)
      dianc   o 'r sŵ
      escape from the zoo

(84)   *gwelodd John y sŵ yr oedd y mwncïod*   *(John saw the zoo (that)*
       saw   John the zoo PT was the monkeys   *the monkeys had*
                                                escaped from it)
      wedi dianc ohono
      after escape from it

The rules for selecting either A or Y (R) are given in considerable detail by traditional grammars of Welsh (see, for instance, Williams, 1959: 221-3). Here we will briefly note that A is used where a noun phrase is relativised as in (83) above, whereas Y (R) is used where the noun from a prepositional phrase, as in (84) above, or an adverbial construction is relativised.

In spoken Welsh these particles rarely occur and we tend to have:

(81)

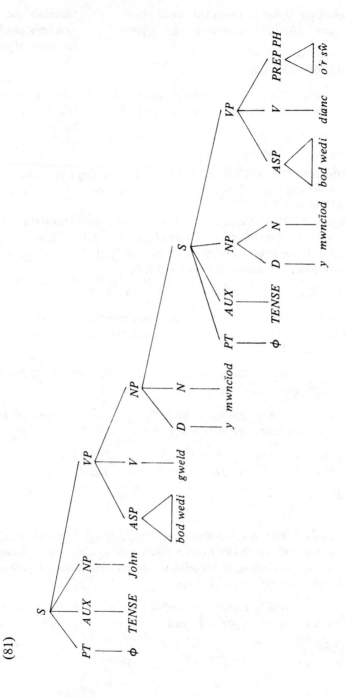

179

(85) mi welodd John y mwncïod oedd wedi
      PT saw John the monkeys was after

      dianc   o 'r sŵ
      escape from the zoo

*(John saw the
monkeys which
had escaped from
the zoo)*

(86) mi welodd John y sŵ oedd y mwncïod
      PT saw John the zoo was the monkeys

      wedi dianc ohono
      after escape from it

*(John saw the zoo
(that) the monkeys
had escaped from)*

The only relative marker in spontaneous Welsh is the SYDD form, as in example (79) above. Other than this, the relative particles are a fairly consistent stylistic marker of formal Welsh.

Note that it is only the MAE (IS) paradigm that involves a special form for relativisation, as indeed it does for inversion (see chapter IX, section 2), interrogation (chapter IX, section 3) and negation (chapter IX, section 4); the MAE (IS) paradigm thus emerges as the most irregular verbal form in Welsh.

5c   Copy pronouns

Relativisation compares very closely with inversion (see chapter IX, section 2) and exhibits similar characteristics. When a noun phrase object is relativised, for instance, a copy pronoun is inserted:

(87)   (i)   'dwi wedi colli y gyllell
             am I after lose the knife

(I've lost the knife)

→ (ii) wyt ti wedi gweld y gyllell?
        are you after see the knife

(have you seen the knife?)

(88)   wyt ti wedi gweld y gyllell dwi
       are you after see the knife am I

       wedi (ei) cholli
       after its   lose

*(have you seen the knife
that I've lost?)*

The pronoun itself is not always consistently realised, although its mutating effect is retained. Again, where the relativised noun is taken from a prepositional phrase, the preposition remains in position, and is inflected if inflection is possible; otherwise there is the possibility of using a copy pronoun:

(89)   'dwi wedi colli'r papur yr oeddwn i 'n
       am I after lose the paper PT was I   I in

       edrych   arno
       look   on (it)

*(I've lost the paper
I was looking at)*

180

(90) dyma   'r dyn yr oeddwn i 'n dadlau am   *(here's the man*
here   is the man PT was   I in argue about   *I was arguing*
about the game
y gem efo fo   *with)*
the game with him

In spontaneous Welsh the preposition sometimes remains uninflected, giving examples such as *'dwi wedi colli'r papur yr oeddwn i'n edrych ar* and *dyma'r dyn yr oeddwn i'n dadlau am y gem efo.*

5d   Relative clause complexity

It is possible to have more than one relative clause modifying the same noun. Consider the following:

(91) (i)   mae'r   dyn yn arwain y parti   *(the man is leading the*
is the man in lead   the party   *party)*

(ii) mae'r dyn yn gwneud trwbl   *(the man is making trouble)*
is the man in   make trouble

On the basis of these two sentences it is possible to have a complex relative clause:

(92) mi welais i 'r dyn sy 'n arwain y parti   *(I saw the man who*
PT saw I the man is in lead the party   *is leading the party*
and who is making
ac   sy 'n gwneud trwbl   *trouble)*
and is   in   make trouble

Similarly, we have occurrences of a relative clause which itself contains a relative clause. Consider the following:

(93) (i)   mae John yn licio'r ferch   *(John likes the girl)*
is John in   like the girl

(ii) mae'r ferch yn dreifio'r car   *(the girl drives the car)*
is the girl in   drive the car

(iii) mae'r car yn gwneud sŵn   *(the car makes a noise)*
is the car in make   noise

On the basis of these three sentences, an example such as the following can be produced:

(94) mae John yn licio'r ferch sy'n dreifio'r   *(John likes the girl*
is John in like the girl is in drive the   *who drives the car*
that makes a noise)
car sy   'n gwneud sŵn
car is   in   make   noise

181

The complexity of the relative clauses in (92) and (94) can be represented by the branching-diagrams in examples (95) and (96) on pages 183 and 184.

In example (92), as the branching-diagram in (95) illustrates, we have a head noun Y DYN (THE MAN) which is relativised twice to give a double relative clause. In deep structure this is represented by using two co-ordinated sentences both of which relate to Y DYN (THE MAN). In example (94), as illustrated by the branching-diagram in (96), the complex relativisation is quite different, in that one relative sentence contains another relative: the relative sentence *sy 'n gwneud sŵn (which makes a noise)* relates to *y car (the car)*, itself part of the relative *sy 'n dreifio 'r car (who drives the car)*.

5e   Adjectives and prepositional phrases

Relative clauses provide the source for two common constituents of noun phrases, *adjectives* and *prepositional phrases*. Consider the following sentences:

(97)   'dwi wedi gweld <u>y   car melyn</u>   *(I've seen the yellow car)*
        am I after   see   the car yellow

(98)   mae'r llyfrau ar y   bwrdd   yn   *(the books on the table*
        is the books on the   table   in   *belong to John)*

        perthyn i John
        belong to John

In the first example the head noun is followed by an adjective, while in the second it is followed by a prepositional phrase. In both cases relative clauses are possible:

(99)   'dwi wedi gweld <u>y   car sy   'n felyn</u>   *(I've seen the car which*
        am I after see   the car is   in yellow   *is yellow)*

(100)   mae'r llyfrau <u>sydd ar y   bwrdd</u> yn   *(the books which are*
        is the books   is   on the   table   in   *on the table belong*

        perthyn i John   *to John)*
        belong to John

By a process of RELATIVE CLAUSE REDUCTION, only the adjective and prepositional phrase remain to produce the examples in (97) and (98). There are certain adjectives like HEN (OLD) and GWAHANOL (DIFFERENT) which occur in pre-modifying position, and special rules must move them from post-modifying position:

(101)   (i)   'dwi wedi gweld car sy 'n wahanol/hen   *(I've seen a car*
               am I after   see   car is in different/old   *which is different/old)*

(cont. on p.185)

182

(95)

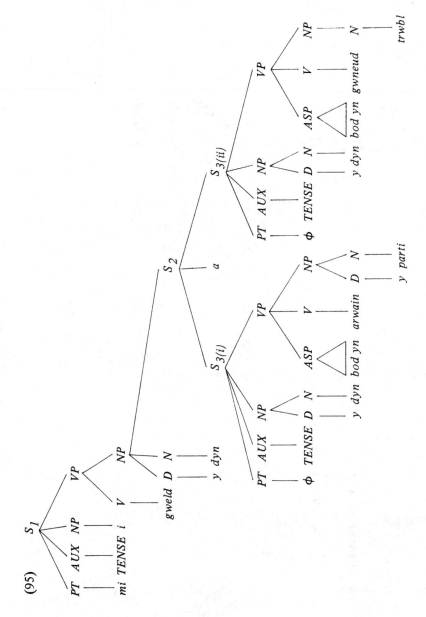

183

(96)

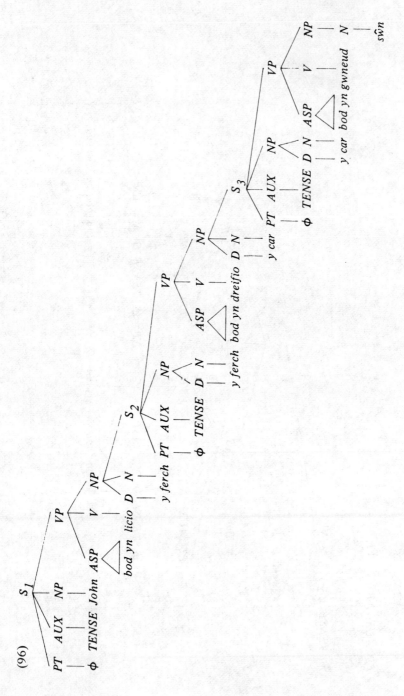

184

	(ii)	'dwi wedi gweld car gwahanol/hen	(I've seen a car
→		am I after see car different/old	different/old)

	(iii)	'dwi wedi gweld gwahanol/hen gar	(I've seen a different/
→		am I after see different/old car	old car)

There are other adjectives for which reduction is obligatory, like PRIF (CHIEF, MAIN), which does not occur in surface structure in a relative clause:

(103) (i)   'rydan ni wedi pasio 'r ffordd sy'n brif   (we've passed the
        are   we after pass the road is the main   road which is main)

→ (ii)   *'rydan ni wedi pasio 'r ffordd brif   (we've passed the
        are   we after pass the road main   road main)

→ (iii)   'rydan ni wedi pasio 'r brif ffordd   (we've passed the
        are   we after pass the main road   main road)

Not all forms occurring in adjectival position, however, come from predicative adjectives in a relative clause. Such is the case with SMOCIWR TRWM (HEAVY SMOKER) and UNION ACHOSION (PRECISE CAUSES). In the first noun phrase the adjective is derived from an adverb:

(104) (i)   mae smociwr yn smocio'n drwm   (a smoker smokes
        is   smoker in smoke in heavy   heavily)

→ (ii)   smociwr sy 'n smocio'n drwm   (smoker who smokes
        smoker is in   smoke in heavy   heavily)

→ (iii)   . . . . . smociwr trwm . . . .   (heavy smoker)
             smoker heavy

Similarly, with the second noun phrase:

(105) (i)   mae'r achosion yn achosi rhywbeth yn union   (the causes
        is the causes   in   cause something in precise   cause something
                                         precisely)

→ (ii)   achosion sy'n achosi rhywbeth yn union   (causes which
        causes   is in cause something in precise   cause something
                                         precisely)

→ (iii)   achosion union   (causes precise)
        causes   precise

→ (iv)   union achosion   (precise causes)
        precise causes

In example (105), the adjective movement rule applies to place UNION (PRECISE) before the head noun.

Adjectives in traditional written Welsh agree with the nouns that they modify in the noun phrase in terms of gender and number. The traditional rules are that singular nouns govern gender concord, producing masculine and feminine forms of certain (but not all) adjectives, while with plural nouns no gender concord arises but certain adjectives (although not all) assume plural forms. The following can illustrate the possibilities with the masculine noun DRWS (DOOR), the feminine DESG (DESK) and the plural noun BOCSYS (BOXES):

(106)   (i)   *drws cryf/trwm/hir/coch*   *(a strong/heavy/long/red*
             door strong/heavy/long/red   *door)*

  (ii)   *desg gref/drom/hir/goch*   *(a strong/heavy/long/red*
             desk strong/heavy/long/red   *desk)*

  (iii)   *bocsys cryfion/trymion/hirion/cochion*   *(strong/heavy/long/red*
             boxes strong/heavy/long/red   *boxes)*

The two adjectives CRYF (STRONG) and TRWM (HEAVY) thus have masculine forms *cryf* and *trwm* and feminine forms *cref* and *trom; hir* and *coch* are examples of adjectives that are unaffected by gender here. All four adjectives have plural forms, giving *cryfion, trymion, hirion* and *cochion.*

Extensive lists of those adjectives which have masculine and feminine forms and those adjectives which have plural forms are given by Williams (1959: 31-8) and Evans (1960: 57-61).

An assessment of the situation in spoken Welsh is difficult because of the different levels of education amongst speakers. But in terms of spontaneous speech, unaffected by the awareness of the possibility of concord which education instils, it is found that the concord of nouns and adjectives is much more restricted than in traditional writing.

Plural forms are very rare as a productive phenomenon and occur primarily in set expressions such as *pethau bychain (little things), dynion duon (black men), mwyar duon (blackberries), storiau byrion (short stories)* and *gwartheg brithion (speckled cows).* The examples in (106) (iii) above would not occur in spontaneous speech; we find that the singular forms occur:

(107)   *bocsys cryf/trwm/hir/coch*   *(strong/heavy/long/red boxes)*
       boxes strong/heavy/long/red

Masculine and feminine forms occur more extensively, and the operation of gender contrasts includes the following: *crwn (round) - cron, dwfn (deep) - dofn, llwm (bare) - llom, trwm (heavy) - trom, byr (short) - ber, cryf (strong) - cref, gwyn (white) - gwen, gwyrdd (green) - gwerdd,* and *hyll (ugly) - hell.* This list includes CRYF (STRONG) and TRWM (HEAVY) exemplified above, but we would not find in spontaneous speech examples such as *cath wleb (wet cat), gardd sech (dry garden)* or *afon seth (straight river)*: rather, we find the masculine forms *cath wlyb, gardd sych* and *afon syth*. With many adjectives the only indication of the noun being feminine is the soft mutation of the adjective, as in the examples just listed.

Adjectives are also traditionally discussed in terms of *degree* - equative degree, comparative degree and superlative degree, as illustrated by the underlined material in the following examples:

(108)   *mae hi cyn oered ag   oedd hi ddoe*   *(it's as cold as it was*
         is she as cold as   was she yesterday   yesterday)

(109)   *mae hi 'n oerach nag oedd hi ddoe*   *(it's colder than it was*
         is she in colder than was she yesterday   yesterday)

(110)   *heddiw ydy'r diwrnod oera'r wythnos yma* *(today is the coldest*
         today is the   day   coldest the week here day this week)

The three degrees have their own characteristics and the details are very well known from traditional grammars. As illustrated by example (108), the equative degree involves pre- and post-occurring equative particles with the adjective medially positioned:

(111)   *EQ PARTICLE ADJECTIVE + EQ SUFFIX EQ PARTICLE*
       cyn   *oer-*   *ed*   *a (g)*

The adjective is inflected by adding the equative suffix -ED. The comparative degree has no-occurring particle but involves an adjective inflected by the comparative suffix -ACH and followed by the comparative particle NA (G):

(112)   *ADJECTIVE + COMP SUFFIX   COMP PARTICLE*
       oer-   *ach*   *na (g)*

The superlative degree has no pre- or post-particles, involving only an adjective inflected by the superlative suffix -A (F):

(113)   *ADJECTIVE + SUP SUFFIX*
       oer-   *a (f)*

The post-occurring degree particles, equative A (G) and comparative NA (G), involve comparison with some other object or entity. The superlative degree is not obviously similar to the equative and comparative degree in these terms. But it could be argued that the superlative degree, too, involves correlation with other objects or entities:

(114)   *heddiw ydy 'r diwrnod oera' o*   *(today is the coldest day*
         today is the   day   coldest of   *of the days of this week)*

         ddiwrnodau 'r   wythnos yma
         days   the   week   here

The prepositional phrase following the superlative adjective marks those objects or entities amongst which the outstanding adjective is superlative.

In addition to an inflectional realisation of degrees of comparison, the same contrasts can be achieved by using analytic or periphrastic patterns. These involve the comparative and superlative degree words MWY (MORE) and MWYA (F) (MOST) (which are themselves comparative and superlative forms of MAWR (BIG)) for the comparative and superlative), and MOR (AS) (also derived from MAWR) for the equative:

(115)   *mae pethau yn edrych mor obeithiol ag o 'r blaen*   *(things look as*
         is things in look   as hopeful as before   *hopeful as before)*

(116)   *mae pethau yn edrych yn fwy gobeithiol nag*   *(things look more*
         is things in look in more hopeful than   *hopeful than before)*

         o 'r blaen
         than before

(117)   *dyma 'r   cynllun sy 'n edrych yn fwya'*   *(this is the plan*
         here is the plan   is in look in   most   *which looks most*

         gobeithiol   *hopeful)*
         hopeful

Choice of the inflected or the analytic system seems to depend upon the syllable length of the adjective for the comparative and superlative. Adjectives of one or two syllables use the inflected system, as with OER (COLD) in examples (108) to (109); whereas adjectives with two or more syllables use the analytic system, as with GOBEITHIOL (HOPEFUL) in examples (115) to (117) above. This rule does not seem to apply with the two alternatives in the formation of the equative degree. Whereas the inflected method may be limited to adjectives of one or two syllables, the uninflected system can apply to adjectives of any number of syllables, as in *mor oer ag oedd hi ddoe (as cold as it was yesterday)*.

The examples of comparatives and superlatives all illustrate *plus degree;* that is, the comparison involves an increase in contrast with other objects or entities. But it is also possible to have *minus degree,* where the comparison involves a decrease. Minus degree with comparative and superlative contrasts does not involve an inflected system but assumes an analytic pattern by using the minus degree words LLAI (LESS) and LLEIA (F) (LEAST) (which are themselves comparative and superlative forms of the adjective BACH (LITTLE)), as illustrated in the following examples:

(118) *mae hi 'n llai oer nag oedd hi ddoe*   *(it is less cold than it*
       is she in less cold than was she yesterday   *was yesterday)*

(119) *heddiw ydy 'r   diwrnod lleia' oer 'r*   *(today is the least cold*
       today is the   day   least cold the   *day this week)*

       wythnos yma
       week   here

In many cases, however, the semantics of the minus comparative degree are achieved by using the equative degree in the negative. Thus, example (118) above could be expressed as follows:

(120) *'dydy hi ddim gyn oered αg oedd hi ddoe*   *(it isn't as cold as it*
       NEG is she NEG as   cold as was she yesterday   *was yesterday)*

This pattern seems to be preferred with adjectives such as TAL (TALL), DEL (PRETTY) and CYFOETHOG (RICH, WEALTHY).

The details of the formation of the various contrasts of plus and minus comparison can be summarised in the following table:

(121)

EQUATIVE		COMPARATIVE	
INFLECTED	*UNINFLECTED*	*INFLECTED*	*UNINFLECTED*
CYN oer-ED A (G)	MOR oer/ obeithiol A (G)	oer-ACH NA (G)	MWY gobeithiol NA (G)
			LLAI oer/ gobeithiol NA (G)

SUPERLATIVE	
INFLECTED	*UNINFLECTED*
oer-A(F)	MWYA(F) gobeithiol
	LLEIA(F) oer/ gobeithiol

The details of the equative contrast in relation to minus degree have been left blank, as possibilities in this area are problematic.

189

Before leaving the question of degree, it can be noted that the equative word MOR and the superlative word MWYA(F) can also occur as intensifiers with adjectives:

(122) 'roedd hi mor oer, mi wnes i wisgo côt arall   (it was so cold,
       was   she so cold PT did I wear coat other   I wore another
                                                             coat)

(123) 'roedd y ffilm mor dda, mi ês i weld o ddwy waith (the film was
       was   the film so good PT went I see it two   time so good, I
                                                             went to see
                                                             it twice)

(124) 'dwi 'n ffeindio gwaith John mwya' diddorol   (I find John's
       am I in find   work John most interesting   work most
                                                           interesting)

(125) mae'r broblem yma yn fwya' od   (this problem is
       is the problem here in most odd   most odd)

The superlative word MWYA' (MOST) in this function may not enjoy widespread use, although it is used by some speakers especially in the expression *mwya' diddorol (most interesting)*. As intensifier-types relating to adjectives, MOR and MWYA(F) are not the same: only the latter can be paraphrased by the intensifier IAWN (VERY), for example:

(126) *'roedd hi 'n oer iawn, mi wneis i wisgo côt arall (*it was very cold, I
           was she in cold very PT did I wear coat other wore another coat)

(127) 'dwi 'n ffeindio gwaith John yn ddiddorol   iawn (I find John's work
       am I in find   work John in interesting very   very interesting)

The intensifier MOR seems to be capable of establishing those circumstance which condition the occurrence of another action. But it can also occur without any consequential action; the action expressed in the accompanying clauses of examples (122) and (123) above could be deleted, giving a simple evaluation of the extent of the cold or the quality of the film.

5f   A possible ambiguity

Finally, we can note a possible ambiguity with relative clauses of the following type:

(128) 'dwi 'n nabod y dyn a welodd y ddynes   (I know the man who
       am I in know the man PT saw   the woman   saw the woman/the
                                                       woman saw)

The ambiguity resides in whether the noun phrases in the relative clause are subjects or objects. In effect, the relative can be derived from either of:

190

(129) (i) *mi welodd y dyn y ddynes*   *(the man saw the woman)*
            PT saw   the man the woman

       (ii) *mi welodd y   ddynes y dyn*   *(the woman saw the man)*
            PT saw the   woman the man

Such examples can be disambiguated however, by using a carrier auxiliary such as
GWNEUD (see chapter V, sections 1 and 2):

(130) (i) *'dwi 'n nabod y dyn y gwnaeth y*   *(I know the man the*
            am I in know the man PT did   the   *woman saw)*

            ddynes ei weld
            woman his see

       (ii) *'dwi 'n nabod y dyn a wnaeth*   *(I know the man who*
            am I in   know the man PT   did   *saw the woman)*

            weld y ddynes
            see the woman

The nature of the surface configurations with a carrier auxiliary allow the noun
phrase subject and noun phrase object to be clearly distinguished.

6 NOUN PHRASE CONSTITUENT STRUCTURE: SUMMARY

The discussion of the noun phrase presented in this chapter is a partial account which
has looked at *nouns, determiners, quantifiers* and *relative clauses* (the source for
demonstratives YMA (HERE), YNA (THERE) and ACW(YONDER), prepositional
phrases, adjectives and many other items). The noun is the one obligatory constituent
of the noun phrase. The quantifiers and determiners occur before the noun in that
order, while relative clauses follow the noun. But all these items are optional additions
to the constituent structure of the noun phrase and can, therefore, be enclosed in
round brackets in the following re-write rule:

(131) *NP* → *(Q) (DET) N (S)*

There are many other items involved in the noun phrase, as the initial illustrative
example (1) suggests, and the account given above is by no means a full discussion of
the noun phrase in Welsh.[1] The rule in (131), detailing the structure of the noun phrase
as discussed in this chapter, can be incorporated into the general set of rules representing
the syntax of Welsh sentences by developing the rules given in (60) of chapter VI as
follows:

(132) (i) *S*   →   *PT AUX NP VP*

(132) (ii) *AUX* → $\left\{\begin{array}{l}\textit{-ITH}\\\textit{-AI}\\\textit{-ODD}\end{array}\right\}$

(iii) *VP* → $(ASP)\left\{\begin{array}{l}V\left\{\begin{array}{lll}\textit{(NP)}&\textit{(PP)}&\textit{(PP)}\\\textit{(PRED.PH)}&&\end{array}\right\}\\COP\left\{\begin{array}{l}\textit{PRED PH}\\\textit{NP}\\\textit{PP}\end{array}\right\}\end{array}\right\}$

(iv) *ASP* → $\left\{\begin{array}{l}\textit{PERFECT}\\\textit{RECENT PERFECT}\end{array}\right\}$ *and/or* $\left\{\begin{array}{l}\textit{PROGRESSIVE}\\\textit{IMMINENT}\end{array}\right\}$

(v) *PP* → *P* *NP*

(vi) *PRED. PH* → $\left\{\begin{array}{l}YN\left\{\begin{array}{l}\textit{NP}\\\textit{ADJ}\end{array}\right\}\\FEL/COP\underline{\quad}NP\end{array}\right\}$

(vii) *NP* → *(Q) (DET) N (S)*

The set of rules given in (132) represent the details of Welsh syntax so far discussed in this book. The entry for the noun phrase is placed last so that it can refer to all the occurrences of a noun phrase in the rules - in (132) (i), (iii), (v), and (vi).

7   THE GENITIVE CONSTRUCTION IN WELSH

7a   Introduction

Apart from the characteristics of sequential ordering and certain aspects of the relationships involved, the nature of the genitive construction in Welsh is not fully understood at this stage. In particular, it is not known how it relates to the structure of the noun phrase. The discussion of the genitive is, however, included in this chapter because of certain superficial connections with the material of the noun phrase.

7b   The structure of the genitive construction

The genitive construction in Welsh can be illustrated by the structures underlined in the following in the following examples:

(133) *mae Mair wedi gweld <u>car yr athro</u>*   *(Mair has seen the*
       is Mair after see   car the teacher   *teacher's car)*

192

(134) *mae John wedi dwyn <u>het merch</u>*   *(John has stolen a*
       is John after steal   hat girl   *girl's hat)*

(135) *mae pawb   yn licio <u>brawd Gwil</u>*   *(everyone likes Gwil's*
       is everyone   in like   brother Gwil   *brother)*

Basically, the genitive construction involves the ordering of a noun which indicates
the thing possessed, which can be labelled *possessum,* and a noun which indicates
the *possessor.* They are ordered in such a way that the possessum precedes the
possessor:

(136) *POSSESSUM*   *POSSESSOR*

       het   *merch*
       brawd   *Gwil*

It is to be noted that features of definiteness involving definite determiners, such as
the definite article, relate only to the possessor. In terms of sequential order, any
definite marker relating to the possessor occurs immediately before the possessor as
in example (133) above, thus adopting the usual position of determiners (see section
3 above) as regards the noun to which that they relate. Thus:

(137) *POSSESSUM*   *DET*   *POSSESSOR*

       car   *yr*   *athro*

The possessum itself is never modified by a definite marker, and sentences such as
the following are impossible:

(138) **mae Mair wedi gweld y car yr athro*   *(*Mair has seen the*
       is Mair after see the car the teacher   *doctor's the car)*

(139) **mae John wedi dwyn yr het merch*   *(*John has stolen a*
       is   John after steal the hat girl   *girl's the hat)*

The possessum is thus always indefinite in genitive constructions. In passing, a
distinction can be introduced between a genitive construction and similar-looking
nominal compounds which can take up an initially-positioned determiner. An example
such as *het plismon (a policeman's hat)* is ambiguous. We can be referring to an
ordinary hat which belongs to a policeman: here we have a genitive construction, and
a definite article only occurs medially to give *het y plismon (the policeman's hat).* Or,
we can be referring to a special sort of hat which is part of a policeman's uniform: in
this sense we have a nominal compound and the determiner can occur initially to
give *yr het plismon (the policeman's hat)* - though, of course, in this case the
determiner cannot occur medially.

7c   The genitive construction and the partitive construction

The *partitive* construction can be illustrated by the underlined items in the following examples:

(140) 'dwi wedi colli rhan o 'r llyfr   (I've lost part of the
       am I after lose part of the book   book)

(141) mae Mair wedi clywed darn o 'r newyddion   (Mair has heard a
       is Mair after hear part of the news   piece of the news)

In these examples, we have a construction which is made up of a noun followed by a prepositional phrase involving the prepositional form O (OF):

(142) NOUN   'O' + NP

       rhan   o 'r   llyfr
       darn   o   newyddion

In each case, the initial noun indicates a *part* of the noun in the noun phrase, hence the label 'partitive construction'. The preposition O (OF) has the function of indicating the partitive relationship between the initial noun and the noun of the prepositional phrase.

The genitive construction and partitive construction in Welsh are quite distinct. Note, in passing, that the first noun of a partitive construction can be preceded by the definite article, as in . . . *y darn o 'r newyddion (. . . the part of the news)*. No attempt has been made to define the semantics of the genitive construction, but that it is different from the partitive construction can be illustrated by comparing the instances in examples (140) and (141) above with the following:

(143) 'dwi wedi colli clawr y   llyfr   (I've lost the cover
       am I after lose cover the book   of the book)

       mae Mair yn licio cynnwys y newyddion   (Mair likes the contents
       is Mair in like   contents the news   of the news)

The genitive construction is not involved in the expression of a partitive relationship.

7d   The genitive construction and the pronominal possessive pattern

It is interesting to compare the genitive construction with the occurrence of the possessive pattern in the noun phrase (see section 3c above):

(145) 'dwi wedi colli 'n llyfr   (I've lost my book)
       am I after lose my book

(146) 'dwi wedi colli ei lyfr o   (I've lost his book)
       am I after lose his book he

194

(147) *'dwi wedi colli llyfr John*   *(I've lost John's book)*
        am I after lose boook John

It can be seen that the personal pronouns positioned finally in the possessive construction in the noun phrase compare sequentially with the positioning of the possessor in the genitive construction. This may explain the possible occurrence of a personal pronoun alone in the possessive construction (mentioned in section 3c above), where the pattern of the genitive construction is retained:

(148) *syniad Mair oedd o*   *(it was Mair's idea)*
        idea Mair was it

(149) *syniad hi oedd o*   *(it was her idea)*
        idea she was it

The noun of the genitive construction is merely pronominalised to produce the possessive-type construction in (149).

8   PRONOUNS

8a   Personal pronouns

Welsh possesses threee formally distinct sets of personal pronouns, which can be illustrated by the underlined items in the following examples:

(150) *'roeddwn i 'n cwyno*   *(I was complaining)*
        was   I in   complain

(151) *yfi   oedd yn cwyno*   *(it was I who was*
        EMPH I was in complain   *complaining)*

(152) *'roeddwn innau   'n cwyno*   *(I too was complaining)*
        was   CONJ I in complain

Traditional names can be used to label these three types. Thus, the pronoun in (150) is a simple pronoun which is best explained negatively in comparison with the other two types. In (151) the pronoun is a *reduplicated* pronoun whose function is an *emphatic* one and, in consequence, typically occurs in the initial position of inverted sentences. In (152) the pronoun INNAU is a *conjunctive* pronoun which implicitly involves a co-ordinated relationship with another person; thus, in this example, the fact that the first person subject was complaining relates to the fact that someone else was complaining. The simple pronouns are selected when neither emphatic nor co-ordinated or conjunctive reference is required.

Within these three types, personal pronouns involve *number* contrast of singular and plural, *person* contrast of first, second and third, and *gender* contrast of masculine and feminine in relation to the third person singular only. The actual forms involved vary according to medium; written and spoken forms differ in certain respects and within the spoken medium further dialect differences are to be found. All these points can be represented in the following table:

(153)

		SINGULAR			
		FIRST	SECOND	THIRD	
				Masc.	Fem.
Simple	S	I-FI-MI	TI/CHDI	(F)O/(F)E	HI
	W	MI	TI	EF	HI
Reduplicated	S	(Y)FI	(Y)TI/(Y)CHDI	(Y)FO/(Y)FE	(Y)HI
	W	MYFI	TYDI	EFE	HYHI
Conjunctive	S	INNAU-FINNAU-(M)INNAU	TITHAU/CHDITHAU	FYNTAU	HITHAU
	W	MINNAU	TITHAU	YNTAU	HITHAU

		PLURAL		
		FIRST	SECOND	THIRD
Simple	S	NI	CHI	N (H) W
	W	NI	CHWI	HWY/HWYNT
Reduplicated	S	(Y)NI	(Y)CHI	(Y) N (H) W
	W	NYNI	CHWYCHWI	HWYNTHWY
Conjunctive	S	NINNAU	CHITHAU	N (H) WTHAU
	W	NINNAU	CHWITHAU	HWYTHAU

S = spoken   W = written

Apart from the written versus spoken contrasts, which will be considered briefly below, there are a variety of choices within the spoken medium, discussion of which introduces a considerable amount of detail. The various choices can be collated as follows.

Firstly, there are syntactic choices, where the selection of a form depends upon the

196

syntactic environment. This applies to the first person singular pronouns simple and conjunctive and is indicated in the above table by dashes: I—FI—MI and INNAU—FINNAU—MINNAU. The 'i' type (I, INNAU) can be illustrated by I. It occurs in two environments, namely, wherever a first person singular inflection occurs in verbal or prepositional forms and in the discontinuous pronominal pattern involving either verbs or nouns. Both environments can be illustrated as follows:

(154) (i) *mi welais i John neithiwr*   *(I saw John last night)*
            PT saw I John last night

       (ii) *'roedd hi 'n dod ata' i*   *(she was coming to me)*
            was she in come to I

(155) (i) *mae o wedi 'ngweld i*   *(he has seen me)*
            is he after my see   I

       (ii) *mae hi wedi colli 'n llyfr i*   *(she has lost my book)*
            is she after lose my book I

In the case of the -ITH inflection and also in the case of the prepositional inflection, the suffix itself ends in 'f' [v] in written Welsh, and any occurrences of FI in this environment can be attributed to the phonetic conditioning produced by the final 'f' [v] of the inflection. Brief exemplification can be given as follows:

(156) *gwelaf   fi John yn dod ataf fi*   *(I see John coming to me)*
       see + ITH   I John in come to   me

As it stands, this example is not an accurate representation of written Welsh, since the pronouns would tend to be deleted (see chapter IX, section 5b), but it will serve to illustrate the point. The 'm' type (MI, MINNAU) occurs after the preposition I (FOR, TO), and can be illustrated as follows:

(157) *mae rhaid i mi/minnau fynd*   *(I/I too must go)*
       is necessity for I/CONJ I go

All other environments see the occurrence of FI or FINNAU and typical instances include object position and comparatives:

(158) *mi welodd John fi/finnau*   *(John saw me/me too)*
       PT saw   John I CONJ I

(159) *mae hi 'n hyn na fi/finnau*   *(she's older than me/me too)*
       is she in older than I/CONJ I

There is, however, an interesting possibility whereby the 'f' [v] type can occur immediately following a verb or noun in place of the 'i' type in the discontinuous pattern:

(160) *mae hi wedi 'mrifo fi*   *(she has hurt me)*
       is she after my hurt i

As the example suggests, this tends to occur where the verb ends in a vowel.

Secondly, there are choices which are entirely conditioned by the preceding phonetic environment. This applies to the simple and reduplicative second person singular pronouns TI or DI and TITHAU or DITHAU, and the simple third person singular masculine pronouns FO or O and FE or E. The following examples illustrate the conditions:

(161) (i)   *mi weli   di/dithau John heno*   *(you/you too will*
             PT see + ITH you/you too John tonight   see John tonight)

       (ii) *mi welaist   ti/tithau John neithiwr   (you/you too saw*
             PT see + ODD you/you too John last night   John last night)

(162) (i)   *mi fyddai   fo/fe yn gweithio bob nos   (he used to work*
             PT used to be   he in   work every night   every night)

       (ii) *mi fydd   o/e yn gweithio bob   nos   (he 'll be working*
             PT will be he in   work   every night   every night)

In the case of TI or DI and TITHAU or DITHAU, the initial consonantal choice of 't' [t] or 'd' [d] is a contrast of voicing, which is governed by the voice features of the immediately preceding inflection. Thus in (161) (i), which is voiced, DI or DITHAU occurs, but in (161) (ii), which is voiceless, TI or TITHAU occurs. In the case of the third person singular, the choice of FO/FE or O/E is determined by the occurrence of a vocalic or consonantal-ending inflection. If the inflection terminates vocalically, as in (162) (i), FO/FE occurs, but if the inflection terminates consonantally, as in (162) (ii), O/E occurs. The exception is the MAE (IS) form, which is followed by O/E even though it involves a vocalic termination:

(163) *mae o/e 'n dod*   *(he's coming)*
       is   he in come

It must be added, however, that there are dialects where FE or FO can occur in this environment to give examples such as *ma' fo/fe 'n dod (he's coming)*.

Thirdly, there are dialectal choices. This applies to the simple and reduplicated third person singular masculine pronouns (F)O or (F)E and YFO or YFE, the simple, reduplicated and conjunctive second person singular pronouns TI or CHDI, YTI or YCHDI and TITHAU or CHDITHAU, and the simple, reduplicated and conjunctive third person plural pronouns NHW or NW, YNHW or YNW and NHWTHAU or NWTHAU.

Fourthly, one should also note that the initial *y* [ə] of the spoken reduplicated pronouns is not always used. Consequently, the same forms as the simple pronoun* sometimes occur in inverted patterns where emphasis is involved.

8b   Possessive pronouns

Possessive pronouns are discussed in section 3c of this chapter. Here, brief consideration can be given to a different type of possessive pronoun which is contained in the traditional paradigm:

(164)   *eiddof (mine)*   *eiddom (ours)*
        eiddot (yours)   *eiddoch (yours)*
        eiddo (his)   *eiddynt (theirs)*
        eiddi (hers)

These forms occur solely in varieties of formal Welsh, and the only regular occurrence is that of the second person plural as a letter-closing device:

(165)   *yr eiddoch   yn gywir*   *(yours truly)*
        the yours   in   true

However, within the formal usage of these forms there are two possible functions. Firstly, they can be used with pronominal reference to represent a possessive relationship of the type discussed in section 3c of this chapter; secondly, they can be used to signify ownership. Examples of both tend to be extremely stylised:

(166)   *pa   dŷ   yw'r eiddoch?*   *(which house is yours?)*
        which house is the yours

(167)   *mae safle can   erw o eiddo 'r fyddin*   *(there is a site of one*
        is   site hundred arces of POSS the army   *hundred acres belonging*
                                                       to the army)

In spontaneous Welsh, both patterns assume different forms. The pronominal substitute type is expressed by using a possessive pattern along with indefinite pronouns UN (ONE) or RHAI (SOME). Example (166) would be rendered as:

(168)   *pa   dŷ   yw 'ch   un chi?*   *(which house is yours?)*
        which house is   yours one you

The paradigm of this type equivalent to that in (164) above is as follows:

(169)   *yn un/rhai i*   *yn un/rhai ni*
        dy un/rai di   *ych un/rhai chi*
        i un/rai o   *i un/rhai nhw*
        i un/rhai hi

Ownership as expressed in example (167) above is conveyed in spontaneous Welsh by the verb PERTHYN (BELONG):

(170)   mae safle can   erw sy 'n perthyn i 'r fyddin   *(there is a site*
        is   site hundred   acres is in belong to the army   *of one hundred*
                                                                        acres which
                                                                        belongs to the
                                                                        army)

Finally, it can be noted that the form EIDDO also occurs as a noun with the meaning of 'property'.

8c   Reflexive pronouns

In Welsh, reflexive pronouns involve a combination of a possessive pronoun (see section 3c above) with the form HUN, HUNAN or HUNAIN. The possibilities of combination produce at least three stylistic and dialectal systems. Traditional grammars (Morris-Jones, 1913: 306-7; Williams, 1959: 76-8) note that some users select HUN with both singular and plural forms while others select HUNAN for singular (including the second plural when it is used respectfully with singular reference) and HUNAIN for plural. There is also a third system used in northern areas, where HUN (again including the respectful use of the second plural) occurs with singular forms and HUNAN occurs with plural forms. These three systems can be represented as follows:

(171)

	(i)	(ii)	(iii)
FIRST SING	*fy hun*	*yn/fy hunan*	*yn/fy hun*
SECOND SING	*dy hun*	*dy hunan*	*dy hun*
THIRD SING	*ei hun*	*'i hunan*	*'i hun*
FIRST PLURAL	*ein hun*	*yn hunain*	*yn hunan*
SECOND PLURAL	*eich hun*	*ych hunain*	*ych hunan*
THIRD PLURAL	*eu hun*	*'i hunain*	*'i hunan*

The system in (171) (i) is recorded in traditional grammars and is thus represented in traditional written forms. The remaining two systems occur in speech and are represented in spoken forms. It can be noted, however, that the written form FY (MY) regularly occurs in speech in the reflexive pattern along with the more usual form YN (MY).

The study of reflexive pronouns is quite a complex subject. Their description here will be conducted on fairly simple lines in relation to the following three contexts:

(172)   *'dwi wedi brifo yn hun*   *(I've hurt myself)*
        am I after hurt myself

(173)   *mae 'r athrawon   'i hunain wedi dod*   *(the teachers themselves*
        is the teachers themselves after come   *have come)*

200

(174) *mae Mair wedi colli 'i goriad 'i hun*   *(Mair has lost*
    is Mair after lose her key   herself   *her own key)*

On the basis of these three examples, the general point can be made that a reflexive pronoun shares the same reference as a noun or pronoun in the same sentence. Thus, in (172) I (I) and YN HUN are identical, in (173) YR ATHRAWON and 'I HUNAIN are identical, and in (174) MAIR and 'I HUN are identical. But within this general function two distinctions can be made. Firstly, examples (173) and (174) above involve emphasis. In the case of (173), which emphasises a noun, the reflexive pronoun can adopt alternative positioning at the end of the sentence:

(175) *mae'r   athrawon wedi dod 'i hunain*   *(the teachers have*
    is the   teachers after come themselves   *come themselves)*

In the case of (174), involving a possessive pattern, no alternative position is possible. But note that similar emphasis can also be produced by using a personal pronoun with appropriate stress:

(176) *mae Mair wedi colli 'i goriad hi*   *(Mair has lost her*
    is Mair after lose her key she   *(own) key)*

As discussed in section 3c above, where the possessor has already been established, the personal pronoun can be left out. Its retention, therefore, produces an emphatic effect. Relevant here is the point discussed following example (63) in the examination of the possessive pattern, that the reflexive pronoun can also be used for emphasis along with the personal pronoun in the possessive pattern: *yn syniad i fy hun oedd o (it was my own idea)* and *ei gar o 'i hun oedd o (it was his own car)*.

Secondly, example (172) is quite different, in that it does not involve emphasis. In this particular instance, the noun phrase in object position has the same reference as that of the subject noun phrase. In these circumstances a reflexive pronoun is compulsory and a pattern involving a personal pronoun is unacceptable:

(177) **'dwi wedi 'mrifo fi*   *(*I have hurt me)*
    am I after my hurt I

(178) **mi fedra' i ngweld i*   *(*I can see me)*
    PT can I my see I

Moreover, when a reflexive pronoun is used in this way, there is no need for a co-occurring possessive pronoun as happens with personal pronouns. The reflexive pronoun tends to occur by itself, as in example (172) above, although it may be that with some verbs a possessive pronoun can also be introduced. Further remarks about reflexive pronouns are also found in the discussion of reflexive verbs in chapter III, section 3a.

8d   Reciprocal pronouns

Reciprocal pronouns are formed in Welsh by combining in sequence the *plural* possessive pronouns with the form GILYDD:

(179)   *yn gilydd (each other)*
        ych gilydd (each other)
        'i gilydd (each other)

Reciprocity is discussed in chapter X, section 2h, and reference is made there to the reciprocal pronouns. Here, we will briefly note that the possessive pronoun agrees with the subject of the sentence:

(180)   *'dan ni 'n nabod yn gilydd*   *(we know each other)*
        are we in know our other

(181)   *'dach chi 'n mynd efo 'ch gilydd?*   *(are you going with*
        are you in go   with your other   *each other?)*

(182)   *maen nhw wedi brifo 'i   gilydd*   *(they have hurt each*
        are they after hurt their other   *other)*

A certain amount of controversy has surrounded these forms in the past, especially when used in the written medium (see Morris-Jones, 1913: 305-6). In particular, it has been argued that the singular EI and not the plural EU should be used for the third plural type - the third singular being the original form in an earlier construction. This problem does not arise in speech, when both have the same pronunciation, as discussed earlier.

8e   Demonstrative pronouns

There are eight forms which are demonstrative pronouns in Welsh and they can be listed as follows:

(183)   *HWN*   *HWNNA*
        HON   *HONNA*
        HYN   *HYNNA*
        (R)HAIN   *(R)HEINA*

As pronouns, these forms can be used where the speaker uses a *spatial* reference; that is, where a physical reference is made to an object or person in the immediate environment:

(184)   *pwy ydy hon?*   *(who is this?)*
        who is this

(185)   *dwi ddim yn licio rheina*   *(I do not like those)*
        am I NEG in like those

202

However, they can also be used with *anaphoric* reference; that is, where the reference is to an object or person expressed in the discourse and not physically present in the environment, as the following example illustrates:

(186)   *dyna syniad John - tydi hwn ddim yn syniad da*   *(there's John's*
        there's idea John   NEG is this NEG in idea good   idea - this isn't
                                                         a good idea)

The most frequent use probably involves spatial reference.

The forms can be sub-divided into those where the reference is to an object which is regarded as being 'near' or 'far' by the speaker. The former gives HWN, HON, HYN and (R)HAIN and the latter gives HWNNA, HONNA, HYNNA and (R)HEINA. These latter forms are derived from a combination involving the first set with the demonstrative determiner (see section 3b earlier) YNA (THERE), thus HWN YNA → HWNNA, HON YNA → HONNA, HYN YNA → HYNNA and RHAI YNA → RHEINA. Contrasts can be illustrated as follows:

(187)   *mae Mair wedi prynu hwn/hwnna*   *(Mair has brought this/that)*
        is   Mair after   buy   this/that

(188)   *faint   ydy rhain/rheina?*   *(how much are these/those?)*
        how much is   these/those

The contrasts of 'far' and 'near' are not absolute but depend upon the speaker's own interpretations. Very often these interpretations are influenced by direction of movement. Thus, a person who is a mile away but is approaching the speaker may be referred to as HWN (THIS) while someone who is very much nearer but is going away from the speaker may be referred to as HWNNA (THAT).

Within the deictic division, a number contrast can be established. The six forms HWN, HWNNA, HON, HONNA, HYN and HYNNA are singular while the two forms (R)HAIN and (R)HEINA are plural.

The singular forms allow distinction of 'animateness', gender and sex. Thus, all human objects can be referred to by HWN or HWNNA and HON or HONNA, while non-human objects can be referred to by HYN or HYNNA. However, there is a certain overlapping of functions. Whereas it is the case that HYN and HYNNA are restricted to inanimate or non-human objects, the other forms HWN, HWNNA, HON and HONNA can refer both to human and to non-human objects, giving:

(189)   *pwy ydy hwn?*   *(who's this?)*
        who is   this

(190)   *beth ydy hwn?*   *(what's this?)*
        what is this

Example (189) refers to a person while example (190) may refer to an animate or inanimate object. If the reference is to a person or animate object, sex distinctions are maintained; HWN and HWNNA refer to males while HON and HONNA refer to females. If the reference is to an inanimate object, gender (see section 2b above) distinctions are maintained. Thus, CADAIR (CHAIR) is referred to as HON while DRWS (DOOR) is referred to as HWN. In the case of the plural reference, these distinctions are not possible and hence there is only a deictic contrast involving two forms as opposed to the six singular forms.

Traditional grammars list a slightly different set of demonstratives:

(191) HWN   HWNNW
       HON   HONNO
       HYN   HYNNY

These types occur in formal Welsh as demonstrative determiners. But, as pointed out in section 3b earlier, spontaneous Welsh uses YMA (HERE) and YNA (THERE) in this function and the traditional demonstratives occur in only a few expressions such as *y flwyddyn honno (that year)* or *yr adeg hynny (that period)*. Even here, however, YMA (HERE) and YNA (THERE) can be used.

8f   Other pronouns

There are a number of items which apparently exhibit a pronominal reference but which are also involved as pre-modifying items in the noun phrase. These include:

(192) *amryw*   *(several)*   *mwy (more)*
       cymaint (as much)   *nifer (number)*
       'chwaneg (more)   *rhagor (more)*
       gormod (too much)   *rhai (some)*
       llai (less)   *tipyn (little, few)*
       llawer (many, much)   *ychydig (little, few)*

Each one of these items can stand alone with apparent pronominal function, for example:

(193) *mae yna <u>chwaneg</u> ar y bwrdd*   *(there's more on the table)*
       is there   more   on the table

(194) *'dwi wedi bwyta <u>gormod</u>*   *(I've eaten too much)*
       am I after   eat   too much

(195) *mae yna <u>rai</u> eraill yn y   gegin*   *(there are some others*
       is   there some others in the kitchen   *in the kitchen)*

In no case, however, does the underlined item replace a noun. Rather, the noun has been deleted and is 'understood':

(196) *mae yna chwanego fwyd ar y bwrdd*   (there's more food
      is there more of food on the table   on the table)

(197) *'dwi wedi bwyta gormod o gacen*   (I've eaten too
      am I after eat too much of cake   much cake)

(198) *mae yna rai eraill o afalau yn y gegin*   (there are some other
      is there some others of apples in the kitchen   apples in the kitchen)

On these terms, such items are not pronominal.

There are other items, however, which have a general and indefinite pronominal reference:

(199) *mae un/dyn yn tueddu i feddwl felly*   (one/a man tends to
      is one/man in tend to think like that   think like that)

(200) *mae pawb yn disgwyl yr un driniaeth*   (everyone expects the
      is everyone in   expect the same treatment   same treatment)

(201) *mae'r peth wedi cyrraedd*   (the thing has arrived)
      is the thing after arrive

(202) *mae'r lle wedi gwagio*   (the place has emptied)
      is the place after empty

The first of these, UN and DYN, are used with a very general reference to refer to anyone who is involved in the activity. It is an interesting point, too, that the second person can be used with a similar reference:

(203) *'dach chi 'n tueddu i feddwl felly*   (you tend to think
      are you in tend to think like that   like that)

The remaining three involve the features of 'human-ness', 'inanimateness' and place, and form a system which involve a variety of contrasts:

(204)   *UN*   *PETH*   *LLE*

	UN	PETH	LLE
(i)	*rhywun*	*rhywbeth*	*rhywle*
(ii)	*unrhywun*	*unrhywbeth*	*unrhywle*
(iii)	*neb*	*dim byd*	*(n)unlle*
(iv)	*pawb*	*popeth*	*pob lle/man*

The first three of these contrasts in (204) (i) - (iii) are discussed in chapter IX, section 4h. The fourth contrast involves 'comprehensiveness' and uses a form of POB (EVERY) as a marker of 'all-inclusiveness'.

Notes to chapter VII

1. It is questionable whether the noun phrase can ultimately be handled satisfactorily by a simple re-write rule of the sort sketched in (132) of this chapter. In view of the occurrence of prepositional phrases within the noun phrases with quantifiers, as presented in this chapter, it may be that some sort of noun phrase recursion is involved:

   (i) *llawer   o   'r dynion*   *(many of the men)*
       many of the men

   (ii)

   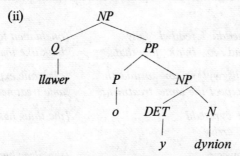

   The problematic nature of the structure of the noun phrase is intensified by the fact that some items occur in more than one position within the same noun phrase, as is the case with numerals:

   (iii) *saith   o bob   deg o gant   o ddynion*   *(seven of every ten of*
         seven of every ten of hundred of men   one hundred men)

   (iv)

   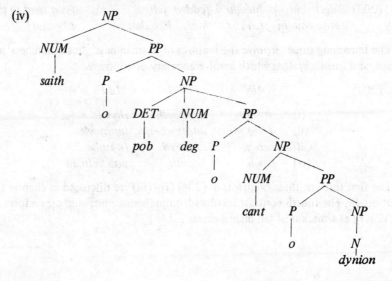

This description has not pursued these points, and has presented the data within a simple framework of linear sequence.

VIII   Remarks on the syntax and semantics of complex sentences

1   INTRODUCTION

1a   The recursive nature of language

Traditional grammar has long recognised that complex sentences are made up of two or more basic sentences (which are usually handled under the headings of principal (or main) clause and various types of subordinate clause). Brief exemplification can be given as follows:

(1) <u>mae John yn gwybod</u> <u>bod Mair wedi derbyn y swydd</u>   *(John knows*
     is John in   know   be   Mair after accept the post   *that Mair has*
                                                                   accepted the
                                                                   post)

(2) <u>'roedd Mair yn gweithio</u> <u>pan oedd John yna</u>   *(Mair was working*
     was   Mair in work   when was John there   *when John was*
                                                                   there)

(3) <u>'roedd John yn canu</u> ac <u>yn dawnsio</u>   *(John was singing*
     was   John in sing and in   dance   *and dancing)*

The significance of complex sentences is that they give clear illustration of the *recursive* nature of language: in the case of examples (1) to (3) above, the complex sentences are produced by re-using the same basic syntactic patterns to create additional varieties of sentence formation. Very brief illustration of the structure of the above complex sentences can be given by the following diagrams:

(4)

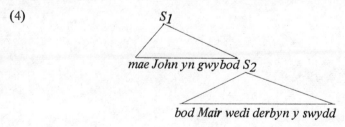

208

(5)

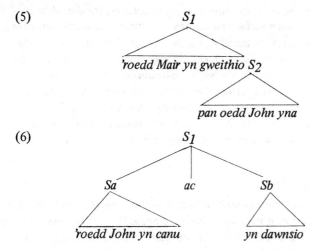

(6)

These diagrams serve to introduce terminology used frequently in this chapter. The first two demonstrate complex structures which contain a higher sentence and a lower sentence, the latter of which is a constituent of the higher sentence; in (4) it is the object while in (5) it occurs as adjunct. The higher sentence is named the *matrix* sentence while the lower sentence is named the *constituent* sentence (alternative labels for the latter are *recursive* and *embedded* sentence). The third diagram contains sentences which can be thought of as occurring on the same level and are known as *conjoined* sentences.

Returning to example (1), it can be seen that it contains two simple sentences *mae John yn gwybod . . . (John knows . .)* and . . . *bod Mair wedi derbyn y swydd (. . . that Mair has accepted the post)*. Each of these sentences can be produced by the came set of basic rules, outlined in chapters II and III. By combining them in a certain manner, the 'new' complex sentence in (1) is produced. The only extra procedure that has to be mastered is that of combining basic sentences to produce a complex sentence. This point helps explain how it is that a native speaker of Welsh can produce and understand an extensive variety of sentence types.

1b   Transformations

In various places in the preceding chapters we have established the following transformations in Welsh:

> the *auxiliary carrier* transformation (chapter III, sections 2b and 2c);
> the *identificatory noun phrase inversion* transformation (chapter III, section 4c);
> the *YNA (THERE) insertion* transformation (chapter III, section 4d);
> the *GAN phrase movement* transformation (chapter III, section 4d);
> the *relative clause reduction* transformation (chapter VII, section 5a).

It frequently happens that the deep structures set up to account for complex sentences are quite different from the surface structures of actually occurring sentences. Consequently, the deep structures are *transformed* by a number of rules so that the correct surface structures are eventually produced. In the course of this chapter, therefore, a variety of additional transformations will be introduced, which produce the surface structures of complex sentences from their deep structures. It will be found that the operations involve three basic processes: (i) *rearrangement,* as in the case of the first two transformations referred to above; (ii) *insertion,* as in the case of the insertion of YNA (THERE); and (iii) *deletion,* as in the case of the relative clause reduction transformation.

1c Types of complex sentence

Although complex sentences are best explained in terms of an abstract deep structure, it makes their presentation easier if they are introduced according to the characteristics of their surface structures. Consequently, we can say that the discussion of complex sentences concentrates upon the following:

(i) complex sentences involving a finite sentence as the constituent sentence, either as a *noun clause* or as an *adverbial clause;*
(ii) complex sentences in which the constituent sentence occurs in the form of a non-finite sentence;
(iii) complex sentences in which the constituent sentence occurs in the form of an infinitival sentence.

The discussion will also consider the following:

predicatival sentences:
passive sentences;
co-ordination;
the occurrence of demonstrative - type sentences.

2 COMPLEX SENTENCES INVOLVING FINITE SENTENCES

2a Introduction : complement and adjunctival recursion

There are a variety of possibilities for the occurrence of finite sentences as constituent sentences. It is useful to begin their description, however, by distinguishing between those that occur in a *complement* position and those which occur in an *adjunctival* position.

The following examples illustrate a variety of finite sentences occurring in complement position:

(7) *'dwi 'n gwybod bod Mair wedi dod yn ôl*   (I know that Mair
    am I in know   be   Mair after come back   has come back)

(8) *'dwi ddim yn gwybod a/os daeth Mair yn ôl*
    am I NEG in know PT came Mair back
    (I don't know
    whether/if Mair
    came back)

(9) *'dwi 'n gwybod pwy ddaeth yn ôl*
    am I in know who came back
    (I know who came
    back)

(10) *'dwi 'n gwybod pryd daeth Mair yn ôl*
     am I in know when came Mair back
     (I know when Mair
     came back)

(11) *'dwi 'n gwybod pam daeth Mair yn ôl*
     am I in know why came Mair back
     (I know why Mair
     came back)

(12) *'dwi 'n gwybod sut daeth Mair yn ôl*
     am I in know how came Mair back
     (I know how Mair
     came back)

(13) *'dwi 'n gwybod lle daeth Mair yn ôl*
     am I in know where came Mair back
     (I know where Mair
     came back)

In each case we have a matrix sentence followed by a constituent sentence in a complement position. Because of their positioning characteristics, constituent sentences of this type can be given the label of *sentential complements.* Examples (7) to (13) above illustrate that sentential complements can be thought of in terms of three types:

    (i) traditionally-labelled *noun clauses,* exemplified by (7);
    (ii) an *A/OS (WHETHER/IF) clause* or *indirect question,* exemplified by (8);
    (iii) *question-type clauses* which can take a variety of forms, as in (9) to (13).

The occurrence of constituent sentences in adjunctival position can be illustrated as follows:

(14) *mi es i pan oedd John yn canu*
     PT went I when was John in sing
     (I went when John
     was singing)

(15) *mi arhosodd Mair oherwydd roedd hi 'n bwrw*
     PT stayed Mair because was she in rain
     (Mair stayed because
     it was raining)

(16) *mi ddaeth John er fod o 'n sâl*
     PT came John although be he in ill
     (John came even
     though he was ill)

(17) *mi eith Mair os daw John*
     PT will go Mair if will come John
     (Mair will go if John
     comes)

Adjunctival recursion thus involves the traditionally-labelled adverbial clauses which begin with types of clausal conjunction; in the above examples we have illustrated the PAN (WHEN) type, the OHERWYDD (BECAUSE) type, the ER (THOUGH) type and the OS (IF) type.

The discussion of constituent sentences is quite complex and, rather than go into detail with all types, we will here concentrate upon the occurrence of *noun clause sentential complements* only. But it should be borne in mind that there are often quite subtle differences between the various types of constituent sentences. This point can be briefly illustrated by the fact that not all sentential complements, for instance, can occur with all matrix sentences:

(18) *mae'n ymddangos bod Mair wedi dod yn ôl*   *(it appears that*
     is in   appear   be   Mair after come back   *Mair has come back)*

(19) **mae'n ymddangos a/os daeth Mair yn ôl*   *(*it appears whether/*
     is in   appear   PT came Mair   back   *if Mair came back)*

(20) **mae'n ymddangos pryd daeth Mair yn ôl*   *(*it appears when*
     is in   appear   when came Mair back   *Mair came back)*

It can be seen from examples (18) to (20) that only noun clauses occur with a matrix sentence of this type[1].

2b   Noun clauses as sentential complements

The discussion of noun clause complements is a complex topic which has received a considerable amount of attention in contemporary linguistic research. We will not review the field (although some indication of alternative treatments is given in the notes) but will present a relatively informal, simplified and selective description. The discussion will concentrate upon the following points:

(i)   surface structure characteristics of noun phrase complements;

(ii)   a distinction between noun phrase complements which are derived from subject position and those which are derived from complement position;

(iii)   the handling of the constituent sentence within the framework of the rules for the syntax of Welsh sentences already established in previous chapters;

(iv)   the occurrence of noun clauses in structures which will be labelled here as *headed noun clauses;*

(v)   the relationship of structures involving noun clauses with the expression of *modal* features.

The first point, concerning surface structure characteristics, is discussed in the ensuing paragraphs of this sub-section, while the remaining points are considered in the following sub-sections.

The following examples illustrate a variety of complex sentences which include a noun clause in a complement position in surface structure:

(21) *mae 'n ymddangos bod Mair wedi dod yn ôl*   *(it appears (that)*
    is in   appear   be Mair after come back   *Mair has come back)*

(22) *mae 'n poeni John bod Mair wedi dod yn ôl*   *(it worries John (that)*
    is in   worry John be Mair after come back   *Mair has come back)*

(23) *mae John yn gwybod bod Mair wedi dod yn ôl*   *(John knows (that)*
    is John in know be Mair after come back   *Mair has come back)*

(24) *mae 'n amlwg   bod Mair wedi dod yn ôl*   *(it is obvious (that)*
    is in obvious   be Mair after come back   *Mair has come back)*

(25) *mae John yn siwr bod Mair wedi dod yn ôl*   *(John is sure (that)*
    is John in sure be Mair after come back   *Mair has come back)*

(26) *y gwir ydy y daw   Mair yn ôl*   *(the truth is (that)*
    the truth is PT will come Mair back   *Mair will come back)*

Before going on to examine the syntax of the constituent sentence, we will look briefly at the matrix sentence itself. It can be seen from the above examples that this occurs in a number of forms.

(i) It can be a verbal sentence, as in examples (21) to (23) above. Verbal sentences, however, can be further sub-divided into:

    (a) those which have an *impersonal* (or *anticipatory* or *expletive*) subject, as in examples (21) and (22);

    (b) those which have a *personal* subject, as in example (23).

(ii) It can be a copula sentence, as in examples (24) to (26). Such copula sentences can be:

    (a) the predicative type, as in examples (24) and (25) which, like the verbal sentences, can involve
      - an impersonal subject, as in (24), or
      - a personal subject, as in (25);

    (b) the identificatory type, as in (26).

The possibilities in the matrix sentence can be summarised with illustration as follows:

(27) (i) *Verbal sentences* *(a)* *impersonal subject* *(mae 'n ymddangos ...)*
                        (b) *personal subject*   *(mae John yn gwybod ..)*

(ii) *Copula sentences* *(a)* *predicative*
                              - impers. subject *(mae 'n amlwg ...)*
                              - pers. subject   *(mae John yn siwr ..)*
                        (b) *identificatory*   *(y gwir ydy ...)*

213

Further details could be added about the types of verbal sentence involved: for instance, the main verbs in the impersonal subject types in (21) and (22) vary according to the number of complements following the verbs. We will not take account of these extra details.

Turning now to the constituent sentence, it is found that this can involve any one of the basic sentences described in chapter III. Here, however, we are only interested in their occurrences as surface constituent sentences and the discussion will concentrate upon two points:

(i) the occurrence of a pre-sentential particle;
(ii) the possibilities of tense contrast.

It can be observed from example (26) above that constituent sentences in complement position may involved the occurrence of the pre-sentential particle Y - this particle could also be referred to as a *complementiser*. It can also be observed that there is no mutation of the verbal form following the particle Y. The particle Y, however, only occurs when the verbal form is inflected and, in addition to (26), further exemplification can be given by the following:

(28) *mae'n ymddangos y bydd   John yn gweithio*   (it appears (that) John
     is in appear   PT will be John in work   will be working)

     mae'n ymddangos yr arhosodd Mair yn hwyr   (it appears (that) Mair
     is in appear   PT stayed   Mair in late   stayed late)

     mae'n ymddangos y medr John el wneud o   (it appears (that) John
     is in appear   PT can John its do   it   can do it)

As can be seen from (28), an 'r' [r] is introduced when the following verbal form begins with a vowel. The particle Y never occurs when the uninflected BOD (BE) is the verbal form, as in (22) to (25) and again in the following:

(29) (i)   *mae'n ymddangos bod Mair yn mynd*   (it appears (that)
            is in appear   be Mair in go   Mair is going)

     (ii)   **mae'n ymddangos y bod Mair yn mynd*   (NO APPROPRIATE
            is in appear   PT be Mair in go   TRANSLATION)

(This point connects with remarks on tense contrasts in the following paragraph, as the BOD (BE) form represents a neutralisation of the tense contrasts supplied by the inflected MAE (IS) and OEDD (WAS) paradigms.) Even when an inflected verbal form occurs, however, as in (26) and (28) above, the particle tends to be deleted in spontaneous speech so that we have:

214

(30) *mae'n ymddangos*   *(it appears (that)*
    is in appear

                    bydd John yn gweithio   *John will be*
                    will be John in work   *working)*

                    medr John ei wneud o   *John can*
                    can John its do   it   *do it)*

It can be seen from (30), however, that the verbal form remains unmutated.

With two significant exceptions, the tense contrasts which are possible in non-recursive sentences are also possible in constituent sentences. Brief illustration can be given by the following:

(31) (i)   *mi fedr John ei wneud o*   *(John can do it)*
          PT can John its do   it

    (ii)   *mi fedrai John ei wneud o*   *(John could do it)*
          PT could John its do   it

(32) (i)   *mi fydd o 'n mynd i'r   pictiwrs bob   nos*   *(he goes to the*
          PT will be he in go   to the pictures every night *pictures every*
                                                              night)

    (ii)   *mi fyddai fo'n mynd i'r pictiwrs bob   nos*   *(he used to go*
          PT would be he in go to the pictures every night   *the pictures*
                                                             every night)

The tense contrasts of (31) and (32) are retained if they occur as constituent sentences:

(33) *mae'n   ymddangos*   *(it appears (that)*
         is   in appear

                    (y) medr John ei wneud o   *John can do it)*
                    PT can   John its do   it

                    (y) medrai John ei wneud o   *John could do it)*
                    PT could John its do   it

                    (y) bydd John yn mynd i'r   *John goes to the*
                    PT will be John in go   to the   *pictures every*
                                                          night)

                    pictiwrs bob nos
                    pictures every night

                    (y) byddai John yn mynd i'r   *John used to go*
                    PT would be John in go   to the   *to the pictures*
                                                          every night)

                    pictiwrs bob nos
                    pictures every night

The exceptions are the MAE (IS) and OEDD (WAS) paradigms, either in copula or in aspectual function (see chapter III, sections 2c and 4b). We will use the latter for illustration here:

(34) *mae John yn gweithio*   *(John is working)*
      is John in work

(35) *'roedd John yn gweithio*   *(John was working)*
      was   John in work

When these sentences occur as constituent sentences, the tense inflections are lost and the base infinitival form BOD (BE) occurs, so that both (34) and (35) are realised as:

(36) *mae'n ymddangos bod John yn gweithio*   *(it appears (that) John is/*
      is in   appear   be John in work   *was working)*

The only possible distinction exists with the retention of OEDD (WAS), which must be preceded by the *'r* form:

(37) *mae'n ymddangos 'roedd John yn gweithio*   *(it appears (that) John*
      is in   appear   was   John in work   *was working)*

But the copula paradigm MAE (IS) never occurs in a sentential complement. The significant point, of course, is that the loss of the tense contrasts in BOD (BE) correlates with the fact that BOD (BE) is never preceded by the recursive particle.

2c   Noun clauses derived from complement position or subject position

So far, the discussion of noun clauses has concentrated upon their surface structure characteristics. In each case the constituent sentence is seen to occur in a complement position, and on this basis the recursive sentence could be generated in the verb phrase of the matrix sentence. But it is possible to distinguish between those sentential complements that are derived from a position in the verb phrase of the matrix sentence and those which are derived from the *subject* position. Even though its surface structure occurrence is in object position, it will be suggested in the following paragraphs that the sentential complement is the *subject* of the matrix sentence in examples (21), (22) and (24), while it is derived from the verb phrase of the matrix sentence in examples (23) and (25).

The following examples each contain a noun clause or sentential complement derived from the verb phrase of the matrix sentence:

(38) *mae John yn gwybod bod Mair wedi dod yn ôl*   *(John knows that*
     is John in know   be Mair after come back   *Mair has come back)*

(39) *mae hwn yn argyhoeddi John bod Mair wedi*   *(this convinces John*
     is this in convince John be Mair after   *that Mair has come*
                                                        back)
     dod yn ôl
     come back

(40) *mae John yn siwr bod Mair wedi dod yn ôl*   *(John is sure that*
     is John in sure be   Mair after come back   *Mair has come back)*

Although it can be shown that each one of these is derived from a deep structure complement, there are a number of differences in other respects - particularly in the occurrences of prepositions in deep structure.

The example in (38) involves a sentential complement which is derived from the object position of the verb phrase of the matrix sentence. This can be illustrated by transforming (38) into an interrogative which queries an object noun phrase (see chapter IX, section 3g):

(41) *beth mae John yn ei wybod?*   *(what does John know?)*
     what is John in its know

The answer to (41) involves the sentential complement of (38), and this suggests that the sentential complement is indeed the object of the sentence. This point can be further illustrated by comparing example (38) with a sentence such as:

(42) *mae John yn gwybod hynny*   *(John knows that)*
     is John in know   that

The sentence in (42) is a transitive sentence which can be represented by a branching-diagram:

(43)

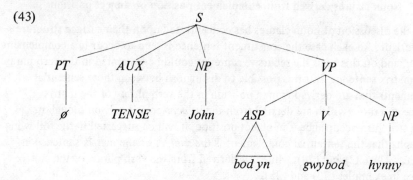

The rules necessary for producing a sentence like (42) include the following:

(44) (i) $S \rightarrow PT \quad AUX \quad NP \quad VP$

    (ii) $VP \rightarrow ASP \quad VERB \quad NP$

In the case of (42), the object noun phrase involves the occurrence of the pronoun HYNNY (THAT). This pronoun is equivalent to the recursive sentence BOD MAIR WEDI DOD YN ÔL (THAT MAIR HAS COME BACK) in (38). It can be argued, therefore, that the object noun phrase of a sentence can involve the occurrence of a sentence. Example (38) above can thus be given a branching-diagram as follows:

(45)

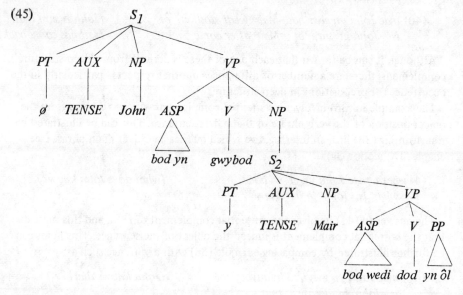

The diagram in (45) clearly shows how the recursive sentence of (38) occurs as a part of the constituent structure of the matrix sentence, and illustrates how the basic resources of the language are re-used in the construction of complex sentences.[2] A number of transformational operations eventually produce the surface structure given in (38) above.[3]

In (39) the sentential complement is derived from a position beyond the object of the matrix sentence. If the sentential complement is queried, it is found that the following example can be produced:

(46) *beth mae hwn   yn argyhoeddi John ohono?*   *(what does this*
      what is this   in convince   John of (it)   *convince John of?)*

It can be seen from (46) that a preposition now occurs before the pronoun which represents the sentential complement. We may therefore suggest that the sentential complement in an example like (39) is derived from a prepositional phrase containing the preposition O (OF) which follows the object of the verb phrase of the matrix sentence:

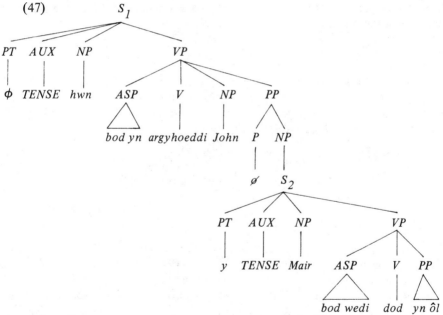

(47)

If the auxiliary carrier transformation is applied to the matrix constituent sentence, a surface structure like the following is produced:

(48)   *mae hwn yn argyhoeddi John o bod Mair wedi dod   *(*this*
      is   this in   convince   John of be Mair after come   *convinces John*

      yn ôl   *of that Mair has*
      back   *come back)*

But such a sentence never occurs with the preposition in this environment in surface structure. There must, therefore, be a further deletion transformation which removes the preposition when a recursive sentence occurs in the prepositional phrase. Such a transformation would contribute towards the production of the appropriate surface structure, as in example (39) above.

A similar explanation can be given to the example in (40), involving a predicative copula sentence as matrix. The interrogative querying the sentential complement again introduces a preposition:

(49) *beth mae John yn siwr amdano*   *(what is John sure about?)*
     what is   John in sure   about (it)

In this case the preposition is AM (ABOUT). It can be suggested that the sentential complement is derived from a prepositional phrase containing AM after the predicative adjective of the verb phrase of the matrix sentence:

(50)

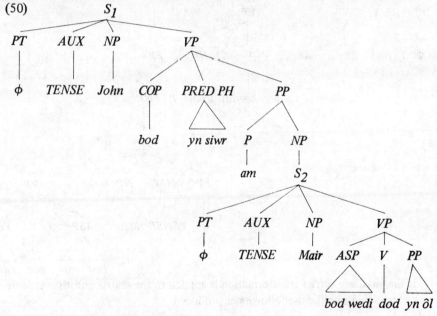

In addition to other transformations, the preposition deletion transformation again applies, because a constituent sentence occurs in the prepositional phrase of the verb phrase.

Returning to the original examples of noun clauses derived from complement position in (38) to (40) above, it can be seen that the matrix sentence can be either a verbal sentence with normal subject or a copula sentence with normal subject. There are, however, restrictions on the verbs which can occur in the former and on adjectives which can occur in the latter. Typical verbs occurring in the verbal sentences include: ADDO (PROMISE), BREUDDWYDIO (DREAM), CASGLU (COLLECT), CLYWED (HEAR), CREDU (BELIEVE), CYDNABOD (ACKNOWLEDGE), CYFADDEF (CONFESS), DEALL (UNDERSTAND), DERBYN (ACCEPT), DWEUD (TELL), DYCHMYGU (IMAGINE), GOBEITHIO (HOPE), GOLYGU (IMPLY), GWELD (SEE), GWYBOD (KNOW), MEDDWL (THINK), OFNI (FEAR), PENDERFYNU (DECIDE), PROFI (PROVE), SICRHAU (ENSURE), SYLWEDDOLI (REALISE) and SYLWI (NOTICE). The list of verbs possible in the verbal sentences is quite lengthy (the above is a very small selection) and, in comparison, the adjectives are small in number, but we can list here AMHEUS (DOUBTFUL), PENDERFYNOL (DETERMINED) and SIWR or SICR (SURE, CERTAIN).

The following examples illustrate sentential complements which occur in complement position in surface structure but which are derived from the subject position of the matrix sentence in deep structure:

(51) *mae'n ymddangos <u>bod Mair wedi dod yn ôl</u>*   *(it appears that Mair*
    is in   appear   be Mair after come back   *has come back)*

(52) *mae'n poeni John <u>bod Mair wedi dod yn ôl</u>*   *(it worries John that*
    is in worry John be   Mair after come back   *Mair has come back)*

(53) *mae'n amlwg <u>bod Mair wedi dod yn ôl</u>*   *(it's obvious that Mair*
    is in obvious be Mair after come back   *has come back)*

The main surface structure characteristic of sentences of this type is that the subject of the matrix sentence is the impersonal HI (SHE = IT). In Welsh, the anticipatory subject is mainly deleted, as in the above examples, so that zero subject occurs. In effect, however, the anticipatory subject, zero or otherwise, is equivalent to the sentential complement and can thus be said to anticipate the latter. This point alone links the sentential complement with the subject of the matrix sentence. A more obvious link, however, is supplied by interrogatives that query the sentential complement, as with example (52):

(54) *beth sy'n poeni John*   *(what worries John?)*
    what is in worry John

The interrogative in (54) takes the form of a subject noun phrase interrogative (see chapter IX, section 3d) and, on this basis, it can be suggested that the sentential complement is the subject of the matrix sentence. The recursive sentence is thus generated in deep structure under the noun phrase subject of the matrix sentence:

(55)

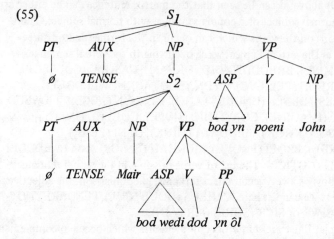

If the auxiliary carrier transformations are applied to both the matrix and constituent sentence, the following surface structure is produced:

(56) *mae bod Mair wedi   dod yn ôl yn poeni John   (*that Mair has come
       is   be Mair after come back in   worry John   back worries John)

But such a complex sentence is not acceptable in Welsh, as the constituent sentence, even though it is derived from subject position, always occurs in complement position in surface structure. Consequently, an important transformation is established, known as the *extraposition* transformation, which moves the constituent sentence to complement position. It is at this point that the impersonal (or anticipatory or expletive) pronoun HI (SHE = IT) is produced by pronominalising the original entry of the constituent sentence. The pronominalisation of the original constituent sentence is optional, however, and sentences like (52) can be produced without an expletive or anticipatory subject.[4]

The other two examples in (51) and (53) likewise involve recursion in the subject position of the matrix sentence:

(57)

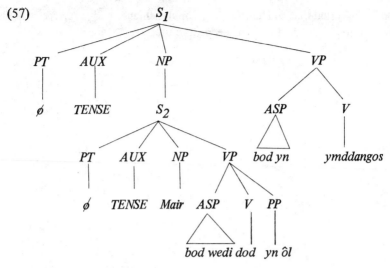

(58)

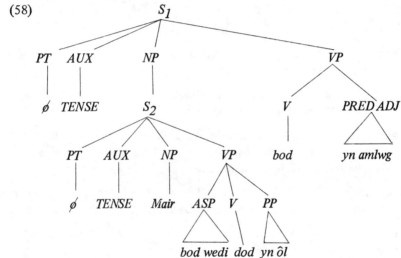

In both cases the extraposition transformation rearranges the constituent sentence so that it occurs in a complement position in the verb phrase.

It can also be suggested that matrix sentences involving identificatory copula sentences are associated with a constituent sentence in subject position. The surface structure of example (26) above is as follows:

(59) *NP   COP   S*

According to the description of identificatory sentences given in chapter III, section

4c, it can be suggested that an identificatory copula sentence with a surface structure like (59) is derived from the following deep structure:

(60)

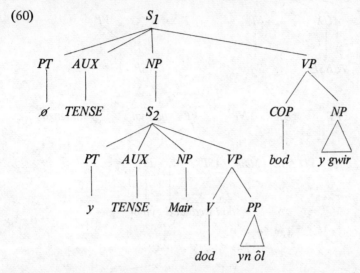

The application of the auxiliary carrier transformation to both the constituent and the matrix sentences produces a derived structure as follows:

(61) *mae y   daw   Mair yn ôl y   gwir*
     is PT will come Mair back the truth

But such a sentence never occurs in Welsh for, as discussed in chapter III, section 4c, the identificatory noun phrase inversion transformation is applied to move the noun phrase from the verb phrase to initial position:

(62) *y gwir bod + TENSE y daw   Mair yn ôl*   *(the truth is that*
     the truth be   PT will come Mair back   *Mair will come back)*

In this environment the MAE (IS) paradigm of the copula form is realised as YDY/YW and the surface structure as in (26) is thus produced.

Noun clauses which are derived from subject position can occur with either a verbal or a descriptive copula sentence with impersonal subject, as described above. The verbs which can occur in the verbal sentences include DIGWYDD (HAPPEN), DILYN (FOLLOW), POENI (WORRY) and YMDDANGOS (APPEAR). The adjectives that can occur in the descriptive copula sentence include AMLWG (EVIDENT), ANHEG (UNFAIR), BRAF (NICE, PLEASANT), CLIR (CLEAR), DA (GOOD), GWIR (TRUE), NEIS (NICE), OD (ODD), OFNADWY (AWFUL), POSIB (POSSIBLE), PWYSIG (IMPORTANT), RHYFEDD (STRANGE, ODD) and SIWR or SICR (SURE, CERTAIN);

an example of a noun is RHAID (NECESSITY). The occurrences of adjectives and nouns is further discussed in section 2f below. The nouns that can occur in initial position in identificatory copula sentences include CYNLLUN (PLAN), DADL (ARGUMENT), FFAITH (FACT), NEWYDDION (NEWS), NIWSANS (NUISANCE), PECHOD (PITY), POSIBILRWYDD (POSSIBILITY), PROBLEM(PROBLEM) and TEIMLAD (FEELING) - some of these are further discussed later.

2d   The handling of the recursive sentence

The discussion of sentential complements derived from the subject position or the verb phrase of the matrix sentence has re-introduced the symbol S to initiate the constituent sentence and, in each case, the constituent sentence has been introduced under a noun phrase (but see note 2). This gives another possibility for the re-writing of the category symbol NP, in addition to those outlined in chapter VII. The possibilities given so far are:

(63) $NP \rightarrow (Q)\ (D)\ N\ (S)$

This rule tells us that a noun phrase is made up of at least a noun with optional pre-modification and post-modification. The discussion of constituent sentences now shows that, in addition to the above, an NP can also *be* an S:

(64) $NP \rightarrow S$

The two rules in (63) and (64) above can be combined as follows:

(65) $NP \rightarrow \begin{Bmatrix} (Q)\ (D)\ N\ (S) \\ S \end{Bmatrix}$

This rule contains the information that a noun phrase is either a noun with optional pre-modification and post-modification, or a sentence.

This extra rule for the construction of Welsh sentences can now be incorporated into the overall rules given in (132) of chapter VII to produce the following:

(66) (i) $S \rightarrow PT\ AUX\ NP\ VP$

(ii) $AUX \rightarrow \begin{Bmatrix} \text{-ITH} \\ \text{-AI} \\ \text{-ODD} \end{Bmatrix}$

(iii) $VP \rightarrow (ASP) \begin{Bmatrix} V \begin{Bmatrix} (NP)\ (PP)\ (PP) \\ (PRED\ PH) \end{Bmatrix} \\ COP \begin{Bmatrix} PRED\ PH \\ NP \\ PP \end{Bmatrix} \end{Bmatrix}$

225

$$\text{(iv)} \quad ASP \quad \rightarrow \quad \begin{Bmatrix} PERFECT \quad and/or \\ RECENT\ PERFECT \end{Bmatrix} \quad \begin{Bmatrix} PROGRESSIVE \\ IMMINENT \end{Bmatrix}$$

$$\text{(v)} \quad PP \quad \rightarrow \quad P \quad NP$$

$$\text{(vi)} \quad PRED\ PH. \quad \begin{Bmatrix} YN \begin{Bmatrix} NP \\ ADJ \end{Bmatrix} \\ FEL/COP - NP \end{Bmatrix}$$

$$\text{(vii)} \quad NP \quad \rightarrow \quad \begin{Bmatrix} (Q) \quad (DET) \quad N \quad (S) \\ S \end{Bmatrix}$$

The introduction of the symbol S within the rules gives the recursive power which provides for the production of noun clauses.

2e   Headed noun clauses

There are a number of nouns in Welsh which can be immediately followed by a noun clause. These nouns include:

(67)   DADL (ARGUMENT)   POSIBILRWYDD (POSSIBILITY)
         FFAITH (FACT)   PROBLEM(PROBLEM)
         NEWYDDION (NEWS)   TEIMLAD (FEELING)

Examples can be given as follows:

(68) 'dwi 'n cytuno efo 'r ddadl   y llwyddith John   (I agree with the
     am I in agree with the argument PT succeed John   argument that
                                                          John will succeed)

(69) 'dach chi wedi clywed y newyddion bod John   (have you heard
     are you after hear the news   be John   the news that
                                                    John is leaving?)
     yn 'madael?
     in leave

(70) mae gen i deimlad bod Mair wedi dod yn ôl   (I have a feeling
     is LOC I feeling be Mair after come back   that Mair has
                                                    come back)

(71) mae'r ffaith y bydd   John yna yn ddiddorol iawn   (the fact that
     is the fact PT will be John there in interesting very John will be
                                                            there is very
                                                            interesting)

(72) mae yna bosibilrwydd bod nhw wedi cyrraedd   (there is a possibility
     is there possibility be they after arrive   that they have arrived)

The whole construction is like a complex noun phrase which has as its head the initial noun (which as a head noun can stand alone), hence the label *headed noun clauses*.

In each case the noun clause defines the noun that it follows. That is, the argument in (68) is that John will succeed and the news in (69) is that John is leaving. On this basis, it can therefore be suggested that headed noun clauses are derived from identificatory copula sentences. Thus the noun phrase complement in (68) can be derived as follows:

(73)

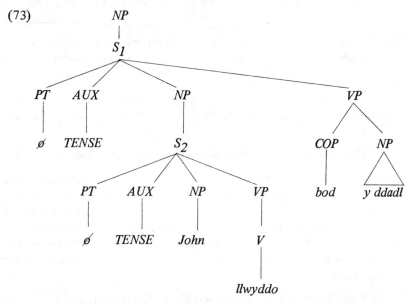

The necessary transformations outlined in section 2c above in relation to example (26) eventually produce:

(74) *y   ddadl   ydy y llwyddith   John* (*the argument is that*
    the argument is PT will succeed John *John will succeed*)

By establishing an extra transformation which deletes copula forms, the noun phrase complement in (68) is produced.

It can be seen from examples (68) to (72) that headed noun clauses occur in a variety of different matrix sentences. Of particular interest, however, is example (71) for, in addition to the pattern given above, we may also have:

(75) *mae'r   ffaith yn ddiddorol y bydd   John yna* (*the fact is*
    is the fact in   interesting PT will be John there *interesting that*
                                         John will be there)

Example (75) shows that the extraposition transformation can apply to the recursive sentence in a headed noun clause in predicative matrix sentences, so that it is re-positioned beyond the predicative adjective. In this instance, however, there is no need to insert a pronominal trace, as the recursive sentence is already represented by the noun FFAITH (FACT). Another example of extraposition applying to the constituent sentence of noun phrase complements is as follows:

(76) *mi glywais i 'r newyddion bod John yn 'madael ddoe*   *(I heard the news*
     PT heard I the news   *be John in leave yesterday*   *that John is leaving*
                                                               yesterday)

(77) *mi glywais i 'r newyddion ddoe bod John yn 'madael* *(I heard the*
     PT heard I the news yesterday be John in leave   *news yesterday*
                                                                that John is
                                                                leaving)

From (77) the constituent sentence can be seen to extrapose beyond a temporal adjunct.

2f   Modal features and propositions in sentences involving subject recursion

A brief glance at the types of sentence which occur as matrix sentences where subject recursion is concerned, as in examples (51) to (53) above, will show that both verbal and copula sentences can occur. The copula sentences are particularly interesting as they supply clear indication of the way in which speakers of Welsh can make a statement on a particular semantic basis. As illustrated by example (53) above, the copula sentences in surface structure assume a descriptive form (see chapter III, section 4b) and are made up of:

(78) *COPULA FORM (HI)   PREDICATIVE ADJECTIVE/NOUN . . .*

The significant point is that there are restrictions on the type of adjective or noun that can occur in predicative position. For instance, we do not find sentences such as:

(79) **mae'n ddel bod Mair wedi mynd*   *(*it is pretty that*
     is in pretty be Mair after go   *Mair has gone)*

(80) **mae 'n drwm bod Mair wedi mynd*   *(*it is heavy that*
     is in heavy be Mair after go   *Mair has gone)*

(81) **mae'n ardd bod Mair wedi mynd*   *(*it is a garden that*
     is in garden be Mair after go   *Mair has gone)*

(82) **mae'n esgid bod Mair wedi mynd*   *(*it is a shoe that*
     is in shoe be Mair after go   *Mair has gone)*

There is, then, a restriction on the types of adjective or noun that can occur in the

228

predicative phrase of the matrix sentence. In addition to AMLWG (EVIDENT, OBVIOUS), in example (53) above, the following occur:

(83) *mae'n <u>bechod</u> bod Mair wedi dod yn ôl*   *(it's a shame that Mair*
      is in shame   be Mair after come back   *has come back)*

(84) *mae'n <u>dda</u> bod Mair wedi dod yn ôl*   *(it's good that Mair*
      is in good   be   Mair after come back   *has come back)*

(85) *mae'n <u>bosib</u>   bod Mair wedi dod yn ôl*   *(it's possible that Mair*
      is in possible be   Mair after come back   *has come back)*

(86) *mae'n <u>debyg</u> bod Mair wedi dod yn ôl*   *(it's likely that Mair*
      is in likely be   Mair after come back   *has come back*

(87) *mae'n <u>ffaith</u> bod Mair wedi dod yn ôl*   *(it's a fact that Mair*
      is in fact   be Mair after come back   *has come back)*

The important point is, however, that there are two different classes of items involved. The first type is represented above by PECHOD (SHAME, PITY) and DA (GOOD). This type presupposes the occurrence of the event and makes a comment upon it. The second type is represented by POSIB (POSSIBLE) and TEBYG (LIKELY) above; these are not commentative adjectives and do not presuppose the occurrence of the event. By contrast, they are concerned with supplying the semantic basis for the making of a statement, and such items include:

(88)   *AMLWG (EVIDENT, OBVIOUS)*
        POSIB (POSSIBLE)
        SIWR (SURE)
        TEBYG (LIKELY)
        FFAITH (FACT)
        RHAID (NECESSITY)

The last two in this list are nouns, as opposed to the others, which are adjectives.

These items represent various features which can be used to make statement on the basis of *obviousness* (AMLWG), *possibility* (POSIB), *certainty* (SIWR), *probability* (TEBYG), *fact* (FFAITH) and *necessity* (RHAID). Thus, when a sentence is produced such as:

(89) *mae'n rhaid   bod Mair wedi dod yn ôl*   *(it is necessary that*
      is in necessity be   Mair after come back   *Mair has come back)*

a *proposition* is made, namely BOD MAIR WEDI DOD YN ÔL (THAT MAIR HAS COME BACK), but this proposition is made on the basis of what evidence there is for believing it to be true. In the above example it is believed to be *necessary* that Mair has come back because there is some evidence which suggests that this must be

229

the case — for instance, the fact that her car may be seen.

The type of evidence that can be used for making a proposition ranges through the various features listed above. The clearest feature is that of *fact* (FFAITH), and an example like (87) above is equivalent to:

(90) *mae Mair wedi dod yn ôl*   *(Mair has come back)*
     is   *Mair after come back*

All the other features tend to be non-factual, based upon the speaker's beliefs or assessment. This latter type of feature is known as a *modal* feature - that semantic feature on the basis of which a non-factual proposition is made. The remainder of this sub-section will look at the syntax of sentences involving modal features. This is a complex topic and part of the aim of this discussion will be specifically to give some indication of the complexity involved in an analysis of modal sentences.

The nature of subject recursion provides a syntactic framework for relating the proposition to the modal feature. Example (89) above is derived from:

(91)

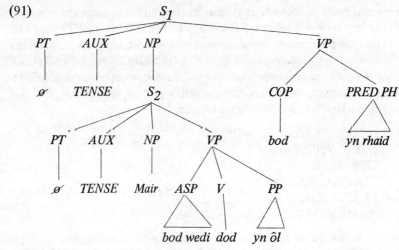

From this we can see that the proposition BOD MAIR WEDI DOD YN ÔL (THAT MAIR HAS COME BACK) is described as a necessity. In this way various propositions can be explicitly associated with the various modal features that occur in predicative position through the syntactic relationships of descriptive copula sentences.

The relationship of a modal feature and a proposition involves the speaker, as it is he who decides on what semantic basis a proposition is likely to occur. The speaker can identify himself by using a GAN prepositional phrase in examples such as:

(92) *mae'n siwr gynna' i bod Mair wedi dod yn ôl*   *(it is certain with me*
     is in sure LOC I be Mair after come back   *that Mair has come back)*

230

(93) *mae'n rhaid   gynna' i bod Mair wedi dod yn ôl* *(it is necessary*
     is in necessity LOC   I be   Mair after come back   with me that Mair
                                                             has come back)

This adds an additional complexity to these sentences. In order to explain the occurrence of the GAN phrase, it can be suggested that the complex sentences which contain the modal items are themselves embedded in a locatival sentence containing a GAN phrase. The resulting deep structure is a fairly complex one consisting of three sentences:

(94)

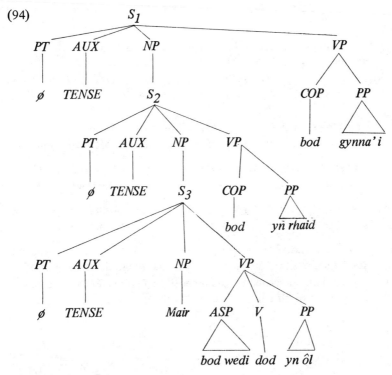

The deep structure in (94), assuming the application of the auxiliary carrier transformation in all three sentences, would produce a structure as follows:

(95) *mae bod bod Mair wedi dod yn ôl yn rhaid   gynna' i* *(that that Mair*
     is   be   be Mair after come back in necessity LOC   I *has come back*
                                                                  is a necessity
                                                                  with me)

Such a sentence does not actually occur, as the copula form of the constituent sentence is deleted and the tense contrasts are carried by the copula form of S_1, giving:

(96) *mae bod Mair wedi dod yn ôl yn rhaid gynna' i* (that Mair has come
    is be Mair after come back in necessity LOC I   back is a necessity
    with me)

In order to make (96) entirely acceptable, the extraposition transformation must be applied to S_3. It is observable, however, that S_3 is extraposed so that it occurs in surface structure beyond the verb phrase of the matrix sentence, as in (93), and does not occur extraposed beyond the verb phrase of S_2 as in:

(97) **mae'n rhaid   bod Mair wedi dod yn ôl gynna' i* (*it is a necessity
    is in necessity be Mair after come back LOC I   that Mair has come
    back with me)

The potential of complex sentences involving modal items to occur with a GAN phrase depends upon the modal item. Thus, GAN is possible with AMLWG (OBVIOUS), SIWR (SURE), TEBYG (PROBABLE) and RHAID (NECESSITY) but not with POSIB (POSSIBLE). Nor is it possible with the non-modal item FFAITH (FACT).

Some of the examples which convey modal features allow a different surface structure, as the following comparison of the occurrence of SIWR (SURE) illustrates:

(98) *mae'n siwr bod John yn gweithio*   (it is certain that
    is in sure be   John in work   John is working)

(99) *mae John yn siwr o fod yn gweithio*   (John is sure to
    is John in sure of be in   work   be working)

It can be seen from the latter example that the subject of the embedded sentence can occur in the subject position of the matrix sentence while the remainder of the sentence is extraposed and preceded by the preposition O (OF). Both sentences can be derived from a deep structure like that of (91) above:

(100)

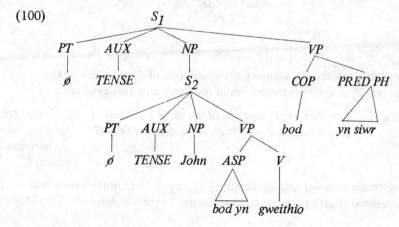

232

In the case of example (98) the normal auxiliary carrier and extraposition transformations are applied:

(101) (i) S_1 *TENSE* S_2 *TENSE John bod yn gweithio* S_2 *bod yn siwr* S_1 →

    (ii) S_1 *TENSE* S_2 *bod John yn gweithio* S_2 *bod yn siwr* S_1 →

    (iii) S_1 *TENSE (hi) bod yn siwr bod John yn gweithio* S_1 →

    (iv) *mae (hi) yn siwr bod John yn gweithio*

But in the case of (99), the constituent sentence is reduced to its subject noun phrase and VP by deleting the PT and AUX:

(102) (i) S_1 *TENSE* S_2 *TENSE John bod yn gweithio* S_2 *bod yn siwr* S_1 →

    (ii) S_1 *TENSE* S_2 *John bod yn gweithio* S_2*bod yn siwr* S_1

The extraposition transformation applies only to the verb phrase of the constituent sentence and the preposition O (OF) is introduced immediately before it in its extraposed position:

(102) (iii) S_1 *TENSE* S_2 *John* S_2 *bod yn siwr o fod yn gweithio* S_1

The original subject of the constituent sentence is now *raised* into the subject position of the matrix sentence:

(102) (iv) *TENSE John bod yn siwr o fod yn gweithio*

The auxiliary carrier transformation now moves the original *bod* of the matrix sentence to initial position to carry the tense feature and (99) above is produced. This type of pattern is possible with SIWR (SURE) as above and TEBYG (LIKELY). But it is not possible with other items such as RHAID (NECESSITY) or POSIB (POSSIBLE):

(103) *mae John yn rhaid   o fod yn gweithio   (*John is necessary*
      is John in necessity of be in   work   to be working)

(104) *mae John yn bosib o fod yn gweithio   (*John is possible*
      is John in possible of be in   work   to be working)

With these items only *complete extraposition* can occur. By contrast, there are two items, BOWND and RHWYM (BOUND), where only *partial extraposition* can occur:

(105) (i)   *mae'n bownd/rhwym bod John yn gweithio (*it is bound that*
          is in bound   be John in work   John is working)

    (ii) *mae John yn bownd/rhwym o fod yn gweithio (John is bound*
          is John in bound   of be in work   to be working)

These various items can thus be characterised as those that allow both partial and complete extraposition, like SIWR (SURE) and TEBYG (PROBABLE, LIKELY); those that allow complete extraposition only, like POSIB (POSSIBLE) and RHAID (NECESSITY); and those that allow partial extraposition only, like BOWND and RHWYM (BOUND).

Modal features can also be conveyed by certain auxiliary verbs (see chapter V, sections 3c and 3d). The feature *possibility* (POSIB), for instance, can also be conveyed by GALLU (CAN) and thus we can compare the members of the following pair:

(106) (i) *mae'n bosib   bod Mair wedi mynd*   *(it's possible that*
            is in possible be   Mair after go   *Mair has gone)*

       (ii) *efallai   bod Mair wedi mynd*   *(it could be that /*
            it + PT + could be Mair after go   *perhaps Mair has gone)*

Both sentences make the proposition on the basis of the modal feature *possibility*. An additional modal feature is also conveyed by the auxiliary verb DYLU in sentences such as:

(107) *mi ddylai bod Mair wedi mynd*   *(Mair should have gone)*
       PT should be   Mair after go

We can describe this modal feature as *likelihood* and say that the proposition BOD MAIR WEDI MYND (THAT MAIR HAS GONE) is made on the basis that it is likely to have happened.

The question of modal features and propositions is an important topic which has only been treated in brief outline here. It gives significant insights into the resources which a speaker of Welsh has for making known the semantic basis on which he makes a particular statement.

3   COMPLEX SENTENCES INVOLVING NON—FINITE SENTENCES

3a   Introduction

The constituent sentence can occur in the following form with certain types of matrix sentence:

(108) *'dwi 'n cofio   John yn gweithio yn y coleg*   *(I remember John*
       am I in remember John in work   in the college *working in the*
                                                             college)

(109) *mi welais i Mair yn gwylltio*   *(I saw Mair getting*
       PT saw I Mair in get mad   *mad)*

(110) *'dwi 'n clywed rhywun   yn gweiddi*   *(I can hear someone*
       am I in hear   someone in shout   *shouting)*

234

The underlined portion constitutes a *non-finite* constituent sentence. That is, no auxiliary carrier occurs and the aspectual marking involves the prepositional form only, the aspectual BOD (BE) (see chapter VI, section 1) being deleted. In the above examples the aspectual form YN (IN) occurs, and this is probably the most frequently occurring form, although instances of WEDI (AFTER) are also found (sometimes in combination with YN (IN)):

(111) 'dwi 'n cofio   John <u>wedi cael damwain</u>   *(I remember John*
      am I in remember John after have accident   *having had an accident)*

(112) 'dwi 'n cofio John <u>wedi bod yn nofio</u>   *(I remember John*
      am I in remember John after be in swim   *having been swimming)*

It is possible to express these latter two examples with an infinitival clause (see section 4 below):

(113) 'dwi 'n cofio John <u>ar ôl iddo</u>   <u>fo gael damwain</u>   *(I remember*
      am I in remember John after for   he have accident   *John after*
                having an
                accident)

(114) 'dwi   'n cofio   John <u>ar ôl iddo</u>   <u>fo fod yn nofio</u>   *(I remember*
      am I in remember John after for   he be in swim   *John after*
                having been
                swimming)

By comparison, the use of the non-finite expression is very colloquial. Verbs which can occur in matrix sentences and contain a non-finite constituent sentence, as illustrated above, include CASAU (HATE), CLYWED (HEAR), COFIO (REMEMBER), GWELD (SEE), LICIO and HOFFI (LIKE) and MWYNHAU (ENJOY). It is interesting to note that they all involve 'experiencing' of some sort.

3b Deriving non-finite sentences

The deep structures set up to explain complex sentences involving non-finites depend largely upon an intuitive understanding of the implications of the non-finite sentence. Here we will look at two possible deep structure sources for non-finites, but some indication is given at the end of this sub-section that there are other possibilities. Firstly, the non-finite sentence can be derived from an adverbial adjunct of the PAN (WHEN) type, briefly mentioned in section 2a above. This is the case with example (108), which can be read as:

(115) 'dwi 'n cofio   John <u>pan oedd o   'n gweithio</u>   *(I remember John*
      am I in remember John when was he in work   *when he was working*
                in the college)

      <u>yn y   coleg</u>
      in the college

In order to produce the surface structure pattern, a reduction transformation deletes PAN (WHEN), the auxiliary carrier and the subject, leaving only the prepositional aspect marker, the remainder of the verb phrase and any adjunctival items. It can be seen that this type of non-finite sentence involves adjunctival recursion of the type briefly sketched in section 2a above.

Secondly, the non-finite sentence can be derived from a relative clause (see chapter VII, section 5), as can be illustrated by example (110) above:

(116) 'dwi   'n clywed rhywun sy'n gweiddi   (I can hear someone
       am I in   hear   someone is in shout   who is shouting)

In this instance the reduction transformation simply applies to the auxiliary carrier SYDD (IS).

In many instances it is somewhat ambiguous whether the non-finite is derived from a PAN (WHEN) clause or a relative clause, as can be exemplified by:

(117) 'dwi   'n cofio   'r bachgen yn reidio beic   (I remember the boy
       am I in remember the boy   in ride   bike   riding a bike)

This example could be derived from either member of the following pair:

(118) 'dwi   'n cofio   'r bachgen pan oedd o 'n (I remember the boy
       am I   in remember the boy   when was he in when he was riding
                                                      a bike)
       reidio beic
       ride   bike

(119) 'dwi   'n cofio   'r bachgen a oedd yn   (I remember the boy
       am I   in remember the boy   PT was in   who was riding a bike)
       reidio beic
       ride   bike

The same transformation applies to both, however, and can thus be named the *non-finite reduction transformation*. In effect, it deletes everything before the aspect marker; in the case of (118) this relates to PAN OEDD O (WHEN HE WAS) and in the case of (119) it relates to A OEDD (WHO WAS).

It should be noted, however, that MWYNHAU (ENJOY) is problematic within the framework of this explanation. An example such as *dwi'n mwynhau'r ferch yn canu'r delyn (I enjoy the girl playing the harp)* is not convincingly derivable from either *dwi'n mwynhau'r ferch sydd yn canu'r delyn (I enjoy the girl who is playing the harp)* or *dwi'n mwynhau'r ferch pan mae hi'n canu'r delyn (I enjoy the girl when she is playing the harp)*. We will not pursue an adequate analysis of MWYNHAU (ENJOY), but it should be noted that there may be much more to an explanation of non-finites than that given here.

236

4   COMPLEX SENTENCES INVOLVING INFINITIVALS

4a   Introduction

Traditional grammars of Welsh note the fact that there are a number of verbs which 'can take another verb as object'. Illustration can be supplied as follows:

(120) 'dwi 'n cofio   siarad efo Mair   (I remember talking
       am I in remember talk with Mair   with Mair)

This account interprets the surface structure of examples like (120) as a complex sentence which is made up of a matrix sentence *dwi'n cofio . . . (I remember . . .)* and an *infinitival* sentence . . . *siarad efo Mair (. . . talk with Mair)* which is the constituent sentence. In terms of surface structure, an infinitive sentence is characterised by the occurrence of a verb, such as SIARAD (SPEAK) in (120), as the major or head word.

Infinitivals roughly share the same syntactic environments as finite sentences and the discussion can proceed along similar lines. Thus, it is found that infinitivals can. occur in a complement position in the verb phrase, as in (120) above, or in an adjunctival position, as in the following example:

(121) mi balais i 'r ardd   cyn/ar ôl gweld Mair   (I dug the garden before/
       PT dug I the garden before/after see Mair   after seeing Mair)

It can be seen from (121) that adjunctival infinitivals can be preceded by various prepositions to convey the various adjunctival notions, such as time in (121). The discussion of infinitivals in this section will centre upon their occurrence in complement position, where it is found that a distinction of subject or complement recursion can be established resembling that of finite sentences (see section 2c above). Within this framework of discussion, reference will also be made to the occurrence of subjects and aspect (see chapter VI) contrasts in infinitivals (and it can be noted that the same characteristics of subject and aspect occurrence are applicable to adjunctival infinitivals).

There are many verbs which can occur in a matrix sentence which contains an infinitival complement in surface structure. In addition to COFIO (REMEMBER) in (120) above, the following can also be listed: ADDO (PROMISE), ANGHOFIO (FORGET), ARFER (GET USED TO), BWRIADU (INTEND), BYGWTH (THREATEN), CEISIO (TRY), CYTUNO (AGREE), DARFOD (FINISH), DECHRAU (START), DEWIS (CHOOSE), DIGWYDD (HAPPEN), DIODDEF (SUFFER), DISGWYL (EXPECT), DYMUNO (WILL), GOBEITHIO (HOPE), GORFOD (HAVE TO), GORFFEN (FINISH), GWRTHOD (REFUSE), LICIO (LIKE), MEDDWL (THINK), METHU (FAIL), MWYNHAU (ENJOY), MYNNU (WILL, WISH), PENDERFYNU (DECIDE), OFNI (FEAR), SMALIO (PRETEND) and TRIO (TRY). For the purposes of reference it is convenient to label a verb with this potentiality as a *catenative* verb. But such a labelling does not necessarily imply a fixed unvariable characteristic of occurrence; the verb COFIO (REMEMBER), for instance, can occur in a matrix sentence with a sentential complement (see section 2 above), or non-finite complement (see section 3 above) or an infinitival complement. There is a special set of verbs, including CAEL (RECEIVE, HAVE), MEDRU (CAN) and GALLU (CAN), which occur in the catenative syntactic environment but have their own semantic and syntactic characteristics. They are usually labelled as *auxiliary verbs;* in chapter V they are discussed in detail and compared with the majority of catenative verbs.

4b   Subject and complement infinitivals

The example in (120) above illustrates the occurrence of an infinitival derived from a complement position in the verb phrase of the matrix sentence. It can be suggested that an infinitival of this type is derived from a finite sentence in deep structure as follows:

(122)

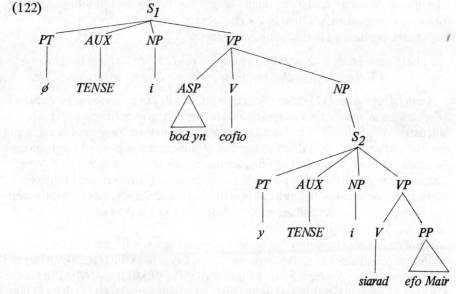

It can be seen from this branching-diagram that the infinitival is produced by the set of rules, described in chapter III, section 5, that produce the basic sentences.[5] As it stands, however, the account of infinitivals given in (122) would produce a sentence such as the following (after application of the auxiliary carrier transformation):

(123)   *'dwi 'n cofio   y   siaradais i efo Mair*   *(I remember that I talked*
         am I   in remember PT talked   I with Mair   *with Mair)*

238

Compared with (120) above, this sentence contains far too much information. Firstly, infinitivals never contain information about the particle or the auxiliary and, secondly, as in (120) above, they can also involve the deletion of subjects. (Examples are given below, however, which illustrate subjects occurring in infinitivals.) Consequently, a transformation is set up which *reduces* the structure of the deep finite sentence in (122) to the surface form of the infinitival, as in (120). This transformation can go under the label of *infinitivalisation transformation*. It compulsorily deletes the PT and AUX with possible retention of the subject NP. An infinitival, then, is basically a verb phrase plus any adjunctival items, with optional retention of the subject noun phrase.

Examples of infinitivals which themselves contain a subject noun phrase can be given as follows:

(124) *mi ddisgwyliodd John i Gwyn weld Mair* *(John expected Gwyn*
      PT expected John for Gwyn see Mair *to see Mair)*

(125) *mi fyddai Mr. Williams yn hoffi* *(Mr. Williams would*
      PT would be Mr. Williams in like *like Mair to open*
                                          the letters)
      i Mair agor y llythyrau
      for Mair open the letters

There are two points which must be made about subjects in infinitivals. Firstly, the subject of an infinitival is always immediately preceded by the preposition I (TO, FOR), as illustrated in the above examples. The infinitivalisation transformation must therefore be modified, so that if the subject is retained the preposition I (TO, FOR) is inserted immediately before the latter.[6] Secondly, the possibility of subject retention depends entirely upon the verb in the matrix sentence. As examples (124) and (125) above illustrate, there are verbs which allow a subject to occur in the infinitival sentence. In addition to DISGWYL (EXPECT) and HOFFI (LIKE) in those examples, other such verbs include CYTUNO (AGREE), DYMUNO (WISH), LICIO (LIKE). MYNNU (WILL, WISH) and OFNI (FEAR). It is significant to note that the subject in the infinitival is *different* from the subject in the matrix sentence. When the two subjects are *identical,* it is found that the subject in the infinitival sentence is typically deleted. Here verbs like DISGWYL (EXPECT) and HOFFI (LIKE) can also occur with infinitivals which have no subject in surface structure, as in the following:

(126) *mi ddisgwyliodd John weld Mair* *(John expected to see Mair)*
      PT expected John see Mair

(127) *mi fyddai Mr. Williams yn hoffi agor y llythyrau* *(Mr. Williams used*
      PT used to Mr. Williams in like open the letters *to like to open*
                                                          the letters)

We have, then, certain verbs which allow either a different subject in the infinitival (which actually occurs) or the same subject (which is deleted). However, there are other verbs, like TRIO (TRY) and DECHRAU (BEGIN), where the subject of the infinitive is always the same as the subject of the matrix sentence. We do not have examples such as:

(128) *'dwi 'n trio i Gwyn siarad efo Mair   (*I try Gwyn to
        am I in try for Gwyn talk with Mair   speak with Mair)

(129) *'dwi 'n dechrau i John aros yma   (*I begin John to
        am I in begin for John stay here   stay here)

Although these verbs are confined to identical subjects, the identical subject in the infinitival sentence does not actually occur for, as we have already seen, it is typically deleted. Thus we do not find examples such as:

(130) *'dwi 'n trio i mi siarad efo Mair   (*I try me to speak
        am I in try for I talk with Mair   with Mair)

Other verbs like TRIO and DECHRAU include ADDO (PROMISE), ARFER ((GET) USED TO), BWRIADU (INTEND), BYGWTH (THREATEN), CEISIO (TRY), DEWIS (CHOOSE), DIODDEF (SUFFER), GOBEITHIO (HOPE), GORFOD (HAVE TO), MEDDWL (THINK), METHU (FAIL), PENDERFYNU (DECIDE) and SMALIO (PRETEND).

The occurrence of an infinitival with a subject noun phrase conveys a past time reference when certain verbs occur in the matrix sentence, as in *mae Mair yn gwybod i John ddod ddoe (Mair knows that John came yesterday)*. The occurrence of this type of infinitival is to be distinguished from the infinitivals with subjects discussed above. Because of its distinctive temporal character, it compares closely with a sentential complement such as *mae Mair yn gwybod bod John wedi dod (Mair knows that John has come)*. This type of infinitival is characterised by the type of verb which occurs in the matrix sentence. Unlike the infinitivals discussed above, it can occur with certain verbs that can also 'take' a sentential complement; we can list here AMAU (SUSPECT), CASGLU (CONCLUDE), CLYWED (HEAR), CREDU (BELIEVE), CYDNABOD (ACKNOWLEDGE), DEALL (UNDERSTAND), GWYBOD (KNOW) and MEDDWL (THINK).

Infinitivals derived from the verb phrase can permit progressive aspect, either with and identical subject or with a different subject, as the following comparisons demonstrate:

(131) (i) *'dwi 'n cofio <u>bod yn chwilio am y goriad</u>* (I remember (I
      am I in remember be in search for the key was) searching

      pan ddaeth Mair i fewn for the key when
      when came Mair in Mair came in)

    (ii) *'dwi 'n cofio <u>chwilio am y goriad</u>* (I remember
      am I in remember search for the key searching for the

      pan ddaeth Mair i fewn key when Mair
      when came Mair in came in)

(132) (i) *mi ddisgwyliodd John i <u>Gwyn weithio</u>* (John expected
      PT expected John for Gwyn work Gwyn to work)

    (ii) *mi ddisgwyliodd John i <u>Gwyn fod yn gweithio</u>* (John expected
      PT expected John for Gwyn be in work Gwyn to be
        working)

In (131) (i), progressive aspect indicates overlapping activity, compared with succeeding activity in (131) (ii) (see chapter VI, section 1b, for functions of the progressive).

Infinitivals which are derived from a complement position are also common when the matrix sentence is a descriptive copula sentence with a personal subject. The situation is complicated by the occurrence or non-occurrence of prepositional forms before the infinitival sentence. Here we will attempt no more than to illustrate some prepositional possibilities, without going into a detailed account of the significance of the prepositions themselves. Typical examples can be given as follows:

(133) (i) *mae John yn awyddus <u>i</u> (fod yn g)weithio* (John is eager to
      is John in eager to be in work (be) work(ing))

    (ii) *mae John yn falch o (fod yn g)weithio* (John is proud to
      is John in proud of be in work (be) work(ing))

Adjectives like AWYDDUS (EAGER) have the preposition I (TO, FOR) occurring before the infinitival, while adjectives like BALCH (PROUD, PLEASED) have O (OF) (and thus compare with modal adjectives like SIWR (SURE) discussed in section 2f above). A third possibility is afforded by adjectives like BODLON (WILLING, CONTENT), which can occur without a preposition:

(134) *mae John yn fodlon (bod yn) gweithio* (John is willing to (be)
      is John in willing be in work work(ing))

It should be borne in mind, however, that BODLON (WILLING, CONTENT) may also 'take' I (TO, FOR) like AWYDDUS (EAGER).

Instances of infinitivals which occur in complement position in surface structure but are derived from subject position in deep structure can be given by the following examples:

(135)   *mae 'n bosib aros yn lle John*   *(it's possible to stay*
       is in possible stay in place John   *in John's place)*

(136)   *mae 'n hawdd siarad*   *(it's easy to talk)*
       is   in   easy   talk

In both instances we have a descriptive copula matrix sentence which clearly displays the zero impersonal subject HI (SHE = IT) typical of surface complements derived from subject position (as was illustrated in the discussion of sentential complements above). The deep structure analyses of both examples can be given as follows:

(137)

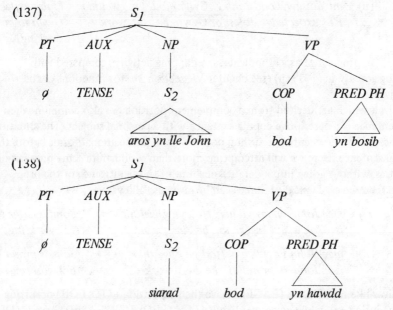

(138)

The infinitivals are basically the subjects of the sentences and are placed in surface complement position through the application of the extraposition transformation.

Up to this point, therefore, infinitivals which are derived from subject position are treated in the same manner as finite sentences derived from subject position, as described in section 2c above. There is, however, a significant difference between infinitivals and finite sentences in this respect. Finite sentences which are produced in subject position are compulsorily extraposed; we do not find examples such as **mae bod John yn dod yn bosib (*that John is coming is possible)*. But in the case of the above infinitivals as they stand, extraposition is optional, as it is possible for the infinitival to remain in subject position in surface structure: *mae aros yn lle John yn bosib (to stay in John's place is possible)* and *mae siarad yn hawdd (to talk is easy).* It thus emerges that finite sentences in subject position in deep structure differ markedly from infinitivals in the possibilities of eventual surface structure positioning.

Infinitivals in subject position are also very common with identificatory copula sentences (see chapter III), as in the following examples:

(139) yr ateb   oedd <u>creu   neuadd Gymraeg</u>   *(the answer was to create*
       the answer was <u>create hall   Welsh</u>   *a Welsh hall)*

(140) y syniad oedd <u>prynu hen geir</u>   *(the idea was to buy*
       the idea was   <u>buy   old cars</u>   *old cars)*

It can be suggested that in both examples the infinitival is derived from subject position in deep structure, as in the following branching-diagram for (139):

(141)

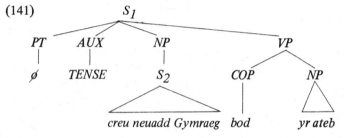

After infinitivalisation (already performed in (141) above), the auxiliary carrier transformation applies and then the identificatory noun phrase movement transformation (see chapter III):

(142) (i)   *TENSE creu neuadd Gymraeg bod yr ateb*
       (ii)   *bod + TENSE creu neuadd Gymraeg yr ateb*
       (iii) *yr ateb bod + TENSE creu neuadd Gymraeg*
       (iv)   *yr ateb oedd creu neuadd Gymraeg*

It is significant to note that the type of noun which occurs in initial position in surface structure is the type of noun which can occur in headed noun clauses (see section 2e above) - and the latter construction is likewise derived from a deep structure like that in (141) above.

The examples so far given of infinitivals which are derived from subject position have involved either the infinitival itself in surface subject position or the impersonal pronoun (typically, zero) with the infinitival extraposed. It is interesting to apply the same general analysis to traditionally-looking transitive-type sentences. Such an example is a sentence involving the verb DIGWYDD (HAPPEN), as in the following:

(143) *mae John wedi digwydd gweld Mair heddiw*   *(John has happened*
     is John after   happen   see   Mair today   to see Mair today)

In traditional terms it could be suggested that JOHN is the subject of the sentence and GWELD MAIR (SEE MAIR) is the object of the sentence. A deeper analysis could suggest that what happened was that John saw Mair and that the subject of the sentence is JOHN GWELD MAIR (JOHN SEE MAIR), giving basically a structure which can be represented by the following 'artificial' sentence:

(144) *mae John gweld Mair wedi digwydd heddiw*   *(John see Mair has*
     is   John see Mair after   happen today   happened today)

In order to represent such an analysis, sentences like (143) stem from a deep structure where the infinitival is derived from a sentence in subject position:

(145)

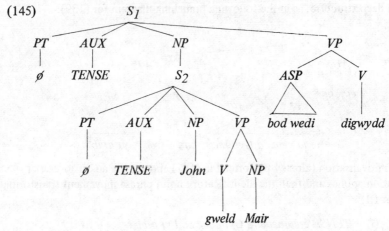

In order to produce the surface structure in example (143) above, a number of transformations are necessary. The infinitivalisation transformation applies to reduce the constituent sentence to JOHN GWELD MAIR (JOHN SEE MAIR), which would eventually produce MAE JOHN GWELD MAIR WEDI DIGWYDD (JOHN SEE MAIR HAS HAPPENED). Such a structure does not occur in Welsh, and in order to produce the surface structure in (143) the partial extraposition transformation is applied to move the verb phrase of the lower sentence, GWELD MAIR (SEE MAIR), to its surface position beyond the verb DIGWYDD (HAPPEN) of the upper sentence. As with the extraposition of infinitivals in descriptive copula sentences with impersonal subjects, described above, no preposition is introduced and the infinitival follows the verb DIGWYDD (HAPPEN). The remainder of the constituent sentence, JOHN, is then raised into the subject position of the matrix sentence, and the surface structure in (143) is achieved.

244

The analysis given above for example (143) is not really surprising, as DIGWYDD (HAPPEN) is one of those verbs which can take a finite sentence as a deep structure sentence (as discussed in section 2c above) and can occur in surface structure of the following form:

(146) *mae'n digwydd bod John yn gweld Mair*   *(it happens that John*
         is in   happen   be   John in see   Mair   *is seeing Mair)*

An example like (146) has roughly the same deep structure source as (143), namely:

(147)

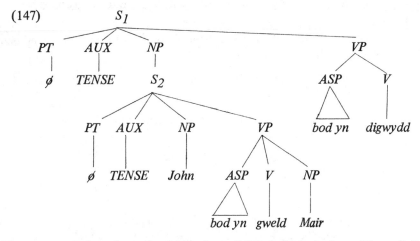

There are a number of transformational possibilities which produce either a finite sentence or an infinitival in complement position. Firstly, if the auxiliary carrier transformation is applied to the constituent sentence, full extraposition is then applied to it, eventually producing a surface structure of the type in (146). Secondly, if the auxiliary carrier transformation is not applied, the infinitivalisation transformation deletes the PT and AUX of the constituent sentence and reduces it to JOHN BOD YN GWELD MAIR. The partial extraposition is then applied and moves the verb phrase only of the constituent sentence to a position beyond the verb DIGWYDD (HAPPEN) of the matrix sentence. The remaining part of the constituent sentence, JOHN, is then raised into the subject position of the matrix sentence to produce a surface structure of the general type given in (143), in this case:

(148) *mae <u>John</u> yn digwydd <u>bod yn gweld Mair</u>*   *(John happens to be*
         is John in happen be in see Mair   *seeing Mair)*

The verb DIGWYDD (HAPPEN), then, can accommodate either a sentential complement with impersonal subject or an infinitival complement with a personal subject which is also the subject of the infinitival.

In the light of the above discussion of infinitivals derived from subject position, it is interesting to speculate on a possible analysis of traditionally-looking transitive sentences which involve the verb DECHRAU (BEGIN). The following example contains a noun phrase subject with an infinitival in complement position:

(149) *mae'r   wal wedi dechrau disgyn*   *(the wall has begun to fall)*
       is the wall after begin   fall

A traditional analysis would say that we have a subject, Y WAL (THE WALL), and a 'verb-noun' DISGYN (FALL), as object. A recent approach, however, makes the suggestion that the subject of the above sentence is in fact Y WAL DISGYN (THE WALL FALL).[7] Notionally, this can be supported by suggesting that what has begun is the whole act of the wall falling, so that basically we have the structure expressed in the following 'artificial' sentence:

(150) *mae 'r wal disgyn wedi dechrau*   *(the wall fall has begun)*
       is the wall fall   after begin

Such an analysis can be represented by a deep structure similar to that given for DIGWYDD (HAPPEN) above in (145):

(151)

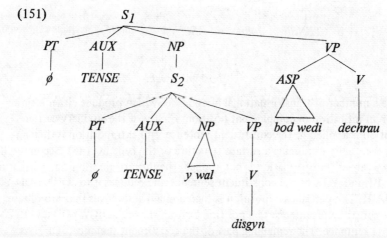

The surface structure in (149) is produced by applying the infinitivalisation transformation to the constituent sentence in (151), thus reducing it to Y WAL DISGYN (THE WALL FALL). The partial extraposition transformation then re-produces the verb phrase DISGYN (FALL) beyond the verb of the matrix sentence and Y WAL (THE WALL) is raised into the subject position of the matrix sentence. Other verbs like DECHRAU (BEGIN) are DARFOD (FINISH), GORFFEN (FINISH) and STOPIO (STOP), in examples such as:

246

(152) mae'r gwynt wedi stopio chwythu   (the wind has stopped
       is the wind after stop   blow   blowing)

(153) mae'r car wedi gorffen/darfod gwneud sŵn   (the car has finished
       is the car after finish/finish make noise   making a noise)

A significant point here is that these verbs form a semantic system which is concerned
with the inception or termination of an activity. Consequently, they can be referred
to as verbs of *temporal aspect,* and relate to the verbs DAL (LAST) and PARHAU
(CONTINUE) which are discussed in sections 4c and 5b below.

Although an example with DECHRAU (BEGIN) like (149) above compares closely
with the occurrence of DIGWYDD (HAPPEN) in (143), distinctions can be made
between the two. Firstly, there is the obvious semantic difference in that DECHRAU
is concerned with aspectual features (of inception) while DIGWYDD is concerned
with the fortituous occurrence of an event. Secondly, there is the syntactic difference,
in that DECHRAU cannot take a sentential complement. Thus, while DIGWYDD can
occur as in (146), we do not find DECHRAU (BEGIN) in a similar structure, as the
following unacceptable example illustrates:

(154) *mae'n dechrau bod y wal yn disgyn   (*it begins that the wall
       is in begin   be the wall in fall   is falling)

The verb DECHRAU (BEGIN) can only occur with an infinitival complement.
Thirdly, there is another syntactic difference - namely, that DECHRAU does not allow
progressive aspect in the infinitival. Whereas DIGWYDD can occur in a structure like
(148) above, DECHRAU is excluded:

(155) *mae'r wal yn dechrau bod yn disgyn   (*the wall is beginning
       is the wall in begin   be in fall   to be falling)

The aspectual restrictions on DECHRAU (BEGIN) can be attributed to the
incompatibility of aspect with the semantics of the verb DECHRAU itself, which is
already involved in a type of aspect in terms of inception, so that the semantics of
progressive aspect proper (see chapter VI, section 2b) in terms of duration are
inappropriate to it.

The distinction between subject and object recursion as far as infinitivals are
concerned correlates with certain facts about the usage of time adverbials with certain
verbs. Consider the following examples:

(156) mi ddechreuodd y wal ddisgyn ddoe/*yfory   (the wall began to
       PT began   the wall fall yesterday/tomorrow fall yesterday/
                                                              *tomorrow)

(157) *mi benderfynodd John weithio yn y ffatri*   *(John decided to*
       PT decided   John   work in the factory   *work in the factory*
                                                          yesterday/ tomorrow)
       ddoe/yfory
       yesterday/tomorrow

The verb DECHRAU (BEGIN) in (156) has been analysed above as involving subject recursion, whereas PENDERFYNU (DECIDE) in (157) involves object recursion. As can be seen from the above examples, DECHRAU with the past tense is restricted to a past time adverb, while PENDERFYNU with the past tense can occur with either a past time or a future time adverb. These facts can be represented by relating the time adverb to the matrix sentence or to the constituent sentence. In the case of the verb DECHRAU (BEGIN), the 'time of starting' and the 'time of the event' must coincide; that is, the adverb relates to the matrix sentence:

(158)

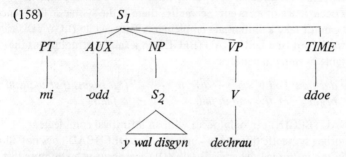

In the case of PENDERFYNU (DECIDE), however, the time of 'making the decision' and the time of 'implementing the decision' can be different. The former is conveyed by the matrix sentence and the latter by the constituent sentence. It can be argued, therefore, that the past adverb DDOE (YESTERDAY), which refers to 'making the decision', occurs in the matrix sentence while YFORY (TOMORROW), which refers to 'implementing the decision', occurs in the constituent sentence:

(159)

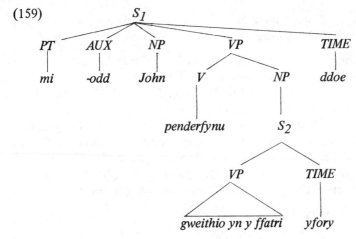

With certain verbs like PENDERFYNU (DECIDE) it is thus possible to have two adverbials. And, indeed, if the adverb in the matrix sentence adopts an initial position it is possible for both to occur in surface structure: *ddoe, mi benderfynodd John weithio yn y ffatri yfory (yesterday, John decided to work in the factory tomorrow)*.

4c   Infinitivals and the preposition I (TO, FOR)

The preposition I (TO, FOR) can occur with infinitivals under certain conditions. The situation has not been fully enough studied to warrant a detailed discussion here. We will merely list the syntactic environments in which I (TO, FOR) occurs, along with typical verbs which occur in those environments. Three verbs, however - DAL (LAST), PARHAU or PARA (CONTINUE) and MYND (GO) - are selected for more detailed discussion.

In the previous sub-section it was seen that I (TO, FOR) occurs when there is a subject in the infinitival clause and also when an infinitival without a subject follows certain adjectives. I (TO, FOR) also occurs in two additional environments: (a) when an infinitival clause follows a noun phrase object, and (b) when an infinitival immediately follows certain verbs. These four environments can be illustrated as follows:

(160)   *mae hi 'n disgwyl i John ddreifio*   *(she expects John to drive)*
         is she in expect for John drive

(161)   *mae hi 'n awyddus i ddreifio*   *(she's eager to drive)*
         is she in eager   to   drive

(162)   *mae hi 'n dysgu John i ddreifio*   *(she's teaching John to drive)*
         is   she in teach John to drive

(163) *mae hi 'n dal i ddreifio*   *(she continues to drive =*
       is she in last to drive   *she's still driving)*

Verbs which can occur in an environment like (162) also include ARGYHOEDDI (CONVINCE), CYNGHORI (ADVISE), DETHOL (SELECT), ENWI (NAME), HELPU (HELP), HYFORDDI (TRAIN), PARATOI (PREPARE), PERSWADIO (PERSUADE) and TEMTIO (TEMPT). A rather special member of this group is the verb CAEL (RECEIVE), which is discussed in relation to passivisation in section 6b below. Verbs which can occur in an environment like (163), in addition to DAL (LAST), include PARA (CONTINUE), MYND (GO), CYTUNO (AGREE) and TUEDDU (TEND).

The two verbs of the third group, DAL (LAST) and PARA (CONTINUE), are particularly interesting. Compare the members of the following pairs:

(164) (i)   *mae Mair yn dal i weithio*   *(Mair continues to work =*
             is   Mair in last to work   *is still working)*

       (ii) *mae Mair yn gweithio*   *(Mair is working)*
             is   Mair in   work

(165) (i)   *mae Mair yn para i ddysgu*   *(Mair continues to teach =*
             is   Mair in last to teach   *is still teaching)*

       (ii) *mae Mair yn dysgu*   *(Mair is teaching)*
             is   Mair in teach

The verbs DAL (LAST) and PARA (CONTINUE) add a feature of endurance or continuity to the basic sentence. It can be tentatively suggested that they are open to an analysis in terms of subject recursion like DECHRAU (BEGIN), STOPIO (STOP), GORFFEN (FINISH) and DIGWYDD (HAPPEN):

(166)

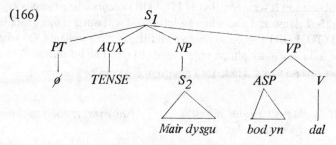

The transformations are identical, involving the reduction of the constituent sentence (already performed in (166)), extraposition of the verb and raising of the subject of the constituent sentence to the matrix sentence. But, in the case of extraposition, the preposition I (TO, FOR) is introduced and distinguishes PARA (CONTINUE) and DAL (LAST) from the other verbs involving this type of recursion.

It is significant, too, that DAL (LAST) and PARA (CONTINUE) form the middle contrast in comparison with DECHRAU (BEGIN) and STOPIO (STOP) or GORFFEN (FINISH):

(167)   *mae John yn dechrau gweithio*   *(John is beginning to work)*
         is John in   begin   work

(168)   *mae John yn para/dal   i weithio*   *(John is continuing to*
         is   John in continue/last to work   *work = is still working)*

(169)   *mae John yn gorffen/stopio gweithio*   *(John is finishing/stopping*
         is John in finish/ stop   work   *working)*

The contrasts thus range through inception and continuation to termination, forming a system of *temporal aspect*.

The verb MYND (GO) in this environment is commonly associated with 'intention':

(170)   *mae John yn mynd i ganu heno*   *(John is going to sing*
         is John in go to sing tonight   *tonight)*

But it also occurs with inanimates where 'intention' is inappropriate as an explanation of its meaning, and with animates in some activities which need not involve 'intention':

(171)   *mae'r wal yn mynd i syrthio*   *(the wall is going to fall)*
         is the wall in go to fall

(172)   *mae Mair yn mynd i grio*   *(Mair is going to cry)*
         is Mair in go   to cry

It seems more reasonable to suggest that this pattern conveys a *developing situation*, the culmination of which can be discerned in various contemporaneous factors. It is also reasonable to suggest that there is a basically locatival pattern which is used to convey the progression towards a certain state of affairs. This explanation can be represented in the following abstract sentences:

(173)   *MAE JOHN YN MYND I JOHN CANU*   *(John is going to John sing)*
         is   John in go   to John sing

(174)   *MAE'R WAL YN MYND I Y WAL DISGYN*   *(the wall is going to*
         is the wall   in go   to the wall fall   *the wall fall)*

(175)   *MAE MAIR YN MYND I MAIR CRIO*   *(Mair is going to*
         is   Mair in go   to Mair   cry   *Mair cry)*

The deep structure configuration thus represents post-verbal recursion and can be illustrated in respect of example (170) or (171) as follows:

(176)

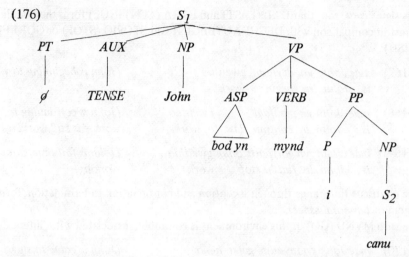

The infinitivalisation transformation then reduces the constituent sentence (already performed in (176)) so that the actual surface structures are produced.

5   PREDICATIVAL SENTENCES

5a   Introduction

In the discussion of the syntax of the verb phrase it was seen that some sentences involve a predicative phrase constituent (see chapter III, sections 3g and 4b):

(177) (i)   *mae Mair yn mynd yn dal*   *(Mair is becoming tall)*
              is   Mair in   go   in tall

       (ii) *mae Mair yn dal*   *(Mair is tall)*
              is   Mair in tall

A predicative phrase is characterised by the occurrence of YN (IN) followed by soft mutation. The same constituent also occurs in a variety of other sentences and three general types can be listed:

(178)   *mae Mair yn edrych yn dal*   *(Mair looks tall)*
         is   Mair in   look   in   tall

(179)   *mae'r ymarfer wedi gwneud Mair yn dal*   *(the exercise has*
         is the exercise after do   Mair in tall   *made Mair tall)*

(180)   *mae'n gas   gan Mair goffi*   *(Mair hates coffee)*
         is   in hateful LOC Mair coffee

A distinction is made here between sentences like those in (177), which are labelled

252

as *predicative* sentences, and those in (178) to (180), which will be labelled slightly differently as *predicatival* sentences. The sentence in (178) differs from that in (179) in that the latter has a noun phrase object. Example (178) can be labelled as *intransitive predicatival* and (179) *transitive predicatival*. The third type in (180) be labelled as a *prepositional phrase-predicatival sentence*.

5b   Intransitive predicatival sentences

The verbs which occur in this type of sentence include EDRYCH (LOOK), SWNIO (SOUND), TEIMLO (FEEL), OGLA (SMELL), DAL (LAST) and PARHAU or PARA (CONTINUE); they can be exemplified as follows:

(181) *mae Mair yn edrych yn dal*   *(Mair looks tall)*
       is   Mair in look in tall

(182) *mae Mair yn swnio 'n dal*   *(Mair sounds tall)*
       is   Mair in sound in tall

(183) *mae'r bwrdd yn teimlo 'n drwm*   *(the table feels heavy)*
       is the table in feel   in heavy

(184) *mae'r pysgod yn ogla 'n ddrwg*   *(the fish smell bad)*
       is the fish   in smell in bad

(185) *mae Mair yn dal yn athrawes*   *(Mair continues as a*
       is   Mair in last in   teacher   *teacher = is still a teacher)*

(186) *mae Mair yn para   'n athrawes*   *(Mair continues as a*
       is   Mair in continue in teacher   *teacher = is still a teacher)*

Superficially, these sentences look as if they could be simple sentences involving no recursion. But it is suggested here that many of them can be interpreted in such a manner that *subject recursion,* as described in sections 2c and 4b above, is involved, although the transformation processes are so severe that only a remnant of the constituent sentence occurs in surface structure. The verbs fall into two groups and each group will be discussed in turn.

The first group involves the verbs of perception - EDRYCH (LOOK), SWNIO (SOUND), TEIMLO (FEEL) and OGLA (SMELL). [8] Compare the members of each of the following pairs:

(187) (i)   *mae Mair yn edrych yn gryf*   *(Mair looks strong)*
             is   Mair in look in   strong

       (ii) *mae Mair yn gryf*   *(Mair is strong)*
             is   Mair in strong

(188) (i)   *mae Mair yn swnio 'n hapus*   *(Mair sounds happy)*
             is Mair in sound in happy

       (ii) *mae Mair yn hapus*   *(Mair is happy)*
             is Mair in happy

(189) (i)   *mae'r bwrdd yn teimlo'n drwm*   *(the table feels heavy)*
             is the table in   feel in heavy

       (ii) *mae'r bwrdd yn drwm*   *(the table is heavy)*
             is the table in heavy

(190) (i)   *mae'r pysgod yn ogla/gwyntio 'n ddrwg*   *(the fish smell bad)*
             is the fish   in smell   in bad

       (ii) *mae'r pysgod yn ddrwg*   *(the fish are bad)*
             is the fish   in bad

It can be argued that the predicatival sentence in (i) of each example makes the
same proposition as the copula sentence in (ii) of each example, only from the
standpoint not of fact but of what is *perceived* to be fact. On this semantic basis,
it can be suggested that predicatival sentences are basically complex sentences which
contain the copula sentences in deep structure. This can be illustrated by considering
EDRYCH (LOOK) in (187) (i) above:

(191)

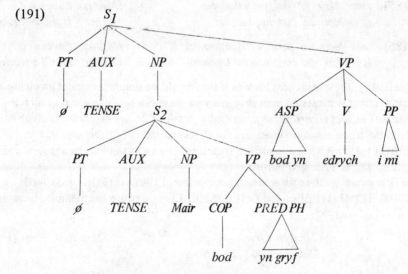

The deep structure, by developing a copula sentence equivalent to MAE MAIR YN
GRYF (MAIR IS STRONG) as the subject of a sentence MAE . . . YN EDRYCH I
MI (. . . LOOKS TO ME), conveys the relationship between a proposition about Mair

254

and the perceptive basis of that proposition. The prepositional phrase of the matrix sentence is necessary to represent the perceiver. As it stands, the account in (191), given the application of the auxiliary carrier transformation to both the constituent and matrix sentence, would produce a surface structure such as:

(192)   *mae bod Mair yn gryf yn edrych i mi*   *(that Mair is strong*
       is   be Mair in strong in look to me   *looks to me)*

Such a sentence does not actually occur in Welsh and a number of transformations must be performed on the deep structure. Firstly, the constituent sentence is reduced to the subject noun phrase and predicative phrase by deleting the PT, AUX and COP by a rule which can be called the *predicatival reduction transformation.* Secondly, the predicative phrase is extraposed beyond the verb EDRYCH (LOOK) of the matrix sentence. The subject of the constituent sentence retains its original position and is raised to occur as the surface subject of the matrix sentence. The prepositional phrase in the deep structure is optionally deleted to produce the surface structure sentence as in (187) (i) above. It is, of course, possible to retain the prepositional phrase to produce examples such as:

(193)   *mae Mair yn edrych yn gryf i mi*   *(Mair looks strong to me)*
       is   Mair in look   in strong to me

It can be seen that the transformational process which produces predicatival sentences is very similar to that which produces complex sentences containing infinitivals derived from subject position. But the reduction of the original deep structure finite sentence is much more drastic, in that the verb is also deleted. It will be shown below, however, that there are some verbs in predicatival sentences which allow the optional retention of the copula BOD (BE).

There may be some uncertainty concerning the occurrence of unmodified *nouns.* Consider the following examples containing EDRYCH (LOOK):

(194)   *mae Mair yn edrych yn athrawes dda*   *(Mair looks a good teacher)*
       is   Mair in look   in teacher good

(195)   *?mae Mair yn edrych yn athrawes*   *(Mair looks a teacher)*
         is   Mair in look   in   teacher

(196)   *mae Mair yn edrych fel athrawes*   *(Mair looks like a teacher)*
        is   Mair in   look   like teacher

As can be seen from (194), a modified noun readily occurs with YN (IN). Given an unmodified noun, however, FEL (LIKE) may be more typical than YN.

The second group of verbs contains PARA (CONTINUE) and DAL (LAST). They are subject to the same contrast with copula sentences:

(197)   (i)   *mae Mair yn para   'n athrawes*   *(Mair continues as a*
                 is   Mair in continue   in teacher   *teacher = is still a*
                                                           teacher)

      (ii)   *mae Mair yn athrawes*   *(Mair is a teacher)*
                  is   Mair in teacher

(198)   (i)   *mae Mair yn dal   yn athrawes*   *(Mair continues as a*
                  is   Mair in last   in teacher   *teacher = is still a teacher)*

      (ii)   *mae Mair yn athrawes*   *(Mair is a teacher)*
                  is   Mair in teacher

The use of these verbs, however, does not represent a departure from the epistemic basis of the copula sentences (and, as the examples in (i) of (197) and (198) show, there is no restriction on the occurrence of a noun only in the predicative phrase). There is no perceiver and the sentences involving DAL (LAST) and PARA (CONTINUE) can be accounted for in the framework proposed in the previous discussion of them in section 4c above:

(199)

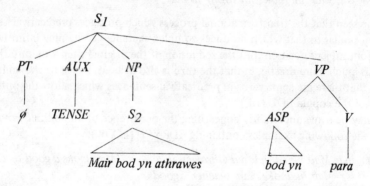

The various reduction, extraposition and raising transformations eventually produce the surface structure as in example (197) (i) above. It is also possible to infinitivalise the constituent sentence and extrapose the copula form BOD (BE) along with the predicative phrase, in which case the preposition I (TO, FOR) is introduced:

(200)   *mae Mair yn para   i fod yn athrawes*   *(Mair continues to*
          is   Mair in continue to be in   teacher   *be a teacher)*

This compares with the extraposition of verb phrases described in section 4c above. The verbs of perception can be discussed in a wider context which involves other related verbs. Consider the following, for instance:

(201) (i)   *'dwi 'n edrych ar Mair*   *(I am looking at Mair)*
             am I in look   on Mair

      (ii) *'dwi 'n gweld Mair*   *(I can see Mair)*
             am I in see   Mair

      (iii) *mae Mair yn edrych yn gryf*   *(Mair looks strong)*
             is Mair in look in strong

In example (201) (i) the activity is pre-perceptive, involving the act which is necessary to achieve perception; in this particular case this act is conveyed by EDRYCH AR (LOOK AT). In example (201) (ii) the receiving end of the perceptive process is conveyed by GWELD (SEE), while in (201) (iii) the predicatival sentence relates the state of affairs which is perceived. The perceptive verbs can all be related to other verbs in this manner as follows:

(202) (i)   *'dwi 'n gwrando ar Mair*   *(I'm listening to Mair)*
             am I in listen   on Mair

      (ii) *'dwi 'n clywed Mair*   *(I can hear Mair)*
             am I in hear   Mair

      (iii) *mae Mair yn swnio'n dda*   *(Mair sounds well)*
             is Mair in sound in good

(203) (i)   *'dwi 'n teimlo 'r bwrdd*   *(I'm feeling the table)*
             am I in feel the table

      (ii) *'dwi 'n teimlo 'r bwrdd*   *(I can feel the table)*
             am I in feel   the table

      (iii) *mae'r   bwrdd yn teimlo'n sych*   *(the table feels dry)*
             is the   table in   feel in dry

(204) (i)   *'dwi 'n ogla/gwyntio 'r pysgod*   *(I'm smelling the fish)*
             am I in smell   the fish

      (ii) *'dwi 'n clywed ogla/gwynt ar y pysgod* *(I can smell the fish)*
             am I in perceive smell   on the fish

      (iii) *mae'r pysgod yn ogla/gwyntio 'n ddrwg* *(the fish smell bad)*
             is the fish   in   smell   in bad

The various verbs can be related as follows:

(205)

Act to perceive	Registration of perception	State perceived
EDRYCH AR (look at)	GWELD (see)	EDRYCH (look)
GWRANDO AR (listen to)	CLYWED (hear)	SWNIO (sound)
TEIMLO (feel)	TEIMLO (feel)	TEIMLO (feel)
OGLA/GWYNTIO (smell)	CLYWED OGLA/ GWYNT (smell)	OGLA/GWYNTIO (smell)

The three groups have their own characteristics. The 'act to perceive' verbs can occur with progressive or non-progressive aspect, while the 'state perceived' type can only occur with the progressive, for example:

(206) (i) *'roeddwn i 'n gwrando ar y gloch* *(I was listening to the*
         was   I in   listen on the bell *bell)*

     (ii) *mi wneis i wrando ar y gloch* *(I listened to the bell)*
          PT did   I listen on the bell

(207) (i) *'roedd y gloch yn swnio 'n uchel* *(the bell sounded loud)*
          was   the bell   in sound in loud

     (ii) **mi swniodd y   gloch yn uchel* *(*the bell was sounding*
          PT sounded the bell   in loud *loud)*

The only exception is EDRYCH (LOOK), where it is possible to have:

(208) *mi edrychodd Mair yn ddel* *(Mair looked pretty)*
      PT looked   Mair in pretty

But this may be a use of EDRYCH (LOOK) which stresses the production of the state by the subject of the sentence, rather than its perception. The 'registration of perception' is characterised by the possibility that some speakers may use the lexical auxiliary GALLU (CAN) (see chapter V, section 3c);

(209) (i) *'dwi 'n gweld/clywed Mair* *(I see/hear Mair)*
          am I in see / hear   Mair

258

(ii) *mi alla' i weld/glywed Mair*   *(I can see/hear Mair)*
   PT can I see/hear Mair

The above examples have dealt with four of the five senses - GWELD (SEE), CLYWED (HEAR), TEIMLO (FEEL) and CLYWED OGLA (SMELL). The fifth one, involving 'taste', patterns differently from these four and can be illustrated as follows. Although there are transitive verbs BLASU (TASTE) and CHWAETHU (TASTE), they are not commonly used in the 'act to perceive', and more typical sentences involve TRIO (TRY) or PROFI (PROVE): *'dwi'n trio/profi'r tatws (I'm trying (i.e. tasting) the potatoes).* The 'registration of perception' can involve two patterns: one is similar to that for 'smell' and involves the verb CLYWED (PERCEIVE) occurring with the nominal BLAS (TASTE), as in *'dwi'n clywed blas tatws ar y cawl (I can perceive the taste of potatoes in the soup);* the other can involve an existential-locative copula sentence with the nominal BLAS (TASTE) modified by a description of the taste as in *mae yna flas tatws ar y cawl (there's a taste of potatoes in the soup).* The 'state perceived' is expressed by the existential-locatival copula pattern involving the nominal BLAS (TASTE), as follows: *mae yna flas neis ar y cawl (there's a nice taste on the soup - i.e. the soup tastes nice).* In some dialects the form TAST(I)O (TASTE) can be used in all three processes.

Finally, we can note that the verb CLYWED (HEAR, PERCEIVE) emerges as a general perceptive verb - replacing GWRANDO (LISTEN), occurring with the nominal OGLA (SMELL) in CLYWED OGLA (PERCEIVE A SMELL), and also occurring with the nominal BLAS (TASTE) in CLYWED BLAS (PERCEIVE A TASTE). It occurs in three out of the five perceptive processes involving the senses. In some dialects, at least, the verb CLYWED can also be used to convey 'feel' in the sense of registering perception, as in *'roeddwn i'n clywed hoelen yn fy esgid (I could feel a nail in my shoe)* and *'roeddwn i'n clywed rhywbeth yn galed (I could feel something hard).* On this basis, the usual English translation of CLYWED as 'HEAR', associating with aural features only, is too narrow an interpretation.

5c   Transitive predicatival sentences

A large number of verbs can occur in a transitive predicatival pattern. It is possible to distinguish various types of relationship involved, and here the discussion will concentrate upon the following:

(210)   *mae Mair yn golchi'r   dillad yn lân*   *(Mair washes the clothes*
          is   Mair in wash the clothes in clean   *clean)*

(211)   *mae Mair yn licio coffi 'n ddu*   *(Mair likes coffee black)*
          is   Mair in like coffee in black

(212)   *mae Mair yn galw John yn ffŵl*   *(Mair calls John a fool)*
          is   Mair in call John in fool

(213)   *mae Mair yn gweld John yn garedig*   *(Mair sees John to be kind)*
          is   Mair in see   John in kind

Although identical in terms of surface structure, these four examples are quite different in terms of their semantics.

Example (210) above is concerned with an activity which changes the state of the referent of the noun phrase Y DILLAD (THE CLOTHES). The sentence proposes that, through the action of washing, the clothes become clean. On this basis, examples like (210) can be associated with an abstract sentence as follows:

(214)   *MAE MAIR YN GOLCHI'R DILLAD FEL BOD HI 'N*   *(Mair washes the*
          is   Mair in   wash the clothes so be she in   *clothes in such a*
                                                          way that she makes
          GWNEUD I 'R DILLAD FOD YN LÂN   *the clothes be*
          do   for the clothes be   in clean   *clean)*

This type of predicatival sentence can be labelled as *causative*. There are a variety of sub-types of causative sentences, and no more will be attempted here than to make some random remarks. The predicative phrase can involve an adjective, as in example (210) above, or a noun. In the case of an adjective, the change involved is in the attributes of the noun which occurs in object position in surface structure. In some instances the predicatival pattern can be replaced by a structure involving an inchoative verb:

(215) (i)   *mae Mair yn gwneud ei sgert yn gwta*   *(Mair is making her*
             is   Mair in do   her skirt in short   *skirt short)*

      (ii) *mae Mair yn cwtogi ei sgert*   *(Mair is shortening*
             is   Mair in shorten her skirt   *her skirt)*

The following examples illustrate the occurrence of a noun in the predicative phrase:

(216) (i)   *maen nhw wedi gwneud John yn gadeirydd*   *(they have made*
             are they after   make John in chairman   *John chairman)*

      (ii) *maen nhw wedi sefydlu   John yn weinidog* *(they have inducted*
             are   they after induct   John in minister *John as a minister)*

260

(iii)   *maen nhw wedi codi John yn flaenor   (they have appointed
         are   they after raise John in deacon   John deacon)*

(iv)   *maen nhw wedi penodi John yn arweinydd   (they have appointed
        are   they after appoint John in conductor   John conductor)*

The change in each case involves alterations of the class-membership characteristics of the noun phrase in object position in surface structure. A significant point is that the noun in the predicative phrase can occur in object position by itself:

(217) (i)   *maen nhw wedi gwneud cadeirydd   (they have made a
              are   they after   make   chairman   chairman)*

(ii)   *maen nhw wedi sefydlu gweinidog   (they have established
        are   they after established minister   a minister)*

(iii)   *maen nhw wedi codi blaenor   (they have appointed
        are   they after rise   deacon   a deacon)*

(iv)   *maen nhw wedi penodi arweinydd   (they have appointed
       are they after appoint conductor   a conductor)*

Quite different are the following sentences, identical in surface structure:

(218)   *maen nhw 'n troi llefrith yn fenyn   (they 're turning milk
        are   they in   turn milk   in butter   into butter)*

(219)   *maen nhw 'n newid y tŷ̂ yn fflatiau   (they 're changing the
        are   they in change the house in flats   house into flats)*

In these examples the change is not of class-membership; it is one of state, whereby the commodity of the noun phrase in object position is converted into another commodity. In this case it is not possible to have the noun in the predicative phrase occurring in object position:

(220)   **maen nhw 'n troi menyn   (*they 're turning butter)
        are   they in turn butter*

(221)   **maen nhw 'n newid fflatiau   (*they 're changing flats)
        are they in   turn   flats*

The above sentences cannot be interpreted as variants of examples (218) and (219) above, although they are acceptable as involving deletion of a predicative phrase *(maen nhw'n troi menyn yn oel (they 're turning butter into oil))*. The verb TROI (TURN) characteristically occurs in complete change causatives and tends to be odd if it occurs in class-membership causatives:

261

(222) *?maen nhw wedi troi John yn arweinydd*   *(they've turned John*
       are they after turn John in leader   *into a leader)*

On the other hand, GWNEUD (MAKE) is a general type of verb in the class-membership variety and tends to be odd if it occurs in the complete change process:

(223) *?maen nhw 'n gwneud llefrith yn fenyn*   *(they're making milk*
       are they in make milk in butter   *into butter)*

However, there are two contexts in which GWNEUD can occur. Firstly, the process of complete change can be viewed from a reverse angle:

(224) *maen nhw 'n gwneud menyn allan o lefrith*   *(they're making butter*
       are they in make butter out of milk   *out of milk)*

(225) *maen nhw 'n gwneud fflatiau allan o'r tŷ*   *(they are making flats*
       are they in do flats out of the house   *out of the house)*

In this case the prepositional sequence ALLAN O (OUT OF) occurs to mark the commodity which is changed, and the resulting commodity occurs in surface object position. Secondly, this same pattern involving GWNEUD (MAKE) and ALLAN O (OUT OF) occurs in a significant variation of the change-of-state process:

(226) *maen nhw 'n gwneud cadeiriau allan o gerrig*   *(they're making chairs*
       are they in make chairs out of stones   *out of stones)*

(227) *maen nhw 'n gwneud ffigurau allan o bren*   *(they're making*
       are they in make figures out of wood   *figures out of wood)*

(228) *maen nhw 'n gwneud dillad allan o bapur*   *(they're making clothes*
       are they in make clothes out of paper   *out of paper)*

The important characteristic of this type of sentence is that there is no ready equivalent TROI (TURN) ... YN (IN) ... pattern:

(229) *?maen nhw 'n troi cerrig yn gadeiriau*   *(they're turning stones*
       are they in turn stones in chairs   *into chairs)*

(230) *?maen nhw 'n troi pren yn ffigurau*   *(they're turning wood*
       are they in turn wood in figures   *into figures)*

(231) *?maen nhw 'n troi papur yn ddillad*   *(they're turning paper*
       are they in turn paper in clothes   *into clothes)*

The reason seems to be that the change involved is not viewed as being 'complete' or 'significant': the stone remains stone even though it occurs in the shape of a chair, whereas the change of milk into butter is viewed as being more substantial.

Example (211) above is not concerned with change of state in any way and a causative paraphrase is inappropriate:

(232) *MAE MAIR YN LICIO COFFI FEL BOD HI 'N   (Mair likes coffee
       is   Mair in like coffee so be she in   in such a way that
                                                           she makes the
       GWNEUD I   'R COFFI FOD YN DDU   coffee to be black)
       make   for the coffee be   in black

Rather, such an example is concerned with *describing* how Mair likes coffee. On this basis it is more satisfactory to think of this type of sentence as involving either a relative clause or a PAN (WHEN) adjunctival clause:

(233) (i)   MAE MAIR YN LICIO COFFI SYDD YN DDU   (Mair likes coffee
             is   Mair in like coffee is   in black   which is black)

       (ii) MAE MAIR YN LICIO COFFI PAN MAE   (Mair likes coffee
             is   Mair in like coffee when is   when coffee is
                                                            black)
             COFFI YN DDU
             coffee in black

It can be recalled that a similar deep structure account was set up for non-finite sentences in section 3b above; consequently, predicative phrases in this context can be related to non-finites. As outlined in chapter VII, section 5e, adjectives are derived from relative clauses in this manner, and a severer reduction transformation would produce:

(234) mae Mair yn licio coffi du   (Mair likes black
       is   Mair in like coffee black   coffee)

The following examples include other verbs which occur in this pattern:

(235) mae Mair yn bwyta tatws   yn oer   (Mair eats potatoes
       is   Mair in eat   potatoes in cold   cold)

(236) maen nhw 'n darlledu 'r rhaglen yn fyw   (they broadcast the
       are they in broadcast the programme in live   programme live)

(237) maen nhw 'n gwerthu tocynnau yn rhad   (they sell tickets
       are they in sell   tickets   in cheap   cheap)

(238) mae hi 'n gwneud tê yn wan   (she makes tea weak)
       is   she in make   tea in weak

Example (238) could also be interpreted as a causative.

Example (212) is different yet again, and is best thought of as involving a relationship which can be represented in abstract form as follows:

(239) *MAE MAIR YN GALW BOD JOHN YN FFŴL*   *(Mair calls that John*
     is   Mair in   call   be   John in fool   *is a fool)*

The relationship can be thought of as *depiction,* and in addition to GALW (CALL) the verb YSTYRIED (CONSIDER) can occur here.

The fourth type is in many ways the most interesting, as it involves the perception or judgement of a state of affairs. In addition to GWELD (SEE), as in example (213) above, CLYWED (PERCEIVE) also occurs, especially in relation to meteorological circumstances:

(240) *mae Mair yn ei chlywed hi 'n oer*   *(Mair feels it to be cold)*
     is   Mair in its perceive it in cold

Examples of this type, involving GWELD (SEE) and CLYWED (PERCEIVE), compare very closely with those involving GALW (CALL) and YSTYRIED (CONSIDER) discussed above. Both sets related to the interpretation of some object, person or state of affairs. Indeed, it is possible to suggest the same deep structure account for GWELD and CLYWED as was suggested for GALW and YSTYRIED:

(241) *mae Mair yn gweld bod John yn garedig*   *(Mair sees that John*
     is   Mair in see   be John in kind   *is kind)*

(242) *mae Mair yn clywed bod hi 'n oer*   *(Mair perceives that*
     is   Mair in perceive be she in cold   *it is cold)*

The reduction of the noun clauses to JOHN YN GAREDIG and HI'N OER would produce the appropriate surface structures (with the re-positioning of the pronoun around the verb in the latter case). They are presented separately here, however, because of semantic differences. The verbs GWELD and CLYWED, as previously discussed, are concerned with perceptive processes, and it is possible to relate their occurrence in the above examples to sentences involving EDRYCH (LOOK) and TEIMLO (FEEL):

(243) *mae John yn edrych yn garedig i Mair*   *(John looks kind*
     is John in look in kind to Mair   *to Mair)*

(244) *mae'n teimlo'n oer i Mair*   *(it feels cold to Mair)*
     is in   feel in cold to Mair

It would be interesting to attempt to relate these latter examples to (241) and (242) above, as both sets involve the same basic message.

5d   Prepositional phrase-predicatival sentences

There are a number of sentences of this type and the following can be listed here:

(245) *mae'n gas   gan Mair goffi*   *(Mair hates coffee)*
       is in   hateful   LOC Mair coffee

(246) *mae'n ddrwg gan Mair am y llythyr*   *(Mair is sorry about*
       is in bad   LOC Mair about the letter   *the letter)*

(247) *mae'n braf ar Mair*   *(it's all right for Mair)*
       is in fine on Mair

These sentences involve a matrix sentence which is a locatival copula sentence, and a constituent sentence which is a descriptive copula sentence.

Consider example (245) above. This sentence involves conveying Mair's attitude towards coffee and it expresses the view that coffee is hateful to Mair. Such an analysis can be repreated by the following 'artificial' sentence:

(248) *mae bod coffi yn gas   gan Mair*   *(that the coffee is*
       is   be coffee in hateful LOC Mair   *hateful is with Mair)*

In terms of deep structure, such a sentence can be said to involve a predicative copula sentence as the subject of a 'possessive' copula sentence:

(249)

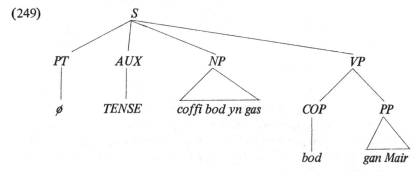

The description of the coffee is conveyed in the constituent sentence, and this is associated with Mair by occurring in the subject position of a locatival sentence involving a GAN phrase. The appropriate surface structure is produced by deleting the PT, AUX and BOD of the constituent sentence, extraposing the noun phrase subject, which is then subject to soft mutation, and raising the predicative phrase YN GAS (IN HATEFUL) to subject position of the matrix sentence. Like CAS (HATEFUL) is the comparative GWELL (BETTER):

(250) *mae'n well   gan Mair goffi*   *(Mair prefers coffee)*
       is in better LOC Mair coffee

These two items form a system of attitude involving the contrast of dislike (CAS) and preference (GWELL).

265

Very similar is example (246); its surface structure can be described as follows:

(251)   *COP + PRED ADJ + PP + PP*

The predicative adjective relates to the referent of the noun in the final prepositional phrase and this sentence can be characterised in deep structure as:

(252)

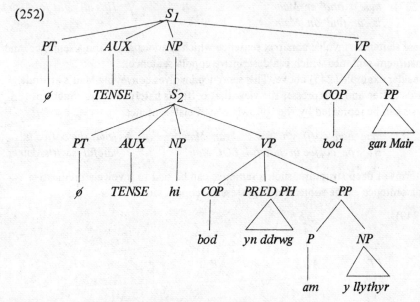

The deep structure assumes the same general form as that given in (249) above. One significant difference, however, is that the subject of the constituent sentence is given as the impersonal pronoun HI (SHE = IT), which in this context can represent a general notion of a 'state of affairs' (compare the analysis of example (247) given below). The constituent sentence is reduced to YN DDRWG AM Y LLYTHYR (IN BAD ABOUT THE LETTER), which would eventually produce MAEN'N DDRWG AM Y LLYTHYR GAN MAIR (IS BAD ABOUT THE LETTER WITH MAIR). However, the prepositional phrase AM Y LLYTHYR (ABOUT THE LETTER) is extraposed beyond MAIR in the matrix sentence, YN DDRWG (IN BAD) is raised into subject position, and the surface structure in (246) is produced. In this case we have admission of default which conveys an expression of apology. Like DRWG (BAD) are PITI (PITY) and GOFID (SHAME), both of which are used to express regret:

(253)   *mae'n biti/ofid gan Mair am   y   llythyr*   *(Mair is sorry about*
          is in pity/   LOC Mair about the letter   *the letter)*

266

These three items are all involved in some form of apology, ranging from apology proper in the case of DRWG to regret in the case of PITI and GOFID.

The third type, exemplified by (247) above, is different in terms of surface structure:

(254)   *COP + PRED ADJ + PP*

There is no extraposed noun phrase and the locative involves the preposition AR (ON). In terms of semantics, it conveys a message to the effect that 'things are fine for Mair'. Thus, it is reasonable to suggest a deep structure like:

(255)   *mae bod hi yn braf ar Mair*   *(that it is fine is on Mair)*
        is be it in fine on Mair

In this deep structure the general state of affairs, or 'things', is represented by the impersonal pronoun HI (SHE = IT) and described as favourable. By embedding in a matrix locatival sentence this description is then associated with Mair. Like BRAF (FINE) is DRWG (BAD):

(256)   *mae'n ddrwg ar Mair*   *(it's bad for Mair)*
        is in   bad on Mair

Slightly different in terms of prepositional occurrence is:

(257)   *mae'n biti drostoch*   *(it's a pity for you)*
        is in pity for you

(258)   *mae'n annifyr i   chi*   *(it's unpleasant for you)*
        is in unpleasant for you

But the same recursive relationships are involved in each case.

6   PASSIVISATION

6a   Introduction

The operation of passivisation is a familiar concept which has been discussed at length in traditional grammar. In Welsh, there are two ways of forming a passive sentence. Consider the following active sentence:

(259)   *mi drawodd Mair y   bachgen*   *(Mair hit the boy)*
        PT hit   Mair the boy

This sentence has an agent as noun phrase subject and patient as noun phrase object. Firstly, the above sentence can be passivised by using CAEL (RECEIVE), so that we have:

(260)   *mi gafodd y bachgen ei daro gan Mair*   *(the boy was hit*
         PT got the boy his hit LOC Mair   *by Mair)*

Secondly, it is possible to use a verbal inflection so that we have:

(261)   *mi drawyd y bachgen gan Mair*   *(the boy was hit by*
         PT was hit the boy   LOC Mair   *Mair)*

Whereas in the active sentence MAIR (the agent) occurs in subject position and
Y BACHGEN (THE BOY) (the patient) occurs in object position, in the passive
sentences their positions are changed. In the process of this change, the agent, in this
case MAIR, is explicitly marked as such by the preposition GAN (LOC).

The function of the passive is to focus attention on the patient as opposed to the
agent, by placing the former in the most prominent (i.e. subject) position.

In traditional grammar, the passive involving CAEL (RECEIVE) is known as the
personal passive and the passive involving the inflection is known as the *impersonal*
passive. In discussing these two types of passive it is important to bear in mind stylistic
consideration, as each relates to different contexts.

6b   The personal (or CAEL) passive

The operation of forming a passive using CAEL (RECEIVE) is complicated. Consider
the number of differences between active and passive sentences by comparing example
(259) with example (260) above: (i) the patient occurs as subject; (ii) the verb CAEL
occurs; (iii) the verb of the active sentence occurs in object position in the passive
sentence, (iv) the original verb is preceded by a possessive pronoun concordant with
the patient, (v) the agent occurs in a final prepositional phrase marked by the
preposition GAN (LOC).

The complexity of the comparison is offset by the fact that the actual passive
pattern is a common one in Welsh. The surface structure of the passive pattern is
superficially a verb phrase of the type V NP PP where, in example (260) above, CAEL
(RECEIVE) is the verb, EI DARO (HIS HIT) is the post-verbal noun phrase and GAN
MAIR (BY MAIR) is the prepositional phrase. The passive pattern thus compares
with familiar examples like:

(262)   *mae'r bachgen wedi cael llythyr gan Mair*   *(the boy has had a*
         is the boy   after have letter LOC Mair   *letter from Mair)*

(263)   *mae John wedi clywed newyddion da gan ei rieni*   *(John has heard*
         is John after hear news   good LOC his parents *good news from*
                                                              his parents)

(264)   *mae Mair wedi prynu côt hir gan ei chwaer*   *(Mair has brought a*
         is Mair after buy coat long LOC her sister   *long coat from her sister)*

The significant point is that there is a functional as well as a formal comparison with the passive pattern. Like the latter, these sentences represent a re-focusing of attention, as they compare with:

(265) *mae Mair wedi anfon llythyr i John*   *(Mair has sent a letter*
       is Mair after send letter to John   *to John)*

(266) *mae rhieni John wedi dweud newyddion da wrtho fo*   *(John's parents*
       is parents John after tell news good to him him   *have told him*
                                                              good news)

(267) *mae chwaer Mair wedi gwerthu côt hir iddi hi*   *(Mair's sister*
       is sister Mair after sell coat long to her her   *has sold a long*
                                                              coat to her)

The passive in Welsh can be explained by viewing the active sentence as a constituent sentence in object position of a matrix sentence containing CAEL (RECEIVE). The details can be illustrated as follows:

(268)

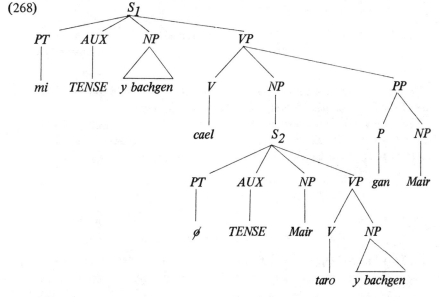

As it stands, the above configuration produces an abstract structure (which can be represented in surface structure terms for convenience):

(269) *mi gafod y bachgen PT tarodd Mair y bachgen gan Mair*   *(the boy had*
       PT had the boy   hit Mair the boy LOC Mair   *that Mair*
                                                                   hit the boy
                                                                   by Mair)

269

In the lower sentence the PT, AUX and subject NP are deleted and the result would be:

(270) *mi gafodd y   bachgen taro y bachgen gan Mair*   *(the boy had hit*
       PT had   the boy   hit the boy   LOC Mair   *the boy by Mair)*

The noun phrase object Y BACHGEN (THE BOY) is pronominalised to give:

(271) *mi gafodd y   bachgen ei daro gan Mair*   *(the boy had his*
       PT had   the boy   his hit LOC Mair   *hit by Mair)*

We have ignored here a variety of other transformational details in order to keep a fairly complex topic as simple as possible.

The personal or CAEL passive is the primary method of forming the passive in spontaneous spoken Welsh. Although the impersonal or inflected passive does occur in speech, its occurrence is by comparison very limited. There are, however, a number of set expressions which use the inflected passive:

(272) *ganwyd y   mab hyna' yn 1951*   *(the eldest son was*
       was born the son oldest in 1951   *born in 1951)*

(273) *agorwyd y   lle 'ma bum mlynedd yn ôl*   *(this place was*
       was opened the place here five year   ago   *opened five years*
                                                         ago)

But, in the main, the personal or CAEL passive is the rule in spoken Welsh and the use of the inflected passive is stylistically marked as formal.

There are a number of restrictions on the use of the CAEL passive. The most general restriction is a *syntactic* one: it mainly applies to a *noun phrase object*. The CAEL passive can apply to simple sentences of the following type:

(274) *mae'r heddlu wedi dal y dyn*   *(the police have*
       is the police after catch the man   *caught the man)*

(275) *mae Mair wedi rhoi'r prês   i 'r capel*   *(Mair has given the*
       is Mair after give the money to the chapel   *money to the chapel)*

(276) *mae'r pwyllgor wedi ethol John yn llywydd*   *(the committee have*
       is the council after elect John in president   *elected John president)*

giving:

(277) *mae'r dyn wedi cael ei ddal gan yr heddlu*   *(the man has been*
       is the man after have his catch LOC the police   *caught by the police)*

270

(278) *mae'r prês wedi cael ei roi   i 'r capel*   (the money has been
       is the money after have his give to the chapel   given to the chapel
                                                          by Mair)
       gan Mair
       LOC Mair

(279) *mae John wedi cael ei ethol yn llywydd*   (John has been elected
       is John after have his elect in president   president by the council)

       gan y pwyllgor
       LOC the council

But the CAEL passive does not readily apply to constituents other than a noun phrase object. The following are unacceptable or at least questionable:

(280) (i)   *mae John wedi eistedd ar y gadair*   (John has sat on
             is John after sit   on the chair   the chair)

       (ii) **mae'r gadair wedi cael eistedd arni*   (*the chair has
             is the chair after have sit   on it   been sat on by John)

             gan John
             LOC John

(281) (i)   *mae Mair wedi sôn am   y llyfr efo John* (Mair has talked
             is Mair after talk about the book with John about the book
                                                            with John)

       (ii) **mae'r llyfr wedi cael sôn amdano*   (*the book has
             is the book after   have talk about it   been talked about
                                                          with John by Mair)
             efo John gan Mair
             with John LOC Mair

(282) (i)   *mae Mair wedi rhoi prês   i 'r capel*   (Mair has given
             is Mair after give money to the chapel   money to the chapel)

       (ii) **mae'r capel wedi cael rhoi prês iddo* (*the chapel has
             is the chapel after have give money to it been given money
                                                          by Mair)
             gan Mair
             LOC Mair

However, we are here in an area of problematic usage: it may be fair to state that accepted practices are sometimes contradicted by colloquial usage in a bilingual society.

There is a further functional restriction within the major syntactic restriction: the CAEL passive only operates upon those noun phrase objects that are patients (see chapter XI, section 2a). Examples (274) to (276) above can therefore be passivised. But consider sentences involving noun phrase objects of the following type:

(283) mae John yn licio Mair   (John likes Mair)
       is John in like Mair

(284) mae'r merched yn deall   hynny   (the girls understand
       is the girls   in understand that   that)

(285) mae pawb yn cofio   'r dyddiad yma   (everyone remembers
       is all   in remember the date here   this date)

In these sentences the verbs involve mental processes or states and passive equivalents are not possible or, at least, uncertain:

(286) *mae Mair yn cael ei licio gan John   (*Mair is liked by John)
       is Mair in have her like LOC John

(287) *mae hynny yn cael ei ddeall   gan y merched (*that is understood
       is that in have its understand LOC the girls by the girls)

(288) ?mae'r dyddiad yn cael ei gofio   gan bawb   (the date is remem-
       is the date   in have its remember LOC everyone bered by everyone)

The CAEL passive is thus functionally, as well as syntactically, restricted.

Traditional grammar has noted that when the perfect aspect marker WEDI (AFTER) occurs, CAEL (RECEIVE) can be left out. Thus:

(289) (i)   mae'r dyn wedi cael ei ddal   (the man has been
             is the man after have his catch   caught)

       (ii) mae'r dyn wedi 'i ddal   (the man has been
             is the man after his catch   caught)

This type of deletion frequently occurs with verbs which involve a change of state, the passive pattern with deleted CAEL (RECEIVE) concentrating upon the state of the patient after the change has occured.

An interesting occurrence of CAEL (RECEIVE) occurs in the following type of example (which may be dialectally distinctive, perhaps being more typical of northern areas):

(290) mae John wedi cael palu'r ardd   (John has had the
       is John after have dig the garden   garden dug)

(291) mi gafodd Mair dorri ei gwallt   (Mair had her hair cut)
       PT had   Mair cut her hair

(292)   *'roedd hi wedi cael glanhau 'r ffenestri*   *(she had had the*
          was she after have clean the windows   *windows cleaned)*

In each case the surface structure is very similar to a passive sentence involving CAEL (RECEIVE), being that of a complex sentence with CAEL as its verb and an infinitival clause in object position. There are, however, a number of significant differences, as will be pointed out in the following discussion.

Firstly, the infinitival clause implicitly involves an agent (see chapter XI, section 2a) who engineers the action. In surface structure terms, the agent can occur in one of two ways, for example:

(293)   *mae John wedi cael rhywun i balu'r ardd*   *(John has had someone*
          is John after have someone to dig the garden   *to dig the garden)*

(294)   *mae John wedi cael palu'r ardd gan rywun*   *(John has had the gar-*
          is John after have dig the garden LOC someone   *den dug by someone)*

In the first instance the agent occurs in the object position of the CAEL sentence and the preposition I (TO) is introduced before the infinitival, following a pattern described in section 4c above. The second instance sees the agent occurring in a post-verbal position in the infinitival clause, where it is preceded by the preposition GAN (LOC), a typical occurrence for an agent as described in section 6a above.

Secondly, the infinitival can occur in a variant pattern, as the following instances illustrate:

(295)   *mae John wedi cael yr ardd wedi 'i phalu*   *(John has had the*
          is John after have the garden after its dug   *garden dug)*

(296)   *mi gafodd Mair ei gwallt wedi 'i dorri*   *(Mair had her hair cut)*
          PT had Mair her hair after its cut

(297)   *'roedd hi wedi cael y ffenestri wedi 'u glanhau*   *(she had had the*
          was she after have the windows after their clean   *windows cleaned)*

Here the infinitival clause itself has been passivised, the original object now occurring initially before the verb and the verb CAEL (RECEIVE) deleted in the infinitival in the context of the perfect aspect marker WEDI (AFTER), as described above. In each case the agent could occur post-verbally in the infinitival clause preceded by the preposition GAN (LOC), for example:

(298)   *mae John wedi cael yr ardd wedi 'i phalu*   *(John has had the*
          is John after have the garden after its dig   *garden dug by*
                                                           someone)
          gan rywun
          LOC someone

Again, this is a typical occurrence of agents in passive sentences.

Examples (290) to (292) above can be derived from a deep structure which is very similar to passive sentences, in that the infinitival can be produced from a constituent sentence in object position. Example (291) can serve as illustration:

(299)

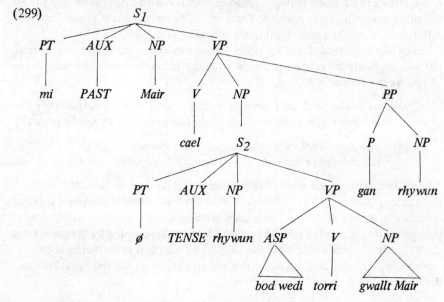

The constituent sentence contains perfect aspect in order to cater for the variant pattern listed in examples (295) to (297). The object noun phrase of the constituent sentence is never identical (or co-referential) with the subject of the matrix sentence, thus distinguishing the eventual surface structure from passive proper. For convenience, the matrix sentence will be considered in surface form and the discussion will concentrate upon the constituent sentence. In deep structure terms it occurs as:

(300) mi gafodd Mair bod rhywun wedi torri   *(Mair had that someone*
       PT had   Mair be someone after cut   *had cut Mair's hair*
                                                     by someone)
       gwallt Mair gan   rywun
       hair   Mair LOC someone

A number of transformations are necessary to produce the various surface structures.

Firstly, deletion transformations are necessary to reduce the constituent sentence to its various surface structure forms. The severest of these deletes everything except the verb, post-verbal constituents and any adjunct constituents. Furthermore, the GAN phrase of the matrix sentence is also deleted. After pronominalising any post-verbal objects, this produces the surface structure as in (291) above. Alternatively, deletion

274

proceeds, as just outlined, except for the GAN phrase of the matrix sentence and the subject of the constituent sentence, giving:

(301) *mi gafodd Mair rhywun torri gwallt Mair*   *(Mair had someone*
       PT had   Mair someone cut hair   Mair   *cut Mair's hair by*
                                                         someone)
       gan   rywun
       LOC someone

In this case, however, two further possibilities apply. Either the GAN phrase is deleted and the subject noun phrase is retained - following this, I (TO, FOR) is introduced before the verb phrase of the constituent sentence to produce an example like (293) above. Or the subject noun phrase is deleted and the GAN phrase is retained to produce an example like (294) above.

Secondly, in order to produce the third possibility in (295) to (297) above, the constituent sentence is itself passivised:

(302) *mi gafodd Mair bod gwallt Mair wedi cael*   *(Mair had that Mair's*
       PT had   Mair be   hair   Mair after have   *hair had had that*
                                                          someone had cut
       bod rhywun wedi torri gwallt Mair   *Mair's hair)*
       be someone after cut   hair   Mair

Pronominalisation throughout produces MI GAFODD MAIR EI GWALLT WEDI CAEL BOD RHYWUN WEDI EI DORRI (MAIR HAD THAT HER HAIR HAD THAT SOMEONE HAD ITS CUT). Deletion in the lowest sentence produces MI GAFODD MAIR BOD EI GWALLT WEDI CAEL EI DORRI (MAIR HAD THAT HER HAIR HAD HAD ITS CUT). Deletion in the middle sentence produces MI GAFODD MAIR EI GWALLT WEDI'I DORRI (MAIR HAD HER HAIR ITS CUT).

The examples considered so far have all involved the action in the infinitival clause being completed. But consider the following examples:

(303) *mae nhw 'n cael paentio'r tŷ*   *(they're having the*
       are they in have paint the house   *house painted)*

(304) *'roedden nhw 'n cael ffitio carpedi*   *(they were having*
       were   they in have cit   carpets   *carpets fitted)*

In each case the main sentence occurs in progressive aspect (see chapter VII, section 1), and the implication is that the activity in the infinitival clause is either in progress or yet to come. On this basis it is inappropriate to have perfect aspect in the constituent sentence (given 'artificially' again):

                                                         (they're having
(305) *maen nhw 'n cael bod rhywun wedi paentio'r tŷ*   *that someone*
       are they in have be someone after paint the house *has painted*
                                                         the house)

(306) *'roedden nhw 'n cael bod rhywun bod wedi*   *(they were having*
         were   they in have be someone be   after   *that someone had*

                                                            fitted carpets)
         ffitio   carpedi
         fit   carpets

Perfect aspect suggests that the action has taken place and does not agree with the aspectual characteristics of the matrix sentence. It is more appropriate to have non-perfect in the constituent sentence:

(307) *maen nhw 'n cael bod rhywun yn paentio 'r tŷ*   *(they're having*
         are   they in have be someone in   paint   the house   *that someone*
                                                              paints the house)

(308) *'roedden nhw 'n cael bod rhywun yn ffitio carpedi*   *(they were having*
         were   they in   have be someone in   fit   carpets   *that someone*
                                                              fitted carpets)

It therefore emerges as a curious fact that the variant pattern involving perfect aspect is yet possible:

(309) *maen nhw 'n cael y   tŷ   wedi 'i baentio*   *(they're having*
         are   they in have the house after its paint   *the house painted)*

(310) *'roedden nhw 'n cael carpedi wedi 'i ffitio*   *(they were having*
         were   they in have carpets after their fit   *carpets fitted)*

There are two possible explanations for the occurrence of the variant passive pattern with this type of sentence. Firstly, it could be based upon the English pattern. Secondly, the degree of reduction which is necessary can only be achieved with the perfect aspect. As pointed out above, the verb CAEL (RECEIVE) in the passive can be deleted if the perfect WEDI (AFTER) occurs. But it is not deletable in the case of the non-perfect, and the only way that the necessary degree of deletion can be achieved is by introducing WEDI.

6c   The impersonal (or inflected) passive

In contrast to the CAEL passive, the inflected passive compares very simply with an equivalent active sentence. Consider example (259) and (261) above. Three changes are involved: (i) the patient occurs as subject; (ii) the agent occurs after the verb, marked by GAN; (iii) the inflectional ending of the verb is changed.

Despite the relative simplicity involved, the inflected passive is not extensively used in spontaneous spoken Welsh. It is primarily found in formal varieties of Welsh, although in such varieties it is used productively and has an extensive range of occurrences. It occurs frequently, for instance, in such items of formal spoken Welsh as news bulletins, and is one of the main stylistic characteristics of traditional written

276

Welsh.

Its simplicity is structural only; in another respect it is relatively complex. One of the main characteristics of spoken Welsh is that it uses an analytic as opposed to a synthetic pattern. The CAEL pattern gives explicit realisation to a variety of features and, in an analytic sense, is simpler than the inflected pattern.

In use, however, the inflected passive is not as restricted as the CAEL passive. The syntactic range of the personal passive is such that it includes prepositional objects as well as ordinary objects. Thus, in addition to noun phrase objects, the inflected passive can apply to the following:

(311) (i) *eistoddodd Mair ar y gadair*   *(Mair sat on the*
            sat   *Mair on the chair*   *chair)*

      (ii) *eisteddwyd ar y gadair gan   Mair*   *(the chair was sat*
            was sat   *on the chair LOC   Mair*   *on by Mair)*

(312) (i) *soniodd y pwyllgor   am   y mater*   *(the committee*
            talked   the committee about the matter   *talked about the*
                                                           matter)

      (ii) *soniwyd   am   y   mater gan y pwyllgor*   *(the matter was*
            was talked about the matter LOC the committee   *talked about by*
                                                        the committee)

In comparing the active and passive sentences, it is interesting to note that the prepositional phrase remains intact, the whole of it following the verb in the passive sentence (or occurring in 'subject position' in the passive sentence) and not just the noun phrase of the prepositional phrase.

The inflected passive also has an important use with complex sentences of the type:

(313) *maen nhw 'n dweud bod y llywodraeth yn mynd* *(they say that the*
       are they in say   be the government in go   *government is*
                                                going to close the
       i gau 'r ffatri   *factory)*
       to close the factory

(314) *maen nhw 'n dadlau bod y wlad   yn well*   *(they argue that the*
       are they in argue be the country in   better   *country is better*
                                                than the town)
       na 'r dre'
       than the town

With such examples it is found that the inflected passive can be used as normal without any further modification; but this is not the case with the CAEL passive:

(315) (i) *dywedir bod y   llywodraeth yn mynd i gau*
            is said be the   government in go   to close

            'r   ffatri
            the factory

            *(it is said that
            the government
            is going to close
            the factory)*

       (ii) **mae bod y llywodraeth yn mynd i gau 'r*
            is   be the government in go to close the

            ffatri   yn cael ei ddweud
            factory in have its said

            *(*that the
            government is
            going to close
            the factory
            is said)*

(316) (i) *dadleuir bod y wlad   yn well   na 'r dre'*
            is argued be the country in better than the town

            *(it is argued that
            the country is
            better than the
            town)*

       (ii) **mae bod y wlad   yn well   na 'r dre'*
            is   be the country in better than the town

            yn cael ei ddadlau
            in have its argue

            *(*that the
            country is better
            than the town
            is argued)*

In spoken Welsh, the normal formulation of a passive involving CAEL (RECEIVE) would not be possible and the unacceptable examples in (315) (ii) and (316) (ii) above must be subjected to another operation to be made acceptable, namely *extraposition* as discussed in section 2c earlier. That is, the constituent sentence which occurs in subject position in the above examples is extraposed beyond the verb DWEUD (TELL, SAY) to produce the examples that would actually occur: *mae'n cael ei ddweud bod y llywodraeth yn mynd i gau'r ffatri (it is said that the government is going to close the factory)* and *mae'n cael ei ddadlau bod y wlad yn well na'r dre' (it is argued that the country is better than the town)*. In spontaneous spoken Welsh, however, the active pattern in sentences of this type is preferred to either acceptable passive pattern and is the normal colloquial usage.

Three inflections exist as possible (although rare) occurrences in speech: -IR, -ID and -WYD. Compared with the possibilities in the periphrastic patterns involving CAEL (RECEIVE), the inflected pattern has to conflate many distinctions which can be made periphrastically. It is possible with CAEL to have:

(317) *mae Mair wedi cael ei gweld gan John*
       is   Mair after have her see   LOC John

       *(Mair has been seen
       by John)*

(318) *mi gafodd Mair ei gweld   gan John*
       PT had   Mair her see   LOC John

       *(Mair was seen by
       John)*

(319)   *'roedd Mair yn cael ei gweld gan John*   *(Mair was being seen*
         was   Mair in have her see LOC John   *by John)*

(320)   *'roedd Mair wedi cael ei gweld gan John*   *(Mair had been seen*
         was   Mair after have her see   LOC John   *by John)*

The inflected passive conflates all these to:

(321)   *gwelwyd   Mair gan John*   *(Mair was seen by John)*
         was seen   Mair LOC   John

Thus, although syntactically less restricted, it loses some of the explicit distinctions which can be made by CAEL.

7   CO-ORDINATION

7a   Introduction

Co-ordination can best be introduced by considering the structures in the following examples:

(322)   *mae Mair yn cysgu a   mae John yn palu'r ardd* *(Mair is sleeping*
         is   Mair in sleep and   is   John in dig the garden *and John is digging*
                                                                        the garden)

(323)   *mae Mair yn crio ond mae John yn chwerthin*   *(Mair is crying but*
         is   Mair in cry but is John in   laugh   *John is laughing)*

(324)   *mae Mair yn prynu tatws   o   'r siop   neu*   *(Mair buys potatoes*
         is   Mair. in buy   potatoes from the shop or   *from the shop or*
                                                    John fetches them
         mae John yn eu nôl nhw   o 'r   dre'   *from town)*
         is   John   in their bring them from the town

In each example two sentences co-occur with each other. As far as co-ordination is concerned they are of equal status, and it is not the case that one recurs within the structure of the other. Rather, we have a situation which can be represented as follows:

(325)

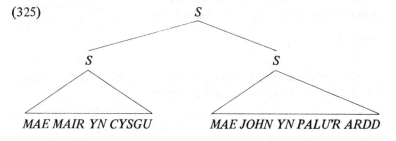

279

In addition to the two co-ordinated sentences we also have various items like A (AND), OND (BUT) and NEU (OR), which are placed between the two sentences:

(326)

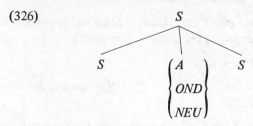

These items are traditionally known as CO—ORDINATING CONJUNCTIONS.

7b   Possibilities involved in co-ordination

Co-ordination is theoretically infinite and it would be possible for a native speaker to spend the rest of his life producing an infinitely co-ordinated sentence. Normally, however, its length is curtailed and, where we have a number of co-ordinated sentences, the co-ordinating conjunctions are usually deleted except for the last one:

(327) *'roedd Mair yn canu'r delyn, 'roedd Gwil yn*
       was   Mair in sing the harp   was   Gwil in   *(Mair was playing the harp, Gwil was playing the guitar, Gwen was playing the piano and John was dancing)*

       canu 'r gitar, 'roedd Gwen yn canu 'r piano
       sing the guitar   was   Gwen in sing the piano

       a 'roedd John yn dawnsio
       and was John in   dance

The possibilities of deletion extend beyond that of merely removing the co-ordinating conjunction. Consider example (327) above. The auxiliary is the same in each case and, after its initial establishment, it too may be deleted, thus producing non-finites (see section 3 above):

(328) *'roedd Mair yn canu 'r delyn, Gwil yn canu 'r*
       was   Mair in sing the   harp Gwil in sing the   *(Mair was playing the harp, Gwil playing the guitar, Gwen playing the piano and John dancing)*

       gitar, Gwen yn canu 'r piano a John yn
       guitar Gwen in sing the piano and John in

       dawnsio
       dance

Moreover, in three of the sentences, the verb is the same, namely CANU (SING); after its initial establishment, this too could be deleted:

(329) *'roedd Mair yn canu 'r delyn, Gwil   y gitar,*   *(Mair was playing*
       was   Mair in sing the harp   Gwil the guitar   *the harp, Gwil the*
       guitar, Gwen the
       Gwen y piano a 'roedd John yn dawnsio   *piano and John was*
       Gwen the piano and was John in   dance   *dancing)*

The final sentence here is quite different and the auxiliary tends to be retained.
It is through a process of deletion that various constituents in a surface structure
sentence are co-ordinated. Consider the following example:

(330) *'roedd John a Mair yn dawnsio ac yn canu*   *(John and Mair were*
       was   John and Mair in dance   and in sing   *dancing and singing)*

In (330) we have co-ordinated noun phrase subject JOHN A MAIR (JOHN AND
MAIR) and co-ordinated verb phrases YN DAWNSIO AC YN CANU (DANCING
AND SINGING). Such a surface ᶜ ructure sentence involves co-ordinated sentences
as follows:

(331)

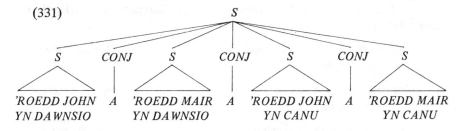

'ROEDD JOHN   A   'ROEDD MAIR   A   'ROEDD JOHN   A   'ROEDD MAIR
YN DAWNSIO   YN DAWNSIO   YN CANU   YN CANU

This would produce a sentence:

(332) *'roedd John yn dawnsio a 'roedd Mair yn dawnsio*   *(John was dancing*
       was   John in dance and was Mair in dance   *and Mair was*
       dancing and John
       a 'roedd John yn canu a 'roedd Mair yn canu   *was singing and*
       and was John in sing and was   Mair in sing   *Mair was singing)*

However, various transformations can eventually produce the surface structure
sentence as in (330).

8   DEMONSTRATIVE SENTENCES

8a   Introduction

The label 'demonstrative sentence' in this context refers to the three forms DYMA
(HERE IS), DYNA (THERE IS) and DACW (THERE (YONDER) IS). The demonstrative
sentence can occur as the matrix sentence in complex constructions:

(333) dyna   ddigwyddodd y   tro hwn   (that's what happened
      that is happened   the time this   this time)

In addition to the above there is also a variety of other possibilities:

(334) dyna   un rheswm pam nad oes gen i gar   (that's one reason why
      that is one reason why NEG is LOC I car   I haven't (got) a car)

(335) dyna   beth ydy'r   trwbl   (that's what the
      that is what is the trouble   trouble is)

(336) dyna   lle mae o   'n mynd   (that's where he's
      that is where is   he   in go   going)

(337) dyma   John yn dod i lawr y ffordd   (here's John coming
      this is John in come down the road   down the road)

The traditional explanation of these forms draws upon etymological facts and suggests that they are the reduced remnants of a previous pattern involving the verb GWELD (SEE):

(338) weli di yma (→ dyma)   (see you here)
      see you here

(339) weli di yna (→ dyna)   (see you there)
      see you there

(340) weli di acw (→ dacw)   (see you yonder)
      se you yonder

If this is the case, the recursion involving the demonstratives can be regarded as object recursion of the above sentences. For example, consider example (333):

(341)

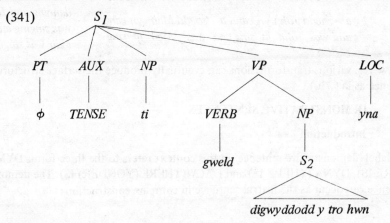

282

The constituent sentence is extraposed beyond YNA (THERE), the matrix sentence is transformed by the auxiliary carrier transformation and reduced, and the surface structure in (333) is produced.

8b   Past historic usage

The last example in (337) involves a non-finite and can be interpreted literally. But of particular interest is the special use of DYMA (HERE IS) with non-finites as follows:

(342) *dyma   fi'n cerdded ar hyd y   stryd*   *(here am I walking*
       this is I in walk   on long the street   *along the street)*

(343) *dyma   Mair yn ateb yn ôl yn syth*   *(here's Mair answering*
       this is Mair in answer back in straight   *back straight away)*

It is possible to interpret these examples as describing a past event. The use of DYMA + non-finite in this fashion is very common in spontaneous spoken narrative of past events. The effect is one of presenting the past happening with the immediacy of a present event. It is frequently referred to as the *historic present*.

Notes to chapter VIII

1.   This formal distinction correlates with a non-factive and factive distinction discussed by Kiparsky and Kiparsky (1970). There is evidence to suggest that noun clauses can occur with factive and non-factive verbs or predicative nouns/adjectives in the matrix sentence, whereas question-type clauses can only occur with factive ones:

(i) (a) *mae'n ofnadwy bod John yn gweithio*   *(its' awful that*
          is in awful   be John in   work   *John works in a*
                                      cold room)
          mewn   'stafell oer
          in a   room cold

    (b) *mae'n ofnadwy lle mae John yn gweithio*   *(it's awful where*
          is in awful   where is John in work   *John works)*

(ii) (a) *mae'n bosib   bod John yn gweithio*   *(It's possible*
          is in possible be John in   work   *that John works*
                                    in a cold room)
          mewn   'stafell oer
          in a   room cold

    (b) **mae'n bosib   lle mae John yn gweithio* *(*it's possible*
          is in possible where is John in work   *where John*
                                        works)

2.   For our purposes all complements, whether finite sentences or infinitivals, are derived from an S which is dominated by an NP. Rosenbaum (1967) distinguishes two types of constituent sentence according to whether they are dominated by an NP or not - *noun phrase complements* (dominated by an NP) and *verb phrase complements*. The possible distinction of the two sorts of complement, although variously discussed in the literature, is not considered; although this may distort the analysis, it considerably simplifies presentation.

3.   Questions of the ordering of transformations are not considered in what is a very informal presentation of transformations.

4.   There are two approaches to sentences of this type. One approach derives these constituent sentences from subject position, involving extraposition, and is witnessed in variant forms in Rosenbaum (1967) and in Kiparsky and Kiparsky (1970). The other approach is exemplified in an unpublished Ph.D dissertation by Emonds (1970), who derives the constituent sentences from a complement position in deep structure and reproduces them in subject position in surface structure by a transformational rule termed *it*-replacement. We follow the extraposition-based approach, but it must be noted that there are variations in this approach, relating to the handling of the impersonal HI (SHE = IT). Rosenbaum (1967), for instance, includes IT in the deep structure in a rule of the following form:

(i)

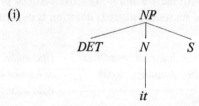

Kiparsky and Kiparsky (1970) introduce impersonal IT (to be distinguished from a factive IT in their analysis) as a pronominal trace for the extraposed sentence. We make a decision of convenience in introducing HI (SHE = IT) through pronominalisation - a decision which is not designed to make a stand on the deep structure or transformational status of IT. The advantage of the extraposition-based approach is that the identity relationship between the impersonal HI (SHE = IT) and the sentential complement is readily explained:

(ii) (a)

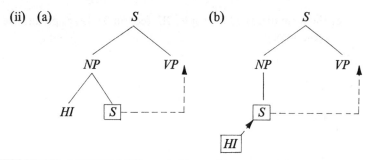

Emonds (1970), in contrast, brings out this relationship by *co-reference:*

(iii)

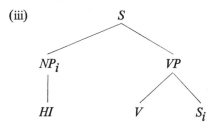

Either the deep structure treatment of HI (SHE = IT) as in (ii) (a) or the generation of HI as a pro-form as in (ii) (b) brings out the relationship between HI and the sentential complement without having to introduce co-referential labelling.

5. The analysis of infinitivals given here as being derived from sentences follows the typical approach of transformational-generative grammarians (e.g. Rosenbaum, 1967). The literature, (e.g. Emonds, 1970) however, witnesses occasional reservations that infinitivals may, in fact, be derived directly from a VP rather than be the remnant of a sentence. It is interesting to note that in traditional Welsh grammar the verbs in infinitivals are referred to as 'verb-nouns' rather than 'infinitives'.

6. The insertion of the preposition I (TO, FOR) in this manner is not really satisfying but will suffice for our purpose.

7. This type of analysis is suggested by Perlmutter (1970) in relation to sentences which contain an inanimate subject. For sentences with animate subject, however, he suggests complement recursion. This is a controversial issue and, in order to simplify matters for the present purpose, only inanimate subjects are considered.

8. Chomsky (1970: 186-7), in a discussion of the English verb FEEL (TEIMLO), gives an alternative analysis which treats these sentences as simple sentences

of the form discussed in chapter III, section 3g, i.e. as predicative sentences in terminology.

IX   Sentential features

1   INTRODUCTION

Recursive operations in language

It is a well-established view of traditional grammar that some sentences are more
elementary or basic than other sentences. In the previous chapter the discussion
centred upon the type of complexity which arises from constituent sentences. In this
chapter we will examine a type of complexity which arises from altering the internal
structure of sentences. Consider, for instance, the following examples:

(1)	'roedd	y	mwnciod	o	'r	sŵ	yn	bwyta'r	*(the monkeys*
	was	*the*	*monkeys*	*from*	*the*	*zoo*	*in*	*eat*	*the*	*from the zoo*
									were eating all
	afalau	*i*	*gyd*						*the apples)*
	apples	*all*							

(2)	'doedd	y	mwnciod	o	'r	sŵ	ddim yn	*(the monkeys*
	NEG + was	*the*	*monkeys*	*from*	*the*	*zoo*	*NEG in*	*from the zoo*
								were not eating
	bwyta'r	*afalau*	*i gyd*					*all the apples)*
	eat	*the apples*	*all*					

The latter example represents a slightly more complex variety than the former but
is derived in basically the same manner. The discussion will examine the ways in which
these related but more complex sentences can be produced.

In chapters III and VIII we have outlined a wide variety of simple and complex
sentence types. The important point is that the native Welsh speaker can produce new
and additional varieties of these various sentences. Consider, for instance, the
following simple sentence:

(3)	*mae*	*John*	*yn*	*palu'r*	*ardd*	*(John is digging the*
	is	*John*	*in*	*dig*	*the garden*	*garden)*

The example in (3) is a simple transitive type pattern and, on the basis of this
pattern, a number of additional varieties can be produced:

(4)	*John*	*sy*	*'n*	*palu'r*	*ardd*	*(it is John who is*
	John	*is*	*in*	*dig*	*the garden*	*digging the garden)*

(5) *ydy John yn palu'r ardd?*   *(is John digging*
     is   John in   dig the garden   the garden?)*

(6) *'dydy   John ddim yn palu'r ardd*   *(John isn't digging*
     NEG is   John NEG in dig the garden   the garden)*

Examples (4) to (6) represent the same basic sentence; the variations are produced by additional *grammatical rules*. These rules can be initially identified by familiar traditional labels: in (4) we have INVERSION, in (5) we have INTERROGATION, in (6) we have NEGATION. It is also possible to make various combinations of these rules and in the following example all three occur:

(7) *nid   John sy 'n palu'r   ardd?*   *(it isn't John who is*
     NEG John is   in dig the garden   digging the garden?)*

Operations like inversion, interrogation and negation enable sentences to be extended into additional varieties. Basically, we have the same pattern recurring in an altered form. This characteristic of language provides a clue as to how the native speaker is able to exercise command over such a wide variety of different sentences.

Phenomena like inversion, interrogation and negation will be referred to as *sentential features* for convenience. The features that we will look at in this chapter will relate mainly to individual simple sentences. We find, however, that various features are mutually contrastive and related features can be listed as follows:

(8) (i)   *Declarative*   .   *interrogative*
     (ii) *Normal*   :   *inverted*
     (iii) *Positive*   :   *negative*
     (iv) *Non-ellipted* :   *ellipted*

The features can also apply to a sentence in various combinations, as illustrated by example (7) above. A basic or elementary sentence is subject to the features on the left-hand side of each contrast. Example (3) above, for instance, is declarative, normal, positive and non-ellipted. Consequently, we can refer to these features as the *unmarked* features of the contrasts. New and additional sentences are produced by one or more of the features on the right of each contrast and, consequently, these can be thought of as the *marked* features.

In this chapter we will be concentrating upon the marked sentence features. The unmarked features will only be referred to in order to clarify the differences produced by the marked features. In addition to the features listed above, we will be looking at IMPERATIVE. Its relationship with other sentential features is slightly more complicated than those of the simple contrasts given in (8) above.

2 INVERSION

2a Introduction

The operation of *inversion* involves *rearranging* the sequence of constituents in a sentence in a specifiable manner so that one or more of those constituents is *fronted* to initial position. Consider the following example of a simple sentence:

(9)	'roedd	Mair	yn	dweud	ei	hanes	wrth	yr	athrawes	*(Mair was telling her story to the teacher)*
	was	Mair	in	tell	her	story	to	the	teacher	

Inversion possibilities produce the following new and additional patterns:

(10) (i)
<u>Mair</u> (a)	oedd	yn	dweud	ei	hanes	*(it was Mair who*
Mair (PT)	was	in	tell	her	story	*was telling her*

wrth	yr	athrawes	*story to the*
to	the	teacher	*teacher)*

(ii)
<u>dweud</u>	ei	hanes	wrth	yr	athrawes	'roedd	Mair	*(telling her story*
tell	her	story	to	the	teacher	was	Mair	*to the teacher*

Mair was)

(iii)
<u>ei</u>	<u>hanes</u>	'roedd	Mair	yn	ei	ddweud	wrth	*(her story Mair*
her	story	was	Mair	in	its	tell	to	*was telling to*

yr	athrawes	*the teacher)*
the	teacher	

(iv)
<u>wrth</u>	<u>yr</u>	<u>athrawes</u>	'roedd	Mair	yn	dweud	*(to the teacher*
to	the	teacher	was	Mair	in	tell	*Mair was telling*

ei	hanes	*her story)*
her	story	

The range of inversion is problematic in some instances and it would be tedious in this context to examine every constituent of every simple sentence type or sub-type to see whether it can be inverted. The aim here is to demonstrate the operation of inversion itself and its productive effects; consequently, the discussion is illustrative rather than definitive.[1]

A brief consideration of the above examples gives some idea of the possibilities involved. The particular example in (9) above is a verbal sentence; copula and copula-prepositional phrase sentences have their own peculiarities in some respects. We can say, however, that the most general inversion possibility is that of the subject noun

289

phrase, illustrated in (10) (i) above. Very general, too, is the inversion of the verb
phrase constituent, exemplified in (10) (ii). With both these inversion possibilities,
generalisations are relatively easy to make. But when we consider the inversion
possibilities of further constituents, more specific statements are required. In the main,
it is possible to invert the post-verbal or complement constituents as in (10) (iii) and
(10) (iv), although the inversion of the verb is problematic. And not all post-verbal
constituents will invert unquestionably, as is shown by the predicative phrase
constituent in the following example:

(11) (i)   *mae Mair yn edrych yn ddel*   *(Mair looks pretty)*
              is   Mair in look   in pretty

      (ii)   *? del   mae Mair yn edrych*   *(it is pretty that*
              pretty is   Mair in look   *Mair looks)*

Despite the various details and problems, we can generalise for our purposes and say
that inversion centres upon the subject noun phrase, the verb phrase constituent and
also the post-verbal constituents without the verb. The possibilities can be represented
as follows:

(12)

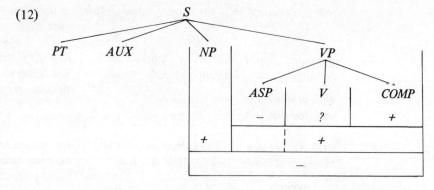

The category COMP(LEMENT) represents all the post-verbal constituents and is, in
fact, an over-simplification. The diagram displays how inversion can be applied to the
subject noun phrase and verb phrase separately and, while the particle and auxiliary
may be affected in terms of their shape (see examples (4) to (6) and (10) (i) above),
they are not themselves inverted. The inversion of the noun phrase-and-verb phrase
together is not possible. Inversion possibilities also exist for the constituents of the
verb phrase, the inversion of the verb itself being problematic as indicated.

The function of inversion is to focus on a constituent by placing it in prominent
initial position. In this way emphasis can be given to a constituent; in particular, it can
be given *contrastive emphasis*. In (10) (i), for instance, it can be emphasised that
MAIR, as opposed to Gwil or John, was telling her story to the schoolmistress; in

290

(10) (ii) that the activity that Mair was engaged on was that of telling her story to the schoolmistress, as opposed to any other activity; in (10) (iii) that it was her story that Mair was telling to the schoolmistress, as opposed to anything else; in (10) (iv) that it was to the schoolmistress that Mair was telling her story, as opposed to anyone else. In this way, inversion can be used to highlight various parts of the message that is being conveyed in the sentence.

2b Some further details

The simplicity of mere movement to initial position is complicated by some additional details which accompany certain inversion patterns.

The inversion of the subject noun phrase raises the following points. Firstly, in traditional formal Welsh a 'relativisation marker' follows the inverted noun phrase:

(13) (i)   *bydd   Mair yn aros   am   John*   *(Mair will be waiting*
            will be Mair in wait for John   *for John)*

(ii)   *Mair a   fydd   yn aros am John*   *(it is Mair who will be*
       Mair PT   will be   in wait for John   *waiting for John)*

(14) (i)   *palodd John yr   ardd*   *(John dug the garden)*
           dug   John the   garden

(ii)   *John a   balodd yr ardd*   *(it is John who dug*
       John PT dug   the garden   *the garden)*

But in spontaneous spoken Welsh the particle A − or Y in appropriate circumstances, see chapter VII, section 5b − does not necessarily occur and (13) (ii) and (14) (ii) above could simply be:

(15) *Mair fydd   yn aros am John*   *(it is Mair who will be*
     Mair will be in wait for John   *waiting for John)*

(16) *John   balodd   yr   ardd*   *(it is John who dug*
     John   dug   the   garden   *the garden)*

In the contemporary spoken language only MAE (IS) is regularly marked by a relativisation marker, in the form of its change into SYDD:

(17) (i)   *mae John yn gweiddi*   *(John is shouting)*
            is John in shout

(ii)   *John sydd yn gweiddi*   *(it is John who is*
       John is   in shout   *shouting)*

Secondly, the inverted subject noun phrase patterns do not follow the usual rules of person and number concord between the subject and the auxiliary carrier. In a normal sentence agreement is necessary:

(18) *'dwi   'n gweld Mair heno*   *(I'm seeing Mair*
      am + I   in see   Mair tonight   *tonight)*

(19) *mae John yn gweld Mair heno*   *(John is seeing Mair*
      is   John in see   Mair tonight   *tonight)*

But in an inverted sentence, the auxiliary item is always the third singular form:

(20) *fi sy 'n gweld Mair heno*   *(it is I who is seeing*
      I   is in see   Mair tonight   *Mair tonight)*

(21) *John sy 'n gweld Mair heno*   *(it is John who is*
      John is in see   Mair tonight   *seeing Mair tonight)*

This rule applies to all auxiliary items in addition to those associated with the MAE (IS) paradigm above. (It is interesting to refer briefly at this point to the view put forward in chapter III, section 4e, that identificatory copula sentences compulsorily undergo subject NP inversion, as in such sentences the auxiliary item is always third singular.)

The inversion of the verb phrase constituent involves special provision for the category of aspect. Firstly, if one or more of the aspect markers YN (IN), AR (ON), WEDI (AFTER) and NEWYDD (NEW) occur, there are two possibilities. The aspect markers AR (ON), WEDI (AFTER) or NEWYDD (NEW) accompany the inverted constituents to initial position:

(22) (i)   *mae John wedi /newydd/ar balu'r ardd*   *(John has/has*
             is   John after /new   /on dig the garden *just/is about to*
                                                           dig the garden)

      (ii)   *wedi /newydd/ar balu'r ardd   mae John*   *(dug the garden*
             after /new   /on dig the garden is John   *has John/just dug*
                                                           the garden has
                                                           John/about to dig
                                                           the garden is
                                                           John)

The aspect marker YN (IN) is deleted in the inverted pattern:

(23) (i)   *mae John <u>yn</u> palu'r   ardd*   *(John is digging*
             is   John in dig the   garden   *the garden)*

      (ii)   *palu'r   ardd   mae John*   *(digging the*
             dig the garden is   John   *garden is John)*

If, however, YN (IN) accompanies another aspect marker, it too occurs in the front:

(24) (i)   *mae John <u>wedi bod yn</u> palu'r   ardd*   *(John has been*
             is   John after be   in dig the   garden   *digging the garden)*

      (ii)   *<u>wedi bod yn</u> palu'r   ardd   mae John*   *(been digging the*
             after be   in dig the   garden is   John   *garden has John)*

Thus, in single occurrences, the aspect feature represented by YN (IN) is un-signalled in an inverted pattern, while the remaining aspect features remain signalled by AR (ON), WEDI (AFTER) or NEWYDD (NEW).

Secondly, if no aspect marker is present and an inflected lexical verb occurs, inversion necessitates the employment of a carrier auxiliary (see chapter V, section 1) to carry the auxiliary material. Consider the following example:

(25) *mi balodd John yr ardd*   *(John dug the garden)*
       PT   dug   John the garden

The verb phrase constituent PALU YR ARDD (DIG THE GARDEN) cannot be inverted to produce:

(26) **palu'r   ardd   -odd   John*   *(*dig the garden*
        dig the garden PAST John   *John -ed)*

A carrier auxiliary like GWNEUD has to be introduced to carry the auxiliary:

(27) *palu'r ardd <u>wnaeth</u> John*   *(it was dig the garden*
                                           that John did)

This use of GWNEUD (DO) is frequently illustrated in traditional grammar and has a very impressive literary heritage; consequently, it is a pattern of considerable prestige. The verb GWNEUD is used with all three lexical verb inflections, but in the spontaneous spoken Welsh of northern areas, the form DDARU can also be used where -ODD occurs:

(28) *palu'r   ardd   ddaru   John*   *(it was dig the garden*
       dig the   garden happened John   *that John did)*

This use of pro-verbs links up with their use in tags and *answer words* (see section 3 on 'interrogation' below and also chapter III, section 1b), where they are also used to carry an inflection in place of a lexical verb.

Finally, we can consider additional details of the inversion of certain post-verbal constituents. When the object noun phrase is inverted (as in (10) (iii) above), a pronoun is inserted before the verb to trace the original object noun phrase constituent:

(29) (i)   mae John yn golchi'r   car   *(John is washing the*
           is   John in wash the car   *car)*

     (ii) y   car mae John yn ei olchi   *(it's the car that*
           the car is   John in its wash   *John is washing)*

This is the usual procedure in formal written Welsh and is widely followed in spontaneous spoken Welsh. Very often, however, only the mutation is realised and the pronoun is not retained:

(30) y   car mae John yn olchi   *(it's the car that*
     the car is   John in wash   *John is washing)*

And in some varieties, both the mutation and the pronoun are dispensed with:

(31) y   car mae John yn golchi   *(it's the car that*
     the car is   John in wash   *John is washing)*

These characteristics of the fronting of the object noun phrase are also found in the *relativisation* of the object (chapter VII, section 5b) and the querying of the object through *interrogation* (see section 3g below). This suggests that the same movement rule is involved in all three cases: again we have evidence of the way in which language makes extensive use of a limited number of resources. A similar situation is found with inversion, questioning and relativisation of the subject noun phrase.

A prepositional phrase constituent in inversion again has two possibilities for positioning the preposition. It can accompany the rest of the prepositional phrase to initial position:

(32) (i)   mae Mair yn cerdded i 'r dre   *(Mair is walking to*
           is   Mair in walk   to the town *the town)*

     (ii) i 'r dre   mae Mair yn cerdded   *(to the town Mair*
           to the town is   Mair in walk   *is walking)*

But it is also possible for the preposition to remain behind, especially when contrastive emphasis is being given to the noun phrase part of the prepositional phrase:

(33) y   dre   mae Mair yn cerdded i   *(the town Mair is*
     the town is   Mair in walk   to   *walking to)*

294

The final positioning of the preposition is common in some varieties of speech and can be further illustrated by the following:

(34) *y tŷ oedden nhw 'n sôn am*   *(the house they were*
     the house were they in talk about   talking about)*

(35) *y tŷ oedden nhw 'n chwilio am*   *(the house they were*
     the house were they in search for   searching for)*

(36) *y tŷ oedden nhw 'n edrych ar*   *(the house they were*
     the house were they in look on   looking at)*

Although these patterns may not occur in formal written Welsh, they are not incorrect and are best viewed in the light of the principles of appropriateness and tolerance.

The operation of inversion or fronting also applies to constituent sentences. The relationship of sentential features in general to constituent sentences is discussed in section 7a below. At this stage we will just make the point that a constituent sentence which has undergone inversion can be preceded by the forms MAI and, in southern areas, TAW.[2] In some areas, particularly in the north, the form NA can also occur. Thus, we find examples such as *mae Mair yn gwybod mai/taw John oedd yn chwerthin (Mair knows that it was John who was laughing)* and *'dwi'n siwr mai/taw chwerthin wneith o (I'm sure that it is laugh that he will do)*. The forms MAI and TAW are not compulsory, however, and in spontaneous speech they can be left out, producing *mae Mair yn gwybod John oedd yn chwerthin* and *'dwi'n siwr chwerthin wneith o.*

2c   Pseudo-clefting

Similar to inversion in effect is another process which can be labelled *pseudo-clefting*.[3] It will be discussed in very brief terms here. Like inversion, pseudo-clefting involves the initial positioning of a particular constituent. The method of achieving this initial positioning is quite different, however. With a sentence like *mae John yn paentio'r drws (John is painting the door)*, pseudo-clefting can involve the subject noun phrase, to produce *yr un sy'n paentio'r drws ydy John (the one who is painting the door is John)*; the noun phrase object, to produce *beth mae John yn ei baentio yw'r drws (what John is painting is the door)*; or the verb phrase, to produce *beth mae John yn ei wneud yw paentio'r drws (what John is doing is painting the door)*. Pseudo-clefted sentences can also permit interchange of the constituents on either side of the copula, producing *John ydy'r un sy'n paentio'r drws (John is the one who is painting the door)*; *y drws ydy beth mae John yn ei baentio (the door is what John is painting)*; and *paentio'r drws ydy beth mae John yn ei wneud (painting the door is what John is doing)*. The actual details of pseudo-clefting are complex. It basically involves an identificatory copula sentence, for discussion of which see chapter III.

3 INTERROGATION

3a Introduction

Another sentential operation is the familiar concept of asking questions. Given a simple sentence such as the following:

(37) mae Mair yn dadlau am   y   gêm efo ei brawd   *(Mair is arguing*
     is   Mair in argue about the game with her brother   *about the game*
                                                   with her brother)

it is possible to produce new and additional varieties such as:

(38) ydy Mair yn dadlau am   y   gêm efo ei brawd?   *(is Mair arguing*
     is   Mair in argue about the game with her brother   *about the game*
                                                   with her brother?)

(39) pwy sy 'n dadlau am   y   gêm efo ei brawd?   *(who is arguing*
     who is in argue about the game with her brother   *about the game*
                                                   with her brother?)

(40) am   beth mae Mair yn dadlau efo ei   brawd?   *(about what is*
     about what is   Mair in argue with her brother   *Mair arguing*
                                                   with her brother?)

(41) efo   pwy   mae Mair yn dadlau am y   gêm?   *(with who(m) is*
     with who(m) is Mair in argue about the game   *Mair arguing*
                                                   about the game?)

These are only a few of the possible question types that can be produced by the operation of *interrogation*. A significant point is that, as with a discussion of inversion, it is possible to organize the various interrogative types by relating them to the constituents of a simple sentence. The various interrogative types relate differently to the types and sub-types of simple sentences. We will use the verbal simple sentences as the main point of reference and make special statements about the other types of simple sentence where necessary.

Interrogatives do not operate upon the particle, although it may be affected by them. Unlike inversion, however, interrogation can operate upon the auxiliary, as (38) above illustrates. Again, unlike inversion, interrogation can operate upon the subject noun phrase-and-verb phrase together by using the verb DIGWYDD (HAPPEN):

(42) beth sy   'n digwydd?   *(what is happening?)*
     what is   in happen

The auxiliary involves the same features, although different in shape, and the question relates to the activity conveyed by the subject noun phrase-and-verb phrase together. Further, interrogation can also apply to the subject noun phrase alone, as illustrated by (39) above, or the verb phrase alone by including GWNEUD (DO):

(43) *beth mae Mair yn ei   wneud?*   *(what is Mair doing?)*
     what is   Mair in its   do

Further interrogation can involve the verb; this cannot be illustrated in relation to example (37) but it is exemplified below. Finally, as examples (40) and (41) above show, interrogation also operates upon the post-verbal constituents. The various possibilities can be seen from the following generalised branching-diagram:

(44)

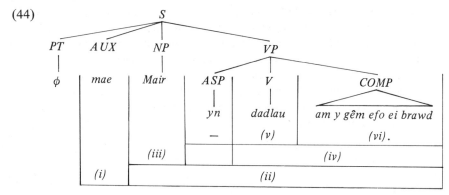

From the diagram, the various interrogatives can therefore be listed as follows:

(i)   auxiliary interrogative;
(ii)   subject noun phrase-and-verb phrase interrogative;
(iii)   subject interrogative;
(iv)   verb phrase interrogative;
(v)   verb interrogative;
(vi)   post-verbal interrogative(s).

In addition to these six types, there are interrogatives relating to the adjunct constituent, and also to the further constituency of the noun phrase. These additional types are discussed briefly in sections 3h and 3j below.

3b   The auxiliary interrogative

The auxiliary interrogative can also go under the label of *yes–no* interrogative, inasmuch as such interrogatives, as in the following example, expect as an answer either 'yes' or 'no':

(45) *oedd Mair yn dadlau am   y   gêm efo*   *(was Mair arguing*
      was   Mair in   argue   about the game with   *about the game*

      ei brawd? – oedd/nac   oedd   *with her brother?*
      her brother – was/NEG   was   *– yes/no)*

Further remarks on the characteristics of this aspect of the auxiliary interrogative are given below. The actual mechanics of forming the auxiliary interrogative in Welsh are basically very simple. The elementary sentence itself remains unaltered and modifications are performed upon (i) the particle, and (ii) the accompanying intonation. As mentioned above, the operation of interrogation does not apply to the particle but does have certain consequences upon it. In spontaneous Welsh, no particle is realised in the main; interrogation is achieved by using the appropriate intonation, as is implied in example (45) above. But in formal Welsh, the particle A occurs, and example (45) would be realised as:

(46) *a oedd Mair yn dadlau am   y   gêm efo ei brawd?*   *(was Mair arguing*
      Q was Mair in   argue about the game with her brother   *about the game*
                                                 with her brother?)

The branching-diagram for an interrogative sentence such as (45) can thus be given:

(47)

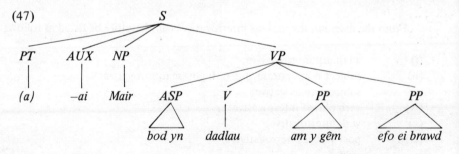

Compared with a declarative sentence with otherwise identical semantic characteristics, interrogatives in Welsh merely involve appropriate particle selection and intonation pattern. There is, however, one exception: the third person form of the MAE (IS) paradigm of the copula BOD (BE) adopts irregular forms in interrogatives. This is the only verbal form in Welsh which adopts a separate form for interrogatives.

298

Where the subject is indefinite, as in existential-copula sentences (see chapter III, section 4d), the form OES (IS) occurs; and where the subject is definite, the form YDY or YM (IS) occurs. All other verbal forms remain unchanged, as the following examples demonstrate:

(48) (a) (i)   *mae yna   gath yn yr   ardd*   *(there's a cat in the*
              is   there cat in the   garden   *garden)*

         (ii)   *oes yna   gath yn yr ardd?*   *(is there a cat in the*
              is   there cat in the garden   *garden?)*

    (b) (i)   *mae John yn yr ardd*   *(John is in the garden)*
              is   John in the garden

         (ii)   *ydy John yn yr ardd?*   *(is John in the*
              is   John in the garden   *garden?)*

(49) (a) (i)   *'roedd yna   gath yn yr   ardd*   *(there was a cat in*
              was   there cat in the   garden   *the garden)*

         (ii)   *oedd yna   gath yn yr ardd?*   *(was there a cat in*
              was   there cat in the garden   *the garden?)*

    (b) (i)   *'roedd John yn yr   ardd*   *(John was in the*
              was   John in the garden   *garden)*

         (ii)   *oedd John yn yr   ardd?*   *(was John in the*
              was   John in the garden   *garden?)*

    (c) (i)   *mi welodd John y   ddamwain*   *(John saw the*
              PT saw   John the   accident   *accident)*

         (ii)   *welodd John y   ddamwain?*   *(did John see the*
              saw   John the accident   *accident?)*

    (d) (i)   *mi ddylai hi   aros*   *(she should stay   )*
              PT should she stay

         (ii)   *ddylai hi   aros?*   *(should she stay?)*
              should she stay

The third person form of the MAE (!S) paradigm reveals itself to be the most 'irregular' verbal form in the Welsh language, not only in interrogatives but also in inversion and negation.

A point of interest is the range of forms that can be used as answer words in contemporary spoken Welsh for the auxiliary (or yes–no) interrogative. According to the traditional statement, the verbal form in the question is repeated in the answer with appropriate person alterations. In contemporary Welsh, this is only the case with the set of 'auxiliary' verbs like BOD (BE), GWNEUD (DO), CAEL (RECEIVE), MEDRU (CAN), GALLU (CAN) and DYLAI (SHOULD) and a very small number of lexical verbs:

(50) *ga' i aros adre? – cewch/na   chewch   (may/can I stay*
     may I stay home   you may/NEG you may   home? – yes/no)

(51) *ddylai hi   fynd? – dylai/na   ddylai   (should she go? –*
     should she go   should/NEG should   yes/no)

The answer form itself involves the person features appropriate for the answerer in addressing the questioner. Thus, if a questioner asks a question about himself in the first person, as in example (50), the answerer replies in the second person, as the subject is the addressee or original questioner. Conversely, second person questions have first person answers. In the case of the third person, as in example (51), the person features remain the same. With an affirmative answer, the answer word is appropriately given without initial mutation. Negative answers, however, are given by placing the negative particle NA(C) (where the C[k] is realised before vowels) before the appropriate verbal form. Under the relevant conditions, the negative particle NA(C) causes aspirate mutation. All these points can be represented in the following table:

(52)

QUESTION	*PERSON CHANGE*	*ANSWER*
ga' i (can I)	*1 → 2*	*cei/cewch (you can); na chei/chewch (you can't)*
cei/cewch (can you)	*2 → 1*	*caf (I can); na chaf (I can't)*
ceith (can he, etc.)	*3 → 3*	*ceith (he, etc. can); na cheith (he, etc. can't)*

Answer words in Welsh reveal themselves to be quite complicated. The interrogativisation of inverted sentences, however, is very much simpler in this respect; the details are given briefly below in section 3k.

The majority of inflected lexical verbs (like RHEDEG (RUN), PRYNU (BUY) or PALU (DIG)) are not used as answer words. In these cases the carrier auxiliary GWNEUD (DO) is employed to provide the answer (compare its use in inversion and in tag questions below):

(53) <u>redi</u>   di   i   'r   siop i   mi?
    will run   you   to   the shop for me

    – *<u>rhedaf</u>/*na   <u>redaf</u>
      I will run/NEG   I will run

     <u>gwnaf</u>/na   <u>wnaf</u>
    I will do/NEG I will do

(will you run to the shop for me? – yes/no)

(54) <u>brynith</u>   hi   'r   gôt 'na?
    will buy   she   the coat there

    – *<u>prynith</u>/*na   <u>phrynith</u>
      will buy/NEG   will buy

    <u>gwneith</u>/na   <u>wneith</u>
    will do/NEG   will do

(will she buy that coat? – yes/no)

(55) <u>bali</u>   di   'r   ardd?
    will dig you   the garden

    – *<u>palaf</u>/*na   <u>phalaf</u>
      will dig/NEG will dig

    <u>gwnaf</u>/na   <u>wnaf</u>
    will do/NEG   will do

(will you dig the garden? – yes/no)

Only in the case of a small number of lexical verbs – DOD (COME), MYND (GO), CAEL (RECEIVE) and GWNEUD (MAKE) – is the verbal form repeated. And even here the carrier auxiliary GWNEUD can be used with DOD and MYND:

(56) <u>ddoi</u>   di   'n ôl yn fuan?
    will come you   back in soon

    –   <u>dof</u>/na   <u>ddof</u>
    will come/NEG will come

    – OR <u>gwnaf</u>/na   <u>wnaf</u>
      will do/NEG will do

(will you come back soon? – yes/no)

(57) <u>ei</u>   di   i   'r   siop i   mi?
    will go   you   to   the shop for me

    –   <u>af</u>/nac   <u>af</u>
    will go/NEG   will go

    OR <u>gwnaf</u>/na   <u>wnaf</u>
      will do/NEG   will do

(will you go to the shop for me? – yes/no)

(58) *ga'*   *i afal?*   *– <u>cei</u> / na <u>chei</u>*   *(can I have an apple?*
     will have I apple   will have/NEG will have   *– yes/no)*

(59) *<u>wnewch</u> chi 'r te? – <u>gwnaf</u>/na <u>wnaf</u>*   *(will you make the*
     will make you the tea   will do/NEG will do   *tea? – yes/no)*

Finally, the familiar point should be noted that DO and NADDO are the answer words used where the -ODD inflection is involved:

(60) *<u>welaist</u> di   John? – <u>do</u>/naddo*   *(did you see John?*
    saw   you John   yes/NEG yes   *– yes/no)*

With these forms, the complexity of auxiliary and person appropriateness does not arise.

The auxiliary interrogatives, however, involve more than straightforward yes–no interrogatives. The yes–no type discussed so far can be regarded as the 'open' sub-type, expecting the answer either 'yes' or 'no'. There are at least two further sub-types, one expecting 'yes' and the other expecting 'no' as an answer. These sub-types are produced by adding tags to the question. Thus:

(61) (i)   *mae Mair yn dadlau am   y gêm*   *(Mair is arguing*
          is   Mair in argue about the game   *about the game*

          efo   ei   brawd, <u>yndydy?</u> – <u>ydy</u>   *with her brother,*
          with her brother, NEG + is   is   *isn't she? – yes)*

    (ıı)   *'dydy Mair ddim yn dadlau am   y gêm* *(Mair isn't*
          NEG + is Mair NEG in argue about the game *arguing about*

          efo   ei   brawd, <u>nac ydy?</u> – <u>nac ydy</u>   *the game with*
          with her brother, <u>NEG is</u>   <u>NEG is</u>   *her brother, is*
                                                      she? – no)

By adding the tag YNDYDY to (61) (i) affirmative expectancy is produced, and by adding NAC YDY to (61) (ii) negative expectancy is produced. The interrogative expecting 'yes' is made up of a positive sentence followed by the appropriate positive answer word preceded by the particle YN(D), as with YND + YDY (IS) in (56) (the D is realised before a vowel). In formal written Welsh YN(D) is replaced by ONI(D). The interrogative expecting 'no' is made up of a negative sentence, with a negative answer form as a tag. Southern dialects possess different methods of forming question tags. In the case of questions expecting 'yes', the tag sees the inclusion of an appropriate personal pronoun more regularly than in northern dialects, as in *wyt ti'n mynd heno, yndwyt ti? (you're going tonight, aren't you?)*. Differences are more marked with questions expecting 'no', as the following demonstrates: *dwyt ti ddim yn mynd, wyt ti? (you're not going, are you?)*. Here the tag not only contains a personal pronoun but also lacks the negative particle NA(C).

302

The tag forms all involve auxiliary verb forms, for example:

(62) ga' i aros, <u>yn   ga' i</u>? – <u>cei</u>   *(I can stay, can't*
     may I stay NEG may I   you may   *I – yes)*

(63) ddylai hi ddim mynd, <u>na   ddylai</u> – <u>na   ddylai</u> *(she shouldn't go,*
     should she NEG go   NEG should   NEG should *should she? – no)*

Where a lexical verb other than the small set of DOD (COME), MYND (GO), CAEL (RECEIVE) and GWNEUD (MAKE) occurs, the pro-verb GWNEUD (DO) is used:

(64) redi   di i 'r siop i mi,   *(you'll run to the*
     will run you to the shop for me   *shop for me, won't*
                                               *you/*won't run*
     <u>yn   gwnei/*yn   redi</u> – <u>gwnaf</u>   *you? – yes)*
     NEG will do/NEG will run will do

(65) brynith   hi ddim y gôt 'na,   *(she won't buy that*
     will buy   she NEG the coat there,   *coat, will she/*
                                               *will buy she? – no)
     <u>na   wneith/*na   phrynith</u> – <u>na   wneith</u>
     NEG will do/NEG will buy   NEG will do

If the -ODD paradigm is involved, the DO or NADDO forms are used as tags, DO becoming YNDO in speech or ONIDO in writing:

(66) welaist ti   John <u>yndo</u>? – <u>do</u>   *(you saw John didn't*
     saw   you John NEG yes   yes   *you? – yes)*

(67) welaist ti mo   John, <u>naddo</u>?   – <u>naddo</u>   *(you didn't see John,*
     saw   you NEG John NEG yes   NEG yes   *did you? – no)*

It is interesting to note another characteristic of southern dialects which occurs with DO and also with tags to existential sentences. It is found that (F)E follows the tag, to give examples such as *mi welaist ti John, yndo fe? (you saw John, didn't you?)* and *mae yna ddigon, yndoes e? (there's enough, isn't there?).* The auxiliary interrogative thus involves at least three sub-types – open, expecting 'yes', and expecting 'no'. It is possible to make further distinctions by varying the intonational pattern on the question, but these details are not pursued here.

One additional variety of a tag question occurs only with the MAE (IS) and OEDD (WAS) paradigms and involves the occurrence of the pre-sentential negative particle ONI(D) only:

(68) *'dydy   'r mynyddoedd yn braf?*   *(aren't the mountains*
NEG + is the mountains in fine   *lovely?)*

(69) *'doedd   hi   'n ddel?*   *(wasn't she pretty?)*
NEG + was she in pretty

The particle ONI(D), where the D is realised before the vowel, is reduced to 'D.
These questions are assumptive, in that they assume agreement and merely proclaim a
particular viewpoint. To that extent they can be viewed as a variety of the
interrogative which expects 'yes'. But they are syntactically distinct, in that they use a
pre-sentential particle without a finally occurring tag and, furthermore, the medially
positioned negative item DIM does not occur even though they involve negation (see
section 4 below).

3c   Subject noun phrase-and-verb phrase interrogative

Brief remarks about the subject noun phrase-and-verb phrase interrogative have already
been given in the general introduction to interrogatives in section 3a above. There it
was shown that the verb DIGWYDD (HAPPEN) can be employed in a structure which
questions the whole activity encompassing the subject noun phrase and the verb
phrase together – an illustration is given in example (42) in relation to example (37).
We can make two other general remarks here. Firstly, the verb DIGWYDD (HAPPEN)
relates to verbal sentences and a different verb is selected for copula sentences (as
will be illustrated shortly). But, even with verbal sentences, the selection of DIGWYDD
(HAPPEN) depends upon the nature of the activity. For instance it is not appropriate
to give *mae John yn licio Mair (John likes Mair)* as an answer to *beth sy'n digwydd?
(what is happening?)*. Secondly, subject noun phrase-and-verb phrase interrogatives
involving DIGWYDD (HAPPEN) are not relevant to the majority of copula or
copula-prepositional phrase sentences. None of the following will do as answers to
(42):

(70) *mae John yn dal*   *(John is tall)*
     is   John in tall

(71) *Mair ydy'r   athrawes*   *(Mair is the teacher)*
     Mair is   the teacher

(72) *mae gan John gar newydd*   *(John has (got) a*
     is   LOC John car new   *new car)*

Neither is a predicatival verbal sentence appropriate:

304

(73) *mae John yn edrych yn dal*   *(John looks tall)*
    is John in look in tall

With *some* of these cases (but by no means all) it is more fitting to relate them to a question of the same general structure, but one which involves the copula verb BOD (BE) and not DIGWYDD (HAPPEN). The copula BOD (BE), however, can be left out:

(74) *beth sy('n bod)?*   *(what is the matter?)*
    what is in be

We can suggest, therefore, that there are two subject noun phrase-and-verb phrase interrogative types, one involving DIGWYDD, as in (42), for the majority of verbal sentences and one involving BOD, as in (74) for many, but not all, of the copula sentences.

3d   Subject noun phrase interrogative

The subject noun phrase interrogative is relatively straightforward and needs little discussion. A significant point is the selection of PWY (WHO) for human subjects and BETH (WHAT) for other subjects:

(75) <u>*pwy*</u> *sydd wedi gwneud hyn? — Mair*   *(who has done this?*
    who is   after do   this   Mair   *— Mair)*

(76) <u>*beth*</u> *sy' wedi gwneud hyn? — y gath*   *(what has done this?*
    what is after do   .this   the cat   *— the cat)*

As illustrated in (75) and (76), moreover, the answers to subject noun phrase interrogatives are frequently made up of a noun phrase only, and there is no need to repeat the remainder of the sentence in the question.

The only complicating factor in the formation of subject noun phrase interrogatives is that the initial placement of the subject noun phrase has repercussions upon the nature of the particle. In the case of the MAE (IS) paradigm, as in examples (75) and (76) above, interrogation results in the change of MAE (IS) to SYDD (as with subject noun phrase inversion — see section 2b above — and subject noun phrase relativisation —see chapter VII, section 5b). In the case of all other auxiliary carriers (see chapter V), the initial placement of the subject noun phrase is optionally followed by the particle A; for example:

(77) (i)   *'roedd John yn gweiddi*   *(John was shouting)*
             was   John in shout

     (ii)   *pwy (<u>a</u>) oedd yn gweiddi?*   *(who was shouting?)*
             who REL was in shout

(78)	(i)	mi fydd Mair yn aros	*(Mair will be staying)*
		PT will be Mair in stay	
	(ii)	pwy (a) fydd yn aros?	*(who will be staying?)*
		who REL will be in stay	
(79)	(i)	mi welodd John Mair	*(John saw Mair)*
		PT saw John Mair	
	(ii)	pwy (a) welodd Mair?	*(who saw Mair?)*
		who REL saw Mair	
(80)	(i)	mi fedr John ddreifio	*(John can drive)*
		PT can John drive	
	(ii)	pwy (a) fedr ddreifio	*(who can drive?)*
		who REL can drive	

In spontaneous speech the particle is not consistently realised, and subject noun phrase interrogatives can simply involve the initial placement of the subject noun phrase in the form of PWY (WHO) or BETH (WHAT). Only the MAE (IS) paradigm consistently marks any formal repercussions for this type of interrogation. We may note that the rules for the realisation of the particle A are exactly the same as those for subject noun phrase inversion and relativisation (see Williams, 1959, for a full description of the particle A/Y in formal Welsh in interrogatives).

3e   Verb phrase interrogative

The verb phrase interrogative is interesting for the way in which the form of the interrogative is related to the role or function of the noun phrase subject. So far, we have illustrated only one type but, on the basis of various relationships, it is possible to set up at least two sub-types. If the subject of the sentence is agent, then it is possible to employ GWNEUD along with a dummy pronoun:

(81)	(i)	mae Mair yn dadlau am y gêm efo	*(Mair is arguing
		is Mair in argue about the game with	about the game
		ei brawd	with her brother)*
		her brother	
	(ii)	beth mae Mair yn ei wneud?	*(what is Mair doing?)*
		what is Mair in its do	
(82)	(i)	mae Mair yn canu	*(Mair is singing)*
		is Mair in sing	

(ii)	*beth mae Mair yn ei wneud?*	*(what is Mair doing?)*
	what is Mair in its do	

If the role of the subject is patient, this type of interrogative is inappropriate. Consider the following sentence, in which something is happening to the subject as opposed to the subject's doing something:

(83)	*mae Mair yn gwaethygu*	*(Mair is worsening)*
	is Mair in worsen	

With this type of subject role it is more appropriate to have an interrogative involving DIGWYDD I (HAPPEN TO) rather than the pro-form GWNEUD (DO):

(84)	(i)	*beth sy 'n digwydd i Mair?*	*(what's happening*
		what is in happen to Mair	*to Mair?)*
	(ii)	**beth mae Mair yn ei wneud?*	*(*what's Mair doing?)*
		what is Mair in its do	

It is therefore necessary to distinguish two interrogative types, agent and patient, illustrated respectively by (81) (ii) and (82) (ii), on the one hand, and (84) (i), on the other. Furthermore, it must also be borne in mind that verbal sentences containing certain verbs do not relate to either of the above interrogatives. Consider, for instance, LICIO or HOFFI (LIKE), where both types are inappropriate:

(85)	(i)	*mae John yn licio Mair*	*(John likes Mair)*
		is John in like Mair	
	(ii)	**beth mae John yn ei wneud?*	*(*what is John*
		what is John in its do	*doing?)*
	(iii)	**beth sy 'n digwydd i John?*	*(*what's happening*
		what is in happen to John	*to John?)*

This is also the case with the majority of copula and copula-prepositional phrase sentences.

3f Verb interrogative

Given a sentence such as:

(86)	*mae Mair yn golchi 'r llawr*	*(Mair is washing the*
	is Mair in wash the floor	*floor)*

It is possible to ask a question specifically about the verb constituent by using the verb GWNEUD (DO) and also introducing the prepositional form I (TO):

(87)   *beth*   *mae* *Mair* *yn* *ei* <u>*wneud*</u> *i* *'r* *llawr?*   *(what is Mair doing*
        what *is*   *Mair* *in* *its* *do*   *to the floor*   *to the floor?)*

The interrogative in (87) is an enquiry about the nature of the action, signalled by the verb, which is performed upon the following noun phrase. There are restrictions on the use of this interrogative type, however, and it does not relate to the following, for instance:

(88)   *mae Mair yn licio John*   *(Mair likes John)*
       is   *Mair* *in* *like* *John*

(89)   *mae Mair yn meddwl am*   *ei*   *chariad*   *(Mair is thinking*
       is   *Mair* *in* *think*   *about* *her* *boy friend*   *about her boy friend)*

(90)   *mae Mair yn dadlau am*   *y*   *gêm efo* *ei* *brawd*   *(Mair is arguing*
       is   *Mair in* *argue*   *about the game with her brother*   *about the game*
                                                    with her brother)

The verb interrogative thus only applies to certain verbal sentences. As far as copula and copula-prepositional phrase sentences are concerned, it is entirely inappropriate.

3g   Post-verbal interrogatives

There are three post-verbal constituents: object noun phrase, prepositional phrase and predicative phrase. Of these three, the noun phrase object is perhaps the most interesting, due to the occurrence of the dummy pronoun in the interrogative sentence (see also remarks on *inversion* of noun phrase object in section 2b above and *relativisation* in chapter VII, section 5b):

(91) (i)   *mae Mair yn golchi 'r*   *car*   *(Mair is washing the*
             is   *Mair* *in* *wash*   *the car*   *car)*

     (ii)   <u>*beth*</u> *mae* *Mair* *yn* <u>*ei*</u> *olchi?*   *(what's Mair*
             what *is*   *Mair* *in* *its* *wash*   *washing?)*

In formal traditional Welsh the pronoun is always used. But in spoken Welsh it is frequently the case that only the mutation is realised, giving:

(92)   <u>*beth*</u>   *mae* *Mair* *yn* <u>*olchi?*</u>   *(what's Mair*
       what *is*   *Mair* *in* *wash*   *washing?)*

It appears, moreover, that the mutation is mainly 'soft' even where the traditional rules of mutation would allow aspirate mutation or determination by an 'understood' object which could well be feminine. For instance, verbs like PALU (DIG), TORRI (BREAK) and CAEL (RECEIVE) are soft mutated and not aspirate mutated:

(93) *be'   wyt ti   wedi (ei) balu?*   *(what have you dug?)*
     what are you after its   dig

(94) *be'   wyt ti   wedi (ei) dorri?*   *(what have you*
     what are you after its   break   *broken?)*

(95) *be'   wyt ti   wedi (ei) gael?*   *(what have you had?)*
     what are you after its   receive

Many speakers use neither pronoun nor mutation, and object noun phrase interrogatives merely have the interrogative word. The interrogative word itself in all cases distinguishes human objects with PWY (WHO) and all others with BETH (WHAT).

The interrogatives relating to the prepositional phrase constituents are essentially enquiries about the nominal part. The interrogative word involved refers to the nominal, while the preposition remains expressed in the interrogation:

(96) (i)   *mae Mair yn chwilio am   John*   *(Mair is searching for*
            is   Mair in search for John   *John)*

     (ii)   *am bwy   mae Mair yn chwilio?*   *(for who(m) is Mair*
            for who(m) is   Mair in search   *searching?)*

(97) (i)   *mae Mair yn dadlau am y   gêm efo* *(Mair is arguing about*
            is   Mair in argue for the game with *the game with her*
                                                    brother)
            ei brawd
            her brother

     (ii)   *am beth mae Mair yn dadlau efo ei brawd* *(about what is*
            for what is   Mair in argue with her brother *Mair arguing with*
                                                           her brother?)

     (iii) *efo pwy mae Mair yn dadlau am y   gêm?*   *(with who(m) is*
            with who is   Mair in argue for the game *Mair arguing*
                                                         about the game?)

(98) (i)   *mae John yn dweud ei hanes wrth Mair*   *(John is telling*
            is   John in tell his story to   Mair   *his story to Mair)*

(98) (ii)   *wrth bwy*   *mae John yn dweud ei hanes?*   *(to who(m) is*
               to   who(m) is   John in tell   his story   John telling his
                                                       story?)

The interrogative word obeys the normal rules of the human : non-human distinction.

There is an additional stylistic point in that traditional formal Welsh usually moves the preposition to the front along with the interrogative word. But in spontaneous spoken Welsh the preposition may occur in final position and only the interrogative word in initial position. Moreover, the finally placed preposition can involve pronominal copying of the object noun phrase through inflection or quite simply remain uninflected with no copying. A common example of this is:

(99)   *be'*   *'dach chi 'n son am(dano)?*   *(what are you talking*
       what are   you in talk about   *about?)*

This pattern exists in spoken Welsh as a fairly productive stylistic possibility and other examples include *beth mae o'n edrych ar (no)? (what's he looking at?)*, *beth wyt ti'n poeni am(dano)? (what are you worrying about?)* and *beth maen nhw'n chwilio am(dano)? (what are they looking for?)*.

The interrogatives relating to the predicative phrase of a sentence may involve more complexity than is suggested here. In this context the discussion will centre upon the possibility of employing SUT (HOW) where adjectives occur and BETH (WHAT) where nouns occur. This can be illustrated with both embedded and non-embedded types of predicative phrase:

(100) (i)   *mae John yn sal*   *(John is ill)*
             is   John in ill

       (ii)   *sut mae John?*   *(how is John?)*
             how is   John

(101) (i)   *mae Mair yn edrych yn iach*   *(Mair looks healthy)*
             is   Mair in look   in healthy

       (ii)   *sut mae Mair yn edrych?*   *(how does Mair look?)*
             how is   Mair in look

(102) (i)   *mae John yn athro*   *(John is a teacher)*
             is   John in teacher

       (ii)   *beth yw John?*   *(what is John?)*
             what is   John

(103) (i)   *maen nhw wedi penodi John yn athro*   *(they've appointed*
              are   they after appoint John in teacher   *John teacher)*

(ii)   <u>*beth*</u> *maen nhw wedi penodi John*   *(what have they*
              what are   they after appoint John   *appointed John?)*

The use of SUT (HOW) by itself, however, is not appropriate for every adjective:

(104) (i)   *mae John yn dal*   *(John is tall)*
              is   John in   tall

(ii)   **sut   mae John?*   *(*how is John?)*
              how is   John

(iii)   <u>*pa   fath o   hogyn*</u> *ydy John?*   *(what sort of boy is*
            what sort of boy   is   John   *John?)*

(iv)   <u>*sut   hogyn*</u> *ydy John?*   *(what sort of boy is*
            how   boy   is   John   *John?)*

As can be seen from (104), with an adjective like TAL (TALL) an interrogative of the form PA FATH O . . . (WHAT SORT OF . . .) or SUT . . . (HOW . . .) followed by a relevant nominal is more appropriate.

3h   Adjunct interrogatives

The adjunct interrogatives are notable for their variety, depending upon the types of adjunct involved. It is noticeable that the interrogative word represents the type of adjunct and, if a preposition is involved, this is used along with the interrogative word:

(105) (i)   *mae John wedi bod yn canu am awr*   *(John has been singing*
           is   John after be in   sing for hour   *for an hour)*

(ii)   <u>*am faint*</u>   *mae John wedi bod yn canu?*   *(for how long has*
           for how much is   John after be in   sing   *John been*
                                                         singing?)

(106) (i)   *mae Mair yn prynu crys i   John*   *(Mair is buying a*
           is   Mair in buy   shirt for John   *shirt for John)*

(ii)   <u>*i   bwy*</u>   *mae Mair yn prynu crys?*   *(for who(m) is Mair*
           for who(m) is   Mair in buy   shirt   *buying a shirt?)*

(107) (i)   *mae o 'n golchi 'r   car am bres*   *(he's washing the car*
           is   he in wash the car for money   *for money)*

(ii)   <u>*am beth*</u> *mae o 'n golchi 'r   car?*   *(what is he washing*
           for what is   he in wash   the car   *the car for?)*

The extensive number of adjunct types affords many other possibilities besides the three illustrated above. Finally, where a prepositional phrase is involved, the preposition may in some instances be retained in final position, as opposed to initial position along with the interrogative word.

3j   Other interrogative types

Other interrogative types are possible in relation to the further constituency of the noun phrase (which is discussed in chapter VII). Here we will briefly note, by way of illustration, the following examples:

(108) (i)   *mae John wedi benthyg car Mair*   *(John has borrowed*
            is   John after borrow   car Mair   Mair's car)

      (ii) *car pwy mae John wedi ei fenthyg?*   *(whose car has*
            car who is   John after its borrow   John borrowed)

(109) (i)   *mae Mair wedi prynu deg o flodau*   *(Mair has bought*
            is   Mair after buy   ten of flowers   ten flowers)

      (ii) *faint   o flodau mae Mair wedi*   *(how many flowers*
            how much of flowers is   Mair after   has Mair bought)

            'u   prynu
            their buy

(110) (i)   *mae o eisiau 'r llyfr mawr*   *(he wants the big*
            is he need   the book big   book)

      (ii) *pa/pwy lyfr mae o eisiau?*   *(which book does he*
            which   book is he need   want?)

In each case, the interrogative word enquires about information contained in the relevant constituent of the noun phrase.

3k   Interrogation and inversion

Of the five interrogative types studied in sections 3b—h and the additional types studied in section 3j, all involve *movement*, with one exception. This is the auxiliary or yes—no interrogative, which merely involves appropriate particle selection and intonation patterns (with special rules to operate upon the MAE (IS) paradigm). The remaining interrogatives involve the occurrence of an interrogative word such as PWY (WHO), BETH (WHAT) or LLE (WHERE) in initial position. These latter types of interrogative exhibit the following features: (i) the occurrence of a particle PA; (ii) the querying of a particular constituent and the representation of the queried constituent in appropriate pronominal form, such as PETH (THING) or LLE (PLACE WHERE); (iii) the occurrence of the queried constituent in initial position, where it follows the particle PA; (iv) appropriate interrogative intonation pattern. The PA particle is not readily discernible in interrogatives in spontaneous spoken Welsh, although its influence is still present in that it conditions mutation of following interrogative pronominal forms (e.g. PA PETH → PA BETH → BETH, or PA LLE → PA LE → B'LE or LLE).

It is suggested here that the particle PA occurs in deep structure in the environment of the constituent that is to be queried. The constituent which is queried is itself realised in indefinite pronominal form, such as PETH (THING), LLE (PLACE WHERE), PRYD (TIME) or MAINT (QUANTITY, SIZE). The particle and pronominal form are then fronted to initial position and the eventual surface structure is given an interrogative intonation pattern. The following branching-diagrams illustrate some of these points:

(111) *beth sy 'n gwneud sŵn?*　　　　　　　　　　*(what's making a*
　　　　what is in make　noise　　　　　　　　　　*noise?)*

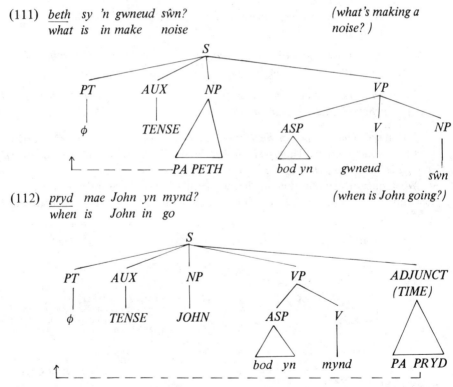

(112) *pryd mae John yn mynd?*　　　　　　　　*(when is John going?)*
　　　when is　John in　go

313

(113) <u>lle</u>   mae Mair yn byw?   *(where does Mair*
      where is Mair in live   *live?)*

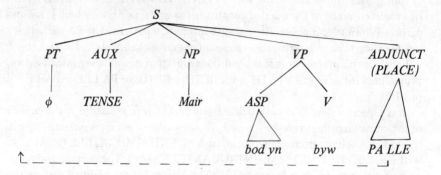

As they stand, the above branching-diagrams would produce interrogatives as
follows:

(114) <u>pa   beth</u> sy 'n gwneud sŵn?   *(what is making a*
      what thing is in make   sound   *noise?)*

(115) <u>pa   bryd</u> mae John yn mynd?   *(what time is John*
      what time is   John in go   *going?)*

(116) <u>pa   le</u>   mae Mair yn byw?   *(what place does Mair*
      what place is   Mair in live   *live?)*

But in spontaneous spoken Welsh there are various rules for realising the particle PA
and following pronouns. Thus, *pa beth* is realised as *beth*, *pa bryd* is realised as *pryd*
and *pa le* is realised as *b'le* or *lle*.

When querying an object noun phrase, the rules listed above are extended to
account for the copy pronoun which is inserted in place of the queried constituent:

(117) <u>beth</u> mae John yn <u>ei</u> baentio?   *(what is John*
      what is   John in its paint   *painting?)*

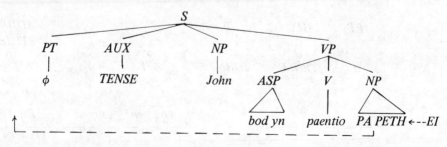

314

In surface structure, the copy pronoun occurs as a possessive pronoun positioned immediately before the verb. As mentioned earlier in the discussion of this type of interrogative, not all dialects use the copy pronoun; some only realise the consequential mutation of the verb, while others have neither pronoun nor mutation.

With regard to the subject noun phrase-and-verb phrase interrogative (see section 3c above), the verb phrase interrogative (section 3e above) and the verb interrogative (section 3f above), the above rules must also allow for the occurrence of linguistic material which is not present in the accompanying answers. This is a complicated area of language study which is not pursued further here.

The movement part of these rules involves the same fronting procedure as in inversion (see section 2 above). A clear similarity can be observed between interrogative and inverted sentences by comparing the following examples:

(118) (i)   *John sy 'n palu'r   ardd*   *(it is John who is*
              John is in dig the garden   *digging the garden)*

       (ii)   *pwy sy 'n palu'r   ardd?*   *(who is digging the*
              who is in dig ·the garden   *garden?)*

(119) (i)   *yr   ardd   mae John yn ei phalu* *(the garden John is*
              the garden   is   John in   its dig *digging)*

       (ii)   *beth mae John yn ei balu?*   *(what is John*
              what is   John in   its dig   *digging?)*

(120) (i)   *yn y   gegin   mae John yn cysgu*   *(in the kitchen John*
              in the kitchen is   John in sleep *is sleeping)*

       (ii)   *lle   mae John yn cysgu?*   *(where is John*
              where is   John in sleep   *sleeping?)*

It can be seen, then, that interrogation involves in part the same operation of movement as inversion — further evidence of the way language maximises the use of a limited number of resources.

The relationship between interrogatives and inverted sentences is seen in another way. A specific question about a particular constituent (which can be identified) may be made by fronting or inverting that constituent to initial position and then giving interrogative intonation to the resulting inverted sentence:

(121) (i)   *mae John yn palu'r   ardd*   *(John's digging the*
              is   John in dig the garden   *garden)*

       (ii)   *John sy 'n palu'r   ardd?*   *(is it John who is*
              John is in dig the garden   *digging the garden?)*

(iii)	*yr ardd* mae John yn ei phalu?	*(is it the garden that*
	the garden is John in its dig	*John is digging?)*

This enables very specific questions to be asked about the information in various constituents of a sentence.

It must be emphasised that questions relating to inverted constituents in this manner are yes—no questions (see section 3b above). In formal welsh, interrogatives of this type have their own interrogative word, AI. It is suggested here that the interrogative item AI is treated like PA (as discussed above): namely, it is introduced in the immediate environment of the constituent to be queried and is fronted along with that constituent to initial position.[4] The branching-diagram for the interrogative in (121) (ii) above could therefore be given as follows:

(122)

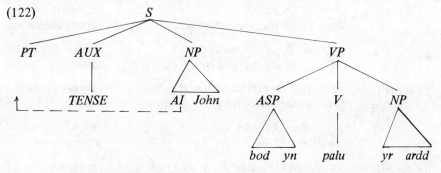

In spontaneous spoken Welsh, the interrogative particle in (122) is rarely realised. Interrogatives of the yes—no type involving inverted sentences are very much simpler than a non-inverted yes—no interrogative, in that there is one affirmative answer word in IE and one negative answer word in NAGE. The complexities of auxiliary and person agreement are thus avoided, the answers to (121) (ii) and (iii) above being either IE or NAGE. Similarly, in the case of conditioned yes—no interrogatives, the formation of the question tags is very much simpler with the inverted types, being either YNTE for 'yes' expectancy or NAGE for 'no' expectancy:

(123)	(i)	*John sy 'n palu'r ardd, ynte – ie?*	*(it is John who is digging the garden, isn't it? – yes)*
	(ii)	*nid John sy'n palu'r ardd, nage? – nage*	*(it isn't John who is digging the garden, is it? – no)*

Again, there are no complexities of person change.

4 NEGATION

4a Introduction

Like the previous grammatical operations, negation is a familiar linguistic concept, much commented upon in traditional writings. Given a *positive* declarative sentence such as:

(124) *mae John yn agor y drws*   *(John's opening the*
      is John in open the door   *door)*

It is possible to produce another related sentence in the form of its *negative* counterpart:

(125) *'dydy John ddim yn agor y drws*   *(John isn't opening*
      NEG is John NEG in open the door   *the door)*

Whereas inversion involves rearrangement, and interrogation involves rearrangement and pronominalisation, negation involves the *addition* or *insertion* of various elements such as DDIM in (125) above into the basic simple sentence.

The traditional grammars have concentrated upon the 'shapes' of the various elements involved in negation and the environments where they occur. In this discussion of negation, the emphasis will be upon the relation of the negative item to the rest of the sentence, and the scope of the discussion will be widened to take into account a greater number of items involved in negation; the traditional emphasis upon the 'shapes' of the various items will play a relatively minor role.

4b Pre-sentential negation

Production of a negative sentence in traditional formal Welsh takes the very simple form of introducing a negative particle initially before a positive sentence. There are five such pre-sentential particles:

(126) *NI(D)*
      ONI(D)
      NA(C)
      NID
      NA(D)

The first four of these particles are associated with other sentential features. Thus NI(D) is used to negate a *statement* (the optional D is selected if the initial sound of the following word is vocalic):

(127) (i) *mae John yn aros*   *(John is staying)*
          is John in stay

(127) (ii)   *nid   yw John yn aros*   *(John isn't staying)*
             $\overline{NEG}$ *is   John in stay*

(128) (i)   *rhedodd John i ffwrdd*   *(John ran away)*
             ran   John away

      (ii)   *ni   redodd John i ffwrdd*   *(John didn't run*
             $\overline{NEG}$ *ran   John away*   *away)*

The particle ONI(D) is used to form a *tag question* (see section 3b above):

(129) (i)   *mae Mair yn mynd*   *(Mair is going)*
             is   Mair in go

      (ii)   *onid yw Mair yn mynd?*   *(isn't Mair going?)*
             $\overline{NEG}$ *is   Mair in go*

The particle NA(C) is used to form negative *imperatives* and negative *answers*:

(130) (i)   *canwch!*   *(sing!)*
             sing

      (ii)   *na   chanwch!*   *(don't sing!)*
             $\overline{NEG}$ *sing*

(131) *a wnewch chwi aros? – na   wnaf*   *(will you stay? – no)*
      Q will   you stay $\overline{NEG}$ I will

The particle NID, where the D is compulsory irrespective of the following phonetic context, is used with *inverted* sentences:

(132) (i)   *John oedd yn gwneud y   trefniadau*   *(John was making the*
             John was in make the arrangements   *arrangements)*

      (ii)   *nid John a oedd yn gwneud y   trefniadau*   *(it wasn't John*
             NEG John PT was in make   the arrangements   *who was making*
                                                             the arrangements)

The particle NA(D) is used in constituent sentences (see chapter VIII, section 2) such as the following:

(133) (i)   *rwyf yn gwybod bod Mair yn mynd*   *(I know that Mair is*
             am I in know   be Mair in go   *going)*

      (ii)   *rwyf yn gwybod nad yw Mair yn mynd* *(I know that Mair*
             am I in know   NEG is Mair in go   *isn't going)*

(134) (i)   *rwyf yn gobeithio y   daeth John ddoe*   *(I hope that John*
             am I in hope   PT came John yesterday *came yesterday)*

(134) (ii)   *rwyf yn gobeithio na   ddaeth John ddoe*   *(I hope that John*
            am I in hope   NEG came John yesterday   *didn't come*
                                                           yesterday)

The relationship of negation with other sentential features is discussed in section 7b below.

The various examples of pre-sentential negation above are mainly characteristic of traditional formal Welsh and are not illustrative of the situation in spontaneous spoken Welsh. A comparison of (127) (ii) above with its spoken equivalent will illustrate the difference:

(135) *'dydy John ddim yn aros*   *(John isn't staying)*
       NEG is John NEG in stay

Spoken Welsh involves what will be called *medial negation* and this is discussed in the next sub-section.

4c   Medial negation

The label 'medial negation', like that of 'pre-sentential negation', is a convenient labelling device based on the position of the negative particles and its significance goes no further than this.

There are four items which are involved in medial negation:

(136) *DIM (= NOT)*
       BYTH (= EVER)
       ERIOED (= EVER)
       HEB (= WITHOUT)

Each one can be illustrated in comparison with a positive sentence:

(137) (i)   *mi fydd   John yn prynu esgidiau newydd*   *(John will be*
            PT will be John in buy   shoes   new   *buying new shoes)*

      (ii)   *fydd   John ddim yn prynu esgidiau newydd* *(John won't be*
            will be John NEG in buy   shoes   new   *buying new shoes)*

(138) (i)   *mi wneith Mair aros adre*   *(Mair will stay home)*
            PT will   Mair stay home

      (ii)   *wneith Mair byth aros adre*   *(Mair will never stay*
            will   Mair ever stay home   *home)*

(139) (i)   *mae o wedi bod yn Llundain*   *(he's been in London)*
            is he after be in London

319

(139) (ii) 'dydy o _erioed_ wedi bod yn Llundain _(he's never been in_
            NEG is he ever   after be in London   _London)_

(140) (i)   mae o wedi cyrraedd   _(he has arrived)_
            is   he after arrive

      (ii) mae o _heb_   gyrraedd   _(he hasn't arrived)_
            is   he without arrive

Before proceeding to discuss each of these negative particles independently, we will briefly consider the use of DIM in relation to the pre-sentential particles.

This comparison, to a large extent, raises stylistic factors. In the main, the actual occurrence of a pre-sentential negative marker like NI(D) is a characteristic of traditional formal Welsh while the occurrence of the medial negative marker DIM is a characteristic of spoken Welsh. Compare the following written examples:

(141) _ni_   redodd John i ffwrdd   _(John didn't run_
      NEG ran   John away   _away)_

(142) 'rwyf yn gwybod _na_   redodd John i ffwrdd   _(I know that John_
      am I in know   NEG ran   John away   _didn't run away)_

(143) _nid_   John a redodd i ffwrdd   _(it wasn't John who_
      NEG John PT ran   away   _ran away)_

with the following examples

(144) redodd John _ddim_ i ffwrdd   _(John didn't run_
      ran   John NEG away   _away)_

(145) 'dwi 'n gwybod redodd John _ddim_ i ffwrdd   _(I know that John_
      am I in know   ran   John NEG away   _didn't run away)_

(146) _nid/dim_ John redodd i ffwrdd   _(it wasn't John who_
      NEG John ran   away   _ran away)_

(The last of these varies, many speakers using NID in both formal and informal situations.) Despite the apparent absence of a pre-sentential marker, it can be argued that spoken Welsh involves a combination of pre-sentential and medial negation for two reasons. Firstly, a pre-sentential element can be said to be present in spoken Welsh to a certain extent in the form of a mutation:

(147) _fydd_ John ddim yn gweithio   _(John won't be_
      will be John NEG in work   _working)_

Secondly, with OEDD (WAS), MAE (IS) and inflected forms of MYND (GO), which all involve initial vocalic sounds, an actual item may be used:

320

(148) (i)   *'dydy John ddim yn gweithio*   *(John isn't working)*
                NEG is John NEG in   work

(ii)   *'doedd   John ddim yn gweithio*   *(John wasn't working)*
                NEG was John NEG in   work

(iii)   *'deith   hi   ddim*   *(she won't go)*
                NEG will go she NEG

The initial 'D in each case can be thought of as a remnant of the pre-occurring NI(D). However, both pre-sentential realisations are always accompanied by medial DIM, which is not the case in traditional formal Welsh.

It should be borne in mind, however, that in some constituent sentences, and with OS (IF) and ER (ALTHOUGH) clauses, the pre-sentential particle NA(D) is used by some speakers without the medial negative marker DIM:

(149) (i)   *'dwi 'n gwybod (y) byddi di   yna*   *(I know you'll be*
                am I in know   PT   will be you there   *there)*

(ii)   *'dwi 'n gwybod na   fyddi di   yna*   *(I know you won't be*
                am I in know   NEG will be you there   *there)*

(150) (i)   *os fyddi di yna, wna i dy   weld ti*   *(if you are there,*
                if will be you there will I your see   you   *I'll see you)*

(ii)   *os na   fyddi di   yna, wna' i ddim*   *(if you aren't there,*
                if NEG will be you there will I NEG   *I won't see you)*

                dy   weld ti
                your see   you

(151) (i)   *er   (y) byddi di   wedi mynd,*   *(although you will*
                although PT will be you after go   *have gone, I'll see*
                you after)

                wna' i dy   weld ti   wedyn
                will I your see you after

(ii)   *er   na   fyddi di   wedi mynd,*   *(although you won't*
                although NEG will be you after go   *have gone, I'll see*
                you after)

                wna' i dy   weld ti   wedyn
                will I your see you after

But even here there are the possibilities of using DIM either along with the pre-sentential particle or without it. Thus, (149) (ii) could also be:

(152) (i)   *'dwi 'n gwybod na   fyddi di   ddim yna*   *(I know you*
              am I in know   NEG will be you NEG there   won't be there)

       (ii)   *'dwi 'n gwybod fyddi di   ddim yna*   *(I know you*
              am I in know   will be you NEG there   won't be there)

Taking all these points into consideration, it can be seen that apart from a few environments the predominant pattern in spoken Welsh is to use the medial DIM with some form of pre-sentential negative marking rather than the pre-sentential particle alone.

As the norm of negative formation in spoken Welsh, DIM is also the *unmarked* negative particle. That is, it can occur with any type of verbal expression, ranging from the variety of inflected lexical verbs to the many periphrastic expressions containing any auxiliary verb and aspect marker, for example:

(153)   *eith/aeth /ai   John ddim*   *(John won't/didn't/*
        will go/went/would go John NEG   wouldn't go)

(154)   *'dydy John ddim yn canu*   *(John isn't singing)*
        NEG is John NEG in sing

(155)   *'dydy John ddim wedi canu*   *(John hasn't sung)*
        NEG is John NEG after sing

(156)   *'dydy John ddim ar   ganu*   *(John isn't about to*
        NEG is John NEG about sing   sing)

(157)   *fydd   John ddim yn canu*   *(John won't be*
        will be John NEG in sing   singing)

(158)   *fydd   John ddim wedi canu*   *(John will not have*
        will be John NEG after sing   sung)

(159)   *fydd   John ddim ar   ganu*   *(John won't be about*
        will be John NEG about sing   to sing)

This point is significant in comparison with the three remaining medial negators BYTH (EVER), ERIOED (EVER) and HEB (WITHOUT), which are restricted by auxiliary and aspectual features.

The occurrence of DIM in a transitive pattern when the verb is inflected involves a slightly different formation:

(160)   *'doedd   John ddim yn palu'r ardd*   *(John wasn't digging*
        NEG was John NEG in dig the garden   the garden)

161) (i)   *phalodd John <u>ddim</u> <u>o</u> 'r   ardd   (John didn't dig
            dug   John NEG of the garden   the garden)

     (ii)   *phalodd John <u>ddim</u> yr ardd   (NO APPROPRIATE
            dug   John NEG the garden   TRANSLATION)

It can be seen from (161) (i) that the object noun phrase following DIM in this context is preceded by the prepositional form O (OF). In the case of a pronoun occurring as object noun phrase, O (OF) occurs in inflected form:

(162) *phalodd John <u>ddim</u> <u>ohono</u> fo   (John didn't dig it)
      dug   John NEG of + it it

As can be seen from (161) (ii), the O (OF) is obligatory in this context but not in a periphrastic expression, as (160) demonstrates. Finally, on this point, we can add that DIM O can be reduced to 'MO giving such examples as *welais i mohono (I didn't see him)*.

On the basis of the discussion of DIM so far, it can be concluded that negation in Welsh involves some sort of pre-sentential marking (either a mutation feature or a remnant of NI(D) if the following sound is vocalic) and the medial occurrence of DIM. The pre-sentential marking can be represented in a branching-diagram as the pre-sentential particle NI(D). The pre-sentential particle causes soft or spirant mutation of the following auxiliary carrier as appropriate. In the majority of cases the particle is deleted, except in those instances such as example (148), where it occurs as the remnant 'D. The medial marker DIM can be inserted by a transformational rule following the selection of the particle NI(D). In each case DIM is inserted *immediately before the verb phrase*. This rule accounts for examples like (144) and (148) above:

(163)

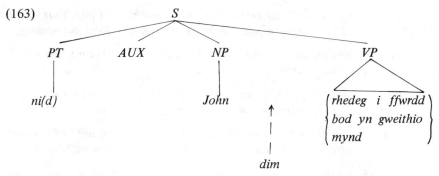

The inserted DIM is subject to soft mutation. In the event of the VP containing an object noun phrase, the preposition O (OF) is introduced before the object noun phrase if the verb itself occurs as an auxiliary carrier. There are two apparent exceptions to this rule of DIM insertion, illustrated by the following comparisons:

(164) (i)   <u>nid/dim</u> John ydy'r   athro   (John isn't the
               <u>NEG</u> John is   the teacher   teacher)

       (ii)   *John ydy <u>ddim</u> yr athro   (NO APPROPRIATE
               John is   <u>NEG</u> the teacher   TRANSLATION)

(165) (i)   does (yna) <u>(d)dim</u> te ar y   bwrdd   (there's no tea
              NEG is there <u>NEG</u>   tea on the table   on the table)

       (ii)   *does (yna) te <u>ddim</u> ar y   bwrdd   (*there isn't tea
               NEG is there tea <u>NEG</u> on the table   on the table)

Unlike previous examples, DIM does not here occur immediately before the verb phrase. But the positioning in these instances is due to other factors. Example (164) (i) is basically an inverted sentence (see chapter III, section 4c) and the rules of negation are those for inverted sentences (as is suggested by the possibility of NID), discussed below. In example (165) (i) DIM can be regarded as a noun phrase determiner, and is thus appropriately positioned immediately before the noun TÊ (TEA).[5]

Slightly different is the use of negation in inverted sentences. As suggested above, either NID or DIM can occur in initial position to negate the inverted constituent. (In some southern dialects, the item NAGE is used in this context. As mentioned earlier, this item otherwise occurs in all dialects as a negative reply to an inverted question.) Consider the possibilities in the following examples:

(166) (i)   'doedd   John ddim yn golchi'r car   (John wasn't washing
               NEG was John NEG in wash the car   the car)

       (ii)   <u>dim/nid</u> y   car oedd John yn ei olchi (it wasn't the car that
               <u>NEG</u>   the car was John in its wash   John was washing)

       (iii) ? <u>dim/nid</u> golchi oedd John y   car   (not washing was
               <u>NEG</u>   wash was John the car   John the car)

       (iv)   <u>dim/nid</u> golchi'r car oedd John   (it wasn't washing the
               <u>NEG</u>   wash the car was John   car that John was)

       (v)   <u>dim/nid</u> John oedd yn golchi'r car   (it wasn't John who
               <u>NEG</u>   John was in wash the car   was washing the car)

In (166) (ii) to (v) the use of inversion along with negation allows the scope of the negative item to be closely defined. It is therefore suggested that the negative item NID/DIM can be treated like PA and AI, as discussed in section 3k above: namely, NID/DIM is introduced in the constituent which is to be negated and the negative item is then inverted to the front along with that constituent. For example:

(167)

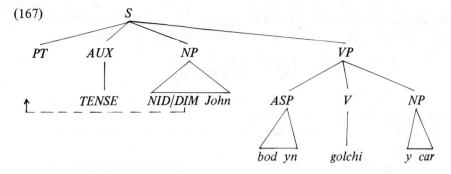

It must be borne in mind that NID/DIM can also occur in the same structure as medial DIM in sentences like the following:

(168) *nid/dim John oedd ddim yn helpu*   *(it wasn't John who*
　　　　 NEG　　 John　 was 　NEG 　in　 help 　　　　　 *wasn't helping)*

The branching-diagram for this example can be given as follows:

(169)

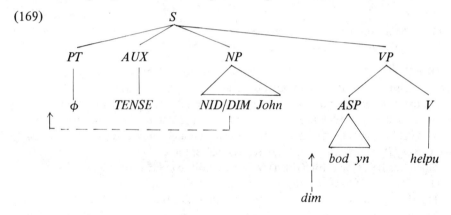

Sentences like (168) above present a situation where the inverted constituent is negated and the following sentence is negated. The negation of the inverted constituent is fairly straightforward, as has been seen, but the negation of the sentence itself has two possibilities: firstly, DIM is inserted by itself as in the above example or, secondly, the pre-sentential NA(D) can occur by itself, giving formal examples such as *nid John nad oedd yn helpu* or, along with medial DIM, giving colloquial examples such as *nid/dim John 'doedd ddim yn helpu* where NA(D) occurs as the reduction 'D. The more typical pattern is the occurrence of medial DIM by itself, even when phonetic conditions would allow the occurrence of the remnant 'D. It is also relevant to point here to examples such as:

325

(170) <u>dim/nid</u> bod John yn golchi'r car   *(not that John was*
      <u>NEG</u>   be John in wash the car   *washing the car)*

(171) <u>dim/nid</u> bod John ddim yn golchi'r car   *(not that John wasn't*
      <u>NEG</u>   be John <u>NEG</u> in wash the car   *washing the car)*

Here the negative element focuses upon all of the sentences including, as (171)
illustrates, a *negative sentence*.

The medial negator HEB (WITHOUT) is relatively easy to explain. Consider the
following sentences:

(172) *mae John wedi cyrraedd*   *(John has arrived)*
      is   John after arrive

(173) *'dydy John <u>ddim</u> wedi cyrraedd*   *(John hasn't arrived)*
      NEG is John <u>NEG</u> after arrive

In example (172) the perfect aspect marker WEDI (AFTER) occurs along with the
negative item DIM. The negator HEB can occur as an equivalent to both of these
forms:

(174) *mae John <u>heb</u>   gyrraedd*   *(John hasn't arrived)*
      is   John <u>without</u> arrive

HEB (WITHOUT) thus emerges as a special negator which also conveys perfect
aspect. As such, it is aspectually restricted and does not occur as freely as DIM. A
distinctive characteristic of the occurrence of HEB (WITHOUT) is the absence of a
pre-sentential negative feature. In example (174), for instance, we have the positive
form MAE (IS), as opposed to a negative form, and an example such as **'dydy John
heb gyrraedd (* not John hasn't arrived)* is unacceptable.

The items BYTH and ERIOED (EVER) are nothing like as simple as HEB
(WITHOUT) and involve an area of language of some complexity.

The first complexity arises out of the fact that BYTH and ERIOED (EVER) involve
a number of uses. Here the discussion will centre upon a single but similar use of each
one, which can be exemplified as follows:

(175) *'dydy Mair byth yn cwyno*   *(Mair never*
      NEG is Mair ever in   complain   *complains)*

(176) *'dydy John erioed wedi nofio yn y   môr*   *(John has never swum*
      NEG is John ever   after swim in the sea   *in the sea)*

This use of BYTH and ERIOED in the above examples can be referred to as
habitual or *durative negation*.

The second complexity arises out of the fact that each item in this use is subject to
auxiliary and aspectual restrictions. The item BYTH (EVER) is, in the main, restricted

to a non-perfect aspect, as the comparison of example (170) above with the following example suggests:

(177) *'dydy Mair byth wedi cwyno   (NO APPROPRIATE
        NEG is Mair ever   after complain   TRANSLATION)

There appear to be two sorts of exception to this tendency. Firstly, when the auxiliary is either BYDD (WILL BE) or BUASAI/BYDDAI (WOULD BE), BYTH (EVER) can occur with both perfect and non-perfect aspect:

(178) (i)   fydd   John byth yn gweithio   (John will never be
                will be John ever in work   working)

       (ii)   fydd   John byth wedi ei gweld hi os   (John will never have
                will be John ever after her see   she if   seen her if he doesn't
                                                                 go tonight)
                nad   eith   o heno
                NEG will go he tonight

(179) (i)   fuasai/fyddai John byth yn brifo neb   (John would
                would be   John ever in hurt no one   never hurt
                                                               anyone)

       (ii)   fuasai/fyddai John byth wedi brifo neb   (John would
                would be   John ever after hurt no one   never have hurt
                                                                 anyone)

Secondly, although the auxiliary verb BU (WAS) is restricted to a non-perfect aspect, BYTH never co-occurs:

(180) *fuodd John byth yn cwyno   (NO APPROPRIATE
         was   John ever in complain   TRANSLATION)

The negative item ERIOED (EVER) is characterised mainly in reverse terms. The general rule is that it co-occurs mainly with perfect aspect, as a comparison of example (177) above with the following example illustrates:

(181) *'dydy John erioed yn nofio yn y   môr   (NO APPROPRIATE
         NEG is John ever   in swim   in the sea   TRANSLATION)

It follows, therefore, that ERIOED (EVER) never co-occurs with BYDDAI (USED TO), which is restricted to a non-perfect aspect:

(182) *fyddai John erioed yn mynd i 'r capel   (NO APPROPRIATE
         used to John ever   in go   to the chapel   TRANSLATION)

However, there is an exception to this general rule, which represents the same aspectual situation as with BYDDAI: namely, although BU (WAS) is restricted to a

327

non-perfect aspect like BYDDAI, it is ERIOED (EVER) that occurs and not BYTH (EVER), as a comparison of example (180) above with the following illustrates:

(183) fu(odd) John erioed yn cwyno   (John had never
       was   John ever in complain   complained)

One can attribute this 'oddity' to the similarity of the retrospective function of the perfect aspect to the past-past function of BU (WAS). As far as the inflected verbs are concerned, BYTH and ERIOED are in a complementary relationship in co-occurrence with -ITH and -ODD:

(184) (i)   weli   di   byth yr un   fath eto   (you will never see
              will see you ever the same sort again   the same again)

       (ii)   *weli di   erioed yr un   fath eto   (NO APPROPRIATE
              will see you ever   the same sort again TRANSLATION)

(185) (i)   *welais i byth neb   fel John   (NO APPROPRIATE
              saw   I ever no one like John   TRANSLATION)

       (ii)   welais i erioed neb fel John   (I never saw anyone
              saw   I ever no one like John   like John)

But ERIOED appears to be excluded from co-occurring with -AI:

(186) *gerddai   John erioed yn bell pan   oedd o   (NO APPROPRIATE
       would walk John ever in far when was   he   TRANSLATION)

       'n ifanc
       in young

(187) *gerddai   John erioed yn bell iawn onibai   (NO APPROPRIATE
       would walk John ever in far very unless   TRANSLATION)

       bod o 'n cael ei dalu
       be he in have his pay

The complexity relating to the occurrences of BYTH and ERIOED can be summarised in the following table:

328

	MAE	OEDD	BU	BYDD	BYDDAI	BUASAI/BYDDAI	-ITH	-AI	-ODD
Non-perfect BYTH	+	+	−	+	+	+	+	+	−
ERIOED	−	−	+	−	−	−	−	−	+
Perfect BYTH	−	−	0	+	0	+	0	0	0
ERIOED	+	+	0	+	0	+	0	0	0

The general rule seems to be that BYTH (EVER) occurs with the non-perfect, while ERIOED (EVER) occurs with the perfect. In the absence of positive aspect marking with the inflected verbs, BYTH occurs with -ITH and -AI while ERIOED occurs with the past tense non-modal -ODD. The significant areas are enclosed in squares and represent ERIOED's occurrence with non-perfect aspect with BU (WAS); BYTH's occurrence with perfect with BYDD (WILL BE), similar to ERIOED; and BYTH's occurrence with perfect with hypothetical BUASAI/BYDDAI, again similar to ERIOED.

Having examined the auxiliary and aspectual restrictions on the occurrence of BYTH and ERIOED (EVER), we can now consider their relationship with negation. It is suggested here that neither of them is a negative marker in itself in the same manner as DIM. Rather, they are both some type of temporal marker co-occurring with other items which are negative markers. This can be made clear by considering ERIOED (EVER) in the following example:

(189) 'dydy John ddim wedi nofio yn y môr erioed (John has never swum
NEG is John NEG after swim in the sea ever in the sea)

From this example, which can be compared with (176) above, it can be seen that the item ERIOED may also occur in sentence final position, and that when it does so the negative item DIM occurs in medial position if the sentence is negative. This example clearly shows the essentially temporal nature of ERIOED, and that the negative features are independently located in other items. It can therefore be suggested that the basic position of ERIOED is sentence final and, by comparing example (189) with (176), it can be further suggested that there is a rule which can move ERIOED into medial position to displace the medial negator DIM. In such circumstances, the marker of negation is either a pre-sentential mutation of the auxiliary carrier or the remnant 'D. The same argument applies to the item BYTH (EVER). Evidence that BYTH occurs in sentence final position with the medially placed DIM is not readily forthcoming, since such examples are not easily acceptable:

(190) ? *'dydy Mair ddim yn cwyno byth*   *(Mair never*
     NEG is Mair NEG in complain ever   *complains)*

However, there are examples of positive sentences where BYTH is positioned finally:

(191) *ydy hi 'n mynd yno byth?*   *(does she ever go*
     is she in go there ever   *there?)*

Even in these examples BYTH can be moved to a medial position. Hence it can be suggested that if a negative marker occurs, BYTH is obligatorily moved to medial position. The two items BYTH and ERIOED will therefore be treated as finally positioned temporal adjuncts which do not themselves mark negation. The negative sentences in (175) and (176) can therefore be represented as:

(192)

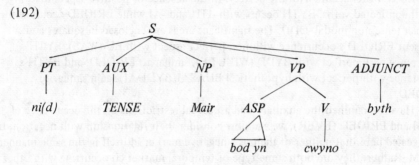

(193)

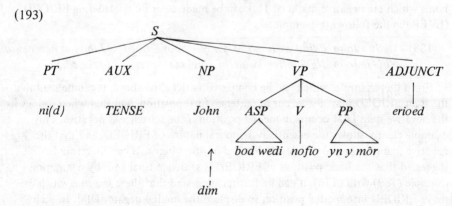

There is another rule, compulsory in the case of BYTH in (192), that if a pre-sentential negative marker occurs, the insertion of DIM can be replaced by the movement of BYTH and ERIOED to medial position immediately before the verb phrase:

(194)

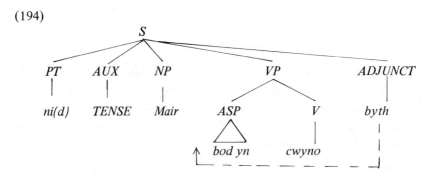

(195)

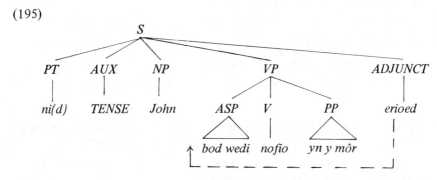

This account illustrates the essentially temporal semantics of BYTH and ERIOED (EVER), and also that the negative marker resides in a pre-sentential feature with or without medial DIM.

4d   Lexical negation

Welsh has a number of verb-nouns with a meaning (or one of several meanings) that involves negation: (NA)CÁU (REFUSE), PALLU (REFUSE, FAIL), PEIDIO (STOP), METHU (FAIL), FFAELU (FAIL). This type of negation, directly involving the meaning of a lexical item, can be called *lexical negation*. The question of lexical negation is a relatively open-ended matter which relates to antonymy, and a number of other items could be included in addition to the four listed above. The four chosen, however, clearly illustrate the concept of lexical negation and a suggestion of other possibilities is only briefly added in the final paragraph of this sub-section.

The verb-noun (NA)CÁU (REFUSE) is used in northern areas to indicate a *lack of volition* (on the part of an animate entity) or a *lack of 'volition-like capability'* (on the part of an inanimate concept):

(196) *mae John yn 'cau ateb*   *(John won't answer)*
       is   John in refuse answer

(197) *mae'r car yn 'cau cychwyn*   *(the car won't start)*
       is   the car in refuse start

In each example volition or volition-like capability is being negated. And this can be clearly seen if the above sentences are paraphrased with the -ITH paradigm (see chapter V, section 2b) in a negative sentence:

(198) *wneith John ddim ateb*   *(John won't answer)*
       will   John NEG answer

(199) *wneith y car ddim cychwyn*   *(the car won't start)*
       will   the car NEG start

(NA)CÁU (REFUSE) also occurs as equivalent to negative -AI in the past:

(200) (i)   *'roedd John yn 'cau ateb*   *(John wouldn't*
             was   John in refuse answer   *answer)*

       (ii) *wnai John ddim ateb*   *(John wouldn't*
             would John NEG answer   *answer)*

(201) (i)   *'roedd y car yn 'cau cychwyn*   *(the car wouldn't*
             was   the car in 'refuse' start   *start)*

       (ii) *wnai 'r car ddim cychwyn*   *(the car wouldn't*
             would the car NEG start   *start)*

The paraphrase involving -ITH (and its past equivalent -AI) clearly shows the negative feature in (NA)CÁU (REFUSE). In southern dialects, PALLU (REFUSE) is used in a similar manner.

For some speakers, it is possible that PEIDIO (STOP) may function like (NA)CÁU above:

(202) *mae John yn peidio ateb*   *(John won't answer)*
       is   John in refuse answer

(203) *mae'r car yn peidio cychwyn*   *(the car won't start)*
       is   the car in refuse start

Whatever the incidence of this particular use of PEIDIO (STOP), two other uses are much more general. Firstly, PEIDIO (STOP) is used in negative imperatives in spoken Welsh, in contrast with the pre-sentential particle NA(C) of formal Welsh:

(204)	(i)	*dos!* go	*(go!)*
	(ii)	<u>*paid*</u> *â mynd* stop with go	*(don't go)*
(205)	(i)	*arhoswch* stay	*(stay)*
	(ii)	<u>*peidiwch*</u> *ag aros* stop with stay	*(don't stay)*

In this use PEIDIO (STOP) (inflected for second person singular and plural) occurs before a verb-noun. Traditionally, PEIDIO (STOP) in this environment is followed by the preposition Â, but this preposition is variously realised or left out by different speakers. Secondly, PEIDIO (STOP) also occurs as the negative marker of infinitivals (see chapter VIII, section 4), as demonstrated in the following examples:

(206)	(i)	*mae John wedi penderfynu aros* is John after decide stay	*(John has decided to stay)*
	(ii)	*mae John wedi penderfynu <u>peidio</u> ag aros* is John after decide <u>stop</u> with stay	*(John has decided not to stay)*
(207)	(i)	*mae Mair wedi trio gweld John* is Mair after try see John	*(Mair has tried to see John)*
	(ii)	*mae Mair wedi trio <u>peidio</u> â gweld John* is Mair after try <u>stop</u> with see John	*(Mair has tried not to see John)*
(208)	(i)	*'dwi wedi addo gweithio'n hwyr* am I after promise work in late	*(I've promised to work late)*
	(ii)	*'dwi wedi addo <u>peidio</u> â gweithio'n hwyr* am I after promise <u>stop</u> with work in late	*(I've promised not to work late)*

The matrix sentence too can be negated, where needed, along with the negative infinitival:

| (209) | *'<u>dydy</u> John <u>ddim</u> wedi penderfynu <u>peidio</u> ag   aros*
<u>NEG</u> is John <u>NEG</u> after decide   stop with stay | *(John hasn't
decided not to
stay)* |
| (210) | *'<u>dydy</u> Mair <u>ddim</u> wedi trio <u>peidio</u> â   gweld John*
<u>NEG</u> is Mair <u>NEG</u> after try stop with see   John | *(Mair hasn't
tried not to see
John)* |

(211)   *'dydwi ddim wedi addo   peidio â   gweithio'n hwyr*   *(I haven't*
          NEG is NEG after promise stop   with work   in late   *promised not to*
                                                                              work late)

The two methods of negating a matrix sentence and an infinitival are therefore quite different.

This situation causes come interesting semantic contrasts when PEIDIO (STOP) occurs with certain uses of some item, namely, the *volition* use of -ITH and the 'obligation' use of RHAID (NECESSARY) and DYLAI (SHOULD). The -ITH paradigm can be used as a general illustration. Consider the following:

(212)   *mi wneith John aros*   *(John will stay)*
          PT will   John stay

One of the interpretations of -ITH here is that of signifying John's willingness to stay. As seen in the discussion of (NA)CÁU (REFUSE) above, -ITH itself can be negated to negate the willingness:

(213)   *wneith John ddim aros*   *(John won't stay)*
          will   John NEG stay

In this sentence the lack of willingness is established. But PEIDIO (STOP) can also be used to negate, not the willingness, but the action signified in the verb phrase:

(214)   *wneith John peidio aros*   *(John will not stay)*
          will   John stop   stay

In this example it can be said that John is willing not to stay; that is, there is positive willingness to perform a negative act (i.e. not to do something). To complete the picture, it is also possible to signify that someone is *not willing* to perform a negative act:

(215)   *wneith John ddim peidio aros*   *(John won't not stay)*
          will   John NEG stop   stay

In this example John's willingness has been negated with DIM and the event with PEIDIO (STOP), signifying that John is *not willing not to do* the action referred to. The same contrasts are possible with RHAID (NECESSARY) and DYLAI (SHOULD) and can be illustrated as follows:

(216) (i)   *mae rhaid   i   ti   aros*   *(you must stay)*
               is   necessity for you stay

(ii)   *mae rhaid   i   ti   <u>beidio</u> ag   aros*   *(you must not stay)*
               is   necessity for you stop   with stay

(iii)   *'does <u>dim</u> rhaid   i   ti   aros*   *(you needn't stay)*
               <u>NEG is NEG</u> necessity for you stay

(iv)   *'does <u>dim</u> rhaid   i   ti   <u>beidio</u> ag aros*   *(you needn't*
               <u>NEG is NEG</u> necessity for you stop   with stay   not stay)

(217) (i)   *mi ddylet ti   aros*   *(you should stay)*
               PT should you stay

(ii)   *mi ddylet ti   <u>beidio</u> ag   aros*   *(you should not stay)*
               PT should you stop   with stay

(iii)   *ddylet ti   <u>ddim</u> aros*   *(you shouldn't stay)*
               should you <u>NEG</u> stay

(iv)   *ddylet ti   <u>ddim</u> peidio ag   aros*   *(you shouldn't not*
               should you <u>NEG</u> stop   with stay   stay)

The first two varieties of each example show a positive obligation towards a positive act in (i) and to a negative act with PEIDIO (STOP) in (ii). The last two varieties show a negative obligation to a positive act in (iii) and to a negative act with PEIDIO in (iv).

The verb-nouns METHU (FAIL) and FFAELU (FAIL) are negative in an antonymic sense:

(218) *'dwi wedi <u>methu</u> â'i wneud o*   *(I've failed to do it)*
        am I after <u>fail</u> with→its do   it

(219) *mae hi   wedi <u>ffaelu</u> ffeindio John*   *(she has failed to*
        is   she after <u>fail</u> find   John   *find John)*

It is possible to compare METHU (FAIL) and FFAELU (FAIL) with either MEDRU (CAN) or LLWYDDO (SUCCEED). Paraphrases of METHU and FFAELU by MEDRU or LLWYDDO directly involve negation:

(220) *'dwi <u>ddim</u> wedi <u>medru/llwyddo</u> i'w wneud o*   *(I've not been able/*
        am I <u>NEG</u> after   car/succeed its do   it   *not succeeded in*
               doing it)

(221) *'dydy hi   <u>ddim</u> wedi <u>medru/llwyddo</u> ffeindio John*   *(she has not been*
        <u>NEG</u> is she <u>NEG</u> after   can/succeed find   John   *able/not*
               succeeded in
               finding John)

The occurrence of the negative in the paraphrases clearly illustrates the negative element in METHU and FFAELU.

The verbs METHU (FAIL) and FFAELU (FAIL) bring the discussion into the realm of lexical negation proper. Other items whose antonyms involve a negative element are COLLI (LOSE) and GWRTHOD (REFUSE):

(222) (i)   maen nhw wedi _colli'r_ gêm   *(they've lost the game)*
                     are   they after lose the game

      (ii)   _'dydyn_ nhw _ddim_ wedi _ennill_ y gêm   *(they haven't won*
              NEG are they NEG after win   the game   *the game)*

(223) (i)   mae hi   wedi gwrthod mynd   *(she has refused to go)*
                   is   she after refuse go

      (ii)   _'dydy_ hi _ddim_ wedi _cytuno_ i fynd   *(she hasn't agreed to*
              NEG is she NEG after agree   to go   *go)*

The discussion will not pursue the relationship of antonyms and negation.

4e   The adverbials CHWAITH (EITHER), BRON (ALMOST), PRIN (RARE), BRAIDD (RATHER) and OND (BUT)

The item CHWAITH (EITHER) can be thought of as the negative counterpart of the item HEFYD (ALSO). Compare the following examples:

(224)   mae John yn aros _hefyd_   *(John is staying also)*
           is   John in stay _also_

(225)   _'dydy_ John _ddim_ yn aros _chwaith_   *(John isn't staying*
         NEG is John NEG in stay _either_   *either)*

The items CHWAITH (EITHER) and HEFYD (ALSO) are restricted respectively to negative and positive sentences – HEFYD is not found in a negative sentence (except in some varieties of southern Welsh) nor CHWAITH in a positive sentence:

(226)   *'_dydy_ John _ddim_ yn aros _hefyd_   *(*John isn't staying*
        NEG is John NEG in stay _also_   *also)*

(227)   *mae John yn aros _chwaith_   *(*John is staying*
        is   John in stay _either_   *either)*

The items HEFYD (ALSO) and CHWAITH (EITHER) are involved in the linking together of similar situations. Thus, with HEFYD (ALSO) in (224) above, John's staying compares with the fact that someone else is staying, while with CHWAITH (EITHER) in (225) John's not staying compares with the fact that someone else is not staying. When pronouns occur in this sort of situation, the comparison can be marked by employing *conjunctive pronouns* so that we have:

(228)   *mae yntau'n aros hefyd*   *(he too is staying)*
        is   he   in stay   also

(229)   *'dydy yntau ddim yn aros chwaith*   *(he isn't staying* ◥
        NEG is he   NEG in   stay either   *either)*

Consequently, HEFYD (ALSO) and CHWAITH (EITHER) can be labelled as *conjunctive adverbs* (respectively positive and negative).

The items BRON (ALMOST) and PRIN (RARE) can be regarded as *semi-negatives*. The item BRON (ALMOST) is also discussed in the chapter on aspect (VI, section 1d). Examples of both can be given as follows:

(230)   *mae hi bron â   chysgu*   *(she's nearly sleeping)*
        is   she nearly with sleep

(231)   *prin 'dwi 'n ei weld o   y   dyddiau 'ma*   *(I scarcely see him*
        rare am I in his see   him the days   here   *these days)*

These items can be said to stand between a positive and negative sentence. The item BRON (ALMOST) thus stands between:

(232)   *mae hi   'n cysgu*   *(she's sleeping)*
        is   she in sleep

(233)   *'dydy hi   ddim yn cysgu*   *(she isn't sleeping)*
        NEG is she NEG in   sleep

Of the two it is nearer the positive than the negative, as it represents an estimation of a developing state of affairs. In (230) above, BRON (ALMOST) occurs as a medially placed adverb in a periphrastic verbal expression. It can also precede an infinitival construction with subject, as in *bron i mi syrthio (I nearly fell)*. In this context, BRON modifies the occurrence of an event rather than a developing situation as in (230).

The item PRIN (RARE) is nearer to the negative, as a paraphrase of (231) above shows:

(234)   *'dwi ddim yn ei weld o   yn aml   iawn y*   *(I don't see him very*
        am I NEG in   his see   him in   often very the   *often these days)*

        dyddiau 'ma
        days   here

But again it does not totally negate the statement. Both items can therefore be regarded as semi-negatives. Positionally, PRIN (RARE) always occurs initially. The item BRON (ALMOST) in spoken Welsh occurs either medially or finally:

(235) (i)   *mae hi <u>bron</u> â chysgu*   *(she's nearly sleeping)*
           is   she   nearly with sleep

    (ii)   *mae hi 'n cysgu <u>bron</u>*   *(she's sleeping nearly)*
           is   she   in sleep   nearly

In some dialects, especially in medial position, BRON (ALMOST) is replaced by JYST (JUST), giving examples such as *mae hi jyst â chysgu (she's nearly sleeping)*.

The item OND (BUT), which is otherwise used as a conjunction (see chapter VIII section 7), has a very clear formal relationship with negation in that its occurrences in examples such as the following are accompanied by a pre-sentential negative feature (either a mutation effect or the remnant 'D):

(236)   *'doedd o <u>ond</u> yn holi   am y prês*   *(he was only asking*
        NEG was he but in   enquire for the money   *about the money)*

Furthermore, in spontaneous speech OND (BUT) frequently occurs with the negative item DIM to form the expression DIM OND, which is reduceable to 'MOND, as in *'doedd o 'mond yn holi am y pres*. The relationship of OND (BUT) with negation in this use is also seen in another respect: tag questions assume a negative form, *'dwi 'mond yn gofyn, nac ydw? (I'm only asking, aren't I?)*, thus indicating a negative feature in this sentence.

The item BRAIDD (RATHER) has a much more tentative connection with negation. Its use can be illustrated by the following example:

(237)   *mae'n oer braidd*   *(it's rather cold)*
        is   in cold rather

It can be suggested that BRAIDD (RATHER) 'dilutes' the full positive statement by adding a form of *diminutive modification*. Formally, however, BRAIDD (RATHER) is not related to the feature of negation.

4f   The adjectives GWIW (FITTING) and GWAETH (WORSE)

The item GWIW (FITTING) invariably occurs in a sentence with a negative feature which is either realised or non-realised:

(238)   *<u>wiw</u> i mi fynd*   *(I daren't go)*
        dare for I   go

(239)   *<u>wiw</u> iddo fo wrthod*   *(he daren't refuse)*
        dare for (he) he refuse

It should be noted that in speech many speakers realise WIW as FIW [viu]. The surface structure of these examples can be given as GWIW ^ INFINITIVAL, where the infinitival contains its own subject. Examples (238) and (239) essentially involve a recursive operation comprising a negated matrix copula sentence and an infinitival clause, NI ∧ COP∧ GWIW ∧ INF. The copula sentences are reduced to GWIW, however, following a common procedure in Welsh that deletes the auxiliary carrier and other material in some matrix copula sentences. The occurrence of OEDD (WAS), however, clearly indicates both the copula form and the negative element in the form of the pre-sentential negative particle 'D:

(240) *'doedd   wiw i   mi fynd*   *(I didn't dare go)*
      NEG was dare for me go

(241) *'doedd   wiw iddo   fo wrthod*   *(he didn't dare refuse)*
      NEG was dare for (he) he refuse

Where BYDD (WILL BE) and BUASAI (WOULD BE) are concerned, they too are realised in surface structure but without an overt negative marker apart from soft mutation:

(242) *fydd   wiw i   mi fynd*   *(I won't dare go)*
      will be dare for me go

(243) *fuasai   wiw iddo   fo wrthod*   *(he wouldn't dare*
      would be dare for (he) he refuse   *refuse)*

The negative feature is also illustrated in paraphrases involving BEIDDIO (DARE); examples (240) and (241) could be paraphrased as:

(244) *allwn i ddim beiddio mynd*   *(I couldn't dare go)*
      could I NEG dare   go

(245) *allai   fo ddim beiddio gwrthod*   *(he couldn't dare*
      could he NEG dare   refuse   *refuse)*

The item GWIW (FITTING) is like RHAID (NECESSITY) and GWAETH (WORSE) (see below) in that it can occur as an answer word and tag:

(246) <u>wiw</u> i mi fynd, na   <u>wiw</u> – na <u>wiw</u>   *(I daren't go, dare I*
      dare for me go   NEG dare   NEG dare   *– no)*

The negative feature is clearly illustrated in the tag and answer word, as they are always negative.

The adjective GWAETH (WORSE) occurs in a surface structure similar to that in which GWIW (FITTING) occurs:

(247) <u>waeth</u> i   mi fynd   *(I might as well go)*
      worse for me go

Like the surface structure for GWIW, it is the remnant of a reduced matrix copula sentence which contains a negative feature. The negative feature can be clearly seen in the way it is reflected in tags and answer words (see section 3b above):

(248) waeth i   mi fynd,   ⎰ na   waeth ⎱   (I might as well go,
      worse for me go   ⎱ NEG worse ⎰   mightn't I?)

                              ⎰ ddim ⎱
                              ⎱ NEG ⎰

The tag is a choice between NA WAETH and the general negative marker DDIM itself. The item GWAETH (WORSE) thus emerges as similar to GWIW (FITTING) and RHAID (NECESSITY) which, like the auxiliary verbs, can occur in tags and answer words. Note that the event in the infinitival clause can be negated by using HEB (WITHOUT), but GWAETH (WORSE) itself still remains negative:

(249) waeth i   mi heb (n) â mynd   ⎰ na   waeth ⎱   (I might as well not
      worse for I without   go   ⎱ NEG worse ⎰   go, mightn't I?)

                                     ⎰ ddim ⎱
                                     ⎱ NEG ⎰

4g Affixal negation

In Welsh there are a number of prefixes which involve negation: DI-, AN- (ANG-, AM-) and AF-. These various affixes can be attached to various words to produce a negative feature, and the negative feature can be illustrated by the possibilities of paraphrase involving DIM:

(250) (i)   mae hi 'n annhaclus [an + taclus]   (she's untidy)
            is she in untidy   un   tidy

      (ii) 'dydy hi ddim yn daclus   (she isn't tidy)
            NEG is she NEG in tidy

(251) (i)   mae John yn afiach   [af + iach]   (John is unwell)
            is John in unhealthy   un   healthy

      (ii) 'dydy John ddim yn iach   (John is not well)
            NEG is John NEG in healthy

It is interesting to note, however, that both DIM and a negative affix can occur. Consider:

340

(252) (i)   *mae'n bosib*   *(it is possible)*
            is   in possible

(ii)   *mae'n <u>am</u>hosib   [an + posib]*   *(it is impossible)*
        is   in impossible in   possible

(iii) *'<u>d</u>ydy hi <u>d</u>dim yn <u>am</u>hosib*   *(it isn't impossible)*
        NEG is she NEG in   impossible

It is unlikely that (iii) is equivalent to (i) on the grounds that two negatives make a positive. Rather, (iii) negates (ii) but is at the same time not (i).

4h   Negation and pronouns

In Welsh there are three sets of pronouns which have a particular relationship with negation:

(253) *RHYWUN (SOMEONE)*   *UNRHYWUN (ANYONE)*   *NEB (NO ONE)*

       RHYWBETH (SOMETHING) UNRHYWBETH (ANYTHING) DIM BYD (NOTHING)

       RHYWLE (SOMEWHERE)   *UNRHYWLE (ANYWHERE)*   *NUNLLE (NOWHERE)*

The 'RHYW' forms in the first two columns are related both formally and semantically. Theoretically, they offer a *specific / non-specific* distinction, as in the following illustrations:

(254) *'dwi wedi gweld <u>rhywun</u> yn gadael y   tŷ*   *(I saw someone leave*
       am I after see   someone in leave   the house   the house)

(255) *mae <u>unrhywun</u> sy 'n meddwl hynny yn wirion*   *(anyone who thinks*
       is   anyone   is in think   that   in silly   that is silly)

In the first example the reference is to an unidentified but *specific* individual while in the second the reference is open to include anyone and is thus *non-specific*. But in spoken Welsh, especially in northern areas, it is frequently the case that the RHYWUN etc. group is used for both specific and non-specific reference, and example (255) above could readily be expressed as:

(256) *mae <u>rhywun</u>   sy 'n meddwl hynny yn wirion*   *(anyone who thinks*
       is   someone is in think   that   in silly   that is silly)

Consequently, the discussion will concentrate upon the RHYWUN etc. group and the particular interest of this group's relationship with NEB (NO ONE), DIM BYD (NOTHING) and NUNLLE (NOWHERE).

The three pronouns RHYWUN (SOMEONE), RHYWBETH (SOMETHING) and RHYWLE (SOMEWHERE) are basically positive, and in normal use they only occur in positive sentences:

(257)   *mae John wedi gweld rhywun*   *(John has seen*
      is   John after see   someone   *someone)*

(258)   *maen nhw wedi gwneud rhywbeth*   *(they've done*
      are   they after do   something   *something)*

(259)   *mae hi wedi mynd i rywle*   *(she's gone*
      is   she after go   to somewhere   *somewhere)*

If the sentences are transformed into negative sentences we find that this group is replaced by NEB (NO ONE), DIM BYD (NOTHING) and NUNLLE (NOWHERE), giving:

(260)   *'dydy John ddim wedi gweld neb*   *(John hasn't seen*
      NEG is John NEG after see   no one   *anyone)*

(261)   *'dydyn nhw ddim wedi gwneud dim byd*   *(they haven't done*
      NEG are they NEG after do   nothing   *anything)*

(262)   *'dydy hi ddim wedi mynd i nunlle*   *(she hasn't gone*
      NEG is she NEG after go   to nowhere   *anywhere)*

It can be said, therefore, that RHYWUN, RHYWBETH and RHYWLE are positive pronouns while NEB, DIM BYD and NUNLLE are their negative equivalents.

There is, however, a special context where RHYWUN (SOMEONE), RHYWBETH (SOMETHING) and RHYWLE (SOMEWHERE) may occur in a negative sentence. In this usage their reference is non-specific and they are further characterised, in northern areas at least, by repetition:

(263)   *wneith hi ddim cysgu efo rhywun [– rhywun]*   *(she won't sleep with*
      will   she NEG sleep with someone someone   *(just) anyone)*

(264)   *wneith hi ddim prynu rhywbeth [– rhywbeth]*   *(she won't buy (just)*
      will   she NEG buy something   something   *anything)*

(265)   *wneith hi ddim cysgu rhywle [– rhywle]*   *(she won't sleep (just)*
      will   she NEG sleep anywhere somewhere   *anywhere)*

Here it is the non-specificness which is being negated, for the suggestion in each case is that certain specific concepts would meet approval.

5   ELLIPSIS

5a   Introduction

It is possible to produce additional varieties of simple sentences simply by leaving out
various constituents:

(266) (i)   *mae John yn paentio'r   drws*   *(John is painting the*
                 is   John in paint   the door   door)

       (ii)   *mae John yn paentio*   *(John is painting)*
                 is   John in paint

(267) (i)   *mae Mair yn dadlau am   y   prês   efo John*   *(Mair is arguing*
                 is   Mair in argue about the money with John   about the money
                                                                     with John)*

       (ii)   *mae Mair yn dadlau am   y   prês*   *(Mair is arguing about*
                 is   Mair in argue about the money   the money)*

       (iii)   *mae Mair yn dadlau efo   John*   *(Mair is arguing with*
                 is   Mair in argue with John   John)*

       (iv)   *mae Mair yn dadlau*   *(Mair is arguing)*
                 is   Mair in argue

The process of leaving out or not realising constituents is known as ELLIPSIS, and
sentences which involve ellipsis can be called *ellipted sentences*. Ellipsis is not
performed without restriction. The next section illustrates some of the possibilities
and limitations involved.

5b   The range of ellipsis

For the convenience of surface structure labelling, ellipted sentences will be divided
into three main types. As with inversion and interrogatives, it is useful to consider the
elliptical possibilities in relation to a generalised branching-diagram. In this way a
general framework can be set up to establish the various possibilities of ellipsis.

Firstly, there is deletion of various constituents excluding the particle, auxiliary and
verb. Since the verbal material is retained, the sentences produced in this manner can
be labelled as *ellipted finite sentences*. The ellipsis applies to the subject noun phrase
and the post-verbal or complement constituents:

(268)

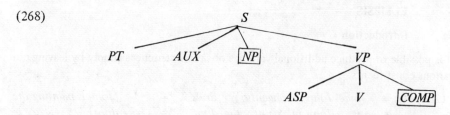

The deletion of the noun phrase subject occurs more frequently in formal written Welsh than it does in spontaneous spoken Welsh, and this type of ellipsis can be interpreted as a stylistic marker of formal written Welsh:

(269) *plygodd Mair ar ei gliniau . . .*   *(Mair bent on her*
    bent Mair on her knees   *knees . . . (she)*

    penderfynodd φ na ddywedai φ   *decided that (she)*
    decided NEG would say   *would not say*

    Weddi'r Arglwydd   *the Lord's Prayer)*
    the Lord's Prayer

The deleted subject is signalled by the sign (φ). The significant point to bear in mind is that ellipsis only occurs if the noun phrase has already been identified. With third person subjects this involves prior textual identification, as in the above examples (where MAIR is established). As far as first and second persons are concerned, context can make the identification apparent:

(270) *felly yr wyf φ yn rhyw dybio . . .*   *(therefore (I) some-*
    therefore am in somewhat imagine   *what imagine . . .)*

(271) *'rydych yn cael ffurflen . . .*   *((you) have a*
    are in have form   *form . . .)*

The deletion of post-verbal constituents is not as clear-cut. There is a wide range of possibilities as can be shown by the following:

(272) *mae John yn meddwl (am y problemau)*   *(John is thinking*
    is John in think about the problems   *(about the problems))*

(273) *mae Mair yn cwyno ((am y bwyd)*   *(Mair is complaining*
    is Mair in complain about the food   *(about the food)*

    (wrth John))   *(to John))*
    to John

(274) *mae Gwil yn palu('r ardd)*   *(Gwil is digging (the*
    is Gwil in dig the garden   *garden))*

The interesting point here is that the deletion of a post-verbal constituent results in greater attention going to the verb, and more highlight is given to the activity involved (as opposed to what the activity is centred upon). But there are problems; not all complements can be deleted. In many cases it depends upon the verb. In example (274) above, object noun phrase deletion is possible but this is not so readily acceptable with TARO (HIT):

(275) *? mi drawodd John (y   wal)*   *(John hit (the wall))*
        PT hit   John   the wall

It would be possible if an adverb were added:

(276) *mi drawodd John yn galed*   *(John hit hard)*
        PT hit   John in hard

A comprehensive survey of the possibilities of post-verbal ellipsis would be too lengthy for our immediate purposes, and it suffices to illustrate some possibilities and restrictions as above.

In the second place, it is possible to isolate the ellipsis of the particle along with the auxiliary verb, producing a *non-finite sentence*:

(277)

Ellipsis of this type can be illustrated as follows:

(278) *. . . a   φ finna'n gweithio mor galed*   *(. . . and me working*
        and I in work   so   hard   *so hard)*

(279) *φ rhywun wedi cwyno?*   *(someone*
        someone after complain   *complained?)*

Both sentences derive from:

(280) *. . . a   'roeddwn inna'n gweithio mor galed*   *(. . . and I was*
        and was   I   in work   so   hard   *working so hard)*

(281) *oes rhywun wedi cwyno?*   *(has someone*
        is   someone after complain   *complained?)*

It is possible to establish two types of non-finites in relation to their linguistic context. The ellipsis may be textually conditioned, where the auxiliary has already had prior establishment in the text. This is the case with example (278) above:

(282)   *'roedd John yn sgwrsio efo Mair a*   *(John was talking*
           was   John in talking with Mair and   *with Mair and me*

           finna'n gweithio mor galed   *working so hard)*
           I   in work   so   hard

Alternatively, the ellipsis can be non-textual, supported solely by reference to the grammar of the language; this is the case with example (281) above. Note that in both cases other possibilities of ellipsis are available, such as subject deletion:

(283)   *mi fuasai'r ŵy yn torri ac*   *(the egg would break*
           PT would the egg in break and   *and run through her*

           φ φ *yn rhedeg trwy   'i bysedd*   *fingers)*
              in run   through her fingers

Or subject and object deletion:

(284)   *wedi gorffen?*   *(finished?)*
           after finish

A third type of ellipsis occurs in *infinitival* sentences, where ellipsis has applied to the particle, the auxiliary, noun phrase subject and aspect marker(s), leaving only the verb and any post-verbal constituents:

(285)

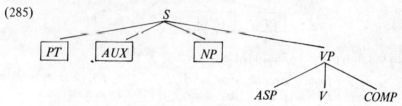

This type of ellipsis can be illustrated as follows:

(286)   *dydy 'r ffaith eich bod chi 'n y   chweched*   *(the fact that you*
           NEG is the fact your be   you in the sixth   *are in the sixth*

           dosbarth ac yn gwisgo bathodyn a <u>gyrru car</u> *form and wear a*
           class   and in wear   badge   and drive car *badge and drive*

           ddim yn eich gwneud chi 'n oddynion   *a car doesn't*
           NEG in your make   you in men   *make you men)*

In the above example GYRRU CAR (DRIVE A CAR) is derived from:

(287)   *...y   ffaith ... <u>eich bod chi 'n gyrru car</u> ...*   *(... the fact that you*
              the fact   your be   you in drive car   *drive a car ...)*

With infinitivals, therefore, it can be seen that the extent of deletion is severe.

6   IMPERATIVE

6a   Introduction

The most familiar realisation of the imperative in Welsh can be exemplified as follows:

(288)   *canwch!*   *(sing!)*
            sing

(289)   *gwranda ar hyn!*   *(listen to this!)*
            listen   on this

In this pattern, the imperative occurs as an inflected form of the verb with second person features. There is, however, no occurring subject noun phrase and the traditional explanation is to say that the subject is 'understood'. There are arguments for suggesting that the subject is deleted, based upon examples such as:

(290)   *gwranda <u>di</u> ar hyn*   *(listen you to this)*
            listen   you on this

In this example the subject actually occurs as underlined, and in comparison it can be suggested that examples like (288) and (289) involve the deletion of the subject.

In the discussion of the imperative presented here, four points will be examined: the semantics of the imperative, the negation of the imperative, the relationship of the imperative and the -ITH inflection, and the person contrasts in the imperative.

6b   The semantics of the imperative

The most familiar use associated with the imperative is that of giving commands. But a number of traditional grammars, including Rowland (1876 : 61) and Williams (1959 : 102), note that the semantics of the imperative range from commands to requests. This can be clearly shown by paraphrasing the above examples of the imperative in (288) and (289) as:

(291)   *'dwi 'n gorchymyn/deisyfu i   chi ganu*   *(I command/request*
            am I in   order/request for you sing   *you to sing)*

(292)   *'dwi 'n gorchymyn/deisyfu i   ti   wrando ar hyn* *(I command/request*
            am I in   order/request for you listen on this you to listen to this)

The possibility of using either GORCHYMYN (COMMAND) or DEISYFU (REQUEST) explicitly illustrates the traditional view of the semantics of the

347

imperative.

The paraphrases in (291) and (292) illustrate something more. When the imperative is used, the *speaker* is performing an action of either giving a command or making a request to an *addressee*. There are two important points here. Firstly, the imperative occurs in the context of a speaker—addressee relationship. The speaker, however, is only signalled in the paraphrases, while the addressee occurs as second person in both the imperative proper (as subject — although frequently deleted) and in the paraphrases (further discussion of person contrasts is given in section 6e below). Secondly, imperatives involve a *performative* feature, where using the imperative means actually performing the act of giving a command or making a request. In this respect, the imperative is similar to the *permission* use of CAEL (RECEIVE) or GALLU (CAN) discussed in chapter V, sections 3b and 3c, and the *suggestion* use of CAEL (RECEIVE) discussed in chapter V, section 3b, as the use of both of these can involve the actual giving of permission and making of a suggestion.

6c   The imperative and negation

The details of negation and the imperative are given in section 4d above. The important point is that the traditional account of forming a negative imperative with NA (C) is not appropriate for spontaneous spoken Welsh, where PEIDIO (STOP) is used. The use of NA (C) is stylistically restricted to very formal Welsh.

6d   The imperative and the -ITH inflection

In terms of the inflectional formation of the imperative, the second person plural, as illustrated by (288) above, is identical with the second person plural of the -ITH paradigm (see appendix). But the second person singular can be distinguished as involving either -A as in (289) above, or the infinitival form of the verb, as in:

(293) *agor y   drws!*   *(open the door)*
      open the door

The details are given in the appendix.

The important point about the relationship of the imperative and the -ITH inflection is semantic rather than concerned with similarity in the shape of the endings. It was pointed out in chapter V, section 2b, that the -ITH inflections can be used with imperative force. It is therefore significant to find that the -ITH inflection carried by the carrier auxiliary GWNEUD (DO) can occur as a tag to imperatives:

(294) *canwch, wnewch chi!*   *(sing, will you!)*
      sing   will   you

348

(295)   *gwranda ar hyn, wnei di!*   *(listen to this, will*
           listen   on this will you   *you!)*

This further illustrates the semantic range of the imperative, as examples of this type approximate to an 'appeal' rather than a 'command', the occurrence of GWNEUD (DO) + -ITH giving support to the 'request' aspect of imperatives. It is important to note, however, that the occurrence of GWNEUD (DO) with imperatives does not follow the normal rules for tags described in section 3b above. The first point to note is that the tag formation for a positive sentence, as described in section 3b above, does not normally occur:

(296)   **canwch, yn   gwnewch chi*   *(*sing, won't you)*
           sing   NEG will   you

(297)   **gwranda ar hyn, yn   gwnei di*   *(*listen to this, won't*
           listen   on this NEG will   you   *you)*

In these circumstances, it is found that the pro-verb GWNEUD (DO) can be repeated without any particle, giving:

(298)   *canwch, wnewch chi!*   *(sing, will you!)*
           sing   will   you

(299)   *gwranda ar hyn, wnei di!*   *(listen to this, will*
           listen   on this will you   *you!)*

In the case of negatives the typical negative tag is normally selected: *peidiwch a chanu, na wnewch chi! (don't sing, will you!)* and *paid a gwrando ar hyn, na wnei di (don't listen to this, will you).* But in some circumstances it may also be possible to use the pro-verb GWNEUD (DO) without a particle as in (298) and (299) above: *paid a dod yn ôl yn gynnar, wnei di! (don't come back early, will you!).*

The occurrence of the -ITH paradigm is also relevant to a discussion of person contrasts in the following sub-section.

6e   Person contrasts

In spontaneous spoken Welsh, the inflected imperative is always second person. But, in traditional Welsh grammar (e.g. Jones, 1913 : 318; Williams, 1959 : 105), the imperative relates to all persons except the first singular. Thus, in formal Welsh, imperatives can relate to third persons:

(300)   *coded   y   gynulleidfa*   *(the congregation will*
           rise + IMP the congregation   *rise)*

Moreover, traditional formal Welsh also allows for an impersonal passive such as the following:

(301) *gweler   tudalen 54*   *(page 54 is to be seen)*
       see + IMP page   54

Neither of these possibilities in this form is productive in spontaneous spoken Welsh (apart from certain dialects); they are stylistic markers of formal Welsh.

Spontaneous Welsh can, however, produce third person imperative equivalents by using other patterns. In particular, as discussed in chapter V, section 2b, the -ITH inflection can be used:

(302) *mi wneith y   gynulleidfa   godi*   *(the congregation will*
       PT will   the congregation rise   *rise)*

Also possible is a pattern of the following type:

(303) *pawb   i   ganu*   *(everyone to sing)*
       everyone to sing

Although both these examples illustrate third person features, they still refer to an *addressee*, as can be shown by the possibilities of paraphrase involving third person characteristics:

(304) (i)   *codwch!*   *(rise!)*
                rise

       (ii)   *mi wnewch chi godi*   *(you will rise)*
                PT will   you rise

(305) *canwch i gyd*   *(all sing)*
       sing   all

The use of non-second person forms, as in (302) and (303), tends to dilute the blunt tone of a direct imperative and, consequently, they are more polite in comparison.

7   GENERAL REMARKS ON SENTENTIAL FEATURES

7a   Sentential features and constituent sentences

Of the five sentential features discussed in this chapter, only three can clearly and regularly apply to both matrix and constituent sentences, namely *inversion*, *negation* and *ellipsis*:

350

(306) *mae Mair yn gwybod mai/taw John sy 'n*   *(Mair knows it is John*
      is   Mair   in   know   <u>it   is   John   is   in</u>   *who is digging the*

      <u>*palu'r   ardd*</u>   *garden)*
      dig   the   garden

(307) (i)   *mae Mair yn gwybod* <u>*nad   ydy John ddim yn*</u>   *(Mair knows that*
                is   Mair   in   know   <u>NEG is   John NEG in</u>   *John isn't digging*

                <u>*palu'r   ardd*</u>   *the garden)*
                dig   the   garden

      (ii)   *mae Mair yn gwybod* <u>*bod John ddim yn*</u>   *(Mair knows that*
                is   Mair   in   know   ` be   John NEG in   *John isn't digging*

                <u>*palu'r   ardd*</u>   *the garden)*
                dig   the   garden

(308) *mae Mair yn gwybod* <u>*bod John yn palu*</u>   *(Mair knows that*
      is   Mair   in   know   <u>be   John   in   dig</u>   *John is digging)*

The range of ellipsis varies, but the relevant point here is that it does occur to some extent.

In the case of the remaining two features — interrogation and imperative — the same possibilities of clear and consistent occurrence in a constituent sentence do not exist. Certainly, in the case of the imperative, it is not possible to have this feature in a constituent sentence:

(309) **mae Mair yn gwybod* <u>*palwch yr   ardd!*</u>   *(*Mair knows dig the*
      is   Mair   in   know   <u>dig   the   garden</u>   *garden!)*

The interrogative feature, however, is problematic. On the one hand, it is not possible to produce a normal yes—no interrogative in a constituent sentence:

(310) **mae Mair yn meddwl ydy John yn palu'r   ardd?*   *(*Mair thinks is John*
      is   Mair   in   think   <u>is   John   in   dig the garden</u>   *digging the garden?)*

On the other hand, there are a number of points which suggest that an interrogative feature can be related to a constituent sentence in certain circumstances. In this discussion, we will briefly highlight three possibilities: (i) *mae Mair yn gofyn* <u>*a ydy*</u> *John yn palu'r ardd (Mair is asking whether John is digging the garden)*; (ii) *pwy mae Mair yn ei feddwl sy'n palu'r ardd? (who does Mair think is digging the garden?)*; and (iii) *mae Mair yn gwybod* <u>*pwy sy'n palu'r ardd*</u> *(Mair knows who is digging the garden)*. The first example contains an A (WHETHER) sentential complement (briefly mentioned in chapter VIII, section 2a), where the A particle can be compared with the interrogative particle of formal Welsh. In this particular example, the verb of the matrix sentence, GOFYN (ASK), has a direct lexical relationship with the feature interrogative and further supports an interrogative interpretation of the consitutent sentence. There are, however, other verbs which can occur in the matrix sentence as the following demonstrates: *'dydy Mair ddim yn gwybod/cofio/sylwi/dweud/a ydy John yn palu'r ardd (Mair doesn't know/remember/notice/say whether John is digging the garden)*. The significant point about the A (WHETHER) clause is that it is possible to substitute OS (IF) for A (WHETHER), as in: *mae Mair yn gofyn os ydy John yn palu'r ardd (Mair is asking if John is digging the garden)* and *'dydy Mair ddim yn gwybod/cofio/sylwi/dweud os ydy John yn palu'r ardd (Mair doesn't know/remember/notice/say if John is digging the garden)*. Indeed, OS (IF) is the typical choice in spontaneous speech. However, it is not possible for OS (IF) to substitute for A (WHETHER) in a normal yes—no interrogative: *a ydy John yn palu'r ardd? (is John digging the garden?)* ≠ *os ydy John yn palu'r ardd (if John is digging the garden)*.

The second example quoted above, *pwy mae Mair yn ei feddwl sy'n palu'r ardd? (who does Mair think is digging the garden?)* is particularly interesting. It illustrates two points. Firstly, the feature interrogative can relate to a constituent sentence, as is demonstrated by the fact that the interrogative word PWY (WHO) relates to the subject of the constituent sentence and the copula form SYDD (IS) occurs (a typical characteristic of subject noun phrase interrogatives). Secondly, however, the constituent sentence cannot itself assume an interrogative pattern in surface structure: thus instead of **mae Mair yn meddwl pwy sy'n palu'r ardd? (*Mair thinks who is digging the garden?)*, the interrogative word PWY (WHO) is moved to the front of the matrix sentence to produce *pwy mae Mair yn meddwl sy'n palu'r ardd?* On this basis, we can again conclude that a constituent sentence cannot assume normal interrogative form (at least in surface structure).

The third example, *mae Mair yn gwybod pwy sy'n palu'r ardd (Mair knows who is digging the garden)*, appears to have an interrogative sentence, PWY SY'N PALU'R ARDD? (WHO IS DIGGING THE GARDEN?) as its sentential complement. It is argued here, however, that the constituent sentence merely involves indefinite pronominalisation and fronting, and is not itself an interrogative.

On the basis of the above discussion, it is possible to distinguish between imperative and interrogative, on the one hand, and inversion, negation and ellipsis, on the other:

(311)

MATRIX ONLY	*MATRIX AND CONSTITUENT*
Imperative	*Inversion*
Interrogative	*Negation*
	Ellipsis

352

Because imperative and interrogative apply only to higher sentences, they can be considered to be quite distinct from the other three, and this point is supported by other evidence discussed in the next sub-section concerning the possibilities of co-occurrence of sentential features.

An interesting phenomenon occurs in relation to the negative feature. Compare the following complex patterns:

(312) <u>'dydy Mair ddim yn gobeithio</u> <u>bod John yn dod</u>   *(Mair doesn't hope*
      NEG is Mair NEG in hope   be John in come   *that John is coming)*

(313) <u>'dydy Mair ddim yn meddwl</u> <u>bod John yn dod</u>   *(Mair doesn't think*
      NEG is Mair NEG in think   be John in come John is coming)*

In example (312) the negative item DIM can only apply to the matrix sentence and negates *Mair's hoping* that John will come. If the constituent sentence is negated, a negative item is inserted in the constituent sentence itself:

(314) <u>mae Mair yn gobeithio</u> <u>bod John ddim yn dod</u>   *(Mair hopes that*
      is   Mair in hope   be John NEG in come   John isn't coming)*

However, in the case of example (313) both interpretations are possible. The negative item in (313) can negate either Mair's thinking or John's coming. In the first interpretation it is syntactically equivalent to (312), but in the second interpretation it is equivalent to (314):

(315) <u>mae Mair yn meddwl</u> <u>bod John ddim yn dod</u>   *(Mair thinks that*
      is   Mair in think   be John NEG in come   'John isn't coming)*

But, unlike GOBEITHIO (HOPE), the negation of the constituent sentence with MEDDWL (THINK) is carried into the matrix sentence rather than left in the constituent sentence. This phenomenon is known as *negative transportation*.

7b   Co-occurrence of sentential features

The discussion of sentential features has established five possibilities: *imperative, interrogative, inversion, negation* and *ellipsis*. In addition to occurring singly, they can also occur in various combinations. There are, however, two restrictions on the co-occurrence of sentential features, one major and one relatively minor.

Firstly, the interrogative excludes the imperative and vice versa: it is not possible to have both a command and an interrogative. Such a situation does exist to a certain extent in the adding of tags to interrogatives:

(316) *agor y   drws, wnei di!*   *(open the door,*
      open the door will you   *will you!)*

But this is better viewed as reinforcement of an imperative than as an instance of the two operating upon the same sentence. It has already been seen that interrogatives and imperatives are distinctive in being restricted to matrix sentences, and this additional characteristic makes them more remarkable. With one important exception, as illustrated in the next paragraph, there is complete freedom of co-occurrence excluding these two. It can thus be suggested that interrogatives and imperatives are somehow more basic, and that the other operations are applied after them.

Secondly, excluding interrogative + imperative, all the operations can co-occur, with the restriction that imperative sentences cannot invert. As example (317) illustrates, interrogative sentences can invert, negate and ellipt, but imperative sentences can only negate and ellipt, as (318) shows:

(317)	*dim John sy 'n palu?*		*(isn't it John who*
	NEG John is in dig		*is digging?)*

(318)	(i)	*palwch yr ardd!*	*(dig the garden!)*
		dig the garden	
	(ii)	*palwch!*	*(dig!)*
		dig	
	(iii)	*peidiwch â phalu'r ardd!*	*(don't dig the*
		stop with dig the garden	*garden!)*
	(iv)	*peidiwch â phalu!*	*(don't dig!)*
		stop with dig	
	(v)	**yr ardd palwch*	*(*the garden dig)*
		the garden dig	

An illustration of the way in which sentential features can combine, and the variety of additional sentence patterns that they produce, can be given as follows:

354

(319)

	Interro-gative	Inver-sion	Nega-tion	Ellipsis	
(i)	−	−	−	−	*mae John yn palu'r ardd*
(ii)	−	+	−	−	*John sy'n palu'r ardd*
(iii)	−	−	+	−	*'dydy John ddim yn palu'r ardd*
(iv)	−	−	−	+	*mae John yn palu*
(v)	−	+	+	−	*nid John sy'n palu'r ardd*
(vi)	−	+	−	+	*John sy'n palu*
(vii)	−	−	+	+	*'dydy John ddim yn palu*
(viii)	+	−	−	−	*ydy John yn palu'r ardd?*
(ix)	+	+	−	−	*John sy'n palu'r ardd?*
(x)	+	−	+	−	*'dydy John ddim yn palu'r ardd?*
(xi)	+	−	−	+	*ydy John yn palu?*
(xii)	+	+	+	−	*dim John sy'n palu'r ardd?*
(xiii)	+	+	−	+	*John sy'n palu?*
(xiv)	+	−	+	+	*'dydy John ddim yn palu?*
(xv)	Imperative	0	−	−	*palwch yr ardd!*
(xvi)	+	0	+	−	*peidiwch a palu'r ardd!*
(xvii)	+	0	−	+	*palwch!*
(xviii)	+	0	+	+	*peidiwch a palu!*

A total of eighteen patterns are involved, seventeen of them being additional variations of the basic sentence in (i) produced by the application of the sentential operations. Even this figure is not exhaustive; in the case of inversion, interrogation and ellipsis, only one of many possible patterns has been produced (see sections 2, 3 and 5 above).

8　PRE-SENTENTIAL PARTICLES

8a　Introduction

As illustrated in the foregoing sections of this chapter, several of the sentential features involve the occurrence of various pre-sentential particles; for example, the fronting movement of subject inversion involves A (although sometimes not realised) as in *John (a) oedd yn gweiddi (it was John who was shouting)* and negation involves NI(D) (again with various realisation rules) as in *'doedd John ddim yn gweiddi (John was not shouting)*. In addition, pre-sentential particles are involved in sentential complements, as discussed in chapter VIII, and relative clauses, as discussed in chapter VII. In this section the aim is to bring together all the pre-sentential particles involved in Welsh sentences, and to list and organise their various uses.

8b　The number and character of pre-sentential particles

The analysis of pre-sentential particles is a complex topic and we will begin simply by listing possible members of this general class in relation to the grammatical context in which they occur. The discussion will proceed initially without regard for stylistic usage, as this information is given in section 8c below. The following table will help to provide a starting point for the discussion:

(320)

			POSITIVE	NEGATIVE
Matrix sentence	*DECLARATIVE*	– *INVERSION*	*mi/fe, etc.*	*ni(d)*
		+ ″	$\left\{\begin{matrix}a\\y(r)\end{matrix}\right\}$	*(nid/dim) . . na(d)*
	INTERROGATIVE –	″	*a*	*oni(d)*
		+ ″	*ai*	*onid*
	IMPERATIVE	–	⌀	*na(c)* NB *peidio*
Constituent sentence	*DECLARATIVE*	–	″	*y(r)*	*na(d)*
		+ ″	*mai/taw* . . $\left\{\begin{matrix}a\\y\end{matrix}\right\}$	*mai/taw* *nid/dim . . na(d)*
Relative sentence	*DECLARATIVE*	–	″	$\left\{\begin{matrix}a\\y(r)\end{matrix}\right\}$	*na(d)*

356

This table gives a total of sixteen grammatical contexts in which a possible (at this stage) pre-sentential particle could occur, depending upon combinations of recursiveness and sentential features. It also illustrates fifteen distinct forms: MI, FE, I, NI(D), A, Y, NID, DIM, ONI(D), AI, ONID, NA(C), NA(D), MAI and TAW. This table can be considerably simplified in two respects. Firstly, a number of the forms listed can be excluded from the class of pre-sentential particle. This applies to those items specifically related to inverted sentences: NID/DIM, AI, ONID, and MAI/TAW. The first three are accounted for as items which are generated in the immediate environment of the constituent that is to be negated (NID/DIM — see section 4c above), questioned (AI — see section 3k above), or both (ONID). The last pair, MAI/TAW, are verbal forms related to the copula verb (see the discussion in section 7a above), and used to introduce inverted sentences. All these items are distinctive in that they do not occur immediately before a sentence but immediately before a constituent which has been inverted to initial position. Thus, one can compare a pre-sentential particle proper such as A or NI(D) as in *a oedd John yn chwerthin? (was John laughing?)* or *nid oedd John yn chwerthin (John wasn't laughing)* with the latter items as in *nid/dim John (a) oedd yn chwerthin (it wasn't John who was laughing)*, *ai John a oedd yn chwerthin (was it John who was laughing?)*, *onid John a oedd yn chwerthin (wasn't it John who was laughing?)* and . . . *mai/taw John a oedd yn chwerthin (. . . that it was John who was laughing)* — and see the positional differences; note, for instance, that the relative particle A in the preceding examples immediately precedes the auxiliary carrier. Secondly, inversion and relativisation can be thought of under the same general heading of fronting, and only one entry is necessary in the table.

In view of these modifications the table can be given in the following simplified and altered form:

(321)

		MATRIX	*CONSTITUENT*
DECLARATIVE	*POSITIVE*	*mi/fe/i*	*y(r)*
	NEGATIVE	*ni(d)*	*na(d)*
INTERROGATIVE	*POSITIVE*	*a*	—
	NEGATIVE	*oni(d)*	—
IMPERATIVE	*POSITIVE*	ϕ	—
	NEGATIVE	*na(c)*	—
FRONTING	*POSITIVE*	—	$\left\{ \begin{matrix} a \\ y(r) \end{matrix} \right\}$
	NEGATIVE	—	*na(d)*

The amended table reduces the grammatical contexts of pre-sentential particles to ten. Basically, the various grammatical contexts involve the features of the traditional category of *mood* (declarative, interrogative and imperative) modified by the contrasts of positive and negative (termed as a category of *polarity* by some linguists), and by *recursiveness* (matrix or constituent). The operation of fronting is slightly different, and it could be argued that it is basically a feature of recursiveness (see note 1) — hence the minus (−) entry under the 'Matrix' column in the above table. The actual details of the combinations and the pre-sentential particles involved can be abstracted from the above table. Examples of their occurrences can be given as follows:

(322) mi oedd John yn chwerthin   *(John was laughing)*
       PT was John in laugh

(323) mae Mair yn gwybod yr oedd John yn chwerthin   *(Mair knows that*
       is Mair in know PT was John in laugh   *John was laughing)*

(324) 'doedd   John ddim yn chwerthin   *(John wasn't*
       NEG was John NEG in laugh   *laughing)*

(325) mae Mair yn gwybod nad oedd John yn chwerthin   *(Mair knows that*
       is Mair in know NEG was John in laugh   *John was not laughing)*

(326) a   oedd John yn chwerthin?   *(was John laughing?)*
       PT was John in laugh

(327) onid oedd John yn chwerthin?   *(wasn't John*
       PT   was John in laugh   *laughing?)*

(328) na chwerthwch!   *(don't laugh!)*
       PT laugh

(329) John a   oedd yn chwerthin   *(it was John who was*
       John PT was in laugh   *laughing)*

(330) y   car yr edrychodd John arno   *(it was the car that*
       the car PT looked   John on it   *John looked at)*

(331) John nad oedd yn chwerthin   *(it was John who*
       John NEG was in laugh   *was not laughing)*

The number of actual distinct particle forms is reduced to nine: MI, FE, I, Y(R), NI(D), NA(D), A, ONI(D) and NA(C).[6] The first three are variants giving MI/FE/I while A, Y, and NA(D) are used in more than one grammatical context each: A_1 (interrogative) and A_2 (fronting), Y_1 (complementiser) and Y_2 (fronting), and $NA(D)_1$ (negative complementiser) and $NA(D)_2$ (negative fronting).

On the basis of the above discussion of pre-sentential particles, we are now in a position to supply details for the re-writing of the pre-sentential particle constituent, PT, of Welsh sentences. There are three points that can be made initially. The first point is that, for our purposes, the particle could be re-written in terms of actually occurring particle forms or it could be related to a set of semantic features (of mood, polarity and fronting) which control the selection of a particular particle. The semantic features involved are illustrated in the table in (321) and the re-writing rule in these terms could be given as follows:

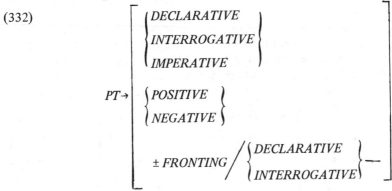

(332)

$$PT \rightarrow \begin{bmatrix} \begin{Bmatrix} DECLARATIVE \\ INTERROGATIVE \\ IMPERATIVE \end{Bmatrix} \\ \begin{Bmatrix} POSITIVE \\ NEGATIVE \end{Bmatrix} \\ \pm FRONTING \Big/ \begin{Bmatrix} DECLARATIVE \\ INTERROGATIVE \end{Bmatrix} \_ \end{bmatrix}$$

The operation of fronting applies only to declarative and interrogative sentences and not to imperatives; this is indicated in the above rule by a contextual restriction. The rule reads that a sentence can be either declarative or interrogative or imperative, and that any one of these can be positive or negative — further, any one of the preceding combinations, with the exception of one containing the feature *imperative*, can be subject to fronting. The second point to make is that, as discussed in section 7a above, there are restrictions on these features in terms of recursiveness: thus *declarative* can occur in both matrix and constituent sentences while interrogative (or, at least its typical surface structure form) and imperative are restricted to matrix sentences. The rule in (332), therefore, represents a comprehensive account of the maximum possibilities but does not discriminate the contexts in which the various possibilities can occur. The third point to make is that, as the columning in the table in (321) indicates, a different particle can occur in matrix and constituent sentences for exactly the same semantic features: thus a positive declarative sentence has a particle MI/FE/I when it is a matrix sentence and a particle Y(R) when it is a constituent sentence. The forms could thus be given in two equivalent sets, one for matrix sentences and the other for constituent sentences:

(333) (i)

$$PT \rightarrow \begin{Bmatrix} mi/fe/i \\ ni(d) \\ a_1 \\ oni(d) \\ na(c) \end{Bmatrix}$$

(ii)

$$PT \rightarrow \begin{Bmatrix} y(r)_1 \\ na(d)_1 \\ a_2 \\ y(r)_2 \\ na(d)_2 \end{Bmatrix}$$

The rule in (333) (i) indicates particles which occur in matrix sentences while that in (333) (ii) indicates those which occur in constituent sentences. For the purpose of this discussion, we may re-write the PT in terms of the occurring forms. This has the advantage of accounting for the restrictions due to recursiveness as well as listing the different particles involved. A rule of the following form can thus be suggested:

(334)

$$PT \rightarrow \left\{ \begin{matrix} \begin{Bmatrix} mi/fe/i \\ ni(d) \\ a_1 \\ oni(d) \\ na(c) \end{Bmatrix} \Big/ \text{Matrix S} \\[2em] \begin{Bmatrix} y(r)_1 \\ na(d)_1 \\ a_2 \\ y(r)_2 \\ na(d)_2 \end{Bmatrix} \Big/ \text{Constituent S} \end{matrix} \right\}$$

The disadvantage, of course, is that this rule does not convey any information about the semantics of any particular particle, but these details can be abstracted from the discussion given above.

The rule in (334) can be incorporated into the overall rules for Welsh syntax given in chapter VIII, section 2d, to produce a set of rules of the following form:

(335) (i) S → $PT \; AUX \; NP \; VP$

(ii) $\dot{P}T$ → $\left\{ \begin{array}{l} \left\{ \begin{array}{l} \left. \begin{array}{l} mi/fe/i \\ ni(d) \\ a_1 \\ oni(d) \\ na(c) \end{array} \right\} \text{Matrix S} \\ \left. \begin{array}{l} y(r)_1 \\ na(d)_1 \\ \left\{ \begin{array}{l} a_2 \\ y(r)_2 \end{array} \right\} \\ na(d)_2 \end{array} \right\} \text{Constituent S} \end{array} \right\}$

(iii) AUX → $\left\{ \begin{array}{l} -ITH \\ -AI \\ -ODD \end{array} \right\}$

(iv) VP → $(ASP) \left\{ \begin{array}{l} V \left\{ \begin{array}{l} (NP) \; (PP) \; (PP) \\ (PRED \; PH) \end{array} \right\} \\ COP \left\{ \begin{array}{l} (PRED \; P\dot{H} \\ NP \\ PP \end{array} \right\} \end{array} \right\}$

(v) ASP → $\left\{ \begin{array}{l} PERFECT \\ RECENT \; PERFECT \end{array} \right\} \; and/or \; \left\{ \begin{array}{l} PROGRESSIVE \\ IMMINENT \end{array} \right\}$

(vi) PP → $P \; NP$

(vii) $PRED \; PH$ → $\left\{ \begin{array}{l} YN \left\{ \begin{array}{l} NP \\ ADJ \end{array} \right\} \\ FEL/COP - NP \end{array} \right\}$

(viii) NP → $\left\{ \begin{array}{l} (Q) \; (DET) \; N \; (S) \\ S \end{array} \right\}$

These rules represent a formulaic summary of many of the points of Welsh syntax discussed in this and the preceding chapters.

8c   Stylistic usage of pre-sentential particles

The occurrence of a particle is determined by the stylistic context — particularly when we consider spontaneous spoken Welsh versus traditional written Welsh. In the main, one must agree with Anwyl (1899 : 178) who says that 'Modern spoken Welsh is characterised by an almost complete elimination of pre-verbal particles . . . ' There are, however, a number of points of detail that can be added to this general statement.

The only particles regularly used in spontaneous speech are MI/FE/I. But the situation seems to be that in the main they do not occur, being only selected for emphasis or narrative effect. The mutation effect of these particles is still present whether or not the particles themselves occur. In traditional written Welsh, however, sentences can occur without a particle of this type and the verbal form can remain unmutated. If a particle is used in written Welsh, FE is generally preferred to MI or I.

The particle NI(D) is quite clearly used solely in traditional written Welsh, and occurs in speech only as the remnant 'D along with medial DIM.

Likewise A (interrogative) is formal and does not occur in speech. The particle ONI(D) (interrogative) is also very formal, and in speech is replaced by a tag question apart from restricted occurrences as a remnant 'D in examples such as *'dydy Mair yn ddel? (isn't Mair pretty?).*

The particle NA(C) (imperative, negative) is very formal even for traditional writing and is replaced by the use of PEIDIO (STOP).

The particle Y(R) (complementiser) occurs in writing; in speech it is mainly left out (although like MI/FE/I it can be used for emphasis).

The negative complementiser NA(D) is likewise mainly found in writing. In speech the medial DIM pattern is used, although NA(D) can occur in some environments as briefly outlined earlier in this chapter.

The particles used in fronting, A or Y(R), are again mainly used in writing and do not extensively occur in spontaneous speech. The particle NA(D) (negative fronting) is rare in speech and occurs primarily in traditional written Welsh; in spontaneous speech medial patterns involving medial DIM are employed.

Notes to chapter IX

1.   Inversion is treated very simply here in terms of the rearrangement of the constituents of a sentence. It could, however, be treated in terms of recursion and relativisation (note the close similarity of inversion and relativisation) so that a sentence such as *y dyn (a) oedd yn chwerthin (it was the man who was laughing)* could be derived from *mae'r dyn a oedd*

yn chwerthin (it is the man who was laughing. This suggestion is implicit in Anwyl (1899 : 177) and, as he points out, can be supported by the occurrence of MAE, spelled MAI, in constituent sentences.

2. As suggested in note 1 above, the forms MAI and TAW could be treated as copula forms in a complex construction — see also Anwyl (1899 : 177).

3. *Pseudo-clefting* is a term used in relation to the grammar of English and refers to sentences such as *what John wanted was a cup of tea.* We may compare this with English sentences like *it was a cup of tea that John wanted*; constructions of this type are referred to as *clefting*. The contrast of pseudo-clefting and clefting is not apparent in Welsh, as the latter is discussed in terms of *inversion*. The use of the term *pseudo-clefting* in relation to Welsh grammar is thus not accompanied by the use of the term *clefting*. We leave open the relationship of pseudo-clefting and inversion in Welsh.

4. Lewis and Pedersen (1961 : 320) suggest that AI involves historically the particle A followed by a form of the copula. Here we have a parallel with the copula character of MAI and TAW as outlined in notes 1 and 2 above, suggesting that interrogative versions of inverted sentences could be treated as complex sentences like the declarative ones.

5. The account of DIM in terms of insertion is a very simple approach. A more significant possibility, however, is one which treats DIM as a quantifier generated within the re-writing rules themselves. This approach could then view the selection of the preposition O (OF) after DIM in certain environments as the normal procedure for a quantifier and would also avoid treating the negation of existential–locatival sentences as exceptional. Negation could then be regarded as a pre-sentential characteristic only, and DIM could be automatically selected through a double negation rule as in *(ni) welais i ddim o John (= I didn't see nothing of John)* — compare *(ni) welais i neb (= I didn't see no one).*

6. As discussed in Anwyl (1899 : 177–8) and Morris-Jones (1913 : 427–9), MI, FE and I are historically derived from initially placed pronouns which were in concord with the subject of the sentence. In contemporary Welsh they occur with all subjects, irrespective of person, number or gender and are treated here as pre-sentential particles.

X   Roles in Welsh sentences

1   INTRODUCTION

In this chapter the discussion will centre on the various functions that the subject noun phrase and the post-verbal constituents of the verb phrase fulfil.[1] By way of initial illustration, consider the following example:

(1)   *mi roddodd John y près i Mair*   *(John gave the money*
       PT give +ODD John the money to Mair   *to Mair)*

The syntax of this sentence is given in chapter III, section 3e; it can be represented here for convenience as:

(2)

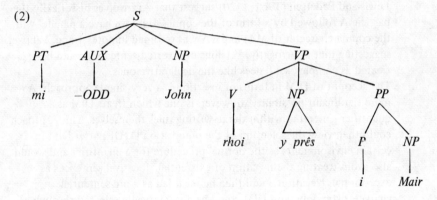

It can be seen from (2) that there are three noun phrases involved in this particular sentence – one of them, MAIR, occurs in a prepositional phrase. Each noun phrase is performing a particular role[2] in the activity of the sentence: the noun phrase JOHN is the *agent* that engineers the action of giving the money; the noun phrase Y PRES (THE MONEY) is directly involved in the giving, and can be said to have the role of *patient* as it is affected by the action of the verb; the giving process is aimed at the noun phrase MAIR in the prepositional phrase, so that MAIR can be said to have the role of *goal*. In this manner, all noun phrases can be described in terms of the roles that are involved in the fulfilment of a particular activity. The verb is of central importance and it is possible to represent the semantics involved by a formula such as:

(3)   *VERB : agent, patient, goal*

The representation in (3) indicates that the sentence conveys an activity that involves agent, patient and goal.[3]

364

The remainder of this chapter will explore some of the roles that are found in sentences, and the syntactic patterns that are used to express them in surface structure. The survey is not comprehensive but selects particular examples for discussion. It is important to bear in mind that the roles themselves are not unique to Welsh. Roles such as agent and patient, for instance, will be found in all languages. The distinctions arise in the way that a particular language represents them syntactically and it is this which may make a particular language unique.

2 ROLES IN WELSH

2a AGENT and PATIENT

In many activities it is common to have an entity which exhibits an active role and an entity which exhibits a passive role. Consider the following sentence, for instance:

(4) *mi olchodd   Mair y   dillad*   *(Mair washed the*
     PT wash + ODD Mair the clothes   *clothes)*

This example is a transitive sentence which has a constituent structure as follows:

(5)

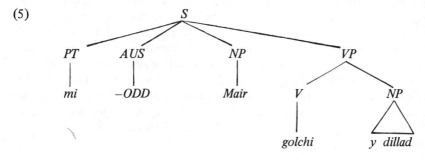

The sentence involves the two noun phrases: MAIR occurring in subject position and Y DILLAD (THE CLOTHES) occurring in object position. In terms of the activity involved, the noun phrase MAIR represents the entity which actually *engineers* the activity and can be labelled as *agent*, while the noun phrase Y DILLAD (THE CLOTHES) represents the entity which is *affected by* the activity and can be described as *patient*. When considering the roles of agent and patient, it is significant that the sentence relates to the following type of interrogative (see chapter IX, section 3f):

(6) *beth   wnaeth   Mair i 'r dillad?*   *(What did Mair do*
     thing do + ODD Mair to the clothes   *to the clothes?)*

The agent element is reflected in the use of the verb GWNEUD (DO) and the patient element is reflected in the use of the preposition I (TO) to mark Y DILLAD

365

(THE CLOTHES). Compare another sentence which has subject and object:

(7) 'roedd *Mair* yn licio'r   dillad   *(Mair liked the*
     was   *Mair* in   like the clothes   *clothes)*

Here it is inappropriate to ask the question *beth oedd Mair yn ei wneud i'r dillad?* *(what was Mair doing to the clothes?)* which suggests that Y DILLAD (THE CLOTHES) in this sentence is not patient; this type of role is, in fact, discussed in section 2c below.

Sentences involving verbs which have an agent and patient can be represented as:

(8) *VERB : agent, patient*

Other verbs in addition to GOLCHI (WASH) which can occur in a sentence involving an agent and patient include GWASGU (SQUEEZE), PALU (DIG), TORRI (CUT), TRWSIO (MEND) and TYNNU (PULL).

Syntactically, this type of sentence is very commonly represented by the transitive pattern discussed in chapter III, section 3b, in which the agent occurs in noun phrase subject position and the patient occurs in noun phrase object position. However, not every transitive pattern involves an agent and patient. Example (7) above has already supplied one illustration of a transitive pattern involving other roles and further exemplification is provided below in the discussion of example (21), in the examples in (32) relating to *instrument*, in the discussion of *stimulus* in section 2c, in examples (54) and (56) regarding location, and in the discussion of *result* in section 2g. Moreover, as the following paragraphs will demonstrate, there are further possibilities for syntactic representation of agent and patient in transitive and intransitive patterns.

Although in Welsh the agent commonly occurs in subject position and the patient in object position, a change of position can be effected by using the passive construction (see chapter VIII, section 6):

(9) *mi gafodd   y   dillad   eu   golchi gan Mair   (the clothes were*
     PT have + ODD the clothes their wash by Mair   *washed by Mair)*

In example (9) above, the patient Y DILLAD (THE CLOTHES) occurs in subject position while the agent MAIR occurs in a prepositional phrase placed finally. It is noticeable that in this type of structure the agent is marked by the preposition GAN, which can therefore be interpreted as a marker of the role agent. It is common for many roles to be marked by a preposition in this manner, and in the course of this chapter this point will be further developed and illustrated. In particular, it will be observed that the inclusion or deletion of the preposition is dependent upon its position: a noun phrase in subject position rarely has prepositional marking while noun phrases occurring after the verb can be marked by a preposition. This phenomenon will arise a number of times in the discussion and provides a basis for making generalisations about the surface structure expression of various roles.

So far, the discussion has concentrated upon agent and patient co-occurring in a transitive pattern. But both can occur alone in subject position in intransitive patterns with certain verbs. Consider the following two sentences:

(10) 'roedd <u>John</u> yn canu   *(John was singing)*
   was John in sing

(11) 'roedd <u>John</u> yn syrthio   *(John was falling)*
   was John in fall

In example (10) JOHN is the agent who engineers the action of singing. Again the interrogative that is associated with this type of sentence is significant:

(12) *beth oedd John yn ei wneud?* *(what was John*
   thing was John in its do   *doing?)*

The selection of GWNEUD (DO) in the question emphasises the role of agent. But in example (11) JOHN does not necessarily engineer the action of falling but, rather, suffers it and can therefore be described as patient. In this instance, the associated interrogative is different:

(13) *beth oedd yn digwydd i John?* *(what was happening*
   thing was in happen to John   *to John)*

The selection of DIGWYDD (HAPPEN) and the preposition I (TO) emphasise that JOHN was affected by some action and that JOHN is patient. It is therefore possible to have patient occurring in either subject or object position. In subject position it is limited to certain verbs like SYRTHIO (FALL) above, DIRYWIO (DETERIORATE) and GWAETHYGU (WORSEN) which can occur in intransitive patterns:

(14) *mae <u>John</u> yn gwaethygu*   *(John is worsening)*
   is John in worsen

(15) *mae'r traddodiadau yn dirywio* *(the traditions are*
   is the traditions in deteriorate *deteriorating)*

Sentences involving only one agent or one patient (as the case may be) can be represented as:

(16) (i)   *VERB : agent*
  (ii)   *VERB : patient*

In both cases an intransitive pattern is used, and the agent or patient is realised in subject position.

There are also sentences in which there are two patients:

(17) *mae'r bws wedi gwrthdaro efo 'r car* *(the bus has collided*
   is the bus after collide with the car *with the car)*

367

In the above example both Y BWS (THE BUS) and Y CAR (THE CAR) are affected by the action conveyed by the verb. They are in a reciprocal relationship in that what Y BWS (THE BUS) does to Y CAR (THE CAR), Y CAR also does to Y BWS. To that extent they are both patients. In this respect, it is significant that both can be expressed as a co-ordinated subject of an intransitive pattern using the same verb:

(18) *mae'r   bws a   'r   car wedi gwrthdaro*   *(the bus and the car*
      is   the bus and the car after collide   *have collided)*

Sentences involving two patients can be represented as:

(19) *VERB : patient, patient*

This type of sentence has two possible syntactic realisations, as examples (17) and (18) above illustrate. In example (17) above, one patient occurs in subject position while the second patient occurs post-verbally and is marked by the preposition EFO/GYDA/Â (WITH). This preposition, however, is not necessarily concerned with marking the role patient. It is frequently used to convey that one noun phrase shares a role with another noun phrase; in other words, it marks *co-participation*. It so happens that, in the above example, two patients are involved. But in the following example two agents are co-participating:

(20) (i)   *'roedd Gwil yn paentio'r   cwt efo Mair*   *(Gwil was painting*
         was   Gwil in paint   the shed with Mair   *the shed with Mair)*

   (ii) *'roedd Gwil a   Mair yn paentio'r   cwt*   *(Gwil and Mair were*
         was   Gwil and Mair in paint   the shed   *painting the shed)*

More will be said about this type of preposition and co-participation later (see section 2h below). In example (18) both patients are co-ordinated in subject position of an intransitive type pattern.[4] Notice that in both examples of co-participation above the preposition occurs only when one of the participants occurs beyond the verb; when both are co-ordinated in subject position, the preposition does not occur.

A different sort of patient is illustrated in a sentence such as:

(21) *mi agorodd   John y   drws*   *(John opened the*
      PT open + ODD John the door   *door)*

It is reasonable to suggest that the object Y DRWS (THE DOOR) is involved in the action of the verb. But a moment's reflection reveals that Y DRWS (THE DOOR) actually performs the action of the verb. The subject JOHN is the agent which causes the action but it is Y DRWS (THE DOOR) which actually realises the action. Thus, it is possible to have:

(22) *mi wnaeth   John i 'r   drws agor*   *(John made the door*
      PT do + ODD John to the door open   *open)*

368

In (22) we clearly see the agent JOHN and also how Y DRWS (THE DOOR) realises and performs the action. It is also possible to have an intransitive structure corresponding to (21):

(23) mi agorodd   y   drws   *(the door opened)*
      PT open + ODD   the door

In (21) Y DRWS (THE DOOR) is the object of a transitive structure. In (23) it is the subject, and this latter sentence conveys largely the same message except that the agent is not signalled. This role must be distinguished from the usual sort of patient role discussed so far, which can be exemplified by:

(24) mi olchodd   Mair y   dillad   *(Mair washed the*
      PT wash + ODD Mair the clothes   *clothes)*

The difference clearly shows itself by the impossibility of:

(25) *mi wnaeth   Mair i   'r   dillad   olchi   *(*Mair made the*
      PT do + ODD Mair to   the clothes wash   *clothes wash)*

(26) *mi olchodd   y   dillad   *(*the clothes washed)*
      PT wash + ODD the clothes

Example (26) is acceptable, but not in the same sense as example (23) above. Its acceptability can be made clearer if an adverb is added, giving *mi olchodd y dillad yn dda (the clothes washed well)*. But such a sentence is a comment upon the manner in which the process of washing was performed upon the clothes and does not imply that the clothes actually realised the action of washing. The role of Y DRWS (THE DOOR) in (21) is both patient and actor; consequently, we can set up a multiple role of *patient / actor*. Sentences involving agent and patient / actor can be represented as:

(27) VERB : (agent), patient / actor

This type of sentence has two syntactic realisations: one involves the occurrence of the actor / patient alone in subject position of an intransitive pattern; the other involves the occurrence of both agent and actor / patient in a transitive pattern, the former in subject position and the latter in object position. The possibility of omitting the agent can be represented in brackets as in (27) above.[5] The role of patient/actor is limited to certain verbs and, in addition to AGOR (OPEN) above, we also have: ARAFU (SLOW DOWN), BERWI (BOIL), BLINO (TIRE), CALEDU (HARDEN), COSI (TICKLE), CYCHWYN (START), CYNHESU (WARM), DEFFRO (WAKE), DIGIO (ANNOY), FFLACHIO (FLASH), FFRWYDRO (EXPLODE), GLANIO (LAND), GWLYCHU (WET), HWYLIO (SAIL), LLENWI (FILL), LLOSGI (BURN), OERI (BECOME COLD), PLYGU (BEND), POENI (WORRY), SEFYLL (STAND), STOPIO (STOP), SIGLO (SWING), SUDDO (SINK), SYMUD (MOVE), TODDI (MELT), TORRI (BREAK), TYFU (GROW). Such verbs as these are discussed also in Watkins (1961 : 189–92).

2b INSTRUMENT

In an activity where something is done to a patient by an agent, it is often the case that an instrument is used:

(28) (i) *mae John yn torri'r   coed   efo 'r fwyell*   *(John is cutting the*
         is   John in cut the wood with the axe   *wood with the axe)*

     (ii) *mi agorodd   John y drws efo 'r   goriad* *(John opened the*
          PT open + ODD John the door with the key   *door with the key)*

     (iii) *mi dorodd   John y bocs efo 'r morthwyl* *(John broke the*
           PT break + ODD John the box with the hammer   *box with the*
                                                                hammer)

In each case the underlined noun phrase involves the role of *instrument*. This role can be more clearly illustrated by the following paraphrase:

(29) (i) *mae John yn defnyddio'r fwyell i dorri'r coed*   *(John is using the*
         is   John in use   the axe   to cut the wood *axe to cut the wood)*

     (ii) *mi ddefnyddiodd John y goriad i agor y   drws*   *(John used the key*
          PT use + ODD   John the key   to open the door   *to open the door)*

     (iii) *mi ddefnyddiodd John y morthwyl i dorri'r bocs*   *(John used the*
           PT use + ODD   John the hammer to break the box   *hammer to break*
                                                                 the box)

In these paraphrases it can be seen how the underlined items are used as instruments in the various activities. In the original sentences, the role of instrument is positioned after the object, where it is marked by a preposition. In example (28) the preposition EFO (WITH) has been used for illustration; but altogether there are three prepositions, EFO, GYDA, Â. The first two tend to be used in spontaneous spoken Welsh and involve a regional choice which is roughly EFO in northern Welsh and GYDA in southern Welsh. Both of these contrast with Â, use of which is a stylistic marker of formal Welsh.

On the basis of the above sentences it can be seen that instrument occurs with at least two other roles, namely, agent and a type of patient. The patient roles can be patient / actor, as in the examples in (28) above or just patient, as in:

(30) *mae Mair wedi golchi'r dillad efo 'r sebon newydd*   *(Mair has washed*
     is   Mair after wash the clothes with the soap new   *the clothes with*
                                                                 the new soap)

370

Sentences involving instruments can therefore be represented as:

(31) *VERB : agent, patient-type, instrument*

In addition to the positioning of an instrument following the object, as in the above examples, we also find the instrument in subject position:

(32) (i) mae'r fwyell yn torri'r coed   *(the axe is cutting*
           is   the axe   in cut the wood   *the wood)*

      (ii) mi agorodd y   goriad y   drws   *(the key opened*
            PT open + ODD the key   the door   *the door)*

      (iii) mi dorrodd   y   morthwyl y   bocs *(the hammer broke*
             PT break + ODD the   hammer the box   *the box)*

When an instrument occurs in subject position, we find that the preposition does not occur. Here the instrument role compares with the agent role, which uses GAN when it is not in subject position but deletes the preposition when it is.

2c STIMULUS

In some activities one of the participants affects the other participant without necessarily engineering the effect:

(33) mae'r   ffrog newydd yn plesio Mair   *(the new dress pleases*
      is   the dress new   in please Mair   *Mair)*

In the above example Y FFROG NEWYDD (THE NEW DRESS) is not an agent; rather, it is a *stimulus*. Significantly, too, it is inanimate, whereas most agents engineering a particular effect are animate. A stimulus, by contrast, can cause an effect without any deliberate action and can therefore be inanimate.

As far as the above sentence is concerned, we find that the stimulus, Y FFROG NEWYDD (THE NEW DRESS), and the patient, MAIR, can reverse positions. When this happens, LICIO / HOFFI (LIKE) is used as the verb in place of PLESIO (PLEASE):

(34) mae Mair yn licio'r   ffrog newydd   *(Mair likes the new*
      is   Mair in like the frock new   *dress)*

The role features remain the same even though their positions have altered: MAIR is still patient and Y FFROG NEWYDD (THE NEW DRESS) is still stimulus. Other examples can be given as follows:

(35)	(i)	*mae* mellt a tharanau *yn dychryn Mair*	*(thunder and lightning*
		is lightning and thunder *in frighten Mair*	*frighten Mair)*
	(ii)	*mae* Mair *yn ofni* mellt a tharanau	*(Mair is afraid of*
		is Mair *in fear* lightning and thunder	*thunder and lightning)*
(36)	(i)	*mae'r* lle *'ma yn synnu* Mair	*(this place surprises*
		is the place *here in surprise* Mair	*Mair)*
	(ii)	*mae* Mair *yn synnu at* y lle *'ma*	*(Mair is surprised*
		is Mair *in surprise to* the place here	*at this place)*

In these two examples we see a change of verb DYCHRYN (FRIGHTEN)
→ OFNI (FEAR), similar to PLESIO (PLEASE) → HOFFI (LIKE), but with
SYNNU (SURPRISE) the same verb is retained and the stimulus is marked by
AT (TO) when it is taken out of subject position. In both cases, however, the role
features are the same, even though their surface structure expression may differ.
Sentences which can be reversed in this manner involve a sort of symmetrical
relationship between the participants and can be labelled *symmetrical propositions*.
Further illustration of symmetry of this type is found in the discussion of the roles
addressee and *topic* in section 2e and *goal* in section 2f below.

With animate beings there is the possibility of an active stimulus, an agent. It would
be possible for someone deliberately to set out to please, frighten or surprise someone
else. Even so, the possibility of positional reversal would still hold, which would
distinguish such patterns from ordinary agent patient patterns.

Of the two noun phrases in examples (33) to (36) discussed above, one has been
distinguished as stimulus. The remaining noun phrase is identified by Langendoen
(1970 : 63–4) as patient but, according to the criterion of interrogative appropriateness introduced in section 2a above, a noun phrase such as MAIR in (33)
or (34) is not a patient like Y DILLAD (THE CLOTHES) in (4) above:

| (37) | *? beth mae'r* ffrog *yn ei wneud i* Mair? | *(what is the dress* |
| | *thing is the* dress *in its do to* Mair | *doing to Mair?)* |

Although the interrogative test does not identify MAIR as patient, the general
notional similarity with Y DILLAD (THE CLOTHES) in (4) above will be preserved
by the label *patient-type*. Propositions of this type will therefore be represented as:

(38) *VERB : stimulus, patient-type*

There are two sets of verbs which can be represented by PLESIO (PLEASE) and
LICIO (LIKE). Both occur in transitive patterns, but with the former the stimulus
occurs in subject position and the patient-type in object position, while with the latter
their positions are reversed.

2d   LOCATION and DIRECTION

The concepts of location and direction are fairly familiar and relatively easy to illustrate. They are also related concepts, in that location involves place and direction involves movement to or from a particular place. The following sentences can serve as initial exemplification:

(39)   'roedd John yn aros <u>yn y   dre</u>   *(John was staying*
        was   John in stay in   the town   *in the town)*

(40)   'roedd John yn cerdded <u>i   'r   dre</u>   *(John was walking*
        was   John in walk   to the town   *to the town)*

In example (39) YN Y DRE (IN THE TOWN) is in fact a locative which relates to the adjunct constituent (see chapter IV) but it serves conveniently as an introductory instance of location here. In (39) John's staying is located in the town while in (40) John's walking is directed towards the town. Following Lyons (1969 : 300, 397) it can be suggested that location is a static feature while direction is a dynamic feature. The dynamic character of direction is emphasised by the fact that verbs of movement are involved. Thus we cannot have:

(41)   *'roedd John yn aros i 'r   dre   (*John was staying*
        was   John in stay to the town   *to the town)*

Location, can, however, contain the dynamic action of movement:

(42)   'roedd John yn cerdded yn y   dre   *(John was walking*
        was   John in walk   in the town   *in the town)*

In this example YN Y DRE (IN THE TOWN) locates the occurrence of John's walking (from one place to another). A place is involved in both cases, but where direction to that place is involved, a directional feature results and verbs of motion are necessary. In addition to CERDDED (WALK) we also have CRWYDRO (WANDER), RHEDEG (RUN), PRYSURO (RUSH). These verbs also describe the type of movement. More neutral verbs of movement are DOD (COME), MYND (GO) and SYMUD (MOVE).

The concepts of location and direction are frequently marked by prepositions. A relatively large number are involved, and by way of illustration we can quote AR (ON), DAN (UNDER), YN (IN), CYFERBYN Â (OPPOSITE), TU BLAEN I (IN FRONT OF), TU CEFN / OL I (BEHIND) and TU MEWN I (INSIDE) as markers of location; and YN ÔL (BACK), YMLAEN (FORWARD), AT (TO), AR ÔL (AFTER), DROS (ACROSS), I (TO) and O (FROM) as markers of direction. An interesting point concerns the familiar I (TO) and AT (TO), where I (TO) can involve entry and AT (TO) can only involve movement towards something or someone. Thus we can have *mynd i'r tŷ (go to the house)* or *mynd at y tŷ (go to the house)* but only *mynd at y meddyg (go to the doctor).* There are, however, a number of examples involving location and direction where a preposition is not employed, and where the place element occurs in object position. In the following sentence we have an example of location:

(43) mae John wedi cyrraedd <u>Llundain</u>   *(John has reached*
      is   John after arrive   London   *London)*

London conveys John's whereabouts and its locatival function is shown by the possibility of using YN (IN):

(44) mae John wedi cyrraedd <u>yn Llundain</u>   *(John has arrvied*
      is   John after arrive   <u>in London</u>   *in London)*

Direction can be illustrated as follows:

(45) mae John yn dilyn <u>y   dynion</u>   *(John is following*
      is   John in follow <u>the men</u>   *the men)*

(46) mae John wedi gadael <u>Llundain</u>   *(John has left*
      is   John after leave   London   *London)*

These are equivalent to:

(47) mae John yn mynd <u>ar ôl y   dynion</u>   *(John is going after*
      is   John in go   <u>after the men</u>   *the men)*

(48) mae John wedi mynd <u>o   Lundain</u>   *(John has gone from*
      is   John after go   <u>from London</u>   *London)*

The paraphrases illustrate the directional element.

The examples we have shown so far have been intransitives involving one other role. We can also have transitive patterns involving two other roles, and directionals of this type contain verbs like DREIFIO (DRIVE), GYRRU (DRIVE / SEND), ANFON (SEND), HEDFAN (FLY), and also the verbs RHEDEG (RUN) and CERDDED (WALK) again. For example:

(49) 'roedd John yn gyrru 'r gwartheg <u>i   'r fferm</u> *(John was driving the*
       was   John in drive the cattle   <u>to the farm</u> *cattle to the farm)*

In this example we have agent JOHN, patient Y GWARTHEG (THE CATTLE) and direction I'R FFERM (TO THE FARM).

Similar patterns with a locatival feature involve verbs like RHOI (GIVE, PUT), GOSOD and DODI (PUT), for example:

(50) mae John wedi rhoi llyfrau <u>ar y   bwrdd</u>   *(John has put books*
      is   John after put   books   <u>on the table</u>   *on the table)*

374

Although this example involves location, there is a direction element to the extent that we are concerned with the eventual location of the patient LLYFRAU (BOOKS). In effect, the books are moved so that they finish up on the table. In these terms, the agent JOHN causes the books to be eventually located on the table. Note, however, that it is the eventual location that is paramount, for such patterns do not readily allow a directional:

(51) *? mae John wedi rhoi y llyfrau i mewn i'r drôr* (*John has put the*
     is John after put the books into the drawer *books into the drawer*)

As locativals, then, RHOI (GIVE, PUT), GOSOD and DODI (PUT) are neutral verbs merely noting that certain objects are placed somewhere. There are also other verbs which give more information about the manner of engineering the eventual location and these include PARCIO (PARK), TAFLU (THROW), GOLLWNG (RELEASE) and GADAEL (LEAVE). A slightly different type is provided by CADW (KEEP):

(52) *mae John yn cadw ei lyfrau yn y drôr* (*John keeps his books*
     is John in keep his books in the drawer *in the drawer*)

As can be seen from this example, CADW (KEEP) is more concerned with maintaining the location than engineering it.

With certain locations an equivalent transitive pattern can be set up. Consider the following sentence:

(53) *mae John wedi rhoi 'r gwin mewn potel* (*John has put the*
     is John after put the wine in bottle *wine in a bottle*)

It is possible to use the nominal POTEL (BOTTLE) as a verb POTELU (BOTTLE) and to conflate (53) into a transitive sentence:

(54) *mae John wedi potelu 'r gwin* (*John has bottled the*
     is John after bottle the wine *wine*)

Verbs like POTELU (BOTTLE) are inherently locatival, conveying at one and the same time the location and the achieving of the location. Other verbs like POTELU (BOTTLE) are CARCHARU (JAIL: RHOI MEWN CARCHAR), PACIO (PACK: RHOI MEWN PAC), and POSTIO (POST: RHOI YN Y POST). Slightly different is TROCHI (IMMERSE) which is equivalent to RHOI MEWN DWR (PUT IN WATER). All these verbs convey both the process of placement and the location of the placement.

Superficially similar are sentences like:

(55) *mae John yn rhoi dŵr ar yr ardd* (*John is putting water*
     is John in put water on the garden *on the garden*)

But in this case the location AR YR ARDD (ON THE GARDEN) is also the patient in the sense that it is affected by the combined action of the verb and the nominal in object position, RHOI DŴR (PUT WATER). This interpretation gains some support by the possibility of asking *beth mae John yn ei wneud i'r ardd? (what is John doing to the garden?)* and giving (55) as an answer. We may thus view YR ARDD (THE GARDEN) as involving a multiple role *patient / location*. It is a characteristic of the role patient / location in this type of sentence that there is also a possibility of expressing RHOI DŴR (PUT WATER) as a verb DYFRO (WATER):

(56) mae John yn <u>dyfro</u> 'r ardd   *(John is watering*
    is John in <u>water</u> the garden   *the garden)*

When the process is expressed analytically as RHOI DŴR (PUT WATER), the patient / location occurs after object position and is marked by a locatival preposition. But when it occurs in object position with a synthetic verb, DYFRO (WATER), the preposition is deleted. Other verbs like DYFRO (WATER) are ACENNU (ACCENT: RHOI ACEN AR), CLORIO (COVER: RHOI CLAWR AR), CORONI (CROWN: RHOI CORON AR), HEMIO (HEM: RHOI HEM AR), FFRAMIO (FRAME: RHOI FFRÂM AR), LLWYTHO (LOAD: RHOI LLWYTH AR), MODRWYO (RING: RHOI MODRWY AR), PLASTRO (PLASTER: RHOI PLASTER AR), PEDOLI (SHOE: RHOI PEDOL AR), PWYTHO (STITCH: RHOI PWYTH MEWN), TOI (ROOF: RHOI TÔ AR). Whereas the previous synthetic verbs like POTELU (BOTTLE) involve the process of placement and location, verbs like DYFRO (WATER) convey both the process of placement and that which is placed, while the location is separately expressed as patient / location:

(57) *POTELU GWIN*   : *RHOI GWIN MEWN POTEL*
       (BOTTLE WINE)   : *(PUT WINE IN A BOTTLE)*

       DYFRO GARDD   : *RHOI DŴR AR ARDD*
       (WATER A GARDEN) : *(PUT WATER ON A GARDEN)*

There are numerous examples of both types in addition to those already given.[6]

The sentences in examples (53) or (54) and (55) or (56) above can be represented as follows:

(58) *VERB : agent, patient, location*

(59) *VERB: agent, patient-type, patient/location*

Both these types can involve a syntactic verb phrase of the form V NP PP with the verb RHOI (GIVE, PUT). Alternative realisations exist through verbalising the location in (58) and the patient-type in (59) and using a transitive pattern. The possibilities can be diagrammatically represented as follows:

376

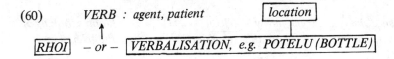

(60)　　　　*VERB : agent, patient*　　　　| *location* |
　　　　　　　　　↑
　　| *RHOI* | *– or –*　| *VERBALISATION, e.g. POTELU (BOTTLE)* |

(61)　　　　*VERB : agent*　　　　| *patient-type* |　　*patient/location*
　　　　　　　　　↑
　　| *RHOI* |　*– or –*　| *VERBALISATION, e.g. DYFRO (WATER)* |

Note that the possibilities of verbalisation relate to the two distinct roles of *location* and *patient-type*[7] and, furthermore, in a RHOI pattern these two roles are positionally distinguishable.

The role of patient / location is also seen in examples such as the following:

(62)　*mae John yn eistedd <u>ar y   gadair</u>*　　*(John is sitting on*
　　　is   John in   sit   on the chair　　　*the chair)*

We can compare this example with the following where we have a locatival adjunct:

(63)　*mae John yn eistedd <u>yn yr   ardd</u>*　　*(John is sitting in*
　　　is   John in   sit   in the garden　　*the garden)*

The difference between the two can be illustrated by interrogatives associated with each type. Questions about patient / location take the following form:

(64)　*beth mae John yn eistedd <u>arno?</u>*　　*(what is John sitting*
　　　thing is   John in   sit   on it　　　*on?)*

Whereas questions about location involve LLE (WHERE):

(65)　*lle   mae John yn eistedd?*　　*(where is John*
　　　place is   John in   sit　　　*sitting?)*

The selection of AR (ON) to mark patient / location is very common, and other examples include:

(66)　*mae John yn sefyll <u>ar y   bwrdd</u>*　　*(John is standing on*
　　　is   John in stand on the table　　*the table)*

(67)　*mae John yn gorwedd <u>ar y   wal</u>*　　*(John is lying on*
　　　is   John in lie   on the wall　　*the wall)*

Moreover, we can also bring in here the verbs that are traditionally listed as being followed by the preposition AR (ON):

(68) *mae John yn edrych <u>ar y teledu</u>*   *(John's looking at*
      is   John   in   look   on the television   *the television)*

(69) *mae Mair yn gwenu <u>ar John</u>*   *(Mair is smiling at*
      is   Mair   in   smile   on John   *John)*

(70) *mae John yn cefnu <u>ar ei ffrindiau</u>*   *(John is forsaking*
      is   John   in   forsake   on his friends   *his friends)*

(71) *mae John yn gwrando <u>ar y radio</u>*   *(John is listening*
      is   John   in   listen   on the radio   *to the radio)*

(72) *mae Mair yn syllu <u>ar y llun</u>*   *(Mair is staring at*
      is   Mair   in   stare   on the picture   *the picture)*

(73) *mae'r dynion yn sylwi <u>ar yr adar</u>*   *(the men are*
      is   the men   in   observe   on the birds   *observing the birds)*

(74) *mae John wedi sbïo <u>ar yr hysbysiad</u>*   *(John has looked at*
      is   John   after spy   on the advertisement   *the advertisement)*

(75) *mae Mair yn canolbwyntio <u>ar ei llaw</u>*   *(Mair is concentrating*
      is   Mair   in   concentrate   on her hand   *on her hand)*

With these examples there is an element of location and also of subjecting that location to a particular process. In so far as they involve a patient / location role, they have the related interrogative too, for example:

(76) <u>*beth*</u> *mae John yn edrych <u>arno</u>?*   *(what is John looking*
      thing is   John   in   look   on it   *at?)*

(77) <u>*beth*</u> *mae John wedi sbïo <u>arno</u>?*   *(what has John*
      thing is   John   after spy   on it   *looked at?)*

There are many other verbs which involve AR (ON) in this fashion, where the patient / location role is not so obvious:

(78) *mae John wedi dylanwadu <u>ar yr hogiau</u>*   *(John has influenced*
      is   John   after influence   on the boys   *the boys)*

(79) *mae Mair wedi blino <u>ar ei gwaith</u>*   *(Mair has tired of her*
      is   Mair   after tire   on her work   *work)*

(80) *maen nhw wedi manylu <u>ar y cynllun</u>*   *(they have given*
      are   they   after detail   on the plan   *details of the plan)*

378

But it can be argued that the **patient** / location role has been utilised to include a number of processes where location is not readily apparent, and that the basic concept of locating a process on an object has been extended beyond its literal use. Sentences involving patient / location can be represented as:

(81) *VERB : agent, patient/location*

The verb phrase in such sentences takes the form V PP, where the patient / location occurs in a post-verbal prepositional phrase.

Another example of a multiple role involving patient and location can be exemplified by the following sentence:

(82) *mi gnociodd   John y   drws*   *(John knocked the*
PT knock + ODD John the door   *door)*

In example (82) Y DRWS (THE DOOR) is affected by the action of the verb and to that extent it is the patient. But it also indicates the *location* of the knocking in the sense that a particular place received the knocking. In this respect, it is significant that we can also have:

(83) *mi gnociodd   John ar y   drws*   *(John knocked on the*
PT knock + ODD John on the door   *door)*

A similar role is found with an example like:

(84) *mi drawodd   John ben Gwil*   *(John struck Gwil's*
PT strike + ODD John head Gwil   *head)*

But here the locatival element only involves a part of the patient. Thus, we say:

(85) *mi drawodd   John Gwil ar ei ben*   *(John struck Gwil on*
PT strike + ODD John Gwil on his head   *his head)*

It is typical of the situation when human nouns are involved that the exact location is specified. It means something entirely different to say:

(86) *mi drawodd   John ar ben Gwil*   *(John struck on*
PT strike + ODD John on head Gwil   *Gwil's head)*

If acceptable, such a sentence tends to be interpreted like (83) above.

2e ADDRESSEE and TOPIC

In many activities described by sentences it is common to find that the activity involves the imparting of information from one person to another. Such is the case in the following sentence:

(87) *mae Mair yn dweud jôc wrth John*   *(Mair is telling a joke*
      is   Mair in   tell   joke to   John   *to John)*

In the above example MAIR fulfils the familiar role of agent responsible for engineering the activity. The activity itself is one of verbal communication and MAIR is the speaker. The other noun phrase, JOHN, is the person addressed and can be conveniently labelled as the *addressee*. Other verbs involving an addressee include LLEFARU (SPEAK), SISIAL and SIBRWD (WHISPER), BALDORDDI (GABBLE),MYNEGI (TELL) and ADRODD (RECITE, RELATE). The role of the object noun phrase is not considered here, but it can be noted that it only involves those entities which can be verbally communicated. Hence only a limited number of nouns can occur, like JÔC (JOKE), STORI and HANES (STORY), ADRODDIAD (REPORT) and CERDD (POETRY). Some of these will be limited to certain verbs, such as CERDD (POETRY) with ADRODD (RECITE, RELATE). Because of the close association with the verb itself, the noun phrase object is frequently left out and only the addressee occurs, giving sentences like:

(88) *'roeddwn i 'n dweud wrth John*   *(I was telling John)*
      was   I in tell   with John

In (88) it is implied that 'something' was being told to JOHN.

The addressee in Welsh is marked by the preposition WRTH (TO) and then occurs finally after the verb or after the noun phrase object if there is one. But it can also occur in subject position by reversing the communication process and looking at the situation from the point of view of the addressee. In this case, the verb CLYWED (HEAR) most frequently occurs, giving sentences like:

(89) *mae John wedi clywed y   stori gan Mair*   *(John has heard the*
      is   John after hear   the story LOC Mair   *story from Mair)*

This type of reverse positioning is possible with other roles and has been introduced in various places above. Welsh therefore affords a fairly general possibility for organising the positioning of the roles from one point of view or another by using either subject position or a post-verbal position. It is also significant that the role in subject position occurs without a preposition, while finally positioned roles are prepositionally marked. Of the three roles involved in this type of activity, two have been identified, namely agent and addressee. The third occurs in object position and can be illustrated by JÔC (JOKE) in (87) above. It is notionally familiar to a *patient* like Y DILLAD (THE CLOTHES) in (4) above, but lacks the formal correlation with interrogatives.

(90) *? beth mae Mair yn ei wneud i   'r   jôc?*   *(what's Mair doing*
      thing   is   Mair in its do   to the joke   *to the joke?)*

380

Consequently, it can be given the general label *patient-type*, as discussed in section 2c above. Sentences involving these three roles can thus be represented as:

(91) *VERB : agent, patient-type, addressee*

With one set of verbs including DWEUD (TELL), the agent is realised in subject position, the patient-type occurs in object position, and the addressee is marked by WRTH (TO) in a prepositional phrase following the noun phrase object. With another set of verbs including CLYWED (HEAR), the positions of agent and addressee are reversed; the agent is marked by GAN (FROM) but WRTH (TO) does not occur with the addressee.

The use of WRTH (TO) as a marker of the addressee must be distinguished from other uses, particularly with sentences such as:

(92) *mae Mair yn glynu papur wrth y wal*   *(Mair is sticking paper*
    is   Mair in stick paper to the wall   *to the wall)*

Such a sentence is syntactically identical with (87) above but the different verb and process involved do not make Y WAL (THE WALL) addressee.

A slightly different syntactic environment for addressee can be illustrated by the following sentence:

(93) *'roedd Mair yn sôn am   y   ddamwain wrth John (Mair was talking*
    was Mair in talk about the accident   to   John about the accident to
                                                     John)

A verb like SÔN (TALK) involves verbal communication and JOHN, marked by WRTH (TO), can again be identified as addressee. In sentences like (93) we have another prepositional phrase rather than noun phrase object and this prepositional phrase identifies the *topic* of the communication. The role of topic is marked by the preposition AM (ABOUT), and a much wider variety of nouns can occur as topic than in the object noun phrase associated with the role of addressee discussed above. Other verbs like SÔN (TALK) which can occur with topic and addressee include ACHWYN (COMPLAIN) and CWYNO (COMPLAIN). Sentences involving these three roles can be represented as:

(94) *VERB : agent, topic, addressee*

The agent is realised in subject position while the topic and addressee occur in post-verbal prepositional phrases, the former being marked by AM (ABOUT) while the latter is again marked by WRTH (TO). In terms of the occurrence of these roles in surface structure there is no strict rule as to the ordering of the prepositional phrases with respect to one other; their arrangement seems to be a matter of emphasis.

2f   GOAL

A sentence such as the following involves three noun phrases:

(95) mae <u>John</u> wedi anfon <u>neges</u>   i   <u>Mair</u>   *(John has sent a*
      is   John after send message to Mair   *message to Mair)*

Of particular interest here is the noun phrase MAIR which occurs in the prepositional phrase in final position. It can be said that JOHN, the agent, has MAIR as the goal of his action and the role fulfilled by MAIR can be consequently labelled as *goal*. The message, in effect, passes from JOHN to MAIR. Other verbs like ANFON (SEND) which involve goal include GYRRU (DRIVE SEND), PASIO (PASS), RHOI (GIVE), BENTHYCA (LEND), GWERTHU (SELL) and TALU (PAY).

In traditional terms, the noun phrase conveying goal is usually described as the *indirect object* or *second object*. In so far as it occurs in a prepositional phrase which follows a noun phrase in object position, goal resembles the roles of location and direction and addressee previously discussed. There is also a notional similarity, as in all cases there is a sense of something passing from one entity to another. This similarity is particularly strong with goal and addressee.[8]

In Welsh, goal is marked by the preposition I (TO) and occurs in a position following the noun phrase object.[9] But the noun phrase goal can also occur in subject position if the action is looked at from another angle. Assuming that MAIR in (95) has actually received the message, then it is possible to say:

(96) mae <u>Mair</u> wedi cael   neges   gan John   *(Mair has received a*
      is   Mair after receive message LOC John   *message from/off*
                                                          John)

When goal occurs in subject position the usual rule of deleting the preposition is involved. And it is significant to notice that, as the agent is moved out of subject position, the preposition GAN is introduced.

When the goal is placed in subject position, the verb CAEL (RECEIVE) is commonly selected in place of the verb used when goal occurs finally. Thus, CAEL (RECEIVE) corresponds to ANFON (SEND), GYRRU (DRIVE, SEND), PASIO (PASS) and RHOI (GIVE). In the case of BENTHYCA (LEND) the same verb can be used in both patterns:

(97) mae Mair wedi <u>benthyca</u> llyfr i   John   *(Mair has lent a book*
      is   Mair after lend   book to John   *to John)*

(98) mae John wedi <u>benthyca</u> llyfr gan Mair   *(John has borrowed a*
      is   John after borrow   book LOC Mair   *book off/from Mair)*

382

It is significant, however, that we can also have:

(99)   *mae Mair wedi <u>rhoi benthyg</u> llyfr i John*   *(Mair has given loan*
       is   Mair after <u>give loan</u>   book to John   *of a book to John)*

(100)   *mae John wedi <u>cael</u>   benthyg llyfr gan Mair*   *(John has received*
       is   John after <u>receive</u> loan   book LOC Mair   *loan of a book off/*
                                                         from Mair)

Here the verbs RHOI (GIVE) and CAEL (RECEIVE) are used to emphasise further the direction from which the process is being described. The verb GWERTHU (SELL) is slightly different in that it has its own verb equivalent PRYNU (BUY):

(101)   *mae Mair wedi <u>gwerthu</u> llyfr i John*   *(Mair has sold a book*
       is   Mair after <u>sell</u>   book to John   *to John)*

(102)   *mae John wedi <u>prynu</u> llyfr gan   Mair*   *(John has bought a*
       is   John after <u>buy</u>   book LOC Mair   *book off/from Mair)*

Irrespective of the verbal idiosyncracies involved, however, one general process remains, and by means of sequencing, prepositional selection and verb type it is possible to look at the process from two angles.

The role of the noun phrase in object position can be characterised as patient-type[10] and the sentence as a whole can be represented as:

(103)   *VERB : agent, patient-type, goal*

One syntactic realisation involves verbs like RHOI (GIVE), etc., where the agent occurs in subject position, the patient-type in object position and the goal in a prepositional phrase marked by I (TO) following the noun phrase object. By selecting another class of verb, exemplified by CAEL (RECEIVE) or other items as outlined above, the goal can occur in subject position and the agent in a post-verbal prepositional phrase marked by GAN (FROM).

2g   RESULT

There are a number of transitive patterns where the referent of the object noun phrase comes about through the action of the verb:

(104)   *mae John wedi gwneud <u>bocs nythu</u>*   *(John has made a*
       is   John after do   box nesting   *nesting box)*

(105)   *mae'r   dynion wedi adeiladu <u>pont   newydd</u>*   *(the men have built a*
       is   the men   after build   <u>bridge new</u>   *new bridge)*

(106)   *mi   greodd   Mair ffasiwn newydd*   *(Mair created a new*
        PT create + ODD Mair fashion new   fashion)

(107)   *mae'r   bachgen wedi cyfansoddi darn o gerddoriaeth*   *(the boy has com-*
        is   the boy   after compose   piece of music   posed a piece of
                                                                   music)*

In each case the object noun phrase results from the activity described by the verb
as performed by the subject noun phrase; consequently, these object noun phrases
have the role of *result*. They can be differentiated from the role of patient in that the
above sentences do not relate to an interrogative of the type *beth mae John wedi ei
wneud i'r bocs nythu? (what has John done to the nesting box?)*, etc.

Sentences which involve result can be represented as:

(108)   *VERB : agent, result*

The verbs which can occur in this type of sentence include ADEILADU (BUILD),
ARLUNIO (SKETCH, DRAW), CLODDIO (DIG), CREU (CREATE),
CYFANSODDI (COMPOSE), CYNHYRCHU (PRODUCE), DYFEISIO (DEVISE),
GWAU (KNIT), GWNEUD (MAKE), PALU (DIG), PEINTIO (PAINT), RHOI (GIVE)
and SEFYDLU (ESTABLISH). The syntactic pattern is a transitive one, with agent in
subject position and result in object position.[11]

2h   CO-PARTICIPATION and RECIPROCITY

A number of roles have been studied and introduced, and we find that a particular role
can participate in an activity with another role of the same kind:

(109)   *'roedd Mair yn peintio'r 'stafell efo John*   *(Mair was painting the*
        was   Mair in paint the room   with John   room with John)*

(110)   *mae'r   bws wedi gwrthdaro efo 'r   car*   *(the bus has collided*
        is   the bus after collide   with the car   with the car)*

In these examples we have agent MAIR, in (109), and patient Y BWS (THE BUS),
in (110), both in subject position. Also involved in the action as agent and patient
respectively are JOHN and Y CAR (THE CAR) and to that extent they can be thought
of as *co-participants*. Co-participant is not a basic role; rather, it identifies two roles of
the same type involved in the same activity.

When one of the co-participants occurs in subject position, the second
co-participant can occur in a prepositional phrase beyond the verb. It is then marked
by the preposition EFO / GYDA / Â (WITH). But it is significant that the second
co-participant can be co-ordinated with the co-participant in subject position:

(111) 'roedd _Mair a   John_ yn peintio'r   'stafell   *(Mair and John were*
      was   Mair and John in paint the room   *painting the room)*

(112) mae'r bws a   'r car wedi gwrthdaro   *(the bus and the car*
      is   the bus and the car after collide   *have collided)*

As illustrated in various places above, it is again seen that when a role occurs in subject position the preposition is not used: thus EFO, etc. (WITH) is dropped in the above examples.

However, if the co-participants occur as objects, we find that co-ordination is used and EFO (WITH) is impossible:

(113) (i)   'roedd Mair yn peintio'r   'stafell _wely_   *(Mair was painting*
              was   Mair in paint the room   bed   *the bedroom and*
                                                              the living room)
              a   'r 'stafell fyw
              and the room live

      (ii)   *'roedd Mair yn peintio'r   'stafell _wely_   *(*Mair was painting*
              was   Mair in paint the room   bed   *the bedroom with*
                                                              the living room)
              efo 'r 'stafell fyw
              with the room   live

Similarly, we find that if more than two co-participants are involved, the second may be marked by EFO (WITH) but additional ones are co-ordinated:

(114) (i)   'roedd _Mair_ yn peintio'r   'stafell   *(Mair was painting the*
              was   Mair in paint the room   *room with John and*
                                                          Gwil)
              efo John a   Gwil
              with John and Gwil

      (ii)   *'roedd _Mair_ yn peintio'r   'stafell   *(*Mair was painting*
              was   Mair in paint the room   *the room with John*
                                                          with Gwil)
              efo John efo Gwil
              with John with Gwil

All three, of course, could be co-ordinated in subject position. We have already seen that EFO (WITH) is also used to mark the instrument. Example (109) above looks very similar to:

(115) 'roedd Mair yn peintio'r 'stafell _efo brwsh mawr_   *(Mair was painting*
      was   Mair in paint the room with brush big   *the room with a big*
                                                             brush)

But EFO BRWSH MAWR (WITH A BIG BRUSH) can be shown not to be co-participant by the impossibility of co-ordination with the subject:

385

(116) *'roedd *Mair a   brwsh mawr* yn peintio'r 'stafell (*Mair and a big
      was *Mair and brush big* in paint the room   brush were painting
                                                        the room)

The test of subject co-ordination nicely distinguishes instrument from
co-participant.

A strong element of co-participation is also seen in examples such as:

(117) *mae Mair yn priodi John*   (Mair is marrying
      is Mair in marry John   John)

In the above sentence, the action is such that what the noun phrase subject does to
the noun phrase object, the noun phrase object also does to the noun phrase subject.
The participants are at one and the same time agent and patient, both engineering and
being affected by the activity of the verb. In short, the activity is *reciprocal*.

Reciprocity exhibits the same characteristics as co-participation, in that both
participants can occur in subject position.

(118) *mae Mair a   John yn priodi*   (Mair and John are
      is Mair and John in marry   getting married)

Verbs like PRIODI (MARRY) are inherently reciprocal and readily occur with
co-ordinated subject as above. Other verbs like PRIODI (MARRY) include CWFFIO,
YMLADD and BRWYDRO (FIGHT). There are, however, many verbs that can involve
reciprocity but cannot occur in the same structures as verbs like PRIODI (MARRY).
Consider GWELD (SEE), for instance. It would be possible for John to see Mair and,
at the same time, for Mair to see John, but this is not expressed by:

(119) *mae Mair yn gweld John*   (Mair can see John)
      is Mair in see John

Rather, we must have a co-ordinated subject with the reciprocal or co-participant
pronoun EI GILYDD (EACH OTHER) in the object position:

(120) *mae Mair a   John yn gweld ei   gilydd*   (Mair and John can
      is Mair and John in see   each other   see each other)

Reciprocity, for the majority of verbs, involves co-ordinated subject with
compulsory occurrence of EI GILYDD (EACH OTHER). But inherently reciprocal
verbs can occur in a transitive structure like that in example (117) above, or with a
co-ordinated subject without EI GILYDD as in (118). Finally, we can add that verbs
like CUSANU (KISS) and CWRDD (MEET) are conditionally reciprocal:

(121) *mae Mair wedi cusanu John*   (Mair has kissed John)
      is Mair after kiss John

386

To involve reciprocity it is conditional that John has returned the gesture and thus we can have:

(122)　*mae* *Mair a　John* *wedi* *cusanu*　　　　*(Mair and John have*
　　　　is　*Mair and John after kiss*　　　　*kissed)*

Like PRIODI (MARRY), there is no necessity for the reciprocal or co-participant pronoun EI GILYDD (EACH OTHER).

3.　ROLES AND SURFACE STRUCTURE

3a　Introduction

In the previous section we have listed and discussed a number of roles. The discussion was by no means a comprehensive one, and many roles have not been mentioned. However, it does illustrate the functional aspect of language and the way in which these functions or roles correlate with surface structures. In this section we will look more closely at the way in which these various roles are expressed in the surface structure of Welsh.

3b　The distribution of roles over the constituents

Chapter III listed different types of verb phrase in terms of their constituent structure. The various roles outlined above can occur in the noun phrase subject and in the various nominal constituents of the verb phrase. Thus, we have roles occurring in subject position, object position, and in indirect object position — involving various constituent types such as noun phrase or prepositional phrase.

However, there are restrictions on the constituents and positions in which the various roles can occur, and the choice very often depends upon the number and type of roles involved. A good example of this can be found by looking at the activity which involves agent, patient/actor and instrument. If all three are expressed, we have a sentence such as:

(123)　(i)　　*mae* *John* *wedi* *torri*　*'r　garreg*　　　*(John has broken*
　　　　　　is　*John after break*　*the stone*　　　*the stone with*
　　　　　　　　　　　　　　　　　　　　　　　　the hammer)
　　　　　　efo　'r　morthwyl
　　　　　　with the hammer

The agent occurs in subject position, patient/actor in object position and the instrument follows in a succeeding position marked by the preposition EFO (WITH). If, however, the agent is not expressed, leaving patient/actor and instrument, we find that the instrument occurs in subject position unmarked by a preposition:

(123) (ii)

mae'r	*morthwyl*	*wedi*	*torri*	*'r*	*garreg*	*(the hammer has*
is	*the hammer*	*after*	*break*	*the*	*stone*	*broken the stone)*

If neither agent nor instrument is expressed, leaving only patient / actor, we find that the latter occurs in subject position:

(123) (iii)

mae'r	*garreg*	*wedi*	*torri*	*(the stone has broken)*
is	*the stone*	*after*	*break*	

There are, then, strict rules determining the distribution of the roles over the constituent structure of the sentence, coupled with the use of prepositions.

Allowing for such rules, it is still possible to choose a particular position for a particular role. The examples in (123) (i) to (iii) above themselves illustrate choice of positioning subject to the rules of distribution. But it is also possible to achieve different positioning by selecting a different verb and prepositional marker. There are a number of examples of choice of positioning in this manner, and its consequences for the traditional notions of 'subject' of and 'object' of a sentence are particularly significant. Traditionally, these terms are used as functional labels where the subject is the 'doer' who imparts something to the object. Even before taking positional criteria into account, it can be seen that a sentence like the following immediately contradicts such a characterisation:

(124)

mae	*John*	*wedi*	*cael*	*damwain*	*(John has had an*
is	*John*	*after*	*have*	*accident*	*accident)*

In this example the subject is JOHN — but here the subject is affected by the action and is patient and not 'doer'. Adequate functional characterisation is best given in terms of roles, and the terms subject and object are best used as positional terms denoting the occurrence of noun phrases at various places in a sentence. Thus, we can talk of subject position, object position and even indirect or oblique object position. This view can be supported by the phenomenon that we have already seen — changing the positions of various roles:

(125) (i)

mae	*John*	*wedi*	*agor*	*y*	*drws*	*(John has opened*
is	*John*	*after*	*open*	*the*	*door*	*the door with*

efo	*'r*	*goriad*	*the key)*
with	*the*	*key*	

(ii)

mae'r	*goriad*	*wedi*	*agor*	*y*	*drws*	*(the key has opened*
is	*the key*	*after*	*open*	*the*	*door*	*the door)*

(iii)

mae'r	*drws*	*wedi*	*agor*	*(the door has opened)*
is	*the door*	*after*	*open*	

388

(126) (i) *mae Mair wedi rhoi prês   i John*   *(Mair has given money*
          is Mair after give money to John   to John)*

      (ii) *mae John wedi cael prês   gan Mair*   *(John has had money*
          is John after have money LOC Mair   off/from Mair)*

(127) (i) *mae Mair wedi dweud y stori wrth John*   *(Mair has told the*
          is Mair after tell   the story to   John   story to John)*

      (ii) *mae John wedi clywed y stori gan Mair*   *(John has heard*
          is John after hear   the story LOC Mair   the story off/*
                                                        from Mair)

(128) (i) *'roedd y bws wedi gwrthdaro efo 'r car*   *(the bus has*
          was the bus after collide   with the car   collided with the*
                                                          car)

      (ii) *'roedd y bws a 'r car wedi gwrthdaro* *(the bus and the car*
          was the bus and the car after collide   had collided)*

(129) (i) *mae'r gôt yn plesio Mair*   *(the coat pleases Mair)*
          is the coat in please Mair

      (ii) *mae Mair yn licio'r gôt*   *(Mair likes the coat)*
          is Mair in like the coat

Despite the fact that their positions alter, the functions of the various noun phrases remain the same. In example (126), for instance, MAIR is agent and can occur in subject position with RHOI (GIVE) and beyond the verb in the case of CAEL (RECEIVE); likewise, JOHN is goal and can occur either in a position beyond the verb in the case of RHOI (GIVE) or in subject position with CAEL (RECEIVE). Terms like subject, object or indirect object, therefore, only indicate positions and do not define functions.

The selection of either subject or object positions, however, does have an effect on the *focus* of the message. By placing a role in subject position, attention is initially focused upon the role in that position and the action is looked at from the point of view of the role in subject position. Thus, in (126) (i), the action is viewed from the point of view of the agent, MAIR, while in (126) (ii) it is viewed from the point of view of the goal JOHN. Positional distribution is therefore important in terms of focusing the message.

3c   **Prepositions**

It has long been held that prepositions denote functions, and in those languages like Welsh which have previously been heavily inflected, prepositions have been used more and more to indicate functions. In the previous sections we have seen how prepositions are extensively used when a role occurs in various post-verbal positions, and below is a list of roles with their prepositions:

(130) *agent*   *GAN/Â*

       instrument   *EFO/GYDA/Â*

       direction   *I, AT, O, etc.*

       location   *AR, O DAN, UWCHBEN, etc.*

       patient/location *AR, YN*

       addressee   *WRTH*

       topic   *AM*

       goal   *I*

Even from the above brief list, we can see how one role can be conveyed by a number of prepositions, or how one preposition can be used to mark several roles.

Prepositions tend to be used when a role is positioned finally. If a role occurs in subject position the preposition is not used. There is, however, one apparent exception to this rule, in a sentence like:

(131) *mae gan John lot o   bres*   *(John has a lot of*
       is   LOC John lot of money   *money)*

Here GAN JOHN occurs in subject position and the preposition is retained. However, as discussed in chapter III, section 4d, a sentence like (131) is derived from a deep structure in which the noun phrase occurs in subject position and the prepositional phrase in complement position, the constituents being re-positioned by the GAN phrase movement transformation.

3d   The transitive structure

The clearest and most explicit surface structure realisation of the roles involved in a particular activity is one in which all of the roles are separately expressed and prepositions are used where necessary. Consider the following examples:

(132) *mae John yn rhoi dŵr   ar yr ardd*   *(John is putting*
       is   John in put   water on the garden *water on the garden)*

(133) *mae John yn rhoi gwin mewn potel*   *(John is putting wine*
       is   John in put   wine in   bottle   *in a bottle)*

Here we can see the various roles individually realised, and the verb phrase is made up of V NP PP. But both messages can be conflated into transitive structures by verbalising one of the roles. Thus, in (132) DŴR (WATER) can be expressed in verbal form as DYFRO (WATER) and in (133) POTEL (BOTTLE) can be expressed as POTELU (BOTTLE). By using these forms, the role and the process involved are expressed all in one:

(134) *mae John yn <u>dyfro</u> 'r   ardd*   *(John is watering*
       is   John in water the garden   *the garden)*

(135) *mae John yn <u>potelu</u> gwin*   *(John is bottling*
       is   John in bottle wine   *wine)*

The transitive structure emerges as a heavily used surface structure configuration which can express a variety of roles. In addition to (134) and (135) we can also list the following transitive types:

(136) *mae Mair wedi golchi'r   dillad*   *(Mair has washed*
       is   Mair after wash the clothes   *the clothes)*

(137) *mae Mair wedi dilyn <u>y   dynion</u>*   *(Mair has followed*
       is   Mair after follow the men   *the men)*

(138) *mae Mair yn licio'r   <u>ffrog</u>*   *(Mair likes the dress)*
       is   Mair in like the dress

(139) *mae John wedi agor <u>y   drws</u>*   *(John has opened*
       is   John after open the door   *the door)*

(140) *mae John wedi gwneud <u>y   drws</u>*   *(John has made*
       is   John after make   the door   *the door)*

The noun phrase object position in the above sentences involves a variety of roles. The surface structure of Welsh does not distinguish the various types in a transitive pattern but other areas of the language illustrate the differences. Example (136) involves the straightforward patient, as discussed in section 2a and relates to the interrogative *beth mae Mair yn ei wneud i'r dillad? (what's Mair doing to the clothes?)*. In (137) Y DYNION (THE MEN) involves a directional element, as illustrated by the paraphrase *mae Mair wedi mynd ar ôl y dynion (Mair has gone after the men)*. In (138) Y FFROG (THE FROCK) is stimulus, and the GWNEUD I (DO TO) interrogative is inappropriate but a symmetrical relationship exists with *mae'r ffrog yn plesio Mair (the dress pleases Mair)*. In (139) the object is patient / actor, as the possibility of an intransitive structure illustrates, *mae'r drws wedi agor (the door has opened)*. In (140) BOCS (BOX) is result and the GWNEUD I (DO TO) interrogative is again inappropriate.

Notes to Chapter X

1. This aspect of the study of sentences is most evident in contemporary linguistics in the writings of Fillmore (1968) and Langendoen (1970), working on case grammar, and of Halliday (1970), working on systemic grammar. The debt to all three will be readily apparent from the discussion, but the responsibility for re-application of their views lies entirely with us (particularly as regards the selection of terminology to represent various functions).

2. This term is borrowed from Langendoen (1970 : 61ff.) and is used here rather than Fillmore's term *case*.

3. The study of syntax and case features represents two quite distinct approaches in contemporary linguistics. The difficulty in treating both together lies in the fact that the theoretical mechanisms of explication are quite different. the discussion of syntax is based mainly on the work of Chomsky while the discussion of the semantics of noun phrases, or case features, is based upon Fillmore (or at least early Fillmore, 1968), Langendoen (1970) and Halliday (1970). We have introduced disparate explicative mechanisms and the display formula in (3) of this chapter is different from that of (2). The system of representation of functions is based on Langendoen (1970) which is slightly different from the use of *case frames* by Fillmore (1968) (for example, (3) of this chapter, ignoring differences of terminology, would be [____ agent + patient + goal] . There is a view that semantic features can act as a 'base' from which syntactic structures may be derived, but no attempt is made to adopt this view as the details of formulation are beyond the immediate aims of this book. We will settle for two different types of discussion, the syntactic approach of Chomsky and the semantic approach of Fillmore.

4. The syntactic pattern in example (17) can be related to the verb phrase type V PP but the details of the pattern in (18) are not worked out here. It may be, however, that such examples are derived from a complex pattern involving co-ordination (see chapter VIII, section 7):

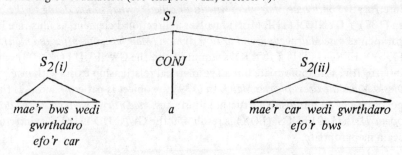

Various transformations can be put forward to achieve, by deletion, the surface structure of (18).

5. This phenomenon is sometimes discussed in the literature under the heading of *ergativity* (e.g. Lyons, 1969:351–2; Anderson, 1968; Halliday, 1970:155–8). A brief reference can be made to the possibility of treating a transitive sentence like (21) as a complex sentence involving a causative sentence containing ACHOSI (CAUSE):

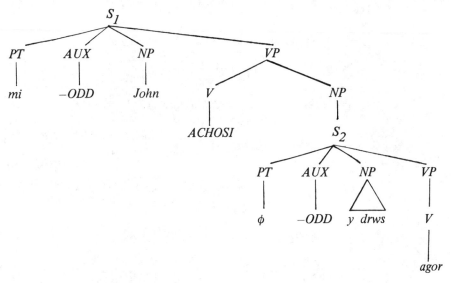

This type of configuration has the advantage of allowing both syntactic patterns in examples (21), (22) and (23) to come from the same source by various transformations. Rather than introduce this complexity, the simplicity of (27) will be maintained. But this is an example of a fairly abstract deep structure accounting for both the syntax and the semantics.

6. It is possible to treat this type of sentence as a complex one involving a causative sentence; we may instance examples (52), (53) and (55):

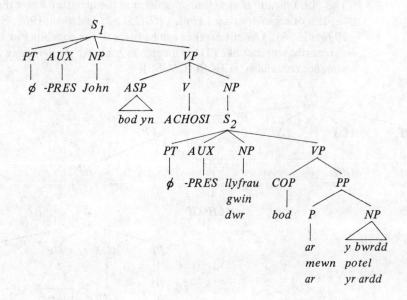

But for the sake of simplicity a superficial approach is maintained. While the branching diagram illustrates the causative element in these sentences, there is still the problem of producing the various surface structures and also producing the various verbs like RHOI (PUT), POTELU (BOTTLE) or DYFRO (WATER). For an example of an apparent simple sentence discussed in terms of a complex sentence, see chapter VIII, section 5, where predicatival sentences are outlined. The reason for treating this latter type of sentence in complex terms is that various distinctions can be made which would be less clear in terms of a simple sentence.

7. Whereas the role of GWIN (WINE) in example (53) can be identified as patient and that of YR ARDD (THE GARDEN) in (55) can be identified as patient / location, DŴR (WATER) in (55) remains problematic. It does not convincingly relate to an interrogative of the type:

(i) *? beth mae **John** yn ei wneud i 'r dŵr?*   *(what is John*
     thing is   John in its do   to the water   *doing to the*
                                                      water?)

Rather, it compares more favourably with:

(ii) *beth mae John yn ei wneud efo 'r dŵr?*   *(what is John*
      thing is   John in its do   with the water   *doing with the*
                                                       water?)

Consequently, it has been given the arbitrary label of patient-type, which allows for its notional similarity with Y DILLAD (THE CLOTHES) in (4) and also its syntactic dissimilarity. A similar point is made in the discussion of *goal*, see note 8 below.

8. With sentences like (95) it is possible notionally to distinguish various types of function in the I (TO) prepositional phrase such as 'recipient' as in (95), or 'beneficiary' or 'sufferer' as in the following sentences:

(i)   *mae John wedi rhoi anrhydedd <u>i Mair</u>*   *(John has given Mair*
      is   John after give honour   to Mair   *an honour)*

(ii) • *mae John wedi rhoi braw <u>i Mair</u>*   *(John has given Mair*
      is   John after give fright to Mair   *a fright)*

It is desirable with this sort of study, however, to characterise the linguistic resources of the sentence rather than the detailed contextual factors of whether one merely receives, benefits or suffers. For in each case the same basic linguistic pattern is used, and to this extent it is better to characterise every instance as goal. In fact, however, one can carry this argument further than has been done in the discussion and characterise goal along with directionals. Their basic linguistic pattern is the same, as the following comparison illustrates:

(iii) *mae John wedi gyrru 'r gwartheg <u>i 'r cae</u>*   *(John has driven*
       is   John after drive the cattle   to the field   *the cattle to the*
                                                             field)

(iv) *mae John wedi anfon y   pr̂es   <u>i Mair</u>*   *(John has sent the*
      is   John after send the money to Mair   *money to Mair)*

The differentiating factors can be distinguished at a more detailed level while at a more abstract level the generalisations can be made. One could likewise include addressee and topic sentences here — they could be distinguished by occurrence of a verb of 'relating', with consequences for prepositional selection.

9. It is also the case that many transitive structures with an apparent patient in object position can be paraphrased by sentences involving the type of surface structure configurations that relate to goal:

(i) *mae John wedi cicio Mair*   *(John has kicked*
    is John after kick Mair   *Mair)*

(ii) *mae John wedi rhoi cic i Mair*   *(John has given Mair*
     is John after give kick to Mair *a kick)*

Moreover, sentences like (i) and (ii) above relate to the interrogative type *beth mae John wedi ei wneud i Mair (what has John done to Mair?)* more readily than sentences like (95) do. The status of MAIR in sentences like (i) and (ii) above is problematic within the framework of the analysis of this chapter and is excluded from the discussion.

10. Langendoen (1970:62–3) identifies the role of the noun phrase in object position, for example NEGES (MESSAGE) in example (95), as patient. Although notionally similar to Y DILLAD (THE CLOTHES) in (4), it does not relate to exactly the same interrogative as the following suggests:

(i) *? beth mae John wedi ei wneud i*   *(what has John done*
    thing is John after its do   to   *to the message?)*

    'r neges?
    the message

(ii) *beth mae John wedi ei wneud efo*   *(what has John done*
     thing is John after its do   with *with the message?)*

     'r neges
     the message

Despite the disparity, the general label patient-type will be used to avoid further complexity.

11. There is a possibility of treating these sentences as complex ones involving a causative sentence:

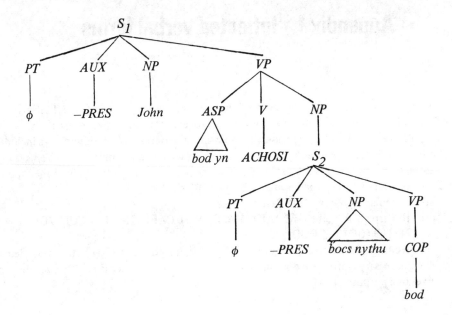

But again the simplicity of the surface structure is maintained for our purpose. For an example of an apparent simple sentence being discussed in terms of a complex sentence (for the reasons given in note 5 above) see chapter VIII, section 5.

Appendix 1 Inflected verbal forms

This appendix attempts to list some of the more generally occurring verbal inflected forms in traditional writing and spontaneous speech. Descriptively, this is a fairly complex task as there is a considerable amount of variation; the following list includes some of the more favoured variants among those which commonly occur. We have not examined all verbal possibilities but have concentrated, as is traditionally done, upon

  (i)   the paradigms of the copula verb BOD (BE);

 (ii)   a regular verb, CANU (SING);

(iii)   the 'irregular' verbs GWNEUD (MAKE, DO), CAEL (HAVE, RECEIVE), MYND (GO) and DOD (COME).

     We have chosen to represent these forms in traditional orthography (modified where necessary) rather than in phonetic script since the former is readily available and serves our purpose.

398

1   MAE (IS)

Traditional written

I	II	III	IV	V
yr ydwyf fi	nid ydwyf i	ydwyf	yr wyf	ydwyf
yr ydwyt ti	nid ydwyt ti	ydwyt	yr wyt	ydwyt
y mae ef, hi	nid ydyw ef, hi	ydyw	y mae, yw	ydyw
yr ydym ni	nid ydym ni	ydym	yr ym	ydym
yr ydych chwi	nid ydych chwi	ydych	yr ych	ydych
y maent hwy	nid ydynt hwy	ydynt	y maent, ynt	ydynt

Northern spontaneous spoken

I	II	III	IV	V
'rydw i	'dydw i	ydw i	'dw i	(y)(n)dw
'rwyt ti	'dwyt ti	wyt ti	'ti	wyt
ma(e) o, hi	'dydy o, hi	ydy o, hi	ma(e)/'dy o, hi	(y)(n)dy
'rydan ni	'dydan ni	ydan ni	'dan ni	(y)(n)dan
'rydach chi	'dydach chi	ydach chi	'dach chi	(y)(n)dach
ma(e)n n(h)w	'dydyn n(h)w	ydyn n(h)w	ma(e)n/'dyn n(h)w	(y)(n)dyn

Southern spontaneous spoken

I	II	III	IV	V
rw i	'dw i	w i	w i	ydw
rwyt ti	'dwyt ti	yw e, hi	ma'/yw e, hi	ydy
ryn ni	'dyn ni	yn ni	'ni	ydyn
rych chi	'dych chi	ych chi	'chi	ydych
ma'n n(h)w	'dyn n(h)w	yn n(h)w	ma'n/yn n(h)w	ydyn

I.   Full forms used in positive declaratives. Note that the third singular sponta-
     neous spoken form (northern and southern) is realised as *ma'* except before
     the pronouns, especially before *e* and *o*, where *mae* occurs; thus we have
     ma' John but *mae e/o*.

II. Full forms used in negatives (declaratives or interrogatives).

III. Full forms used in positive interrogatives.

IV. Contracted forms used in positive and negative declaratives and interrogatives
     (third person alternatives relate to these features).

V.   Answer words to yes-no interrogatives.

2   OEDD (WAS)

Traditional written

I

oeddwn i
oeddet ti
oedd, ydoedd ef, hi
oeddem ni
oeddech chwi
oeddynt hwy

Spontaneous spoken

I	II
oeddwn i	*o'n i*
oeddet ti	*o't ti*
oedd o/e, hi	*o(e)dd o/e, hi*
oedden ni	*o'n ni*
oeddech chi	*o'ch chi*
oedden n(h)w	*o'n n(h)w*

oe = [oɪ] or [o:]
e = [ɛ] or [a]

I.   Full forms:
- (a)   positive declaratives: can be preceded by *'r* in speech or *yr* in writing;
- (b)   positive interrogatives: can be preceded by ∅ in speech or *a* in writing;
- (c)   negative declaratives: can be preceded by *'d/'t* in speech or *nid* in writing;
- (d)   negative interrogatives: can be preceded by *'d/'t* in speech or *nid* in writing.

II. Contracted forms:
- (a)   positive declaratives: can be preceded by *'r*;
- (b)   positive interrogatives: can be preceded by ∅;
- (c)   negative declaratives: can be preceded by *'d/'t*;
- (d)   negative interrogatives: can be preceded by *'d/'t*.

3   BU (WAS)

Traditional written	Spontaneous spoken
bum	*(PT) fûs (s = [ʃ])*
buost	” *fuost*
bu	” *fu(o(dd))*
buom	” *fuon*
buoch	” *fuoch*
buont	” *fuon*

Note that answer words are *do* and *naddo*.

4   BYDD (WILL BE or non-past habitual)

Traditional written	Spontaneous spoken
byddaf	*(PT) fydda'*
byddi	” *fyddi*
bydd	” *fydd*
byddwn	” *fyddwn*
byddwch	” *fyddwch*
byddant	” *fyddan*

Imperative

bydd/bydda
byddwch

Notes: (a)   First singular, at least, can be reduced to *'dda' i*, as in *'dda' i 'na rŵan (I'll be there now)*.

(b)   In answer words there is no mutation with affirmatives and first singular occurs as *byddaf*.

5 BYDDAI (WOULD BE or past habitual)

Traditional written	Spontaneous spoken
byddwn	*(PT) fyddwn*
byddit	" *fyddet*
byddai	" *fydde*
byddem	" *fydden*
byddech	" *fyddech*
byddent	" *fydden*
	$e = [ɛ]$ or $[a]$

6 BUASAI (WOULD BE)

Traditional written

buaswn
buasit
buasai
buasem
buasech
buasent

Spontaneous spoken

	I	II
(PT)	*faswn*	*'swn*
"	*faset*	*'set*
"	*fase*	*'se*
"	*fasen*	*'sen*
"	*fasech*	*'sech*
"	*fasen*	*'sen*

$a = [a]$ or $[ə]$ $e = [ɛ]$ or $[a]$
$e = [ɛ]$ or $[a]$

I.   Full forms.
II.   Contracted forms - do not occur with PT. Note that corresponding full forms for southern Welsh have a different contraction, *buswn*, etc.

402

Traditional written

canaf	canwn	canaswn	cenais
ceni	canit	canasit	cenaist
can	canai	canasai	canodd
canwn	canem	canasem	canasom
cenwch	canech	canasech	canasoch
canant	canent	canasent	canasant

Spontaneous spoken

(PT)	gana'	(PT)	ganwn
"	gani	"	gane̱t
"	ganith/iff	"	gan̲e
"	gan̲wn	"	gan̲en
"	ganwch	"	gane̱ch
"	ganan'	"	gan̲en'

(PT)	gan'swn	(PT)	ganis
"	gan'se̱t	"	ganist
"	gan'se̱	"	ganodd
"	gan'sen	"	gan'son
"	gan'se̱ch	"	gan'soch
"	gan'sen	"	gan'son

w = [u] or [a]   e = [ɛ] or [a]   e = [ɛ] or [a]

Imperative

cana
canwch

Southern Welsh

(PT)	ganes
"	ganest
"	ganws
"	gan(s)on
"	gan(s)och
"	gan(s)on

Note: In spontaneous speech, the paradigms in the second and third columns are used for the same functions (see chapter V) although they may be dialectally distinguished. This note also applies to the remaining verbs listed below.

Traditional written

gwnaf	gwnawn	gwnaethwn	gwneuthum
gwnei	gwnait	gwnaethit	gwnaethost
gwna	gwnai	gwnaethai	gwnaeth
gwnawn	gwnaem	gwnaethem	gwnaethom
gwnewch	gwnaech	gwnaethech	gwnaethoch
gwnant	gwnaent	gwnaethent	gwnaethant

Spontaneous spoken

(PT)	'na'	(PT)	'nawn	(PT)	'neuthwn	(PT)	'nês
"	'nei	"	'naet	"	'neuthet	"	'nêst
"	'neith/'naiff	"	'nai	"	'neuthe	"	'nâth
"	'nawn/'nân	"	'naen	"	'neuthen	"	neuthon
"	'newch	"	'naech	"	'neuthech	"	'neuthoch
"	'nan	"	'haen	"	'neuthen	"	'neuthan

eu = [eɨ] or [ə] eu = [eɨ] or [ə]
th = [θ] or [s] th = [θ] or [s]
e = [ɛ] or [a]

Imperative	Southern Welsh	Southern Welsh	Southern Welsh
gna	(PT) 'nelwn/en	(PT) nelse	(PT) netho
gnewch	" 'nelet	" nelset	" nethot
	" 'nele	" nelse	" nâth
	" 'nelen	" nelsen	" nethon
	" 'nelech	" nelsech	" nethoch
	" 'nelen	" nelsen	" nethon

See note under CANU (SING) above for the relationship of second and third columns of spontaneous speech.

9   CAEL (RECEIVE, HAVE)

Traditional written

caf	*cawn*	*cawswn*	*cefais*
cei	*cait*	*cawsit*	*cefaist*
caiff	*cai*	*cawsai*	*cafodd*
cawn	*caem*	*cawsem*	*cawsom*
cewch	*caech*	*cawsech*	*cawsoch*
cânt	*caent*	*cawsent*	*cawsant*

Spontaneous spoken

(PT)	*ga'*	*(PT)*	*gawn*	*(PT)*	*geuthwn*	*(PT)*	*gefis/gês*
"	*gei*	"	*gaet*	"	*geuthet*	"	*gefaist/gêst*
"	*geith/gaiff*	"	*gai*	"	*geuthe*	"	*gafodd/gâth*
"	*gawn/gân*	"	*gaen*	"	*geuthen*	"	*gawson*
"	*gewch*	"	*gaech*	"	*geuthech*	"	*gawsoch*
"	*gân*	"	*gaen*	"	*geuthen*	"	*gawson*

eu = [eɨ] or [ə] aw = [aʊ] or [ə]

th = [θ] or [s] s = [s] or [θ]

e = [ɛ] or [a]

Southern Welsh   Southern Welsh

(PT)	*gelwn/en*	*(PT)*	*geson*
"	*gelet*	"	*gesot*
"	*gele*	"	*gâs*
"	*gelen*	"	*geson*
"	*gelech*	"	*gesoch*
"	*gelen*	"	*geson*

See note under CANU (SING) above for the relationship of second and third columns of spontaneous speech.

Traditional written

af	awn	aethwn	euthum
ei	ait	aethit	aethost
â	âi	aethai	aeth
awn	aem	aethem	aethom
ewch	aech	aethech	aethoch
ant	aent	aethent	aethant

Spontaneous spoken

(PT)	a'	(PT)	awn	(PT)	euthwn	(PT)	ês
"	ei	"	aet	"	euthet	"	êst
"	eith/aiff	"	âi	"	euthe̲	"	âth
"	awn/ân	"	aen	"	euthe̲n	"	euthon
"	ewch	"	aech	"	euthe̲ch	"	euthoch
"	ân	"	aen	"	euthe̲n	"	euthon

$e = [\varepsilon]$ or $[a]$ $th = [\theta]$ or $[s]$

Imperative	Southern Welsh		Southern Welsh	
dos/cer	(PT)	elwn/en	(PT)	etho
ewch/cerwch	"	elet	"	ethot
	"	ele	"	âth
	"	elen	"	ethon
	"	elech	"	ethoch
	"	elen	"	ethon

See note under CANU (SING) above for relationship of second and third columns of spontaneous speech.

406

11   DOD (COME)

Traditional written

deuaf	deuwn	daethwn	deuthum
deui	deuit	daethit	daethost
daw	deuai	daethai	daeth
deuwn	deuem	daethem	daethom
deuwch	deuech	daethech	daethoch
deuant	deuent	daethent	daethant

Spontaneous spoken

(PT)	ddo'	(PT)	ddown	(PT)	ddeuthwn	(PT)	ddois
"	ddoi	"	ddôt	"	ddeuth<u>e</u>t	"	ddoist
"	ddaw/ddoith/ddoiff	"	ddôi	"	ddeuth<u>e</u>	"	ddoth/
							ddaeth
"	ddown/ddôn	"	ddoen	"	ddeuth<u>e</u>n	"	ddeuthon
"	ddowch/ddewch	"	ddoech	"	ddeuth<u>e</u>ch	"	ddeu<u>t</u>hoch
"	ddôn	"	ddoen	"	ddeuth<u>e</u>n	"	ddeu<u>t</u>hon

e = [ɛ] or [a̅]   th = [θ] or [s̅]

Imperative	Southern Welsh		Southern Welsh	
tyd	(PT)	ddelwn/en	(PT)	ddetho
dewch/dowch	"	ddelet	"	ddethot
	"	ddele	"	ddâth
	"	ddelen	"	ddethon
	"	ddelech	"	ddethoch
	"	ddelen	"	ddethan

See note under CANU (SING) above for relationship of second and third columns of spontaneous speech.

Appendix 2   Inflected prepositions

This appendix lists some of the most general forms in formal writing and spontaneous speech of the inflected prepositions. Each listed preposition is detailed in horizontally arranged paradigms with the written forms listed in the first line and the spoken forms listed in the lower lines.

	1 sing.	2 sing.	3 sing. masc.	3 sing. fem.
AM	amdanaf	amdanat	amdano	amdani
	amdana'	amdan$\begin{Bmatrix}a\\o\end{Bmatrix}$t	amdano	amd$\begin{Bmatrix}a\\e\end{Bmatrix}$ni
AR	arnaf	arnat	arno	arni
	arna'	arn$\begin{Bmatrix}a\\o\end{Bmatrix}$t	arno	arni
AT	ataf	atat	ato	ati
	ata'	atat	ato	ati
DAN	danaf	danat	dano	dani
	dana'	dan$\begin{Bmatrix}a\\o\end{Bmatrix}$t	dano	d$\begin{Bmatrix}a\\e\end{Bmatrix}$ni
DROS	drosof	drosot	drosto	drosti
	drosta'	drost$\begin{Bmatrix}a\\o\end{Bmatrix}$t	drosto	drosti
GAN	gennyf	gennyt	ganddo	ganddi
	g$\begin{Bmatrix}e\\i\end{Bmatrix}$n	g$\begin{Bmatrix}e\\i\end{Bmatrix}$n	ganddo	ganddi
	g$\begin{Bmatrix}e\\i\\y\end{Bmatrix}$nna'	gynn$\begin{Bmatrix}a\\o\end{Bmatrix}$t	g$\begin{Bmatrix}e\\i\\y\end{Bmatrix}$nno	g$\begin{Bmatrix}e\\i\\y\end{Bmatrix}$nni
	gynno'			

1 pl.	2 pl.	3 pl.

$$\text{1 pl.} \qquad\qquad \text{2 pl.} \qquad\qquad \text{3 pl.}$$

amdanom

$amdan \begin{Bmatrix} a \\ o \end{Bmatrix}$

amdanoch

$amdan \begin{Bmatrix} a \\ o \end{Bmatrix} ch$

amdanynt

$amdan \begin{Bmatrix} y \\ a \end{Bmatrix} n'$

arnom

$arn \begin{Bmatrix} a \\ o \end{Bmatrix} n$

arnoch

$arn \begin{Bmatrix} a \\ o \end{Bmatrix} ch$

arnynt

$arn \begin{Bmatrix} y \\ a \end{Bmatrix} n'$

atom

$at \begin{Bmatrix} a \\ o \end{Bmatrix} n$

atoch

$at \begin{Bmatrix} a \\ o \end{Bmatrix} ch$

atynt

$at \begin{Bmatrix} y \\ a \end{Bmatrix} n'$

danom

$dan \begin{Bmatrix} a \\ o \end{Bmatrix} n$

danoch

$dan \begin{Bmatrix} a \\ o \end{Bmatrix} ch$

danynt

$dan \begin{Bmatrix} y \\ a \end{Bmatrix} n'$

drosom

$drost \begin{Bmatrix} a \\ o \end{Bmatrix} n$

drosoch

$drost \begin{Bmatrix} a \\ o \end{Bmatrix} ch$

drostynt

$drost \begin{Bmatrix} y \\ o \end{Bmatrix} n'$

gennym

$g \begin{Bmatrix} e \\ i \\ y \end{Bmatrix} nn \begin{Bmatrix} a \\ o \end{Bmatrix} n$

gennych

$g \begin{Bmatrix} e \\ i \\ y \end{Bmatrix} nn \begin{Bmatrix} a \\ o \end{Bmatrix} ch$

ganddynt

$g \begin{Bmatrix} e \\ i \\ y \end{Bmatrix} nn \begin{Bmatrix} y \\ o \end{Bmatrix} n'$

	1 sing.	2 sing.	3 sing. masc.	3 sing. fem.
HEB	*hebof* *hebdda'*	*hebot* *hebdd* $\begin{Bmatrix} a \\ o \end{Bmatrix}$ *t*	*hebddo* *hebddo*	*hebddi* *hebddi*
I	*i* *i*	*i* *i*	*iddo* *iddo*	*iddi* *iddi*
O	*ohonof* *ohon* $\begin{Bmatrix} a \\ o \end{Bmatrix}$ *'*	*ohonot* *ohon* $\begin{Bmatrix} a \\ o \end{Bmatrix}$ *t*	*ohono* *ohono*	*ohoni* *ohoni*
RHWNG	*rhyngof* *rh* $\begin{Bmatrix} y \\ w \end{Bmatrix}$ $\begin{Bmatrix} ngdd \\ ngth \end{Bmatrix}$ *a'*	*rhyngot* *rh* $\begin{Bmatrix} y \\ w \end{Bmatrix}$ $\begin{Bmatrix} ngdd \\ ngth \end{Bmatrix}$ $\begin{Bmatrix} a \\ o \end{Bmatrix}$ *t*	*rhyngddo* *rh* $\begin{Bmatrix} y \\ w \end{Bmatrix}$ $\begin{Bmatrix} ngdd \\ ngth \end{Bmatrix}$ *o*	*rhyngddi* *rh* $\begin{Bmatrix} y \\ w \end{Bmatrix}$ $\begin{Bmatrix} ngdd \\ ngth \end{Bmatrix}$ *i*
TRWY	*trwof* *trwydda'*	*trwot* *trwydd* $\begin{Bmatrix} a \\ o \end{Bmatrix}$ *t*	*trwyddo* *trwyddo*	*trwyddi* *trwyddi*
WRTH	*wrthyf* *w(r)tha'*	*wrthyt* *w(r)th* $\begin{Bmatrix} a \\ o \end{Bmatrix}$ *t*	*wrtho* *w(r)tho*	*wrthi* *w(r)thi*
YN	*ynof* *yna'*	*ynot* *yn* $\begin{Bmatrix} a \\ o \end{Bmatrix}$ *t*	*ynddo* *yn(dd)o*	*ynddi* *yn(dd)i*

1 pl.	2 pl.	3 pl.
hebom	*heboch*	*hebddynt*
$hebdd\begin{Bmatrix}a\\o\end{Bmatrix}n$	$hebdd\begin{Bmatrix}a\\o\end{Bmatrix}ch$	$hebdd\begin{Bmatrix}y\\o\end{Bmatrix}n'$
i	*i*	*iddynt*
i	*i*	*iddyn'*
ohonom	*ohonoch*	*ohonynt*
$ohon\begin{Bmatrix}a\\o\end{Bmatrix}n$	$ohon\begin{Bmatrix}a\\o\end{Bmatrix}ch$	$ohon\begin{Bmatrix}y\\o\end{Bmatrix}n'$
rhyngom	*rhyngoch*	*rhyngddynt*
$rh\begin{Bmatrix}y\\w\end{Bmatrix}\begin{Bmatrix}ngdd\\ngth\end{Bmatrix}\begin{Bmatrix}a\\o\end{Bmatrix}n$	$rh\begin{Bmatrix}y\\w\end{Bmatrix}\begin{Bmatrix}ngdd\\ngth\end{Bmatrix}\begin{Bmatrix}a\\o\end{Bmatrix}ch$	$rh\begin{Bmatrix}y\\w\end{Bmatrix}\begin{Bmatrix}ngdd\\ngth\end{Bmatrix}\begin{Bmatrix}y\\o\end{Bmatrix}n'$
trwom	*trwoch*	*trwyddynt*
$trwydd\begin{Bmatrix}a\\o\end{Bmatrix}n$	$trwydd\begin{Bmatrix}a\\o\end{Bmatrix}ch$	$trwydd\begin{Bmatrix}y\\o\end{Bmatrix}n'$
wrthym	*wrthych*	*wrthynt*
$w(r)th\begin{Bmatrix}a\\o\end{Bmatrix}n$	$w(r)th\begin{Bmatrix}a\\o\end{Bmatrix}ch$	$w(r)th\begin{Bmatrix}y\\o\end{Bmatrix}n'$
ynom	*ynoch*	*ynddynt*
$yn(dd)\begin{Bmatrix}a\\o\end{Bmatrix}n$	$yn(dd)\begin{Bmatrix}a\\o\end{Bmatrix}ch$	*yn(dd)yn'*

References

Anwyl, E. (1899). *A Welsh Grammar for Schools*, Part II, *Syntax*. London: Swan, Sonnenschein.

Anderson, J. (1968). 'Ergative and nominative in English', *Journal of Linguistics*, 4 (1), 1-32.

Bach, E., and Harms, R. T., eds (1968). *Universals in Linguistic Theory*. New York: Holt, Rinehart.

Bierwisch, M., and Heidolph, K. (1970). *Progress in Linguistics*. The Hague: Mouton.

Chomsky, N. (1957). *Syntactic Structures*. The Hague: Mouton.

———— (1965). *Aspects of the Theory of Syntax*. Cambridge, Mass.: MIT Press.

———— (1970). 'Remarks on nominalization', in Jacobs and Rosenbaum (1970).

Emonds, J. (1970). 'Root and structure-preserving transformations'. Cambridge, Mass.: Massachusetts Institute of Technology (unpublished Ph.D. dissertation).

Evans, J. J. (1960). *Gramadeg Cymraeg*. 2nd ed. Aberystwyth: Gwasg Aberystwyth.

Fillmore, C. J. (1968). 'The case for case', in Bach and Harms (1968), pp. 1-88.

Halliday, M. A. K. (1961). 'Categories of the theory of grammar', *Word*, 17, 241-92.

———— (1970). 'Language structure and language function', in Lyons (1970), pp. 140-65.

Jacobs, R. A., and Rosenbaum, P. S. (1967a). *Grammar*, vol. 1. Boston, Mass.: Ginn.

———— (1967b). *Grammar*, vol. 2. Boston, Mass.: Ginn.

————, eds (1970). *Readings in English Transformational Grammar*. Waltham, Mass.: Ginn.

Jones, M. (in preparation). 'The verbal phrase in Welsh'. To be submitted as a Ph.D. thesis.

Katz, J. J., and Postal, P. (1964). *An Integrated Theory of Linguistic Descriptions*. Cambridge, Mass.: MIT Press.

Kiparsky, P., and Kiparsky, C. (1970). 'Fact', in Bierwisch and Heidolph (1970).

Lakoff, G. (1971). 'On generative semantics', in Steinberg and Jacobvits, eds (1971), pp. 232-96.

Langendoen, D. T. (1969). *The Study of Syntax*. New York: Holt, Rinehart.

———— (1970). *Essentials of English Grammar*. New York: Holt, Rinehart.

Lyons, J. (1969). *Introduction to Theoretical Linguistics*. Cambridge University Press.

————, ed. (1970). *New Horizons in Linguistics*. Penguin.

McCawley, J. D. (1968). 'The role of semantics in a grammar', in Bach and Harms (1968), pp. 125-69.

Morris-Jones, J. (1913). *A Welsh Grammar, Historical and Comparative*. Oxford: Clarendon Press.

Perlmutter, D. M. (1970). 'The two verbs begin', in Jacobs and Rosenbaum (1970).

412

Richards, M. (1938). *Cystrawen y Frawddeg Gymraeg*. Cardiff: Gwasg Prifysgol Cymru [University of Wales Press].
Rosenbaum, P. S. (1967). *The Grammar of English Predicate Complement Constructions*. Cambridge, Mass.: MIT Press.
Ross, J. R. (1969). 'Auxiliaries as main verbs', in Todd (1969).
––––– (1970). 'On declarative sentences', in Jacobs and Rosenbaum (1970).
Rowland, T. (1876). *A Grammar of the Welsh Language*. 4th ed. Wrexham: Hughes & Son/London: Simpkin, Marshall.
Steinberg, D. D., and Jacobvits, L. A., eds (1971). *Semantics: an Interdisciplinary Reader in Philosophy, Linguistics and Psychology*. Cambridge University Press.
Todd, W. (1969). *Philosophical Linguistics*, Series I. Evanston, Ill.: Great Expectations.
Watkins, T. A. W. (1961). *Ieithyddiaeth*. Cardiff: Gwasg Prifysgol Cymru [University of Wales Press].
Williams, S. J. (1959). *Elfennau Gramadeg Cymraeg*. Cardiff: Gwasg Prifysgol Cymru [University of Wales Press].